Savoring

A NEW MODEL OF
POSITIVE EXPERIENCE

Savoring

A NEW MODEL OF
POSITIVE EXPERIENCE

Fred B. Bryant
Loyola University Chicago

Joseph Veroff
University of Michigan

LEA

LAWRENCE ERLBAUM ASSOCIATES, PUBLISHERS

2007 Mahwah, New Jersey   London

Lawrence Erlbaum Associates, Inc., Publishers
10 Industrial Avenue
Mahwah, New Jersey 07430
www.erlbaum.com

Cover design by Tomai Maridou

Library of Congress Cataloging-in-Publication Data

Bryant, Fred B.
   Savoring : a new model of positive experience / Fred B. Bryant,
Joseph Veroff.
        p.   cm.
   Includes bibliographical references and index.
   ISBN 0–8058–5119–4 (cloth : alk. paper) — ISBN 0–8058–5120–8
(pbk. : alk. paper) 1. Positive psychology. I. Veroff, Joseph, 1929–
II. Title.
   BF204.6B79   2006
   150.19'8—dc22   2006007924

Books published by Lawrence Erlbaum Associates are printed on acid-free
paper, and their bindings are chosen for strength and durability.

To

MERRILEE MILES BRYANT,

who showed me the secrets of savoring.

—FBB

Contents

Permissions

The authors gratefully acknowledge permission for the use of the following material:

Blackwell Publishers (Oxford, UK) for adaptations of Table 1 (pp. 780–782) and Figure 1 (p. 787) from Bryant, F. B. (1989). A four-factor model of perceived control: Avoiding, coping, obtaining, and savoring. *Journal of Personality, 57,* 773–797.

"Children's Savoring Beliefs Inventory," adapted from Cafasso, L. L. (1994). *Uplifts and hassles in the lives of young adolescents.* Unpublished master's thesis, Loyola University Chicago, Chicago, IL. Used by permission of Dr. Lynda Cafasso.

"somewhere i have never travelled, gladly beyond." Copyright 1931, © 1959, 1991 by the Trustees for the E.E. Cummings Trust. Copyright © 1979 by George James Firmage, from COMPLETE POEMS: 1904–1962 by E.E. Cummings, edited by George J. Firmage. Used by permission of Liveright Publishing Corporation.

Taylor & Francis, Ltd. (London, UK) for an adaptation of Table 4 (pp. 186–187) from Bryant, F. B. (2003). Savoring Beliefs Inventory (SBI): A scale for measuring beliefs about savouring. *Journal of Mental Health, 12,* 175–196. [http://www.tandf.co.uk]

The Houghton Mifflin Company for "The Most Sacred Mountain" by Eunice Tietjens from THE SECOND BOOK OF MODERN VERSE, edited by Jessie B. Rittenhouse, Copyright 1919 by Houghton Mifflin Company.

Preface

Most people learn to cope with what life has to offer them and to accept what comes their way. They generally learn to survive whatever challenges they face in growing up, making a living, relating to others, and being an adult in a changing world. Some of them even find some degree of happiness and satisfaction from what they are doing in their lives. And yet there remains a gnawing question for many of them: What is it all about? What meaning do people attribute to being alive in the shapes and colors that their lives take?

That turns out to be a hard question to answer without trivializing the predicament in which human beings find themselves. Each of the answers offered by thinkers from various philosophical persuasions makes some sense. Philosophers and sages tell people to find love, find beauty, find truth, find community, find God, find your sexual self, find your spiritual self. A smorgasbord of worldly advice offers these and other prescriptions.

What we present in this book is not such a direct answer. We advocate learning how to cultivate savoring, or the capacity to attend to, appreciate, and enhance the positive experiences in one's life. With that capacity, people can better enjoy love, truth, beauty, community, God, sexuality, spirituality, or whatever preferred values and individual goals they deem important. Thus, we think savoring is a boon to positive fulfillment in life. And yet it is a neglected topic in psychology. Our major mission in this book is to increase the scientific focus on processes of savoring, in order to make savoring a legitimate topic of systematic inquiry in psychology. Secondarily, we offer some prescriptions for expanding people's capacities to savor their lives, given the assumptive framework and research results we present.

It is with some embarrassment that we admit we first stumbled on the topic of savoring not from any astute psychological analysis of the human condition, but from a logical statistical analysis of the structure of psychological well-being. We were trying to simplify the multiple ways that people reveal how they feel about their ongoing lives. We had available the many different answers that people gave in reporting how they felt about their lives in response to a national survey of subjective mental health. Among other survey questions were people's reported happiness and worries; their various psychological and physical symptoms; their level of satisfaction; their morale about the future; their self-esteem; their sense of personal control. Some 25 such measures seemed to us to capture different aspects of people's views about the quality of their lives. What might these measures represent in simpler terms? To answer this question, we used statistical analytic techniques to explore how these 25 indexes were intercorrelated, and we found six basic factors or dimensions of psychological well-being that underlay people's subjective self-assessments: happiness, satisfaction, self-confidence, feelings of vulnerability, physical strain, and uncertainty.

We reasoned, however — and here's where simple logic came in — that there had to be a yet-unmeasured dimension of psychological well-being having to do with controlling one's own positive experiences, not really "happiness" or "satisfaction," but the sense that one can actively engage life with enjoyment. After all, we had measures of one's sense of being able to cope with difficulties presented by life, particularly in the specific questions about self-confidence and feelings of vulnerability included in the national survey. Shouldn't there also be a parallel dimension concerning one's sense of being able to activate pleasure and good feelings in life? That was our logical reasoning in 1984, when we first published our thinking about this dimension.

One of us (Fred) picked up on that idea and embarked on a systematic study of what he soon called *savoring*. His empirical work is a major foundation for many of the ideas and propositions in the chapters that follow. We present several measurement instruments he developed over a number of years to assess beliefs about savoring and ways that people report they savor positive experiences. We describe Fred's experiments in inducing savoring, and correlational studies by Fred and his students that show how people differ in ways of savoring. This volume is the first time that some of these studies appear in print.

The other member of this duo (Joe) dropped the topic of savoring for 14 years until he retired and found himself in the throes of considering life's meaning more personally (which is the wont of people when they retire) and returned to the topic of savoring as a personal quest. He began to record for himself the times he savored an experience and the processes that seemed to be involved experientially. With that newfound phenomenological orientation to the process, he pestered his wife, children, and grandchildren, and Fred to do the same. Fascinated by what they told him about their savoring moments, he asked Fred whether they might join forces in writing a monograph on savoring, where he could find a home for some of these qualitative data on savoring. Fred agreed, and the idea for this book was born. Together we have sought instances in other research and in literary and artistic efforts that illustrate moments of savoring in people's lives. All of this we use to help highlight the issues that need to be raised in considering what savoring is all about.

Of late, there has emerged a vibrant new discipline within the field of psychology known as "positive psychology." Researchers are now beginning to develop the relevant theoretical concepts and measurement tools to define this emerging area of study. Constructs of positive affect, happiness, optimism, hope, life satisfaction, flow, inspiration, resilience, flourishing, virtue, and a few others have been proposed as the conceptual bedrock on which to form the foundations of positive psychology. It is within this field that a concept such as savoring belongs.

With this book, we intend to introduce students, researchers, and theorists in psychology and related disciplines to savoring as a process in human experience. Although this book is designed to serve as a text for undergraduate and graduate courses in positive psychology and psychological adjustment, it is also designed as a resource for social, personality, and clinical psychologists who wish to investigate phenomena within the field of positive psychology. The book provides a theoretical framework and set of related research tools for understanding and studying savoring as a critical process underlying positive experience.

Indeed, among psychologists studying positive psychology, there has been relatively little analysis of the processes underlying positive experience. It is as if positive emotions are assumed to flow naturally as consequences arising from positive events or from positive personality styles. What the fledgling field of positive psychology lacks are cogent ideas about the dynamics of positive experience, ideas about the processes that link positive events or positive personality styles with positive emotions. Without formal models of such processes, psychology lacks an understanding of the dynamics of positive feelings.

We wrote this book partly to fill the need for understanding some of these dynamics within positive psychology. In the first chapter, we cover some of the existing concepts in psychology that are relevant to such dynamics, including mindfulness, flow, and meditation. Although these are important specific processes, they do not generally capture the broad class of processes on which we wish to focus. Instead, we propose the term *savoring* to refer to processes through which people actively derive pleasure and fulfillment in relation to positive experience. And we highlight the major ways in which savoring unfolds in people's lives.

We begin by laying the conceptual groundwork to serve as a theoretical foundation for a psychology of savoring. We explicate what we mean by the term *savoring,* and we distinguish it from a variety of related but separate constructs, including mindfulness, meditation, daydreaming, time work, positive emotions, aesthetic responses, intrinsic motivation, and flow. We also discuss major conceptual issues central to the construct of savoring, including relevant domains of positive experience, the degree of conscious awareness and intentionality involved, how savoring is engaged and halted, and various social and cultural influences on savoring.

In subsequent chapters, we discuss many different forms of savoring, as well as factors that influence both the appearance of savoring and the intensity and duration of positive affect it produces. Particularly important factors are the role of time in the form of memories and anticipatory capacities that contribute to savoring across the life span. Indeed, we have reserved an entire chapter for these issues. We also consider the relevance of savoring in understanding important human concerns, or ways in which savoring might influence romantic love, friendship, mental and physical health, creativity, and spirituality. These are contexts where savoring processes can have critical effects. It is not our intention to cover all possible theoretical or practical issues related to concepts of savoring. On the contrary, we want this book to stimulate further theoretical clarification and generate additional empirical work on this vital part of human life.

Besides building the theoretical scaffolding for a psychology of savoring, this book also provides researchers with a set of validated measurement instruments for use in studying savoring. In particular, the appendixes include copies of instruments assessing: (a) perceived control in avoiding and coping with negative outcomes, and in obtaining and savoring positive outcomes; (b) the perceived capacity to savor positive experience through anticipation, enjoying the moment, and reminiscing, for use with adults (the Savoring Beliefs Inventory) as well as children (the Children's Savoring Beliefs Inventory); and (c) specific thoughts and behaviors (i.e., cognitive and behavioral savoring strategies) in which people may engage in response to positive events (the Ways of Savoring Checklist). We also provide detailed instructions and SPSS syntax files for scoring each of these measurement instruments. We have included these appendixes in order to facilitate systematic empirical research on savoring.

It would be ingenuous for us not to admit from the very beginning that we also want this book to present ideas and information about savoring that might be guidelines for people who seek to expand their own capacities for enjoyment. In the final chapter of this book, we draw together the implications of the model we develop for increasing the role that savoring plays in peoples' lives. Along the way, we also present preliminary research on strategies for inducing and enhancing savoring.

We owe a great deal to many different people who helped make this book possible. For their astute comments and advice on earlier drafts of this manuscript, we thank Ken Sheldon, Laura A. King, and Jack Bauer. Martin Seligman also gave us a much-needed shot in the arm in the critical early stages of this project, and his encouragement, advice, and support have been invaluable. Over many years, Fred's wife, Linda Perloff, and Joe's wife, Jody Veroff, provided constant intellectual and emotional support regarding this project. Linda also edited the text and references with great care at the eleventh hour, and we are deeply indebted to her. We also thank Darrin Lehman, whose critical insights and unwavering belief in the importance of savoring as a psychological construct have for more than two decades been a powerful source of inspiration and creativity. In the same way, Bob Kerns contributed exceptional energy and imagination from the start, and his limitless creativity has been inspirational. In addition, Jackie Allen was instrumental in creating some of the measurement tools we present, and we gratefully acknowledge her contributions. We are grateful to Senior Editor Debra Riegert, Senior Book Production Editor Debbie Ruel, Editorial Assistant Rebecca Larsen, and Copy Editor Patricia Ferenbach of Lawrence Erlbaum Associates for their astute advice and guidance throughout this project.

Also instrumental in shaping our thinking about savoring have been Maria Arne, Scott Arne, Bob Bjornsen, Kristin Bjornsen, Mary Ann Bjornsen, George Bryant, Denise Davidson, Jerry Delo, Libby Douvan, Frank Fisher, Larry Grimm, Catherine Haden, Riadh Hamdane, Dave Handley, Rick Hanna, Eaaron Henderson-King, Donna Henderson-King, Jim Johnson, Paul Jose, Dave Klingel, Jaime Kurtz, Tracy Lindberg, Andrew MacLeod, Darryl Maybery, Dan McAdams, Bob McWilliams, David Mitchell, Paul Moser, Victor Ottati, Evelyn Perloff, Judy Perloff, Richard Perloff, Robert Perloff, Alfred Pfister, Sydney Reed, Robert Russell, Joe Rychlak, Constantine Sedikides, Mike Smith, Nancy Smith, Harry Upshaw, Paul Yarnold, and Chuck Yopst, whose stimulating intellectual conversations and insights about savoring have enriched this book immeasurably.

Over the years, numerous graduate and undergraduate students at Loyola University Chicago have helped in collecting and coding data for our research on savoring. Although we cannot name all of these individuals here, they include Cathi Barnett, Jen Brockway, Lynda Cafasso, Juliana Carravetta, Lynn Davidson, Rebecca Devlin, Angela Dimanno, Juliana Fruzzetti, Yanghui Han, Neely Herman, Scott King, Mike Meehan, Ingrid Mejia, Todd Miller, David Morgan, Lynn Morgan, David Njus, Meghanne Reilly, Tim Ritchie, Liz Sanders, Steve Serio, Shaista Shaik, Reena Sharma, Jon Sherwell, Colette Smart, Milena Tatic, Fran Weaver, and Brian Whang. In particular, Adam DeHoek and Carrie Ericksen provided an extraordinary level of assistance in managing the research process, proofreading earlier versions of this manuscript, cross-checking references, locating sources for quotations, and obtaining copyright permissions. We are indebted to all of these individuals for their help throughout this project. Without their support, encouragement, and inspiration, our work would not have been possible.

1

Concepts of Savoring:
An Introduction

There is no duty we so underrate
as the duty of being happy.
—Robert Louis Stevenson (1881)

Who are the people who truly experience well-being in their lives? Those who have fulfilled basic needs for food, shelter, sex, family, work, and health, you might say. Yet, even if basic needs are fulfilled, that does not necessarily imply that people automatically feel good about their lives. The proportion of Americans who describe themselves as "happy" has not changed since the 1950s, even though average "real income" has more than doubled during that time (Easterbrook, 2003). Even with basic needs fulfilled, some people see possible stress and misfortune looming around every corner, and they remain anxious about their lives. And even if people have the ability to weather the storms about which they are anxious, this does not necessarily help them notice or appreciate the positive aspects of their lives.

Being able to handle adversity is vital in life, but having a capacity to cope seems not to be the same as having the capacity to enjoy life. In other words, just because people are *not down,* doesn't mean they're *up.* Considering only stress, coping, and distress omits from the picture positive experiences and personal capacities that comprise the central topics of the growing field of positive psychology. What about attaining authentic happiness (Seligman, 2002a), experiencing positive feelings like joy and pleasure (Fredrickson, 2001), flourishing (Keyes & Haidt, 2003), feeling hope (Snyder, 2002) or optimism (Segerstrom, 2001) toward the future, or having a sense of satisfaction in response to what one has done or accomplished (Diener & Diener, 1995)? Aren't these critical emotional states that also feed into people's overall well-being? Although this book is not directly about these emotional states, it features a major process by which people bring about, appreciate, and enhance these positive experiences. We call this process *savoring*.

OUR INITIAL NOTION
OF A SAVORING CONCEPT

As we noted in the preface, our earlier work on subjective mental health (Bryant & Veroff, 1984) led us to conclude that something vital was missing from the literature on psychological well-being. In particular, the process of coping with stress had no positive counterpart. But if people make self-assessments of their ability to handle negative experiences in their lives, then surely they must also make self-assessments of their ability to enjoy positive experiences. We contend that savoring is this missing process — the positive counterpart of coping.

This book and the conceptual analysis and empirical research presented in it are meant to fill this gap in the literature. We posit that people have capacities *to attend to, appreciate, and enhance the positive experiences in their lives.* This is the basic conceptual definition of savoring we use throughout this book. We call those capacities, *capacities to savor,* and the processes underlying those capacities, *savoring.*

From research on coping (see Compas, Connor, Osowiecki, & Welch, 1997; Lazarus & Folkman, 1984), we know that people use a range of different types of coping strategies to handle stress. For example, people may use active problem solving, social support, prayer, cognitive reappraisal, formal help seeking, wishful thinking, escape-avoidance, denial, or substance abuse to help them cope with their problems. Some of these approaches to coping may even involve active attention to the good things in one's life, what seems like savoring, but such mechanisms were seen in the coping literature as "breathers" or "sustainers," or as ways to avoid stress, not as ways to heighten positive experiences for their own sake (Lazarus, Kanner, & Folkman, 1980). Within the mental health literature, theorists and researchers have been careful to distinguish the process of coping, that is, the thoughts and behaviors that people use to modify stressful circumstances and to minimize potential threat, from its outcome, that is, the consequences of coping. This important distinction has guided theory and research on stress management and adjustment, and it has been valuable in helping us better understand the processes involved in dealing with anxiety, depression, misfortune, and illness.

But when it comes to happiness, joy, elation, and delight; when it comes to satisfaction, gratification, meaning, and fulfillment; when it comes to pleasure, rapture, gratitude, and bliss, there is little knowledge about the processes through which these positive states come about. As a result, we know practically nothing about the processes through which people derive joy in their lives. Clearly, people actively engage in thoughts and behaviors before, during, and after positive experiences, and these thoughts and behaviors influence how strongly these experiences are felt, just as people's thoughts and behaviors in response to stress influence their subsequent levels of distress. But there are no terms in the social science literature to denote these positive processes directly.

Just as in the literature on coping and distress, however, we must be careful to distinguish between the process of attending to joy and the joy itself. We needed a word to denote the positive counterpart of coping. This term had to refer to the *processes* rather than to the *outcome* of enjoyment, and it had to convey the dynamic, interactive, transactional nature of positive emotions. There were many words that came to mind, each of which captured a different flavor of the process. Some words were rich in meaning but narrow in scope, and were more specific to particular circumstances: rejoicing, reveling, delighting, basking, and luxuriating, for example. Other words were broader and more general, and seemed to convey more clearly the notion of a positive process: appreciating, cherishing, enjoying, relishing, and savoring, for instance.

We settled on the term *savoring* because for us it most vividly captures the active process of enjoyment, the ongoing interplay between person and environment. The word savoring also conveys metaphorically a search for the delectable, delicious, almost gustatory delights of the moment. Although the term fits more intuitively with attending to a sensory experience such as taste, we mean to extend it to attending to more complex cognitive associations. Our extension of the term savoring beyond mere sensation to include cognitive reflection is consistent with the etymology of the word "savor," which comes from the Latin word *sapere* meaning "to taste," "to have good taste," or "to be wise." Thus, we define the concept of savoring as going beyond the experience of pleasure to encompass a higher order awareness or reflective discernment on the part of the individual.

We would speak of savoring if people were attending to how much well-being they are deriving from their accomplishments or from their social connections. We would speak of savoring if people were attending to their pleasurable communion with nature or to their uplifting transcendence in God, taking pleasure from doing a difficult task, reflecting on the joy of watching their children grow up, or from countless other positive feelings. Indeed, the Oxford Unabridged Dictionary (Simpson & Weiner, 1989) also notes two major definitions of the verb "to savor (savour)." The first one is with regard to appreciating the enjoyment of the taste of food, but the second is with regard to appreciating the enjoyment of *any* experience. It is with that second meaning that we proceeded with our analysis of savoring.

Earlier References to Savoring-Like Processes

We are not the first social scientists to discuss concepts related to savoring. The earliest references to a savoring-like process that we can locate come from the literature on economics. In 1789, Bentham (1789/1948) included among the determinants of subjective utility the enjoyment currently derived from anticipating future gratification. Another early acknowledgement of people's awareness of future joy is from Marshall (1891), who noted "the pleasures of expectation" (p. 178). In a similar vein, Jevons (1905) noted "three distinct ways . . . in which pleasurable or painful feelings are caused: (1) By memory of past events; (2) By the sensation of present events; (3) By anticipation of future events" (p. 3). Jevons (1905) termed the latter phenomenon *anticipal pleasure,* which he considered to be the most critical determinant of economic behavior.

Analyzing the anticipation of a planned vacation, Jevons (1905) framed several interesting psychological hypotheses about temporal changes in the intensity of anticipal pleasure:

> The intensity of the anticipation will be greater the longer the holiday; greater also, the more intensely one expects to enjoy it when the time comes. In other words the amount of pleasure expected is one factor determining the intensity of anticipal pleasure. Again, the nearer the date fixed for leaving home approaches, the greater does the intensity of anticipal pleasure become: at first when the holiday is still many weeks ahead, the intensity increases slowly; then, as the time grows closer, it increases faster and faster, until it culminates on the eve of departure. (p. 64)

In a more up-to-date economic analysis of pleasure, Loewenstein (1987) specifically used the term *savouring* to refer to "positive utility derived from anticipation of future consumption" (p. 667), and provided an elaborate mathematical model of the anticipation and valuation of delayed consumption. Extending Jevons' (1905) and Lowenstein's (1987) analyses, we use the term *savoring* to denote the process of deriving pleasure in any one of the three temporal orientations, although we focus on the positive feelings that savoring evokes in the here and now. There is a paradox here: Although savoring can occur only in the moment, it may focus on past or future moments.

ASSUMPTIVE FRAMEWORK
FOR A MODEL OF SAVORING

Distinguishing Savoring From Pleasure

By the term savoring, we mean something different from mere pleasure, although savoring and pleasure are intimately connected concepts. When one savors, one is aware of pleasure and appreciates the positive feelings one is experiencing.

But by experiencing pleasure, one does not necessarily savor. Attentive and appreciative awareness of the pleasure must also occur or we would not consider the experience to involve savoring. As we emphasize later in this chapter, some degree of mindfulness (Langer, 1989) and meta-awareness (Schooler, 2001; Schooler, Ariely, & Loewenstein, 2003) has to be attached to an experience for it to be savored, at least in our sense of the word.

In considering the concept of pleasure, Russell (2003) argued that "pleasure is the most neglected topic in psychology, at least in relation to claims about its importance" (p. 161). Although some theorists view pleasure as a unitary construct—for example, as global subjective "experience" utility in decision making (Kahneman, Wakker, & Sarin, 1997), or as the satisfaction of visceral drives in physiology (Cabanac, 1992)—other theorists have adopted a multidimensional perspective and have proposed a variety of different typologies of pleasure. For example, Duncker (1941) distinguished three basic types of pleasures: sensory pleasures derived from physical sensations (e.g., the taste of wine, the feel of a Jacuzzi); aesthetic pleasures derived from sensations expressive of reactions to natural or human-made phenomena (e.g., a panoramic vista, an orchestral symphony); and accomplishment pleasures derived from the attainment of something desirable (e.g., receiving an award, winning an athletic competition). Other writers have highlighted additional varieties of pleasure, including social pleasures derived from the company of others (Dube & Le Bel, 2003; Kubovy, 1999; Tiger, 1992), pleasures of the body versus pleasures of the mind (Kubovy, 1999; Tiger, 1992), pleasures of anticipation (Loewenstein, 1987), and pleasures of memory (Bentham, 1781/1970).

Clearly, however, we are not mindful of all our pleasures. As Brown and Ryan (2003) noted, one may be aware of stimuli without these stimuli being at the center of attention. Even eating can be pleasurable without savoring, if there is no conscious attention focused on the sensations of pleasure as they are being experienced. Savoring involves not just the awareness of pleasure, but also a conscious attention to the experience of pleasure.

It would thus be hard to speak of savoring for one of the most intense human pleasures, sexual orgasmic gratification, because in the immediacy of that sexual response, mindful elaborated attention to the experience is often relatively absent. Poets and novelists may sometimes be mindful of that fleeting elusive phenomenon, but for most people, the experience of physical release dominates awareness. Pleasure indeed, but usually not in the category of a savoring experience. In fact, mindfulness about sexual activity can interfere with continuing a pleasurable sexual response. Many men and women lose their arousal when they closely attend to what they are doing and experiencing. Much sexual savoring, however, can occur in the anticipatory buildup to sexual release and in the afterglow of sexual gratification. Indeed, sexual savoring often occurs in the sensuous enjoyment of one's own body or in looking at the female or male body, or in touching or being touched in a sensuous way. Later we discuss such experiences as a form of savoring we term *luxuriating*. But rarely would we think of ongoing orgasm as eliciting sexual savoring.

In addition to their role in much of sexuality, the five senses give us many pleasures and at the same time easily lend themselves to savoring. Ackerman (1990), in *The Natural History of the Senses,* strives to do exactly what we wish to do in this book: make people more systematically aware of the joys of the senses, to become more mindful of them and how they operate in our experience. Ackerman (1990) presents the case of a woman who lost her capacity to smell, a sensory experience to which we generally pay little attention. When this woman recovered her sense of smell through medication, she found herself intoxicated with the smells of her everyday life, including the scent of her husband, smells of which she was unaware or that she had taken fully for granted. All of us can imagine being without one of our senses in this way, and this heightened awareness can then make us more fully conscious of the pleasurable things we see, hear, smell, touch, or taste. The process of appreciating this "missing sense" exemplifies what we mean by the term savoring.

Domains of Savoring

Just as the domains of pleasure are infinite, so too are the domains of savoring infinite. The domains to which we direct our attention when we savor know few bounds. Bearing this out is a study by Lowe (2002) in which people were asked to describe what gave them pleasure. Lowe (2002) used the Mass Observation Archive at the University of Sussex, in which a panel of several thousand volunteers had been recruited to respond to particular directives several times a year to write about various aspects of British life. A directive in 1993 asked these recruits about "all the nice things that happen to them and to report on ten things that gave them pleasure, from simple occasions to extravagant treats — and to describe them in detail." This directive instructed respondents to attend to what gives them pleasure, close to what we mean by savoring. An admittedly biased sample of only 387 responded. Those who did respond were mostly middle-aged or older, with only 13% under age 40. More women than men responded.

Despite the sample's lack of representativeness, the diversity of the types of things written about as sources of pleasure is startling. Men's top-ranked category was "Food and Drink," closely followed by "Music," "Reading," "Family/Children." For women, additional top-ranked sources of pleasurable experiences were "Entertainment," "Home/Garden," "Nature/Scenery." But although many of the responses can be categorized into a simple set, that set would not begin to cover what most people wrote about. A short list of some of the responses also includes: "Love/Sex," "Exercise/Sport," "Friends," all of which were mentioned relatively often, and "Memories," "Art," "Spiritual/Religious," "Smells," "Sounds," and "Humor," all of which were mentioned relatively infrequently.

If you look even more closely at what people wrote, a more diverse picture of people's "pleasures" emerges. Under food and drink, one person spoke of her "afternoon tea"; another of "fresh brown bread with cheddar cheese"; many spoke of chocolate. Here is what one respondent said about enjoying good wines:

> Good wine can make me feel orgasmic. The nose, taste and glow one gets can be overwhelming. I have occasionally had wine so delicious it has almost brought tears to my eyes. The ability to taste different spices, fruits, flowers, herbs within one glass of wine differentiates good wines to bad wines for me and a good wine requires time and thought to be fully enjoyed.

Notice how this response directly implicates savoring processes in its emphasis on a deliberate, conscious awareness of the pleasures of taste.

Some responses are not at all easily categorized. One respondent derived pleasure from taking a break:

> In later life I had a friend in the scrap metal business. Some Sunday afternoons, when he was free of account books and ledgers, he would call at my door and ask if I wanted to "go lean on a gate." He would drive in his car a few miles into the country before he found a quiet lane, and then he would stop, and leave the car and quite literally "lean on a gate." Most often we found ourselves looking across a field of sheep or cows against a dark backcloth of trees, and we would smoke and stare and talk a little. My friend called this simple pleasure "taking the creases out."

That response would be hard to categorize with most of the others, but could perhaps be viewed as "Stress Reduction," "Nature/Scenery," or "Camaraderie." In other words, the types of domains for savoring can vary enormously. Individuals are highly idiosyncratic about what they find pleasurable.

So are cultures. When asking people to identify events in their lives that are positive experiences, Lindberg (2004) found that East Asian Japanese, compared to European North Americans, identify a higher proportion of interpersonal events and a lower proportion of events deemed to be leisure activities. Other research on cross-cultural differences in positive emotional experience has found that Italians report more social interactions involving talking with others and feelings of interpersonal intimacy, whereas Scots, in contrast, report more positive feelings associated with relaxation and being alone (Duncan & Grazzani-Gavazzi, 2004). It stands to reason, therefore, that it would also be hard for us to create an exhaustive categorization of what all people everywhere savor.

Along these lines, previous theorists and researchers have noted that different types of pleasure-eliciting activities are associated with different types of pleasurable experiences, and that these in turn are also associated with different personality dimensions (Berenbaum, 2002; Meadows, 1975). For example, compared to other activities, social activities are more likely to evoke cheerfulness and are more strongly linked to extraversion, and intellectual activities are more likely to evoke enchantment and are more strongly linked to openness to experience (Berenbaum, 2002). It is not our intention to develop a comprehensive classification scheme for categorizing the variety of experiences that people savor and the correlates of these savoring responses. Nevertheless, later in this book we highlight some personality types that may be more likely to experience savoring under certain conditions.

A Mindful Fluid Process for the Here and Now

In addition to its direct connection to pleasurable experiences, a savoring experience can also be characterized as a mindful state. In contrast to other mindful, self-regulatory activities, however, savoring is in the moment, in the here and now. Although there is a chain of associations that can be elicited in savoring, none of them necessitates a future reward. If people attend too much to the future for their social and ego needs, we argue, they are in danger of interrupting the experience of savoring and are really enhancing other goals instead.

However, we do not rule out thinking about savoring in the future as a way to enhance the savoring of the present moment. For example, while savoring an ongoing visit with a close friend, one could think about later telling family members about the visit and could anticipate savoring this in the future. That awareness of the future can augment savoring the present visit with one's friend. Or one could currently be in a neutral affective state, and the mere anticipation of savoring an upcoming event might elicit savoring in the present.

While we are on the topic of anticipating future savoring as an adjunct to present savoring, we should speak of *dreams* of savoring, or delightful fantasies that may or may not come true. These dreams themselves can be savored in the present. A wonderful example of someone savoring positive fantasies occurs in Eliza Doolittle's song "Wouldn't It Be Loverly?" from the musical *My Fair Lady*. Alone, chilled, and destitute, she relishes fantasies about the simple pleasures that are missing in her life—having her own room, a large comfortable chair, a supply of chocolates, and a fire by which to warm herself—and imagines how "loverly" it would be to possess such things.

One doesn't have to be a poor, cold, friendless flower girl like Eliza Doolittle to have such dreams, dreams that make a person feel good just to have them in one's mind. Less in the realm of fantasy, most of us know what it is like to have savoring images while planning for a vacation, looking forward to Spring during the Winter, anticipating the arrival of loved ones, and thinking about revisiting places and experiences savored at some earlier time. Most people can enjoy thinking about their own daydreams and thoughts about the future, however outrageous these fantasies may be. In the here and now, they can savor them.

As an aside, it can be noted that sometimes vacations, planned encounters, and visits with others are not as sweet or thrilling as they were imagined in one's dreams. Indeed, certain styles of (over)anticipation, such as idealizing the future experience, may well predispose people to be disappointed when the positive event actually occurs. In chapter 6, we discuss a fascinating set of ideas and studies (Mitchell & Thompson, 1994; Mitchell, Thompson, Peterson, & Cronk, 1997) that focuses on the tendency people have to enjoy the present less, compared to the enjoyment they expected to experience and also compared to the enjoyment they remember later.

We suggest that people can *choose* to bring savoring processes into their future lives when they feel bereft of them in the present. Along these lines, a friend recently mentioned that he was going to teach his son to be spontaneous, which to us seems to be a contradiction in terms. In contrast, planning to savor is something different from planning to be spontaneous. We contend that planning to savor in the future may be successful. Although, more often than not, savoring comes out of the unplanned impromptu moment, we spell out ways that cognitive and behavioral processes can be invoked to set up conducive conditions for savoring to occur in the future, processes based on what people psychologically go through when they are savoring in the present.

Just as anticipating the *future* can become part of savoring in the present, reconsidering the *past* can also be brought to bear on what people are currently savoring. Many of us spend at least some time attending to and appreciating positive experiences from the past. In chapter 6, we highlight two common processes in savoring the past — namely, reminiscence and story-telling — that can augment people's savoring of ongoing positive experience.

Freedom From Social and Esteem Needs

When do we savor our experiences in life? Joe noticed in his retirement that he had more time and inclination to savor once he was freed from his work responsibilities. He wrote the following in his notes about savoring:

Outside the window framing my computer monitor are the lush greens of early summer mornings in Michigan. The sun gently illuminates shades of the verdant wild marsh on my left, thicker textured woods in front of me, and grazes three cedars and one small ash tree on my right. I can barely see the sky. I gaze at the scene awaiting the inevitable bird that interrupts the landscape with more flashy color. I'm not disappointed. A cardinal, solitary at the moment but sometimes with a mate, does his thing beneath the yew branches. A mourning dove perches on a dead limb of a willow in the marsh, and goes through a preening display for a good five minutes. I am savoring this ten-minute interruption from the ordinary flow of life, looking around me, and appreciating the visual blessings of the life I lead in the natural world. Had I been outside, I'm sure my appreciation of this scene would extend to the sounds and smells, and the almost erotic feel of the sun on my arms.

This is what it is all about, I tell myself. Savoring life. Enjoying its everyday bounty. This is what I wasn't doing in my life before retirement. This is what I'm now doing before I die. For so long I had been too busy as an academic researcher-professor-administrator at the University of Michigan to savor everyday life. Who had time to

*savor when you led a busy, involved, responsible professional life in the United States
at the turn of the 20th century?*

We assume that savoring may take a willingness to shed pressures from
performance and others' evaluations and to discard one's own expectations for
achievement and social well-being to let savoring happen. Given the rich bounties that come from savoring experiences, it is surprising how committed we
all seem to be to fulfilling such pressures and expectations for ourselves, even
though they often impede us from either launching into savoring activities or
letting our minds indulge in savoring respites from our ongoing responsibilities. Perhaps it is because savoring is so rewarding that men's and women's puri-
tanical souls rise up in protest. It is false, we assert, that savoring comes only to
those who have the leisure to savor or who have fully met all responsibilities and
major needs.

We assume that a person's own sense of social responsibility or personal
search for love and recognition often stand in the way of savoring experiences.
Will one allow oneself to indulge in savoring when there remain so many things
one *has to do* as a responsible, mature, loving adult?

A dear friend of ours rarely lets herself feast on pleasure because she is too
concerned about what her family needs. Even if no one is knocking on her door
for consolation or help, she imagines that they might be. Sooner than savor,
she would make plans to help someone. Fred's wife, Linda, has experienced that
herself in planning and preparing birthday parties for their children when they
were younger. She rarely savored the games and festivities she organized for
the celebration because she was so busy worrying about the social dynamics
of the party. It was only the next day, when she was without external obliga-
tion, that she could watch the videotape of the party and savor the celebration
retrospectively.

Obviously, there are differences in who takes on these overriding social
responsibilities or other standards for performance that interfere with savoring.
Perhaps we need an extended psychoanalysis of people to know the underlying
root of intense concerns with social responsibility. We only wish to highlight
here that we assume that concerns for doing the responsible thing often interfere with savoring, whether these concerns be moralistic, altruistic, rational, or
irrational in the situations we face.

Beyond concerns for social responsibility, are there other concerns that often
impede savoring? We could draw on Maslow's (1954) theory of the hierarchy of
motives to understand when savoring occurs. We could suggest that not just with
social responsibilities, but with every other concern in the hierarchy of motives,
if a need is unmet—if we're hungry, unsuccessful, frustrated, oppressed, or
unloved—then savoring cannot easily occur. Again, while there is some truth
in that, we don't believe it helps explain *all* conditions of savoring. Someone in
chronic pain might have trouble focusing on savoring a positive moment, but

we argue that, under certain conditions, that person could savor the pleasure of a thoughtful gift or revel in the innocent humor expressed by a child. A hungry person can savor the few morsels that he or she has or the blessings that exist in other domains of life. An unloved person can forget his or her rejection for a moment and enjoy, if not wallow in, music. Blues is a form of music that can speak to and be especially savored by those who feel unloved. At the time of the death of loved ones, most of us savor our memories of them. No doubt, people in the throes of rejection or mourning may be unable to switch to the savoring modality easily. But even in these circumstances we assume it is not impossible to savor.

Gratification of any need can of course be savored, if a person self-consciously attends to its gratification for any length of time beyond a fleeting moment. The feelings of achievement on receiving an award, the glow of good fellowship in getting together with friends, the joy of having won a point in an intellectual argument, sexual release, and many more positive experiences can be savored if people can stop to consider in some way the pleasures these gratifications give them. These gratifications can even be vicarious. If one's children, one's parents, or other loved ones experience something wonderful in their lives, most of us may vicariously experience that as something wonderful, and savor it.

In Yiddish there is a word for that vicarious savoring—one *kvells* over a loved one's accomplishment, which means that the person reaps and holds in consciousness some pleasure from what the loved one has done. There can be similar vicarious savoring from the accomplishments of a protégé, a mentor, or a colleague. A colleague's accomplishments, however, can often invite comparison to oneself, which can immediately raise concerns about one's own achievements and hence might stand in the way of savoring the colleague's accomplishment. In the same way, sibling rivalry often prevents true savoring of a brother or sister's accomplishments. The experience of *schadenfreunde,* in which one takes malicious delight in the misfortunes of others (R. H. Smith, 2000), represents yet another wrinkle in the complex fabric of savoring.

In another set of notes on savoring upon retirement, Joe suggested that he wanted to grab all the savoring moments he could in retirement while he still had his capacity to get around and before physical immobilization took over. On reflection, Joe now thinks this is a short-sighted view of savoring. Even if his range of activity is depleted in the future, his capacity to savor is not diminished. Only the realm of what is savored changes. For the elderly, losses in physical capacities do not vitiate a variety of other positive experiences—for example, what the future has in store for grandchildren not yet born, great-grandchildren in the offing, music unheard, books unread.

Technically, it would be difficult to call an end to savoring unless we totally capitulate to simple stereotypes about the grim fate of the disabled in our society. To be sure, physically challenged individuals have their problems, but these difficulties do not infuse every aspect of their lives. This analysis suggests that one of the main tasks of adaptation to disability, beyond learning to cope with one's limitations, is learning to find new ways to fulfill one's limitless capacity to savor life. As Helen Keller, who was deaf and blind, noted (Schoeneck, 1987, p. 2):

> What we once enjoyed
> We can never lose.
> All that we love deeply
> Becomes a part of us.

We return to the study of savoring among the elderly in chapters 6 and 7.

The Focused Nature of What Is Savored

When we present our model for savoring in chapters 3 through 6, we will suggest that in savoring something, people are *focusing attention* on their subjective experience. The focused mindfulness in savoring enables people to consider their ongoing experience as being something more than just their impulsive personal feelings and sensations. The fact that savoring sometimes occurs rather spontaneously can make it feel as if such focusing is being controlled mysteriously from the outside, and it may also lead us to see the savored experience as sometimes "outside" ourselves, a phenomenon we later refer to as world-focused savoring. Consider, for example, the sudden appearance of rainbows and how awestruck people generally are at seeing them. This is not to say that to savor, one has to focus on an external object. On the contrary, the attentional focus of savoring can also be primarily on an internal thought, feeling, or sensation—a phenomenon we later refer to as self-focused savoring. We merely wish to suggest that in savoring, people partially set a positive experience apart from their immediately attending self, such that the attending self interacts more directly with the focused experience, whatever that experience might be. Along these lines, Lambie and Marcel (2002) have distinguished between the *first-order consciousness* of phenomenal experience and the *second-order consciousness* of personal awareness, or "introspective awareness or appreciation of one's emotions" (p. 220). Thus, savoring by virtue of its state of mindful meta-awareness is an experience of second-order consciousness.

Although we have said that savoring requires a kind of immediacy, we are also saying that the immediacy experienced need not be totally self-oriented. Certainly it can be an individually derived experience that no one else senses in quite the same way, but it still is something that one can "look at," as if it were an event, a circumscribed experience that involves more than just instinctive sensory experiences. Savoring daydreams and fantasies is likewise the process of enjoying internal images that have taken on some focused reality. When fantasies become the dominant experience people savor in their lives, however, this situation can raise concerns about their ability to interact with others. But for a person to savor such fantasies some of the time seems to be a very human process that we should recognize and tolerate in ourselves and others.

It is important to consider how clearly focused the experience of savoring is. This is an important dimension we consider in the next chapters. The savoring process is somewhat like treating a personal internal feeling as if it were an external object. A person can go from merely tasting a glass of wine as an undefined positive experience, to something much more complex, attending to what is being tasted, appreciating that good taste, and thereby savoring the experience. The tasting has then become more clearly focused, albeit still a reaction to a subjective experience. A proposition that we consider is that the most clearly focused experiences of savoring are those most easily prolonged and most easily reinvoked at later times, while those savoring experiences that are least clearly focused are short-lived and least available for future reflection in other contexts.

In focusing attention, a person is being mindful; and in being mindful, according to Langer (1989), one is open to new ways of perceiving and categorizing experience. In the case of a savoring experience, this means being complexly aware of the experience of pleasure, delight, joy, contentment, awe, pride, or other positive feelings. Sometimes people can deliberately adopt a conscious strategy to pay attention to their pleasures, but more often they find themselves just attending in a savoring way without any strategic deliberation about it. In summary, besides being a mindful enjoyment and appreciation of a positive experience, savoring also involves: (a) a sense of immediacy, of something occurring in the here and now; (b) freedom from social and esteem needs as major, motivating concerns; and (c) some focused and mindful connection to the experience, and not just the experience of hedonistic pleasure or various ego gratifications. This triad of characteristics forms the core assumptive foundation of savoring processes.

DEFINITION OF KEY CONCEPTUAL TERMS RELATED TO SAVORING

In explicating the nature of savoring, we use three interrelated conceptual terms, the definitions of which are important to specify and distinguish clearly and precisely. These key terms are: savoring experiences, savoring processes, and savoring responses or strategies. At the broadest level, a savoring experience represents the totality of a person's sensations, perceptions, thoughts, behaviors, and emotions when mindfully attending to and appreciating a positive stimulus, outcome, or event, along with the accompanying environmental or situational features of that encounter. Examples of savoring experiences include a tourist viewing the Egyptian Pyramids from the back of a camel, a diner tasting an exotic dish in a gourmet restaurant, and a hiker soaking in a hot tub under the stars after a long day of backpacking.

At the intermediate level, a savoring process is a sequence of mental or physical operations that unfolds over time and transforms a positive stimulus, outcome, or event into positive feelings to which a person then attends and savors. Savoring processes involve noticing and attending to something positive, interpreting and responding cognitively or behaviorally to this stimulus (with savoring responses or strategies), experiencing positive emotional reactions as a consequence, attending to these positive feelings in an appreciative way, and often repeating this sequence of operations iteratively over time in a dynamic transactional cycle. Along these same lines, Folkman and Lazarus (1985) have distinguished between coping processes (that change over time as people transact with the environment) and coping responses or strategies (which are specific cognitions or behaviors that influence the coping process).

Different savoring processes regulate different positive emotional states. For example, the savoring process of marveling regulates awe, thanksgiving regulates gratitude, basking regulates pride, and luxuriating regulates physical pleasure. Within negative psychology lie parallels to the concept of savoring processes in positive psychology, such as the coping processes of mourning in response to grief and psychosocial adjustment in response to a disabling injury or accident.

At the microlevel, a savoring response or strategy is a specific, concrete thought or behavior in which a person engages in reaction to a positive stimulus, outcome, or event. These cognitive or behavioral responses moderate the impact of positive events on positive emotions by amplifying or dampening the intensity, or prolonging or curtailing the duration, of positive feelings. Savoring responses are operational components of the savoring process. For example, the savoring process of basking often entails specific cognitive savoring responses reflecting self-congratulation, in which one thinks about how impressed others are by one's personal accomplishments or how long one has worked for the particular outcome. Paralleling the concept of savoring responses, the coping literature includes the concept of specific coping responses, such as talking to others about one's feelings, trying not to think about one's problems, or making a plan to change the situation, each of which may be part of several different coping processes.

Relating these three key savoring-related terms to one another, we believe that different savoring experiences initiate different savoring processes, which themselves include different types of savoring responses moderating different positive emotions. In chapter 4, we distinguish a variety of different types of savoring responses or strategies in exploring the structure of savoring. In chapter 5, we explicate several basic savoring processes and present an integrative conceptual framework for understanding these phenomena.

SAVORING PROCESSES CONTRASTED WITH SIMILAR PHENOMENA

We have argued that savoring requires three important preconditions: a sense of immediacy in the here and now; freedom from social and esteem needs as motivations; and focused mindful attention to positive experience. These three prerequisite criteria for the occurrence of savoring are the building blocks of the model of savoring that we explicate more fully in the next few chapters. Before we begin, however, we recognize that these assumptive criteria raise questions about how to distinguish savoring processes from other processes that have emerged in similar conceptual spheres of positive psychology. In broadly staking out what we mean by savoring, we realize we share common conceptual ground with at least nine related but different phenomena currently in the positive psychology literature: mindfulness, meditation, daydreaming, emotional intelligence, time work, positive emotions per se, aesthetic responses, intrinsic motivation, and flow. Let us briefly highlight the similarities and differences between savoring processes and these related phenomena.

Savoring and Mindfulness

In her book, *Mindfulness,* Langer (1989) put psychologists in touch with a way of thinking about consciousness that had previously been neglected — namely, the way people gear themselves to being alert about their changing environmental contexts. According to Langer, when people are mindful, they are open to generating new ways of looking at the world and are not controlled by routines and habitual ways of observing. Along these lines, Thera (1972) described mindfulness as "the clear and single-minded awareness of what actually happens to us and in us at the successive moments of perception" (p. 5). Other theorists have defined mindfulness as "an enhanced attention to and awareness of current experience or present reality" (Brown & Ryan, 2003, p. 822), typically characterized by "open" or receptive consciousness (Deikman, 1982; Martin, 1997).

When people savor, they too are mindful of their experience, but their attention does not remain totally open to incoming or internal stimuli. Instead, the savoring process involves a more restrictive focus on internal and external stimuli associated with positive affect. In that sense, savoring is a narrower concept than mindfulness.

Increased mindfulness has been linked to positive emotional states and increased well-being (Brown & Ryan, 2003). There is also experimental evidence to support the connection between focused attention and savoring. For example, instructing people to attend to the physical sensations they experience while eating chocolate produces greater reported pleasure, compared to performing a distraction task while eating chocolate (Le Bel & Dube, 2001). Indeed, an increased awareness of pleasurable sensations lies at the very heart of savoring.

Savoring and Meditation

We can draw a similar distinction between savoring and another conscious process: *meditation.* Both are processes involving how people focus their attention, but there is a crucial difference. Savoring focuses attention on the consciousness of feelings or the arrangement of ideas that elicit feelings. Meditation, according to Shapiro (1980), focuses attention in a nonanalytic way, either on a single object (concentrative meditation) or on all possible internal or external stimuli (mindfulness meditation). In either kind of meditation, people consciously intend to transcend themselves and to enter into the flow of consciousness. Shapiro, Schwartz, and Santerre (2002) noted a third category of meditation, contemplative meditation, that involves opening up to a "larger self." One can see, therefore, that, like the process of mindfulness, meditation of any sort focuses less deliberately on feelings as the target of attention. Feelings are not always directly involved in meditation as they are in savoring. People who meditate may feel good after the process, but during the process their feelings are not necessarily the focus of their attention. People who savor, by contrast, deliberately attend to positive feelings and to those experiences that are making them feel good.

For example, transcendental meditation (TM) allows one to experience a relaxed and enjoyable state that draws attention inward and quiets the mind while also increasing one's level of alertness (Bloomfield, Cain, & Jaffe, 1975). Although TM practitioners experience thoughts and feelings while meditating, they are taught to disengage from these sensations in order to achieve a state of pure awareness, which consists of being alert without being aware of anything except awareness itself. Indeed, one is taught "never to interrupt the ongoing process of meditation by analyzing thoughts which arise during the practice" (Bloomfield et al., 1975, pp. 25–26).

Savoring, on the other hand, entails a deliberate contemplation of one's own inner experience. Rather than turning away from positive thoughts and feelings that arise in the moment, when one savors, one intentionally reflects on these experiences, mulling them over, "swishing them around" in one's mind, so to speak, as one would savor a fine wine on one's palate. In the process, one explicitly acknowledges associated thoughts and feelings that arise, further enhancing enjoyment.

Savoring and Daydreaming

Earlier, we noted that when people savor daydreams and fantasies, they are enjoying internal images that have taken on some "objective" reality. But this is not to say that daydreaming is necessarily a form of savoring. On the contrary, daydreaming is characterized by a stream of thought that turns attention inward and that is no longer determined by one's immediate surroundings or current task (Singer, 1981). Furthermore, daydreaming has been conceptualized as unpremeditated and without goal or purpose (Klinger, 1990), whereas savoring has the clear, deliberate goal of amplifying or prolonging positive emotional experience.

Consider the special case of "positive daydreaming" (Langens & Schmalt, 2002), in which people generate cognitive imagery that "enacts the successful attainment of personal goals" (p. 1726). Research has found that the emotional consequences of positive daydreaming depend on an individual's level of fear of failure. For those high in fear of failure, a positive daydream can actually signify the likely absence rather than presence of future positive outcomes. For these people, becoming aware of the absence of desired goals in this way can ultimately produce a negative mood and some goal disengagement as a form of mood repair (Langens & Schmalt, 2002). For people low in fear of failure, in contrast, daydreaming about attaining personal goals signifies the likely presence of future positive outcomes and provides a motivational incentive to strive toward those goals, thereby increasing goal commitment (Langens & Schmalt, 2002).

Clearly, people may or may not savor positive daydreams, depending on their characteristic expectations regarding failure. Indeed, anticipating future positive outcomes may well make people feel demoralized or depressed if they believe that they are unlikely to attain these outcomes (MacLeod, Pankhania, Lee, & Mitchell, 1997). To savor a positive daydream, one must be mindfully aware of the feelings of pride, joy, pleasure, or fulfillment that it provides and must consciously reflect on these good feelings. Thus, just because one is daydreaming does not mean that one actually savors the experience.

Savoring and Emotional Intelligence

As a process underlying the management of positive emotions, savoring shares some connections with emotional intelligence, or "the ability to monitor one's own and others' emotions, to discriminate among them, and to use the information to guide one's thinking and actions" (Mayer & Salovey, 1993, p. 433). Higher levels of emotional intelligence have been linked to greater positive affect and psychological well-being (Goleman, 1995; Salovey, Mayer, Goldman, Turvey, & Palfai, 1995; Schutte, Malouff, Simunek, McKenley, & Hollander, 2002). Savoring, like emotional intelligence, involves awareness and regulation of emotions, as well as the use of emotional cues to direct thoughts and behaviors.

Savoring also shares common ground with the narrower constructs of *mood attention* (Salovey et al., 1995) and *mood awareness* (Swinkels & Giuliano, 1995), which encompass both mood monitoring and mood labeling. However, although savoring requires people to be aware of their positive feelings, people may or may not explicitly label these feelings. Nonetheless, just as the ability to understand what one is feeling facilitates the regulation of negative emotion (Barrett, Gross, Christensen, & Benvenuto, 2001), we expect that the ability to discriminate among different types of positive feelings — for example, joy, awe, pride, serenity, or gratitude — facilitates savoring.

Although previous theorists and researchers have devoted a great deal of attention to the self-control of negative emotion, little work has been done on the regulation of positive emotion (Gross, 1999). The prevailing assumption has been that people are generally motivated to avoid, prevent, or curtail bad feelings and to obtain, generate, or prolong good feelings (Klinger, 1982; Kokkonen & Pulkkinen, 1999; Zillmann, 1988), resulting in what has been termed "a unidirectional effort to achieve a pleasurable state of mind" (Erber, Wegner, & Therriault, 1996, p. 757). The scant evidence that does exist suggests that happy people tend to avoid things that would reduce their positive feelings (Freedman, 1978; Isen, 2000; Wegener & Petty, 1994).

Emotional intelligence involves the adaptive harnessing of emotions in oneself and others (Salovey & Mayer, 1989–1990; Schutte, Malouff, Hall, et al., 1998). Likewise, savoring may be either adaptive or maladaptive depending on the contexts in which it occurs. To devote attention to savoring a landscape while driving in fast-moving, bumper-to-bumper traffic, for example, may not be adaptive. Thus, people may savor in emotionally intelligent or unintelligent ways, and they can learn healthier ways of savoring their lives. Indeed, deficits in the separate domains of monitoring, understanding, or regulating positive emotions might well require different therapeutic interventions. We return to this point in chapter 8 when we discuss how to enhance savoring.

Savoring and Time Work

A relatively new concept that relates closely to savoring is the notion of *time work,* or the management of temporal experience. Characterized by purposeful, agentic self-determination, time work has been defined as individual or interpersonal efforts to create or regulate particular kinds of temporal experience (Flaherty, 1999, 2003; Garfinkel, 1967). Flaherty (2003) identified five main forms of time work in which people engage, involving attempts to control or manipulate the duration, frequency, sequence, timing, or allocation of temporal experience. The deliberate effort to control perception through time work resembles the mindful customizing of positive experience through savoring.

The temporal variable of duration is a case in point. In particular, Flaherty (2003) noted that "some individuals find themselves in (or anticipate) pleasurable circumstances, and they want to prolong the experience" (p. 22). Clearly, this represents one kind of savoring, in which people consciously strive to hold onto positive experiences and make them last longer. For example, Flaherty (2003) interviewed a young female respondent who described how she savors a weekend:

> I always try to make the good days last a little longer by spacing [out] the things I'm going to do . . . so that there's always something waiting to be done. I'll also try to make the days seem longer by making it a point to stop in the middle of it and think about what I am doing and what I still have left to do, and for a while at least, put time on hold. (p. 22).

A 54-year-old female respondent used a similar strategy to prolong enjoyment of a vacation: "I try to slow down my breathing, visually take in my surroundings, be aware of being in the present moment, be grateful for this time to be peaceful and relaxed, and enjoy my surroundings or activity" (Flaherty, 2003, pp. 22–23). As Flaherty (2003) observed, "Whereas those who want to accelerate the perceived passage of time imagine or remember other circumstances, those who wish to prolong their experiences concentrate on the here-and-now of the current situation" (p. 23). Clearly, savoring by prolonging or lingering in happy moments represents a way of increasing the perceived duration of positive experience. But savoring can also entail thoughts and behavior aimed at intensifying positive experience, independent of its duration. Thus, savoring may involve time work, but not necessarily.

Savoring and Positive Emotions

If the distinction between savoring and both mindfulness and meditation rests on the fact that the process of savoring deals with positive feelings, then how do we distinguish savoring from positive feelings or emotions themselves? As we said earlier in distinguishing savoring and pleasure, savoring is a mindful process that attends to the pleasurable affect, but it is not identical to pleasure, however closely tied it is to positive affect. Fredrickson (2001) developed an elegant theory of positive emotions (e.g., joy, contentment, pride) that involve people's entire thought–action repertoire, including attention to and curiosity about the world around them. Nevertheless, in Fredrickson's conceptualization of positive emotions, the focus is on the elicitation and strength of the feeling and its consequence. She does posit, however, that a positive emotion broadens what we may attend to. In a certain sense, we are suggesting that such broadening may involve savoring processes that amplify positive emotions. If a savoring process is elicited when a positive emotion is experienced, then savoring could very well be the mediating mechanism through which a person's cognitive repertoire is expanded when a positive emotion is experienced. Furthermore, when people savor, they often broaden the range of feelings they can have and the contexts in which these feelings occur. At any rate, savoring processes and positive emotions are closely allied, but we should be careful to distinguish them as being distinctly separate phenomena.

Savoring and the Aesthetic Response

Let us consider in some detail aesthetic pleasures, or positive feelings people have in the presence of naturally occurring or creatively formed beauty. Philosophers call these experiences *aesthetic reactions*. Analysts of aesthetics have defined the *aesthetic response* in many different ways. The definition we prefer is: to receive a communication of feelings through the arrangement of visual, auditory, and other sensory modes or through the arrangement of words and ideas in written or oral forms. It is a very human response to be moved by a painting, a song, a poem, or other works where the person who created the work intends to reveal and communicate feelings. There does not have to be a one-to-one correspondence between the feelings that the creative person intended and the feelings the observer experiences. What is important is that there is a transfer of feelings in the process of communication.

When such an aesthetic response occurs, can one speak of the person who has that response as savoring? We say "yes," if the person is being mindful of the experience and not simply reacting with emotion. People can be aesthetically overwhelmed with deep emotional awe when hearing a Bach chorale without attending to the various nuances of the sound that inspired that awe. However, when people become mindful of the nuances of the experience as they are listening, we say they are savoring the music. In many instances, aesthetic responses are savored in this way, but in many instances they are not. Humans are often moved by a work of art and indeed profoundly affected by it, perhaps experiencing awe and transcendence, without having the mindfulness required for savoring.

Consider the following excerpt from the collected writings of Richard Feynman, perhaps the finest physicist of our time, in which an artist and a scientist each contemplate the beauty of a flower:

> I have a friend who's an artist and he's sometimes taken a view which I don't agree with very well. He'll hold up a flower and say, "Look how beautiful it is," and I'll agree, I think. And he says — "you see, I as an artist can see how beautiful this is, but you as a scientist, oh, take this all apart and it becomes a dull thing." And I think he's kind of nutty. First of all, the beauty that he sees is available to other people and to me, too, I believe, although I might not be quite as refined aesthetically as he is; but I can appreciate the beauty of a flower. At the same time I see much more about the flower than he sees. I can imagine the cells in there, the complicated actions inside which also have beauty. . . . Also the processes, the fact that the colors in the flower evolved in order to attract insects to pollinate it is interesting — it means that insects can see the color. It adds a question: Does this aesthetic sense also exist in lower forms? Why is it aesthetic? All kinds of interesting questions which shows that a science knowledge only adds to the excitement and mystery and the awe of a flower. (Robbins, 1999, p. 2).

Feynman's observations clearly illustrate the difference between a purely aesthetic response to the flower's beauty and the deliberate process of savoring that beauty.

But how about the reverse question? When people are savoring, can we automatically say that they are having an aesthetic experience? We say "no" in answer to that question. Savoring does not mean that a person is necessarily mindful of the arrangement of stimulation. In contrast to aesthetic responses — such as enjoying a painting or being moved by a play — when savoring, the form of our associations is not critical. When people rather randomly consider the beauties of the landscape they are viewing, they may be savoring but not having an aesthetic experience. Sometimes a person perceives a landscape in a more aesthetic way, and we humorously call it "nature imitating art." An Ansel Adams photograph, however, might reflect the artist's savored appreciation of the formal aspects of nature. Indeed, some critics have suggested that in photographing a landscape, Ansel Adams purposefully captured his experience of a moment in time in a setting, as if he were trying to communicate what he savored about the scene. Therefore, when observers aesthetically appreciate one of his photographs, they may well experience the same savoring Adams experienced in appreciating the formal structure of the landscape he caught on film and brought to life in the darkroom.

Empathy or identification with characters in plays and novels can also lead to savoring, if the characters are having positive feelings. In literature, on the stage, or in a film, if a character experiences a triumphant moment after overcoming adversity, we may be particularly moved by vicarious joy. Indeed, many people report being especially choked up at those times, particularly if the words used to convey the feelings have a grand sweep. We might term it "delicious schmaltz." The familiar "lump in the throat" (known as *globus hystericus* in medical terms) reflects this type of vicarious response. Humor in literature can also be savored, as can the pleasure in just getting to know a character more fully. Indeed, many people savor the mere pleasure of reading, even sad stories, because it takes them out of their everyday world for a brief while. "Addicted" readers are often let down when a particularly good read is finished. Addicted film buffs might say the same about the end of a well-crafted, engrossing movie. Thus, in many ways, savoring and having aesthetic responses can be overlapping experiences.

We do not wish to suggest, however, that all aesthetic reactions involve savoring. The buildup and release of tension in reading or viewing tragedies may involve savoring processes, but it is unlikely. Aristotle long ago posited that in good tragedies there is a purging of emotions that comes from experiencing the drama. It would be hard to coordinate this view with our conception of savoring as a process of mindfully appreciating a positive experience. Nevertheless, if the emotional purging in a tragedy brought a pleasurable sense of relief that one could mindfully appreciate, then one might well be able to savor this positive state.

Savoring and Intrinsic Motivation

In motivational psychology, there is a body of literature suggesting that human beings often behave as if there were no clear external reward for their activity other than a sense of their own competence (White, 1959) with a clear internal attribution for their behavior, or what has been termed *intrinsic motivation* (Deci, 1975). In response to our explication of savoring, the reader might begin to think of this concept as either a set of processes that have no external motivating agents or a set of activities that are intrinsically motivated.

One could ask why people savor, and possible answers would seem to include that they feel competent when they savor, or that they like being guided not by external rewards but by their own appreciative reactions to what they are experiencing.

These answers to the question of why people savor do not cover the heart of the experience of savoring. Competence may be involved in savoring experiences, but many other human needs can also be part of savoring. As noted earlier, people can savor their sociability as well as their mastery; they can savor their aesthetic reactions to external stimuli as well as their own internally generated experiences. Furthermore, if competence reigns as the basis for behavior, then concerns about competence may well interfere with savoring, just as when any other ego or esteem needs become dominant.

In addition, important to the idea of intrinsic motivation is the notion that one attributes the particular activity not externally, but to oneself. As far as we can tell, the attribution of causes of positive experiences that one savors is irrelevant to whether savoring processes occur in the first place. For instance, one might savor a spectacular sunrise as it slowly tinges the clouds crimson with alpenglow—a positive experience for which one might feel absolutely no personal responsibility. Nevertheless, it may very well be that one can better prolong savoring in settings where one is intrinsically motivated to act. In any event, savoring is a phenomenon distinctly separate from intrinsic motivation.

Savoring and Flow

Finally, we should consider the conceptual overlap between savoring and Csikszentmihalyi's (1975, 1990, 2002) conception of *flow experiences*. In a brilliant analysis of what humans truly find gratifying in their activities, Csikszentmihalyi has argued and presented considerable evidence that optimal "flow" experiences occur when people engage in activities that provide persistent but not overwhelming challenges to their efficacy. In such activities, people lose both themselves and a sense of time passing; and their attention is totally centered on the task at hand. Hobbyists, artists, and writers often have that experience when they become engrossed in what they are trying to create. Even at work or in everyday life, one can have these flow experiences if one is challenged appropriately, but at the same time feels that he or she is being efficacious.

When people lose themselves in their activities in that way, we could easily say they are savoring their activity. And yet we hesitate to call these flow experiences "savoring." Compared with a savoring experience, flow activity implies far less conscious attention to the experience. It is almost as if flow has its own self-generating motivation without the intervention of any extraneous mindfulness, much like many sexual activities. Mindfulness seems not to be a necessary condition for flow. Indeed, Nakamura and Csikszentmihalyi (2002) contend that intense self-awareness disrupts the process of flow.

More importantly, as Csikszentmihalyi (1975, 1990, 2002) speaks of flow, it involves issues of efficacy and challenge that keep the person engrossed in the experience. Flow occurs when a person's skills perfectly match the demands of the task at hand; when task demands exceed one's skills, the result is anxiety, and when the person's skills exceed task demands, the result is boredom (Csikszentmihalyi, 1975, 1990). Accomplishing a task or solving a problem is thus part of flow experiences. When concerns about performance dominate one's attention, however, they can interfere with flow. Likewise, we have explicitly argued that concentration on any ego needs, including mastery or competence, as mentioned earlier, can also interfere with savoring. Thus, the processes that maintain flow and the processes that maintain savoring may well have some similarity.

Finally, we recognize that one can savor a flow experience if one can focus one's attention on the experience as it is happening or just after it has happened. And yet we caution that if one is savoring a flow experience, then the process of focusing on the positive feelings that flow engenders while it is occurring might undermine the ongoing experience of flow. Research on flow suggests that people are not explicitly aware of the pleasure they are feeling at the time that flow occurs. Indeed, Csikszentmihalyi (1999) has argued that awareness of pleasure in flow activities may only happen afterwards:

> Strictly speaking, during the experience of [flow] people are not necessarily happy because they are too involved in the task to have the luxury to reflect on their subjective states. ... But afterwards, when the experience is over, people report having been in as positive a state as it is possible to feel. (p. 825)

Further linking savoring and flow, there is evidence that individuals high in trait absorption — that is, the "disposition to enter under conducive circumstances psychological states that are characterized by marked restructuring of the phenomenal self and world" (Tellegen, 1992, p. 1) — experience stronger aesthetic responses than those low in trait absorption (Wild, Kuiken, & Schopflocher, 1995). Along these lines, Wild et al. (1995) speculated that people high in absorption prefer to devote more attention to affect than to other attentional objects, a tendency that might well facilitate the process of savoring. Thus, people more prone to absorptive flow experiences may also be more adept at savoring. We return to the concept of flow in chapter 4, when we discuss absorption as a type of savoring strategy.

PREVIEW OF UPCOMING CHAPTERS

In this chapter, we staked out what the concept of savoring is generally about and we examined a number of other concepts to which savoring is related. We noted how savoring is both alike and different from these other concepts. In the next four chapters, we get to the heart of the psychology of savoring. We begin by presenting the critical issues that a model of savoring must confront (chapter 2), and in so doing, we highlight several reports of savoring experiences that illustrate these issues. We then discuss the central premises of the model (chapter 3); report the results of research on the various types of cognitive and behavioral savoring strategies that people use in response to positive events (chapter 4); and present an integrative conceptual framework for understanding different kinds of savoring processes, including four primary forms of savoring (i.e., marveling, thanksgiving, basking, and luxuriating) that people encounter in their lives (chapter 5). We then consider the role of time in relation to savoring (chapter 6) and discuss how savoring relates to a variety of vital human concerns, including love, marriage, friendship, mental and physical health, creativity, meaning, and spirituality (chapter 7). Finally, in chapter 8, we consider the model's implications for helping people enhance savoring in their lives.

2

Critical Issues for a Psychology of Savoring

*The most visible joy can only reveal itself
to us when we've transformed it, within.*
—Rainier Rilke (1923/2005)

What should constitute a psychology of savoring? That most everyone savors at one time or another seems incontrovertible. But when does savoring happen? Can a person control when or how it happens? Can people savor the past or the future? Are there different kinds of savoring experiences? What processes go on when it happens? What influences the intensity of the experience? Can other people be involved in what seems to be a very private experience? Indeed, are there cultural differences in savoring processes? These are a few of the conceptual questions any formal model for the psychology of savoring must address. Beyond these concerns is an important pragmatic issue for us as social scientists: How should we go about measuring features of the savoring process for systematic study? In this chapter, we first discuss important conceptual issues relevant to a psychology of savoring and then in a final section address the need to establish means of measurement.

CONCEPTUAL ISSUES

In this introductory section, we highlight six major conceptual issues raised by the questions just asked, issues we address more fully in the model for savoring we develop in the next four chapters of this book. Clearly, these are not the only issues we need to consider, but they are the ones that we have found arise immediately when we introduce the general nature of our inquiry.

The first two questions that commonly arise concern the perceptions implicated in savoring processes. As Issue 1, we ask: Does savoring refer only to sensory events such as taste, as the term *savoring* commonly connotes, or can savoring refer to more complex cognitive events? As Issue 2, we ask whether savoring has to involve conscious awareness. Issue 3 addresses the questions of how savoring processes in general are engaged and halted. As Issue 4, we discuss a critical aspect of Issue 3: What is the role of intentionality in starting and stopping the process of savoring? Issue 5 examines the critical dimension of time and whether people can savor the past or the future. And finally, Issue 6 addresses questions concerning the social and cultural nature of savoring. As we present these issues, we feature several qualitative reports of savoring experiences, in order to make the relatively abstract issues we discuss more concrete. Now, let us consider these six critical conceptual issues.

Issue 1: Are Savoring Experiences Limited to Simple Sensory Events, or Can an Awareness of Complex Thoughts Also Be Savored?

It is perhaps easiest to think of savoring as a process applied to only one sensory experience at a time, such as tasting a particularly rich dessert one craves or listening to the latest CD by a favorite musical performer. And yet there is nothing about our initial definition of savoring that suggests it has to be limited to only one sensory experience at a time, or for that matter, to only experiences that are sensory. Clearly, there are times when absorbing a visual stimulus and listening to an aural stimulus simultaneously would enhance the appreciation of each of them. From the comfort of home, viewing a wild storm brewing up over a lake can be a visually beautiful experience. If you then add the sounds of the wind and the rain on your roof, they make for special savoring. So do sounds combined with visual images. Many of us have savored intriguing performances of *sons et lumieres* [sounds and lights], as well as excerpts from Disney's film, *Fantasia,* that are remarkable in the use of dual sensory modes. Indeed, good musical scores can help audiences savor the visual details of a movie scene.

Do savoring experiences involve only sensory events? No, many of us would say. A person can savor a psychological state without clear connection to one of the senses. Consider these passages from Nichols' (1987) *A Fragile Beauty,* describing a walk he took on the mesa behind his ranch in Taos, New Mexico, after a wintry snowfall:

> I pass black and brown cows mournfully standing around, wondering what next?
> Steam boils out of their nostrils. Mountains are bleached from top to bottom,
> and their whiteness merges with the snowy mesa, and the snowcover travels west

until it fades into the cerulean blue atmosphere. . . . Right now the arctic mood belongs solely to me. I own the mountains; the sky begins expanding an inch above my shoulders. The solitude creates a rapture inside me. Creak, creak, my boots advance. Until, for the last time, I halt, turning a circle, gazing all around. I don't want to lose it, I suppress feelings of loss. Perhaps I can't ever reproduce the satisfaction of this moment; maybe I'll never again have such reverence for life. It doesn't matter. The most precious gifts often dissolve off my fingertips within a moment of their triumphs. . . . We are touched by magic wands. For a fraction of just one day, life is perfect, and we are absolutely happy and in harmony with the earth. The feeling passes much too quickly. But the memory — and the anticipation of other miracles — sustains us in the battle indefinitely. (pp. 74–76)

While extraordinarily attentive to what he sees as he inspects the world of his mesa, Nichols also reveals to the reader other ongoing processes: an "arctic mood," "a rapture" of solitude, a "reverence for life," being in "harmony with the earth," and "the anticipation of other miracles." His savoring experience was indeed complex, both sensory and ideational. Thus, there may be any number of cognitive associations people have at the same time they are experiencing sensory phenomena. When a person savors the beauty of a painting, it may not be merely because of the feelings that the painting's visual imagery evokes, but also because of the many other associations the painting evokes.

Looking at Cezanne's oil painting, *The Card Players,* for example, a viewer can attend to and appreciate the soft subtlety of the multicolored textures of the three players' clothes and the elegant integration of all five figures in the design of the canvas. These and other visual absorptions can induce savoring. But that is not all. The viewer also can attend to the meaning of the two observers of the game, and get caught up in an imagined story about the event. Both the visual artistry and the viewer's own imputed meanings and reactions to those meanings can, together, contribute to the savoring.

Indeed, a person can also savor something without *any* sensory cue at all. One can attend to the wonderful elegance of a mathematical proof, or to the joys of reading a suspenseful melodrama, or to the many simultaneous pleasures experienced at a family reunion. These experiences are complex targets of attention. Certainly, there may be some cognitive limit to how many different dimensions one can be mindful of and savor at any given moment. Nevertheless, a person in a mindful state can cognitively absorb many facets of positive experience at once.

A reasonable question to ask is whether one savors more intensely if what is savored is a simple sensory experience as opposed to a more complex one that has many facets. For example, is viewing and enjoying a work of art savored more fully and intensely if a person engages in intellectual appraisals of it, its context, data about the painter, or more information about the process used in executing the art? Recall from chapter 1 Feynman's intellectual reactions that enhanced his savoring of the beautiful flower beyond the purely aesthetic reactions of the artist. To put it more generally, is it true that the more you know about what you are savoring, the more powerful will be the savoring you experience?

At chamber music concerts, there are often elaborate program notes not only about the performers, but also about the particular pieces being performed. Joe observes that sometimes he reads these notes carefully before the performance and sometimes he does not. The question is, does this preview affect his savoring of the music? We say, yes it does — sometimes for the good, and sometimes for the bad, as far as savoring is concerned. On one hand, intellectual aids can give the listener various templates to use in being mindful of the music. As a result, the listener may hear and appreciate different patterns, and the experience may therefore become richer. On the other hand, one may begin searching for elements in the music that the program notes describe, and this search can distract one from experiencing the overall gestalt of the music. In these latter instances, one's preoccupation with the cognitive search could diminish savoring.

Our conceptual analysis also applies to reading books for enjoyment. Knowing the allusions an author intended expands the possible information communicated. Understanding a play on words, grasping the structure of a novel and seeing it unfold, or comprehending the role a piece of literature played in the author's own psyche are not all absolutely necessary for the enjoyment of reading, but each element can add something to the overall savoring experience. However, once the reader begins to attend to these matters as the dominant approach to reading, then the emotional aesthetic savoring reaction is jeopardized. Having read Joyce's *Ulysses* in college as a set of puzzles to be carefully decrypted, we both can attest to the way in which an intellectual emphasis on reading can destroy a book's emotional impact. Both of us naively wondered what all the fuss was about that particular book. Although it was interesting, it did not appeal to us as much as did Dostoyevski's novels, in which we also considered intellectual themes, but not to the exclusion of savoring the story being told.

Perhaps the same can be said in general about the relationship between the amount of available information pertaining to any experience being savored and the subsequent degree of savoring. More information can sometimes enhance savoring, and sometimes diminish it, depending on whether the additional information sharpens or dulls attention to the basic perceptions that arise in savoring. We thus seek to establish conditions in our model of savoring that clarify when such mindfulness of new information will magnify as opposed to lessen savoring.

Issue 2: Does Savoring Necessarily Reflect Conscious Awareness?

It would seem that as soon as we identified savoring as the process of *attending to* positive feelings, then we would immediately imply that savoring involved conscious awareness. But if one examines a recent scholarly text on attention, such as Styles' (1997) *The Psychology of Attention,* one soon becomes aware of multiple meanings of the concept of attention, each of which is a valid form of attention with supporting data, and only some of which imply conscious processing. There may be some automatic processing of sensory cues, for instance, that can easily be retrieved, but at the time of processing was not attended to consciously. Such automatic processing is also considered attending. We thus follow suit and permit nonconscious processing to occur within the sequence of savoring experiences, but we contend that *some* conscious awareness of the overall process must exist before we would label the processing involved as savoring.

What, then, might this "conscious awareness of some overall process" be? How should we define it? This is a perennial question that cannot be answered easily. Styles (1997) lists many different ways that scientists have tried to define consciousness and suggests that these multiple modes of consciousness are correlated with different modes of attention. Incorporating this perspective, we suggest that savoring always involves a particular kind of consciousness, identified by the person's ability to recount the positive experience that has been savored. Without a person telling us that he or she has savored something, we have no independent measure of savoring. Much as we would like to speak of a cat wallowing in a bed of catnip as an instance of savoring, we cannot do this without some magical language of communication. Purring comes close, but it won't do.

Therefore, we speak of savoring as occurring only in humans, and only when they can tell another person, or perhaps themselves, during a positive experience or later in a diary or through other self-reports, about the experience of attending to their own positive feelings. For this reason, we think that verbal qualitative reports about savoring experiences are critical to any inquiry about savoring. We intentionally feature these accounts as some of the "data" relevant to understanding savoring processes. In addition, we include quantitative data among the evidence we present, although these data focus on the systematic use of people's answers to self-report questions about what they have experienced. In other words, our systematic empirical research is also based on verbal reports about what people were aware of when they were savoring a particular positive event or experience. Nevertheless, emerging research on comparative metacognition suggests the intriguing possibility of studying cognitive self-awareness behaviorally in both humans and animals (Smith & Washburn, 2005).

Issue 3: What Forces Are at Work That Impel a Savoring Experience or Call It to a Halt?

This is a very basic issue, one that is difficult to explicate in a model of savoring, but one that we must address if we are to understand the construct of savoring. This issue concerns the conditions that put the processes of savoring into operation in the first place, and once initiated, eventually shut down the experience.

In classical mechanistic philosophical jargon, this issue concerns first the "prime mover" of the savoring process, and second, how the savoring experience is satiated. Within our own conceptual framework, this issue concerns how a savoring experience begins to enter one's consciousness and then fades from one's awareness. Clearly, the experience has to involve a pattern of sensory or cognitive cues that are vivid enough for us to be mindful of them on one hand, and pleasurable enough to be coded as a positive experience on the other. And when that vividness and pleasurableness recede, satiation of savoring must then occur.

But how does this process happen? That is the key question. And our model does not have a completely resolved answer. In fact, we feature two levels of thinking about an answer: one, a somewhat biomechanistic model; the other, a model based on expectancy-value theory.

First, we consider the biomechanistic approach. We suggest in our model that several assumptions borrowed from theories of curiosity and the pleasure of novelty (see Arkes & Garske, 1982, pp. 172–195) are helpful in understanding how patterns of sensory and cognitive cues emerge and then fade from awareness as savoring experiences. These assumptions derive from optimal-level theory, a conceptual framework that suggests people inherently prefer a level of stimulation that is optimal for them, and that people arrange their world to attain that optimal level of stimulation. We develop this idea more fully in chapter 3. For now, we wish to illustrate the particular phenomena of savoring that prompted us to consider such an idea in the first place.

Consider an activity that Joe's wife, Jody, has spoken to us about as a powerful savoring moment in her life—swimming in the cool waters of the lake in front of her house on a warm summer day. She speaks of being aware of the sensations on her skin, her easy movement, the soft feel and the sweet smell of the water, being surrounded by the gentle landscape, experiencing a total pleasure of being one with the world. There are so many changing patterns of stimulation while swimming that the savoring can be extensive. Dobb, a science writer, spoke of a similar sense of savoring in *The New York Times Magazine* (August 30, 1998). As he described it:

> Whenever I chance upon water, I am seized by the desire to plunge in. Nothing compares to the exquisite embrace of complete immersion, when all of the skin is stimulated simultaneously. What's more, the mind, submerged long enough, assumes the shape of the water. It dilates, becomes fluid, and that, too, is a source of enormous pleasure. (p. 64)

Indeed, one can ask why does Jody or Edwin Dobb ever stop swimming? In fact, Dobb raised the possibility that he tends to linger too long for his own good, a tendency he argues extinct animals might have had that would have hastened their extinction. Mountaineers have described a similar phenomenon known as "rapture of the heights," in which a climber is unable or unwilling to leave the ecstasy of a high vista and remains rooted in place sometimes to the point of being trapped by darkness or inclement weather (Macfarlane, 2003). Aside from becoming tired when people swim, we can suggest that they become habituated or adapted to the patterns they savor as they swim, at which point the patterns no longer hold a strong pull on their curiosities and sense of pleasure. People might then focus their attention elsewhere, and the savoring ends. Thus, a theory of a change in stimulation, such as the ideas found in optimal-level theory, often seems relevant to the question of what makes savoring start and stop.

To frame savoring processes in terms of optimal-level theory, however, tends to ignore the person as an actor weighing choices implicitly or explicitly for the pleasure these various choices can bring. Carver (2003) suggested that pleasure often serves as a sign of goal attainment, which, in turn, provides a cue for people to stay in a goal region or move on in pursuit of other tasks. This brings us to a conceptual orientation for savoring processing that depends on what is called an expectancy-value position. In that viewpoint, savoring a particular event or experience describes a rather complex cognitive activity, one that always involves feelings and thoughts.

A theory to account for savoring, one can argue, must therefore look closely at both feelings and thoughts at any given moment. Expectancy-value theories, which dominated psychology during the last part of the 20th century, are just such theories. These theoretical models posited that to explain any complex human behavior, one had to recognize two important aspects of human tendencies: (a) situational and dispositional *expectancies* about the situations people are in; and (b) situational and dispositional *values* people have within those situations. In chapter 3, we expand on such ideas for considering savoring processes a bit further.

Issue 4: What Is the Role of Intentionality in the Savoring Process?

In order to savor, do people have to have savoring in mind as a goal? Must they intend to enjoy what they are attending to? Or, on the opposite side of the coin, if they do intend to savor, does this interfere with the savoring process? Our answer to each of these three questions about intentionality is, "No, not necessarily."

We present a model of savoring that does not necessarily presume any intention to savor, although we do presume a conscious awareness of savoring. However, people often employ strategies of savoring to prolong their savoring or to intensify it. These savoring strategies are often intentional at the time they are employed. For example, a study of semistructured interviews about the joys of eating concluded, "People who enjoy eating have the explicit intention to enjoy, they eat slowly and focus upon salient features of foods and environment, and they often engage in social activities before, during, and after the meal" (Macht, Meininger, & Roth, 2005, p. 137). Thus, people may deliberately structure and respond to positive experiences in ways that maximize their hedonic benefits.

Along these lines, under Issue 5 next, we present an extended example of savoring in which Fred recounts his experience on reaching the summit of Snowmass Mountain in the Colorado Rockies. He describes in careful detail the variety of steps he took to capture the fleeting moments and to freeze the experience in his memory. In this instance, there was clear evidence of Fred's deliberate intention to savor. But not every moment of savoring in people's lives will be as intentional as Fred's was. Sometimes the savoring process just happens, willy-nilly.

Can being so intentional in savoring backfire? We think so. In savoring, there is a constant interplay of cognitive attending and positive feelings. We assume thoughts and feelings need to be in some subtle balance in people's experience if savoring is to occur. Should cognitive processes get too heavily weighted by one's intentional strategies to implement savoring, then the positive feelings we seek to experience in savoring can fade. We have already mentioned such a phenomenon when we noted in chapter 1 that sexual arousal can diminish if the aroused person thinks too much about the process of maintaining sexual pleasure.

Indeed, there is some empirical evidence that focusing too closely on the levels of one's positive feelings can interfere with enjoyment. In particular, Schooler et al. (2003) found that instructing participants to continually evaluate levels of enjoyment when listening to music can reduce overall enjoyment. As Nathaniel Hawthorne allegedly noted, "Happiness is as a butterfly which when pursued is always beyond our grasp, but which, if you will sit down quietly, may alight upon you" (Cook, 1997). Yet, if one goes about it the right ways, we argue, one need not wait passively for the butterfly of happiness to land on oneself, but rather can actively hunt for and capture the joy of the moment. We return to this point in chapter 3 when we discuss the importance of attending to one's positive feelings in a way that does not short-circuit the affective experience while one is trying to savor the ongoing event.

Because being strategic about savoring can backfire, and one can undermine the possibility of savoring by thinking about the process too much, what does this say about any goals we might have to develop ways of enhancing savoring? It forewarns us that we need to integrate the complex interplay between the expectancies and feelings that go into any savoring process. Our final chapter on enhancing savoring (chapter 8) is as much about strategies for avoiding over-intellectualization within savoring contexts as it is about strategies for opening vistas of pleasure to which to attend.

Issue 5: How Does One's Time Perspective on the Past or Future Bear on the Topic of Savoring?

We have stated that savoring is an experience of the here and now. If so, then when people savor, do they shut off any attention to the past or future? This narrowed temporal perspective seems unlikely, for we all carry around with us memories of and associations to past events and circumstances, as well as potential thoughts about the future. These remembrances and anticipations can likely be part of any present-focused savoring. But how? Our next chapters tackle that difficult question in some detail.

To illustrate how the past and future can enter and enrich a savoring experience, we present next an extensive account of what Fred wrote when Joe asked him to share some critical savoring moments in his life. His story is of savoring the moment on reaching the top of Snowmass Mountain (14,092 feet) in the Elk Range of the Colorado Rockies. He wrote this particular passage in his diary shortly after returning to base camp from the summit. His account speaks of the many facets of joys he attended to, one of which we have just discussed in considering the issue of his intentionality at the summit, and others to which we return in further explications of savoring. For now, however, the reader should notice the images of the past and future that infuse this savoring account:

A vast ocean of snowy summits stretches as far as the eye can see in all directions. Like whitecaps on a frozen sea, wave after wave of silver-tipped crests merge with green-blanketed valleys in the distant haze. My friends and I stand silent and in awe, marveling at the cosmic tapestry spread out before us, drinking in the magnificent panorama. We have climbed all day from a camp far below to reach this rocky highpoint. We have surmounted thousands of feet of steep, fractured granite and icy snow to get here. We have each trained for months beforehand to prepare our bodies and minds for the struggle, walking and running hundreds of miles over the weeks, doing thousands of pushups and sit-ups, toughening ourselves for what we'd face. We have planned, imagined, and anticipated this moment for years. Twice before we have been unsuccessful in trying to climb the mountain, and finally here we are! And all of these efforts now culminate in a few, precious minutes together breathless on a remote mountaintop. I embrace my friends and tell them how very happy I feel, and how much it means to me to share this with them. We remind each other how much we wanted this moment, how special it is. We laugh and shout for joy together. Then we each draw apart to be alone for a few minutes, each by himself in the clouds.

I look back into the past and remember how long I've looked forward to this moment. The realization that it is here now intensifies my joy. I remember an earlier time when a back injury effectively crippled me and made it doubtful whether I'd ever climb again. I remember how much I wanted to climb again back then. I imagine what it would have been like never to have reached this mountaintop. To be here now, to stand on the summit of my dreams despite all odds, is made even sweeter by contrast.

I look ahead into the future and remind myself that a time will come when I'll no longer be physically able to climb mountains. I imagine what it will be like to savor summits no more, to look back longingly and gratefully for what I once had. Indeed, what if this is the last summit I ever experience in the mountains? To be here now, to be able to reach the mountaintop, is even more glorious by contrast.

I give thanks to God in a silent prayer for the blessings I am enjoying. I thank the Creator for giving me life, for enabling me to enjoy this moment, for creating the beautiful earth and these magnificent mountains, for giving me friends with whom to share this experience. Tears of joy well up in my eyes, as I realize how special the gift of this experience is, and how much I have to be grateful for.

I have a strong sense of the fleetingness of the moment, and I make special efforts to capture it. I want to remember this moment for the rest of my life, so I build the memory of it actively and deliberately. I slowly turn in a circle and let my eyes seek out what they find attractive. I notice tiny details in the overwhelming expanse beneath me: a wrinkled quilt of emerald and olive patches is a forest of aspen and spruce; a thin, silver ribbon zigzagging through the shadows is a river; a handful of silver coins strewn randomly on the floor is a group of lakes near our camp. All these things and more I notice, as I make a mental movie of what surrounds me.

I take a deep breath in the thin, cold air and slowly let it out. I notice a sharp, pungent scent, and seeking out its source, find a lone lavender Sky Pilot growing between the boulders beneath my feet. I close my eyes and listen to the wind, as it rushes up the mountain from the valley below. I sit down between the highest boulders and relish the ecstasy of lying motionless in the warm sun. I reach for a rock the size of a matchbox to take back as a souvenir, a keepsake of this moment. Its rough, pitted texture feels like sandpaper. I get a strange urge to smell the stone, and as I sniff it, its strong musty odor triggers a flood of ancient images. I get a sense of how long it must have rested in this place, the eons it has been here. More than ever, I realize just how precious this glorious moment is and how much I want to hold onto it for all time.

I think of my loved ones back home — my wife, my children, my parents, my brother, my friends — and a wave of joy sweeps over me. If only they could be here with me on the summit right now. What would I want them to see and feel, what is it that I wish I could share with them? I drink it all in again, noticing each part of the moment that I find pleasurable.

I want them to see what I see. I stand up and raise my camera, peering through the viewfinder to frame a memory. I slowly rotate 360 degrees, taking photographs in an overlapping sequence. I imagine how much fun it will be to share these images with my friends and loved ones back home. My heart leaps at the thought of sharing this moment with them.

I think of my late grandfather, my Daddy Jack, whose spirit of adventure lives on in me. How much he would have loved this place, this wild sanctuary of rugged beauty. What joy it would have been to share it with him. How proud he would be of me now.

Then the wind shifts and picks up speed, as the weather begins to change. The first loud rumble rolls in from the west, a thunderous warning of what is to come. We each take a final glance around us, hastening to seize the moment, knowing full well that we shall never be here again.

Notice that in Fred's dramatic savoring experience, elements of past memories come surging forth that seem to be part of the whole experience being savored: preparing endlessly for the moment of reaching the summit; recalling how much he wanted to do this and to overcome the handicap that a crippling back injury had given him; thinking about his friends and family, particularly Fred's grandfather, who had inspired him to begin climbing in the first place.

How much do these contribute to the richness of this savoring experience? No doubt, a great deal.

In fact, intriguing empirical work by Mitchell et al. (1997) demonstrates that the affective evaluation of pleasant memories can be more positive than when these events actually occurred. Mitchell and Thompson (1994) called this phenomenon *rosy retrospection*. For some kinds of positive experiences, savoring the past through rosy retrospection might produce a more intense emotional response than savoring the present as it is unfolding.

On the other hand, there is also evidence that waxing nostalgic in general (Sedikides, Wildschut, & Baden, 2004), or using memorabilia or cognitive imagery in particular to facilitate recall of positive memories (Bryant, Smart, & King, 2005), can increase people's current levels of happiness. In other words, looking back on good times from the past may well sweeten the present. Although we have stated that savoring is a phenomenon of the here and now, we believe that a model of savoring has to permit such memories to enter the picture.

In the same way, Fred's experience on the summit of Snowmass Mountain includes various types of future anticipations that also seem to be part of his savoring. He and his fellow mountain climbers had looked forward to their mountaintop moment for years. Although Fred does not state this in his narrative account, it would not be hard to imagine that before the trip, he and his fellow climbers had savored the experience with great relish in anticipating being together on the summit. In fact, one wonders whether anticipating the experience so intensely and for so long might have actually heightened the extent of their savoring of the moment when it finally occurred.

There were also thoughts of the future at the very moment of savoring, anticipating sharing the moment with others and anticipating trying to recall the experience in days to come. Indeed, Fred's desire to hold onto the exhilaration he felt on the summit, to capture it and preserve it forever, motivated him to carefully craft a memory of it while he was actually experiencing it. In order to do this, he began to scrutinize his environment in search of memorable details. This process of active memory building undoubtedly helped him to notice pleasurable things he might not have seen otherwise, to examine them in minute detail, to "swish them around" in his mind, and to extract from them the essence of their pleasurableness.

Fred claims that these memories actively formed on the summit of Snowmass Mountain remain vibrant and accessible to him even today. In fact, the small pitted rock he retrieved from the mountaintop still sits on his desk, and when he holds the keepsake and sniffs it, he reports, it triggers the same flood of vivid memories and intense feelings he originally felt on the summit. A conceptual model of savoring must consider not only reminiscence, but also anticipatory processes, along with certain other anticipatory savoring that could be even more positive than the savoring that occurs at the moment—a phenomenon that Mitchell and Thompson (1994) termed *rosy prospection*. In chapter 6, we discuss both *rosy prospection* and *rosy retrospection* in relation to savoring, and we spell out in detail the implications these temporal effects have for the affective quality of positive experience.

Within Fred's description of his savoring on reaching the summit are many references to people in his life—his wife and children, his parents, his brother, his grandfather, his friends back home, and his fellow climbers. There is also a mention of the importance of God in savoring. What role do others play in the dynamics of savoring, given that we usually think of savoring as a very private experience? This question is the focus of the next critical issue we discuss.

Issue 6: In What Ways Do Our Relationships With Other People Enter Into Our Savoring Experiences?

Other people can play many different roles in our savoring experiences. A person can so savor the way she feels about someone that she can pleasurably make that person the sole object of her attention. Rubin (1973) long ago identified such exclusivity as one of the most important behavioral distinctions between loving and liking a romantic partner. In loving a person, one often cannot avoid keeping one's eyes focused on the loved one, or gazing at the person for extended periods with obvious relish. The postmodern cinematic adaptation of Romeo and Juliet (1996, directed by Baz Luhrmann) brilliantly portrays the love-at-first-sight meeting of the star-crossed lovers as an extensive visual tracking of each other's faces through a giant fish tank. During this gazing sequence, the filmgoer cannot help but be impressed that these two are falling deeply in love. When a person is the center of savoring, as is the case in gazing, this harkens back to what we posited in Issue 1—anything, any sensory experience, any cognitive ideation or association can become the object of savoring. There is no reason to exclude a person, a group of people, or thoughts about God from that formulation.

Savoring a relationship can have interactive consequences with the person or persons who make up that relationship. When savoring does apply to a person, then it can be a strong causal force in affecting an interpersonal transaction. Basking in one's love, luxuriating in sexual contact, lingering with friends in sweet companionate talk, and thinking about one's fulfillment as a parent are all instances of interpersonal savoring. Such savoring is often reciprocated, which can be stimuli for further savoring. This phenomenon of reciprocal savoring is at the heart of another of Joe's reports of a special kind of savoring experience he calls contagious "reverberating laughter":

> *An instance of interactive savoring occurs for me in laughing with someone about some situation or joke that strikes us both as being especially funny initially, and then when the laughter continues and becomes mutually contagious, we set each other off in a reverberating circuit. The uncontrolled giddiness comes on suddenly and unexpectedly. This savoring of something funny with another person in this spontaneous*

way can continue for several minutes. It is a delightful shared human experience. My partner-in-laughter and I can feel very bonded, since being overwhelmed with laughter is not happening to anyone else but the two of us. In fact, there can be mild irritation by others that my partner and I are sharing something to the exclusion of them. Being aware of the irritation often pulls us out of the spiraling fun. The savoring is interrupted. It is clear that our respective savoring of laughter had inspired each other to continued glee.

A more complex and less frivolous savoring comes when people feel connected to others as part of the savoring experience. When Fred felt connected to his fellow climbers, when he felt connected to God, the overall savoring moments were intensified and prolonged. In another one of his reports of favorite savoring moments, Joe speaks of savoring letters he and his wife receive from their children, and the special possibility for savoring that they hold. This is what Joe remembers:

For a number of years, my children and I used to write what we call a chain letter. I would write to one of my kids who then enclosed my letter and his/her letter in a letter to another sibling, who, in turn, added his/her letter to the previous two in a letter to a third sib, and so on, until it all would come back to me with my having received five letters in addition to my own original letter. The next cycle was repeated by my keeping the first letter I wrote and including a new one along with all the letters from the five Veroff kids. This went on for ten years. It came around about two or three times a year. Reading them all together was a great joy for me. Although some of the news was old, the combined letters gave us all a chance to be in touch with the way our family was thinking about their lives — myself included.

I used to savor reading these letters when they came. I didn't read them instantly. I would find a quiet moment when I could linger a bit with them, and read them in order and let the words roll very slowly over me like a long warm, gentle shower. I read each one slowly. Sometimes they were highly sentimental, and I couldn't hold back the tears. Sometimes they were profoundly insightful about what had been happening to them and the world around them, and I was amazed. I could almost feel the children gathered in the room in which I was reading.

I would show the letters to Jody. She experienced the same emotional tugs, even though she did not contribute a letter to the chain. She, too, savored the experience. The fact that we both savored the same things and spoke of our savoring to each other intensified the joy we each felt. These good feelings came from the multiple associations we had with the ideas the letters expressed, and the evidence of the goodness of our children's lives, for which we felt both an enormous gratitude and a quiet pride. After all, they were our legacy, and by their own words they were telling us that the legacy is flourishing. We used to feel very rich. This was thus a complex mindfulness of feelings. Mostly we feel very connected.

These savoring moments from the chain letter thus involved complex social feelings — pride, a vicarious pleasure in the lives of children, a sense of legacy unfolding, and a connection with one's distant family who are felt as being very much present. Such a diverse set of thoughts is probably not unusual for anyone who takes time out in some way to think about someone they love and the joys this person creates. Often this savoring process requires an intentional slowing down of one's flow of experience. Notice that Joe did not want to read the chain letter quickly or in a circumstance that would force him to read it inattentively. Might that be what happens in many instances of savoring, that people put their mind's camera into slow motion? As Flaherty (2003) noted with respect to the management of temporal duration, "Those who wish to prolong their experiences concentrate on the here-and-now of the current situation" (p. 23). In the next chapters, when we expand the model for savoring, we often use such social connections as instances of savoring, and within them we again highlight how savoring processes require a deliberate focus on what one is feeling or experiencing.

Although we have considered how social ties can infuse our savoring experiences, we should also note that social ties can interfere with savoring. In particular, culture may profoundly influence one's general attitude toward positive experiences, as well as specific thoughts and behaviors in response to those experiences. In a dissertation on similarities and differences in savoring across culture, Lindberg (2004) compared the responses of North American and Japanese students to questions about savoring experiences in their lives. Confirming a priori hypotheses, North American and Japanese students showed largely equivalent factor structures underlying their beliefs about their ability to savor positive events in their lives, suggesting that the concept of savoring has the same meaning across the two cultures. Lindberg (2004) also found that savoring related comparably to personality and subjective adjustment in the two cultural groups, suggesting that the construct of savoring as developed in research with Western samples generalizes to East Asian samples.

However, Lindberg (2004) also found cross-cultural differences in savoring. Confirming a priori predictions, East Asian respondents reported a lower capacity to derive joy by anticipating, savoring the moment, and reminiscing, compared to North American respondents. In addition, North Americans more strongly endorsed cognitive and behavioral savoring responses that amplify or prolong enjoyment (e.g., Self-Congratulation, Behavioral Expression, and Sensory Perceptual Sharpening); and East Asians more strongly endorsed savoring responses that dampen or curtail enjoyment (i.e., Kill-Joy Thinking). East Asians also reported several novel savoring strategies not seen in North American samples, including Making Greater Effort, Increasing Activity, Increasing Knowledge, and Continuing Connection with Others Involved. Lindberg's (2004) findings are generally consistent with other research that has found both elements of universality and cultural variation in the experience of positive feelings (Kitayama, Markus, & Kurokawa, 2000; Oishi, Diener, Napa Scollon, & Biswas-Diener, 2004).

Clearly, culture has a major impact on the quality of savoring experiences. Lindberg's (2004) work suggests that Japanese students may deliberately avoid intensifying their savoring moments, and may even actively seek to reduce the intensity and duration of enjoyment. Compared to North American respondents, East Asian respondents not only placed less value on enjoying the moment, but also more strongly believed that good events are inevitably balanced by future negative events (Ji, Nisbett, & Su, 2001). An ancient Chinese proverb reflects this concern: "Extreme happiness begets tragedy."

Other research supports the notion of East–West cultural differences in savoring. Reviewing the cross-cultural literature on happiness, for example, Uchida, Norasakkunkit, and Kitayama (2004) concluded that North Americans tend to define happiness in terms of personal achievement and strive to maximize positive affect, whereas East Asians tend to define happiness in terms of interpersonal connectedness and strive to maintain balance between positive and negative affect. Thus, happiness is best predicted by self-esteem in North American cultural contexts, but by "perceived embeddedness of the self in a social relationship" (Uchida et al., 2004, p. 223) in East Asian cultural contexts.

We have argued that physical, social, and esteem needs must be minimized for people to focus on enhancing savoring. Certainly, cultural norms that discourage too much savoring can also operate. But other needs for self-esteem maintenance can occur in any culture.

For example, Joe and his wife recall how they recently prepared a fine lunch for visiting friends, a meal they could not savor despite all the tasty dishes they had prepared: sauteed chanterelles on crisp crusted Italian bread, sorrel vichyssoise, curried chicken salad, green salad with arugula and basil, and orange almond torte topped with whipping cream. It tasted fine to them, they said, but they were busy listening to their friends, trying to make them feel at home, and worrying by any indication that their dinner guests might not like the menu they planned. Thus, fear of failure and concern about pleasing others dominated their attention, leaving little attentional room for savoring the food. This conclusion is consistent with evidence cited in chapter 1 that people high in fear of failure typically experience negative emotions, engage in mood repair, and get little or no joy of anticipation when they think about positive goal attainment (Langens & Schmalt, 2002). Joe and his wife derived many social pleasures from their lunch with friends, but their positive experiences were not in the savoring mode with respect to either the ongoing camaraderie during the meal or the pleasures of eating.

It is important to realize that our conceptualization of savoring distinguishes between the experience of savoring the connection with others and the straightforward experience of enjoying the gratifications of social needs. As with other pleasures, it is one thing to experience social pleasure and quite another thing to savor the pleasure we derive from that social connection. If we attend to the social pleasure with a savoring orientation, then there is no reason why savoring cannot occur. But often in social pleasures, as in sexual pleasures, a person is so immersed in the positive experience that savoring does not occur. Again, this is because we assume that for a positive experience to be savored, some awareness of the self as a "perceiver" (or some degree of meta-awareness) must exist.

By the way, Joe and his wife reported that the next day they dined on the leftovers from their luncheon and at that point took their time with their meal and truly savored the tasty concoctions they had created. Clearly, it is easier to be mindful of enjoyment when one's attention is not directed elsewhere.

Summary of the Conceptual Issues

In this chapter, we introduced six critical issues with respect to savoring that we address more fully in the next three chapters. Although these are not the only issues that our theoretical model addresses, we believe they are the most important. These conceptual issues concern the ways in which (a) complex cognitive events as well as sensory processes are savored; (b) experiences arise and become satiated in human consciousness in the first place; (c) savoring reflects conscious awareness; (d) the process of savoring may or may not reflect a person's intention to savor; (e) memories of the past and anticipations of the future operate in savoring; and (f) relationships with people and culture bear on experiences of savoring.

These are complex issues that cannot be explicated briefly with a few words or phrases. Instead, in the chapters ahead, we carefully weave more complete answers to these questions into the conceptual fabric of our model of savoring.

MEASUREMENT ISSUES

Although we believe that highly detailed, verbal self-reports of savoring experiences are a valid way to assess savoring, as scientists we are also trained to gather systematic quantitative assessments. In this book, we rely not only on the qualitative data we have presented thus far, but also on quantitative measurements. These quantitative assessments include both people's beliefs about their ability to savor positive experience and their reports about specific ways in which they savor positive events. Fred has devoted many years of research to developing valid and reliable quantitative tools for studying savoring.

Savoring Beliefs

These quantitative measurement instruments focus on two different concepts integrally related to savoring. The first of these key concepts is the notion that people make self-evaluations of their capacity to enjoy positive experiences. We refer to people's subjective perceptions of their personal ability to enjoy positive experience as beliefs about savoring capacity, or *savoring beliefs*. We assume that people's beliefs about their savoring capacity have something to do with their actual ability to savor positive experiences. We describe two measurement tools for assessing people's savoring beliefs: the five-item unidimensional Perceived Ability to Savor Positive Outcomes scale (PASPO; Bryant, 1989); and the 24-item, three-factor Savoring Beliefs Inventory (SBI; Bryant, 2003).

Both the PASPO and the SBI provide global total scores for use in summarizing overall beliefs about savoring ability. However, the SBI also provides three separate eight-item temporal subscales assessing Savoring Through Anticipation, Savoring the Moment, and Savoring Through Reminiscence. Scores on these respective subscales reflect people's self-evaluations of their ability to savor positive events prospectively, concurrently, and retrospectively.

Savoring Responses

A second key savoring-related concept for which Fred has developed a multidimensional conceptual model and measurement instrument is the notion that people engage in a variety of different thoughts and behaviors while they are experiencing a positive event. We refer to these cognitive and behavioral reactions to ongoing positive experience as *savoring responses* or *strategies*. These "ways of savoring" reflect different patterns of response to positive events that may or may not influence the intensity or duration of one's actual enjoyment of these events.

The *Ways of Savoring Checklist (WOSC)* is a 60-item, multidimensional measurement tool for assessing savoring responses to positive experiences. This instrument consists of ten subscales or dimensions of savoring: Sharing With Others, Memory Building, Self-Congratulation, Comparing, Sensory-Perceptual Sharpening, Absorption, Behavioral Expression, Temporal Awareness, Counting Blessings, and Kill-Joy Thinking. These 10 ways of savoring embody the same set of strategies for regulating enjoyment found in people's responses to open-ended questions in earlier pilot testing. And the same dimensions of savoring have emerged consistently in numerous samples.

Although the 10 WOSC dimensions cover a diverse array of thoughts and behaviors, we are not suggesting that these particular dimensions of savoring are exhaustive of all savoring responses. On the contrary, there are obviously more than 10 different ways to savor positive experiences. Indeed, some ways of savoring are undoubtedly unique to specific cultures—as Lindberg (2004) found among Japanese students—and these additional ways of savoring are not included in the 60-item WOSC. Other untapped ways to enhance savoring include becoming more childlike, humorous, or aware of coparticipants' joy; other unmeasured ways to suppress savoring include making upward comparisons, and negating or ignoring positive feelings. Nevertheless, the 10 WOSC subscales provide a broad comprehensive profile of the cognitive and behavioral savoring responses of young adults to positive events. This makes the WOSC a potentially useful tool for researchers interested in studying savoring responses.

But how do savoring beliefs relate to savoring responses? In general, how do people's beliefs in their capacity to savor relate to what they think and do in response to ongoing positive experiences? First, we expect that people who believe they can savor the moment (based on their SBI scores) will engage in different types of thoughts and behaviors, or exhibit a different pattern of savoring responses (on the WOSC), compared to people who report less ability to savor. We further assume that these different patterns of savoring responses produce differences in the level or duration of people's actual enjoyment.

In addition, we assume that people are aware of how well they can savor positive experiences in their lives, and that this self-awareness manifests itself in the form of beliefs about their personal capacity to savor (i.e., savoring beliefs). As argued in the literature on subjective well-being (Andrews & Withey, 1976; Campbell, Converse, & Rodgers, 1976; Diener, 1984, 1994), people may be their own best judge in assessing the quality of inner subjective experience. Extending this logic, people's savoring beliefs should be a useful indicator of how well they can actually savor positive events.

Yet, how capable people believe they are of savoring positive experiences is not necessarily identical to how capable people *actually* are of savoring positive experiences or how much enjoyment they are currently experiencing in their lives. Some people may feel perfectly capable of enjoying themselves, but may actually be largely unable to do so, whereas other people who are unable to enjoy their lives are well aware of their hedonic deficits. One's perceived savoring capacity and one's current level of enjoyment are not necessarily the same.

Although researchers may be tempted to use reported levels of positive affect to assess savoring ability, this approach is inadequate for several reasons. First, among people who are fully capable of savoring, some may report less positive affect due to lower baseline levels or "hedonic set-points" (Diener & Diener, 1996; Headey & Wearing, 1992; Lykken, 1999). Furthermore, there are individual differences in the extent to which people express their positive emotions (Bryant, Yarnold, & Grimm, 1996; Larsen & Diener, 1987; Weinfurt, Bryant, & Yarnold, 1994).

In addition, equating reported positive affect with savoring ability does not distinguish people who believe they cannot savor positive events despite their best efforts from people who believe they can savor positive events, but have chosen temporarily to forego such pleasure in favor of other pursuits. If researchers use levels of positive affect to gauge savoring ability, then both types of people would be classified as equally low in savoring capacity. Yet, clearly the former group lacks some of the basic skills necessary for positive functioning, whereas the latter group does not (Bryant, 2003).

Likewise, retrospection is not necessarily the same as actual experience. What people recall in relation to recent positive events may well differ from what they actually thought and did or how much they actually enjoyed these events (e.g., Mitchell & Thompson, 1994).

Ultimately, we believe that whether or not people actually have the ability to savor positive experience is more critical than whether or not people believe they can savor, just as we believe that whether or not people actually have the ability to cope with negative experience is more critical than whether or not people believe they can cope. But we also recognize the utility of measuring people's beliefs about their capacity to savor positive outcomes as a means of indirectly assessing actual savoring ability. Let us now briefly describe each of the three measurement instruments with which we have investigated savoring, for we draw on each in our subsequent discussions of the model of savoring.

The Ability to Savor Positive Outcomes

In 1989, Fred published a research paper on one way to assess savoring processes (Bryant, 1989). In this research, he generated a set of self-report items to measure four different types of perceived control: (a) the perceived ability to avoid negative outcomes; (b) the perceived ability to cope with negative outcomes; (c) the perceived ability to obtain positive outcomes; and (d) the perceived ability to savor positive outcomes. These four kinds of items were shown to define four separate factors in confirmatory factor analyses of responses given by 524 college students. The Perceived Control Questionnaire from this study appears in Appendix A; and Fig. 2.1 presents the four-factor model that emerged from the confirmatory factor analyses (see Bryant, 1989).

The four factors reflect the four different processes originally hypothesized, two concerning perceived control over external events (Avoiding and Obtaining) and two concerning perceived control over internal feelings (Coping and Savoring). Furthermore, multiple regression analyses using these four scales to predict subjective mental health supported the scales' discriminant validity. Whereas the two factors assessing control over feelings (Coping, in the case of negative feelings; and Savoring, in the case of positive feelings) are minimally related to each other, they are differentially related to other indexes.

It was also clear that Savoring, like Obtaining, related more strongly to indexes of subjective well-being than to indexes of subjective distress. Savoring, however, was significantly related to general happiness, whereas Obtaining was not. These latter results suggest that perceived control over positive emotions is more important to feeling happy than is perceived control over positive events. This is an important aspect of savoring to keep in mind, especially when we consider ways to enhance savoring. Positive events may set the stage for people to experience savoring. But evidently positive events alone are not enough to bring about happiness. People need to be able to attend to and appreciate the positive feelings that emerge from positive events. Truly, it is as the French writer François de La Rochefoucauld (1694) aptly noted, "Happiness does not consist in things themselves but in the relish we have of them."

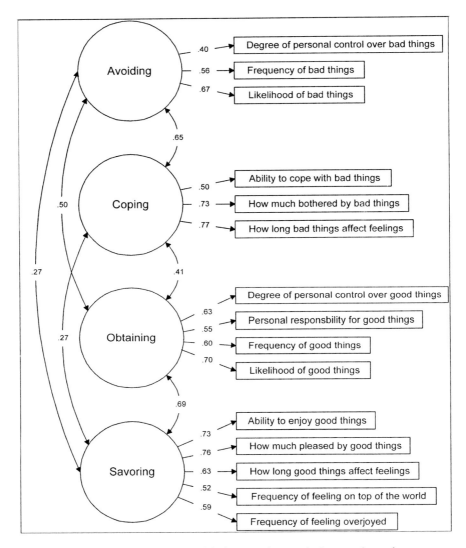

FIG. 2.1. The Four-Factor Model of Perceived Control. These results are from a confirmatory factor analysis, $\chi^2(84, N = 524) = 434.82$. The 15 perceived control items are enclosed in rectangles, and the four perceived control factors are enclosed in circles. Curved, double-arrow-headed lines represent correlations among factors, and straight, single-arrow-headed lines represent standardized factor loadings. Cronbach's alpha for each of the perceived control factors was .60 for Avoiding, .70 for Coping, .71 for Obtaining, and .78 for Savoring. Adapted from Bryant (1989, p. 787) with permission from Blackwell Publishing. See Appendix A for a copy of the actual items used in this analysis.

The Savoring Beliefs Inventory (SBI)

A much more complex view of savoring went into the development of Fred's next instrument for assessing savoring processes (Bryant, 2003). Realizing that there is not only the process of *savoring the moment* but also the processes of *savoring in anticipation* and *savoring in reminiscence,* Fred constructed separate eight-item scales for past-, present-, and future-focused modes of savoring. For each temporal mode, four of the self-report items were worded positively (e.g., "I know how to make the most of a good time"), and four were worded negatively (e.g., "I find it hard to hang onto a good feeling"). Table 2.1 presents the 24 SBI items clustered by valence within temporal domain; and the actual instrument appears in Appendix B, along with detailed instructions for scoring the SBI in Appendix C.

Confirmatory factor analyses using a sample of 415 college students indicated that the best-fitting model for the SBI included three factors reflecting the temporal forms of savoring, along with two "method" factors reflecting positively worded and negatively worded items. Five subsequent studies evaluated the convergent and discriminant validity of the SBI in relation to a battery of other measures, including: (a) personality assessments such as Eysenck and Eysenck's (1975) scales of extraversion and neuroticism; (b) control beliefs such as Rotter's (1966) measure of Internal-External Control of Reinforcement; and (c) subjective adjustment such as Bryant and Veroff's (1984) scales of Gratification and Depression. Examining total score as well as the subscale score for each time frame, Fred found a great deal of evidence for the construct validity of the SBI. Table 2.2 reports these validity coefficients.

The results in Table 2.2 are too plentiful to describe here, but the pattern of construct validation is impressive. As just one example of the discriminant validity of the subscales, Fred found that the SBI Anticipating subscale was more strongly related to Scheier and Carver's (1985) measure of optimism than were the other two temporal subscales. We return to these validational data in the course of discussing evidence for some of the conceptual propositions we develop in subsequent chapters.

Results of an additional longitudinal study (Bryant, 2003, Study 5) further demonstrate the SBI's discriminant validity prospectively. Providing crucial evidence for the validity of these assumptions, Bryant (2003, Study 5) used earlier SBI scores to predict later reported experiences just before, during, or just after a Christmas vacation. Within each of the three time frames, the relevant SBI subscale generally predicted behaviors and affects more strongly than did the subscales associated with the other two temporal orientations. Thus, there is prospective evidence that savoring beliefs are predictive of reported savoring experiences in relation to the past, present, and future.

TABLE 2.1
Items Composing the Savoring Beliefs Inventory (SBI)

Savoring Through Anticipation (α = .77)

Positively worded items:

1. Before a good thing happens, I look forward to it in ways that give me pleasure in the present.
7. I feel a joy of anticipation when I think about upcoming good things.
13. I can enjoy pleasant events in my mind before they actually occur.
19. I can make myself feel good by imagining what a happy time that is about to happen will be like.

Negatively worded items:

4. I don't like to look forward to good times too much before they happen.
10. For me, anticipating what upcoming good events will be like is basically a waste of time.
16. It's hard for me to get very excited about fun times before they actually take place.
22. When I think about a pleasant event before it happens, I often start to feel uneasy or uncomfortable.

Savoring the Moment (α = .78)

Positively worded items:

5. I know how to make the most of a good time.
11. When something good happens, I can make my enjoyment of it last longer by thinking or doing certain things.
17. I feel fully able to appreciate good things that happen to me.
23. It's easy for me to enjoy myself when I want to.

Negatively worded items:

2. It's hard for me to hang onto a good feeling for very long.
8. When it comes to enjoying myself, I'm my own "worst enemy."
14. I can't seem to capture the joy of happy moments.
20. I don't enjoy things as much as I should.

Savoring Through Reminiscence (α = .80)

Positively worded items:

3. I enjoy looking back on happy times from my past.
9. I can make myself feel good by remembering pleasant events from my past.
15. I like to store memories of fun times that I go through so that I can recall them later.
21. It's easy for me to rekindle the joy from pleasant memories.

Negatively worded items:

6. I don't like to look back at good times too much after they've taken place.
12. When I reminisce about pleasant memories, I often start to feel sad or disappointed.
18. I find that thinking about good times from the past is basically a waste of time.
24. For me, once a fun time is over and gone, it's best not to think about it.

Note. Items are listed by their number in the SBI questionnaire. The response scale for the SBI ranges from 1 (strongly disagree) to 7 (strong agree). Reported for each SBI subscale is Cronbach's alpha (α), a coefficient of internal consistency reliability. For SBI total score, α = .90. See Appendix B for a copy of the SBI, and Appendix C for instructions for scoring the SBI. See Savoring Beliefs Inventory (SBI): A Scale for Measuring Beliefs About Savouring by F. B. Bryant (2003), *Journal of Mental Health, 12,* 175–196.

TABLE 2.2
SBI Construct Validity Coefficients From Five Studies

Criterion Measures	Study	SBI Factor Scores			
		Anticipate	Savor the Moment	Reminisce	Total
I. Individual differences:					
Affect intensity	2	.21*	.21*	.17*	.27*
	3	.49**	.31*	.49**	.48**
Extraversion	4	.34*	.44**	.33*	.42**
Optimism	4	.56**	.41**	.42**	.50**
Hopelessness	4	-.48**	-.33*	-.37**	-.41**
Neuroticism	1	-.22*	-.30*	-.23*	-.26*
	2	-.18*	-.48**	-.30*	-.38**
Guilt	3	-.19*	-.34*	-.13	-.26*
Shame	3	-.12	-.19*	.04	-.09
Physical anhedonia	4	-.52**	-.52**	-.50**	-.56**
Social anhedonia	4	-.50**	-.58**	-.48**	-.57**
Social desirability	3	.07	-.01	-.04	-.01
II. Control Beliefs:					
Internal locus of control	4	.25*	.32*	.31*	.31*
Self-control	3	.19*	.23*	.23*	.24*
Obtaining	1	.29*	.41**	.34*	.41**
	2	.23*	.37**	.44**	.44**
Savoring	1	.35**	.51**	.39**	.49**
	2	.40**	.67**	.53**	.63**
Avoiding	1	-.04	.15	-.09	.02
	2	.05	.20*	.17	.18
Coping	1	.04	.40**	.12	.23*
	2	-.06	.35**	.29*	.21*
III. Subjective adjustment:					
Present happiness	1	.08	.37**	.20*	.25*
	2	-.03	.28*	.21*	.20*
Gratification	1	.29*	.39**	.28*	.39**
	2	.21*	.45**	.39**	.37**
Self-esteem	1	.30*	.39**	.23*	.39**
	2	.10	.42**	.28*	.30*
Strain	1	-.02	-.19*	-.03	-.09
	2	-.16	-.46**	-.33**	-.33**
Perceived vulnerability	1	.00	-.16	-.02	-.06
	2	-.06	-.23*	-.27*	-.20*
Depression	1	-.12	-.34**	-.11	-.25*
	2	-.11	-.40**	-.28*	-.31*
Happiness intensity	3	.24*	.59**	.26*	.45**
	6	.48*	.60**	.46*	.56**
Percent of time happy	3	.38**	.58**	.39**	.55**
	6	.47*	.60**	.46*	.61**

Note. Tabled are Pearson product-moment correlation coefficients relating SBI scores to scores on criterion measures. Sample sizes varied slightly within studies 1–4 due to incomplete data for some respondents and were as follows: Study 1 ($N = 82$–90); Study 2 ($N = 104$–112); Study 3 ($N = 58$–82); Study 4 ($N = 69$–84); and Study 6 ($N = 36$). Adapted from Table 4 (pp. 186–187) of Bryant, F. B. (2003). Savoring Beliefs Inventory (SBI): A scale for measuring beliefs about savouring. *Journal of Mental Health, 12,* 175–196, with permission from Taylor & Francis, Ltd. [http://www.tandf.co.uk]

*$p < .05$, one-tailed unadjusted **$p < .05$, one-tailed Bonferroni-adjusted (i.e., unadjusted one-tailed $p < .0004$).

The Ways of Savoring Checklist (WOSC)

Having developed a measure of perceived savoring capacity, the next goal was to investigate people's savoring responses to positive events. This third step in developing psychometric tools to measure savoring involved moving from (a) global self-assessments of the capacity to savor prospectively, retrospectively, or in the moment, to (b) self-reports of specific cognitive and behavioral strategies individuals use to regulate their enjoyment of ongoing positive experiences. With this goal in mind, Fred constructed the Ways of Savoring Checklist (WOSC), with which respondents indicate the degree to which they engaged in 60 thoughts or behaviors in connection with a particular positive event. The 60-item WOSC also includes an initial set of 12 questions assessing cognitive appraisals of the target positive experience, and 2 final quesions assessing the level and duration of enjoyment.

Table 2.3 presents the WOSC items clustered by subscale, the full measure appears in Appendix D, and detailed instructions for scoring the WOSC appear in Appendix E. Table 2.3 also reports an index of internal consistency reliability (Cronbach's alpha) for each WOSC subscale. In general, the WOSC subscales show reasonable reliabilities in a large sample of undergraduates ($N = 1,136$).

The WOSC parallels the format and procedure of the Ways of Coping Checklist (Folkman & Lazarus, 1980), with which respondents focus on a stressful event and indicate the extent to which they engaged in 66 thoughts and behaviors in response to that event. Although critics have raised questions about the Ways of Coping Checklist (e.g., Stone, Greenberg, Kennedy-Moore, & Newman, 1991), results emerging from it have been especially important in clinical and health psychology. For example, people who use coping strategies that focus on the source of stress (i.e., problem-focused coping) rather than on feelings resulting from stress (i.e., emotion-focused coping) often show better psychological adjustment; and people who confront stressful problems directly are often better adjusted than people who deny or avoid problems, particularly when these problems are controllable (Lazarus & Folkman, 1984).

Administering the WOSC to many samples, Fred has discovered a reliable set of savoring strategies encompassing different combinations of the 60 items (see Table 2.3). We describe these savoring dimensions in more detail in the chapter on types of savoring strategies (chapter 4), which features in-depth results from the WOSC. There, we also consider more directly how savoring beliefs and savoring responses relate to one another.

Summary of Measurement Issues

A challenge in studying savoring processes systematically is to stake out valid ways of assessing the phenomena we have posited conceptually. We have asserted that savoring processes should reflect verbal reports of people's awareness of their

TABLE 2.3
Items Constituting the Ten Subscales of the
Ways of Savoring Checklist (WOSC)

Sharing with Others (6 items; α = .86):
1. I thought about sharing the memory of this later with other people.
11. I looked for other people to share it with.
21. I expressed to others present how much I valued the moment (and their being there to share it with me).
31. I hung around with others who know how to have a good time.
40. I physically expressed my feelings to others (hugging, touching).
47. I talked to another person about how good I felt.

Memory Building (7 items; α = .89):
2. I tried to take in every sensory property of the event (sights, sounds, smells, etc.).
12. I thought about how I'd reminisce to myself about this event later.
22. I consciously reflected on the situation—took in details, tried to remember them, made comparisons.
32. I labeled specific details of the situation explicitly—tried to find out what it was that I was enjoying and note each aspect explicitly.
41. I took mental photographs.
48. I tried to memorize my surroundings.
53. I took photographs with a camera to capture the experience.

Self-Congratulation (7 items; α = .84):
3. I reminded myself how long I had waited for this to happen.
13. I reminded myself what a relief it was.
23. I told myself how proud I was.
33. I told myself how impressed others must be.
42. I thought about what a triumph it was.
49. I told myself why I deserved this good thing.
54. I thought about what a good time I was having.

Comparing (7 items; α = .78):
6. I thought back to events that led up to it—to a time when I didn't have it and wanted it.
16. I thought about ways in which it could have been worse.
26. I focused on the future—on a time when this good event would be over.
36. I reminded myself that others who were involved in the event were also thinking and feeling the same way.
45. I compared myself to others (asked myself "Am I enjoying this as much as they are?").
51. I made associations with other past pleasant events and reminded myself of them.
55. I thought about how things might never be this good again.

Sensory-Perceptual Sharpening (4 items; α = .73):
7. I tried to focus on certain sensory properties in particular (perhaps blocking out others).
17. I opened my eyes wide and took a deep breath—tried to become more alert.
27. I tried to slow down and move more slowly (in an effort to stop or slow down time).
37. I concentrated and blocked out distractions; I intensified one sense by blocking another.

Absorption (4 items; α = .74):
8. I thought only about the present—got absorbed in the moment.
18. I closed my eyes, relaxed, took in the moment.
28. I made myself relax so that I could become more absorbed in the event or activity.
38. I just went through the experience one moment at a time and tried not to look too far ahead.

Continued

TABLE 2.3 *(Continued)*

Behavioral Expression (6 items; α = .82):
 5. I jumped up and down, ran around or showed other physical expressions of energy.
 15. I laughed or giggled.
 25. I tried to speed up and move more quickly.
 35. I sighed or made other verbal sounds of appreciation to help myself savor the moment (e.g., saying mmm, aahh, humming or whistling).
 44. I screamed or made other verbal expressions of excitement.
 50. I touched myself—rubbed my stomach, clapped my hands, etc.

Temporal Awareness (5 items; α = .82):
 4. I reminded myself how transient this moment was—thought about it ending.
 14. I thought how I wished this moment could last—reminded myself how I must enjoy it now because it would soon be over.
 24. I reminded myself that it would be over before I knew it.
 34. I reminded myself that nothing lasts forever so I must enjoy this now.
 43. I thought about how fast the time was passing.

Counting Blessings (3 items; α = .72):
 9. I reminded myself how lucky I was to have this good thing happen to me.
 19. I thought about what a lucky person I am that so many good things have happened to me.
 29. I said a prayer of thanks for my good fortune.

Kill-Joy Thinking (7 items; α = .80):
 10. I told myself why I didn't deserve this good thing.
 20. I thought about ways in which it could have been better.
 30. I withdrew and inhibited my feelings (stiffened up).
 39. I told myself how it wasn't as good as I'd hoped for.
 46. I reminded myself of other places I should be or of other things I should be doing instead.
 52. I thought about other things that were hanging over me, problems and worries that I still had to face.
 56. I thought about things that made me feel guilty.

Note. Items are listed by their number in the WOSC questionnaire. These ten savoring dimensions are based on a principal-axis factor analysis (with promax rotation) of the responses of 1,136 college undergraduates. Respondents are instructed first to think about a recent positive event and to describe it in writing. They then read a list of 60 statements representing "things that people might think or do while they are going through positive events," and are asked to use a 7-point scale (1 = definitely does not apply; 4 = applied somewhat; 7 = definitely applies) to indicate the extent to which each statement characterizes what they thought and did when they experienced the positive event in their written description (see Appendix D for a copy of the actual instrument and Appendix E for detailed scoring instructions). Reported for each WOSC subscale is Cronbach's alpha (α), a coefficient of internal consistency reliability. There are three unscored WOSC items (57–60) that do not fall on any of the subscales and a final "blank" item (61) that allows respondents to list and rate an additional savoring response they might wish to add to the checklist.

attention to positive experiences. And it is for this reason that people's full-scale narrative accounts, either in response to our requests for their experiences about savoring, or in spontaneous self-reports available in their autobiographical writing of one kind or another, are of special interest in our investigation of savoring. These accounts include verbatim reports of our own experience. Such qualitative data — and we do not hesitate to treat these self-reports as "data" — are important as evidence supporting the conceptual issues that we cover in this book.

Nonetheless, refined analyses of the dimensions and processes involved in savoring are better handled using quantitative data. To this end, we use results from a number of quantitative assessments that are amenable to standard statistical analyses. In the second section of this chapter, we briefly described three such instruments that Fred has developed: the 5-item Perceived Ability to Savor Positive Outcomes Subscale (PASPO; Bryant, 1989); the 24-item Savoring Beliefs Inventory (SBI; Bryant, 2003), and the 60-item Ways of Savoring Checklist (WOSC). The quantitative indicators derived from these three assessment devices, together with the additional qualitative data, provide the basic empirical evidence for many of the assertions we make about savoring processes.

To close this chapter, we end by drawing together these various measurement tools conceptually into a unifying set of postulates. Note that the first two instruments — the PASPO and the SBI — both reflect the same underlying characteristic, the perceived capacity to savor positive experience. Section II of Table 2.2 reveals that scores on the global PASPO are most closely related to beliefs about savoring the moment, but are also positively related to savoring via anticipation and reminiscence. The PASPO thus provides a brief, reliable index of perceived overall savoring capacity (Bryant, 1989; Wood, Heimpel, & Michela, 2003), whereas the SBI provides reliable measures of perceived savoring capacity with respect to the three temporal domains, as well as a global total score (Bryant, 2003).

Underlying all three measurement instruments are four basic assumptions:

- People savor positive experiences in characteristic ways (as reflected in the WOSC)
- People's characteristic ways of savoring influence their levels of positive affect in response to positive events (as reflected in reported enjoyment)
- People are aware of how well they are actually able to savor positive experiences
- People can assess their personal ability to savor (as reflected in the PASPO and SBI).

In contrast to measures of savoring beliefs (i.e., the PASPO and SBI), the WOSC assesses specific thoughts and behaviors in response to positive events. Because these responses may influence enjoyment, they are assumed to relate to people's actual savoring ability, as well as to people's savoring beliefs — assumptions we test empirically in chapter 4. Note that the WOSC focuses exclusively on savoring the moment, and not on anticipating or reminiscing. Although we recognize the potential to develop checklists to assess ways of anticipating and reminiscing, we have focused primarily on savoring the moment because enjoying the present is the essence of savoring. Nevertheless, we have also developed detailed survey instruments for assessing the content, antecedents, consequences, and styles of positive reminiscence (Bryant et al., 2005; Bryant, Yarnold, & Morgan, 1991). And we have also completed some pilot work on a Ways of Anticipating Checklist (WAC). We hope that the PASPO, SBI, and WOSC will be useful to researchers interested in studying ways of savoring positive experiences.

3

Toward a Model
for Savoring

No man is happy who does not think himself so.
—Publilius Syrus (42 B.C./1856)

What are the important factors that control savoring processes? The answers to this question form the heart of a psychology of savoring. Most of what we discuss is new and is meant to pave the way toward building that psychology, but it is hardly an integrated model of savoring. Because we have only limited empirical documentation to report from our own work and the work of others on the phenomena we discuss, what we assert here should be considered as only initial propositions. Nevertheless, what follows in this chapter reflects the understanding we have accumulated over the years from our research in motivation and subjective mental health, as well as from our specific forays into studying savoring empirically. Much work remains to be done before psychologists know as much about the processes of savoring and how these are integrated as they do about the processes of coping. We hope that our initial propositions help facilitate this work.

We outline our conceptual propositions under three major sets of factors critical to a psychology of savoring: (a) conditions that give rise to savoring; (b) factors affecting the quality and intensity of the positive affect experienced; and (c) factors affecting attention to the positive affect experienced. Although these three sets of factors are not entirely independent, for the sake of clarity we present them one at a time and indicate how they might be interrelated. Because this presentation is highly abstract, we illustrate the propositions we make with savoring experiences we presented in the last chapter, as well as other examples of savoring.

CONDITIONS THAT GIVE RISE TO SAVORING

As we noted in the previous chapter, there are an infinite variety of situations that people savor. Although the contexts for most of them can be classified under certain common life situations — eating and drinking, love and sex, being in nature, sports and exercise, work and leisure, contact with the arts, reading, to name some of the most prominent — there are also a host of situations people savor that are either difficult to classify into a single category or highly idiosyncratic. Some savoring experiences seem to have a certain spontaneity about them; others, such as what we sometimes experience on vacations or during a sumptuous meal, can be well planned. This diversity of experience makes it a Herculean task to identify the triggering conditions for savoring. One could well say the same thing about attempts to catalog the innumerable situations with which people are forced to cope throughout their lives.

Nevertheless, there are undoubtedly common psychological mind-sets that permit people to attend to and appreciate their pleasure in a savoring way. We have already described one of these sets in chapter 1, where we delimited the savoring process as occurring when social and esteem needs are not pressing, particularly any demands that evoke a sense of social responsibility. It is then a logical next step to state that a necessary condition for savoring is the relatively weak activation of social and esteem needs.

Imagine a high-energy business meeting in which a person, let's call him Archibald, is intensely arguing a viewpoint concerning a new company policy. In the midst of this high-powered meeting, it would be hard for Archibald to shift into a savoring mind-set in which he could appreciate for any length of time the positive experiences of friendship that might be occurring at the meeting. Archibald's social needs for influence and his esteem needs for achievement take precedence in this particular situation. On the other hand, another person at the same meeting, let's call her Alice, who has little at stake in what is going on, could sit back and savor the friendship of someone at the meeting, the professional manner in which the meeting is being conducted, or even some rich fantasies she may be having about her love life.

In our initial definition of savoring, we also highlighted savoring as being a process in the here and now in which people focus their attention on positive feelings. These conceptual elements imply that there is an immediacy to whatever is being savored, a demand on the person's perceptual and cognitive scanning that may be so strong as to automatically elicit some degree of savoring. The sudden image of a marvelously vivid, multicolored sunset, the melodious resonance of a perfectly executed sweet aria, the mouth-watering fragrance of freshly baked bread — these simple pleasures make some degree of savoring virtually unavoidable. Even so, all of us can imagine situations in which we might be so self-absorbed that we would not even notice these powerful situational stimuli. As Wordsworth wrote in 1806 (Goodman, 1990, p. 119):

> The world is too much with us. Late and soon,
> Getting and spending we lay waste our powers.
> Little we see in nature that is ours.
> We have given our hearts away, a sordid boon.

Let us think again of Archibald arguing his viewpoint in the policymaking meeting noted earlier. Suppose Alice interrupted him and told an exceptionally funny joke. On one hand, we could imagine that, for at least a moment, Archibald might attend to the joke and might savor Alice's humor, even though his social and esteem needs were still on the line. The joke might press into his consciousness for a brief moment and "demand" savoring, despite his other goals. On the other hand, we can also imagine Archibald being so immersed in the meeting that he could not, for even a second, let any humor intrude.

Thus, even with vivid immediate sensory experiences or a wildly humorous joke, we still must consider when internal or external conditions "demand" savoring. Yet we are hard pressed to state these conditions in abstract terms. Certainly not having anything to distract us from savoring *is* a necessary condition, but it is obviously not a sufficient condition for savoring to occur in our responses. What actually triggers a savoring mode, if there are no active needs to interfere with savoring?

One powerful force for savoring comes from modeling others who are savoring an ongoing experience and hence alerting us to it. We all have loved ones or those we hold in high esteem who, at a particular time, are clearly savoring something, and directly or indirectly invite us to share that pleasure. Think of a superb teacher you have known in the past. Such gifted educators have a contagious enthusiasm that manifests itself in their own savoring of their subject matter with such palpable intensity that their students are caught up in the same delightful savoring and pursue the topic further, even without direct encouragement or pressure from the teacher. And yet such modeling need not be involved in the initiation of all savoring. Something more general must be involved.

BACKDROP THEORETICAL PERSPECTIVES ON THE DYNAMICS OF SAVORING

Most of what we present as the theoretical basis of savoring involves specific concepts about how savoring processes work. However, we also wish to offer some heuristic theoretical perspectives to serve as a backdrop for understanding the process of savoring. As noted in the last chapter, we need one set of concepts to help us understand dynamic processes *as savoring is occurring* (i.e., optimal-level theory), and another set of concepts to help us understand dynamic processes *as savoring is being chosen as a goal state not yet attained* (i.e., expectancy-value theory). Let us first consider optimal-level theory.

Optimal-Level Theory as a Heuristic for Understanding Ongoing Savoring Processes

In the last chapter, we proposed to use a theory of preferences for stimulation that has been in psychology for many years to help frame the dynamics of savoring as a person is in the midst of a savoring experience. This is basically a simple idea concerning arousal. Specifically, Berlyne (1960) noted that infants automatically attend to a novel visual stimulus that is not too discrepant from stimuli they have just been seeing. If the stimulus is not discrepant at all, then it is uninteresting to them; and if it is too discrepant, then they avoid attending to it. In other words, humans have a built-in preference or motivation to attend to a moderate level of stimulation (Berlyne, 1966).

For our purposes in thinking about savoring, we would add that these moderate discrepancies are especially likely to be *appreciated and savored.* We thus assume, using optimal-level concepts, that the individual will be motivated to attend to these moderately discrepant stimuli, and once such moderate discrepancies are noted, the individual will continue to attend to these stimuli and savor them as long as they remain moderately discrepant.

As people get used to any pattern of positive stimulation, their interest in such stimulation eventually wanes, and they attend elsewhere. It is as if the affective experience of savoring can easily peter out, or become satiated to some extent over time. What at first is very arousing, delicious, or wonderful to contemplate eventually begins to lose its attractiveness, not because of any external interference, but merely because of the passage of time. Eventually, we all become adapted to a specific experience of pleasure so that it loses its dynamism and appeal. The first taste of a rich dessert may be intensely appreciated, but with repeated mouthfuls, the pleasure diminishes. In some cases, the dessert may even become too rich for one's palate.

Along these lines, many years ago Helson (1964) introduced the notion of an "adaptation level" for sensory responses. Others have extended this idea to affective responses as well (e.g., Brickman & Campbell, 1971; Brickman, Coates, & Janoff-Bulman, 1978). A person gets used to a sound that at first was grating. People also can get used to mild pain in a way that sometimes permits them to ignore the pain. Likewise, a person can get used to a savored stimulus. We are arguing here that people often adapt or habituate to a pleasure they are savoring, such that what initially was highly pleasurable loses its intensity merely with the passage of time.

The speed of adaptation to pleasurable stimuli might be a function of various factors concerning the quality and number of the sensory dimensions involved. If an experience being savored is a relatively simple taste, then we would not expect the savoring to last long. But if an experience is complex, involving multiple sensory and cognitive dimensions, such as what Fred experiences during his mountaintop moments, then there can be automatic shifts of focus to different dimensions before habituation occurs and the savoring dissipates.

If this reasoning is correct, then one could interpret the various cognitive and behavioral strategies people adopt as tools for maintaining or even enhancing their ongoing savoring.

However, working out the particular parameters needed to assess people's ongoing adaptation levels to patterns of stimuli, particularly to complex patterns, is a difficult task. Most of the time, we are not in a position to do that. Furthermore, the definition of a moderate discrepancy is almost always difficult to pin down in advance, if we were to get more serious about using optimal-level theory in a predictive way. Although it has always been an intuitively appealing theory, the optimal-level framework has promoted little explicit research. Thus, we use optimal-level theory here merely as a heuristic tool because it makes sense in explaining how and why an individual aroused to attend to positive experience might savor that experience in the first place and might prolong the savoring experience as it unfolds. We adopt optimal-level theory as a backdrop paradigm, until a more compelling conceptual framework emerges.

Expectancy-Value Thinking and Choosing to Savor

Using optimal-level thinking as a model for the ebb and flow of savoring may strike the critical reader as rather mechanical. Indeed, at first we wanted to describe conditions under which savoring would be automatically evoked or would disappear by the automatic changing flow of one's conscious images. Our thinking thus far reflects that mechanistic bias. And yet we know that people can intentionally savor or deliberately make themselves focus on aspects of their conscious awareness that bring about savorable experiences. Unfortunately, we know of no good psychological theory of intention, or *will*, as James (1890/1981) called it, to help us understand savoring as a willful phenomenon. Seligman (2002a) has resurrected will as a sine qua non of what he identifies as human "virtues," which are important variables to be explored in establishing a comprehensive positive psychology. In particular, he notes that people must intend to do whatever gets labeled as a virtue.

We also would like to resurrect will as a construct that underlies much savoring activity. In the sections that follow, we sometimes use a notion of intention or will in considering how people manipulate their own internal world to regulate the experience of savoring.

As a general orientation to the factors that may be important to any choice activity, whether it involves savoring or not, we have found useful certain ideas from the expectancy-value position, described briefly in chapter 2. Expectancy-value theories derive from cognitive approaches to motivation and, as such, outline the psychological forces *within* the person that are critical in determining which choice out of an array of choices the person selects. These theories focus largely on *expectancies* and *values* for each possible activity in a person's repertoire of available choices. By values, we generally mean the goals that people have when performing a particular activity in a given situation. These goals can be conceived in situational terms, in which case they are often called *incentives;* or they can be conceived in dispositional terms, in which case they are often called *motives* (see Veroff & Veroff, 1980). By *expectancies,* we mean the perceived probability of attaining the goals in the situation, which again can be purely situational or can be based on general dispositional characteristics of the person, such as one's characteristic level of optimism or pessimism (Scheier & Carver, 1985, 1992) or dispositional hope (Snyder, 1994, 2002). If at any moment in time one could isolate a limited set of possible tendencies that a person can choose to perform, then each tendency would have motives, incentives, and expectancies as forces determining its strength. The simple prediction then would be that the person will choose or perform the strongest tendency in the situation, until the tendency of a different activity emerges at the top of the person's hierarchy of tendencies.

In everyday life, we can rarely plot the potential array of tendencies that people can choose. As a result, this basic conceptual model of choice has largely been used for simplified laboratory experiments, including much work on level of aspiration and persistence conducted in the confines of the laboratory (see Weiner, 1992).

For now, we are only suggesting that in order to understand what impels a person to decide to attend to the pleasures of a given activity (or to savor), we need to know three pieces of information for each tendency the person has in a moment in time to act in a certain way: (a) the nature and strength of the person's incentive for such attending; (b) his or her general motive to attend to pleasures; and (c) his or her expectancy that if the activity is performed, it will be successful in attaining a savoring experience. These factors would be involved in determining the strength of all possible tendencies active at a moment in time. Whichever tendency has the strongest force would be the one most likely chosen and enacted.

Among those tendencies to act at a given moment in time might be a tendency controlled by savoring incentives and motives and by the expectation that performing that action would lead to successful attainment of savoring incentives. If such a tendency is the strongest at a moment in time, then it will most likely be chosen. This is an exceedingly complex conceptual perspective and was presented merely as an assumed general backdrop for thinking about a person's motivation to choose a particular savoring alternative, just as we presented optimal-level theory as an assumed general backdrop for understanding ongoing savoring.

In lieu of working through these very generalized backdrop perspectives, we turn instead to more middle-level theoretical constructs, which are more manageable in helping shape a model of savoring. We have grouped these concepts into two major categories: (a) factors affecting the intensity of enjoyment experienced in savoring; and (b) factors affecting the attention paid to the enjoyment experienced.

FACTORS AFFECTING THE INTENSITY OF ENJOYMENT EXPERIENCED

We consider six different factors that affect the intensity of enjoyment experienced in savoring: the duration of the experience; the stress-reducing capacity of the experience; the complexity of the experience; the degree of attentional focus during the experience; the degree of balance in self-monitoring; and how socially connected the experience is.

Duration of the Experience

We hesitate to mention a simple-minded idea that the longer a positive experience lasts, the greater chance one has to savor it. And yet this simple notion is important to note, for it implicates an important proposition about savoring. Often when people are savoring, they feel that they are slowing down time or, put another way, stretching out their experience. Indeed, people often get the feeling they are making the most of the moment when they slow down the positive experience or linger in it, to try to make it last longer.

In the preceding chapter, Joe spoke of wanting to slow down his experience in reading his family's chain letter, so that he could appreciate it more fully. He would make sure he read the letter when he was not in a hurry to do other things, during a quiet moment purposely set aside to enjoy the experience. Savoring seems to go hand in hand with the experience of time passing more slowly. When people are in a rush, it is possible for them to enjoy an event, but perhaps only briefly. Savoring is then minimized. We have noted how people typically have a sense that the perceived world is going past them more slowly than usual when they are in a mindful savoring mode. When this happens, they are more embedded in the processing of their experience so that they sense more and attend more closely to details than if they perceived the world in their usual "mindless" disregard for ongoing experience.

To slow down is to allow oneself time to savor. In their 1966 hit song, "Feelin' Groovy," Simon and Garfunkel advised people to slow down and not move too fast, in order to make the morning last. In this song, they urged people to decelerate the pace of living in search of fun and "groovy" feelings, as they called them. A slower pace may well foster an appreciative orientation.

We have noticed that the stylish fast-framing that occurs in much of modern cinema and television programming sets a pace for processing that, while exciting, permits precious little time for savoring. As a result, whenever a movie's framing slows down, a person can embrace the images more intimately and lovingly. Once a person becomes adapted to a given pace of processing, however, then the slowing down can seem boring, like reaching an adaptation level to moderately discrepant stimulation.

Undoubtedly, there are strong individual differences in the processing pace that facilitates optimal savoring. It is for this reason that reading remains one of the most reliable activities for savoring artistic expression. We all can read at our most comfortable pace, retrace a phrase or a sentence in order to enjoy what is being conveyed with increased pleasure, or compare particular passages with each other to gain new insight and enrich appreciation.

In a similar vein, much of the joy of climbing mountains comes from slowly making one's way up a mountain at a pace that allows one to notice every detail both in one's surroundings and in oneself. The steep terrain and thin air at higher altitudes force the climber to move more slowly than normal, and to adopt a rhythmic, Zen-like approach to upward movement. This snail-like pace affords the opportunity to notice minute environmental details that one would otherwise miss — the shimmering of snow crystals, the humming of small insects, the screaming of ravens, the piping of marmots, the delicate scent of alpine wildflowers, the distant roar of the wind. These unexpected small things seem to have an almost other-worldly beauty that brings intense joy when the climber views them with full attention. In the same way, the slow upward crawl to higher elevations encourages the climber to scrutinize thoughts and feelings in a more intense light, stripping away successive layers of self-deception to unmask the true inner self (Shulman, 1992).

It is not so easy to slow down to savor. The pace of life catches us in a whirl, so much so that even highly enjoyable moments, those for which one has set time aside, may be examined too quickly and only briefly encountered. When visiting a new place in a foreign country, for example, tourists often try to cram in as many sights as possible in a short period of time, so that they can "do" what good tourists are expected to do in that place. People run from one tour-book attraction to another, without having the time to appreciate sufficiently any one attraction. Under these circumstances, one can say that people's savoring is reduced. If tourists spent a longer time at a museum or cathedral or sat for a longer time at a vista overlooking a city, then they might savor that museum, or that cathedral, or that vista more fully.

When experiencing a savoring moment, people can employ an act of will to intentionally slow down the pace of their activity and notice smaller units of what they are experiencing, as if they were putting a video tape in slow motion. We are not saying that a longer and more focused period for savoring necessarily makes an experience more intense. But often it does.

Some experiences are by their nature fleeting, and an attempt to slow down such experiences might be futile. A spectacular shooting star might streak across the night sky and vanish in less than a second. An unexpected compliment from a stranger might be over by the time one perceives it. When hiking over a hill of lilacs, a person can be met headlong by the sweet wonderful fragrance that lilacs in full bloom exude. But that smell to be savored soon recedes from conscious-ness as we adapt to the atmospheric aroma. The stimulation causing the aroma is still there, but is not sensed as strongly as it was at first. It would be difficult to put the waxing and waning of the aroma into slow motion. One's intense savoring might be limited to less than a minute, if that long. We again invoke principles from optimal-level theory to suggest that the hiker approaching a group of lilac bushes gets adapted to the stimuli so that the fragrance no longer interests the hiker. In the case of many instances of olfaction, good or bad, perceivers literally become adapted to the smell.

Other experiences do not end or fade so quickly, and the longer they last, the more people can bring a multitude of associations and feelings into play, the more they can pick up new facets of the experience. Recall Fred's description of his savoring experience when reaching the top of Snowmass Mountain. He lingered in this savoring moment, remembering how much he had longed to climb the mountain (i.e., recalled anticipation), attending to new and different things about the current experience, as well as thinking about the joys he would later have in telling others about it (i.e., anticipated recall).

Next we discuss the dimension of complexity of the savored experience, which is highly correlated with the duration of the experience. With complex experiences, the duration of the experience can become extended and hence affect the quality and perhaps the intensity of the savoring. Adopting optimal-level thinking, we suggest that more complex stimuli take longer to reach an adaptation level where moderate discrepancies subside and make the person inattentive to the experience. Thus, greater complexity may prolong the duration of a positive experience.

And yet a situation that combines many different positive experiences at one time may tax a person's capacity to savor it fully. Along these lines, experi-mental evidence indicates that, given a choice, people prefer to separate rather than combine two positive events — that is, the so called "gain-savoring" effect (Linville & Fischer, 1991). "Consider two positive events, such as receiving two manuscript acceptance letters. Receiving both letters on the same day is likely to produce a real high, a sense that things could not be better. On the other hand, if the letters arrive on different days, one may more fully savor the pleasure of each acceptance, and there is the added advantage of having two distinct positive experiences instead of one" (Linville & Fischer, 1991, p. 5). Linville and Fischer (1991) further proposed that:

> . . . people possess limited gain-savoring resources that are consumed in the process of experiencing positive events that occur in close temporal contiguity but that are also naturally renewable over time. These resources include time, cognitive resources, and physical energy and consummatory capacity (e.g., in eating or drinking). For example, savoring a positive event may involve cognitive processes such as cognitively elaborating the event and its implications for one's goals and for one's self-evaluations, replaying the event, imaging others' reactions, and savoring the emotional high that is associated with the event. Such cognitive processes require time and considerable cognitive resources. (pp. 9–10)

Thus, the capacity to savor requires attentional resources, the use of which people seek to maximize by choosing to separate or combine events, depending on which approach produces the more favorable anticipated emotional outcome (Linville & Fischer, 1991). Likewise, people may slow down or linger while savoring in order to maximize their use of attentional resources.

Another way to speak of slowing down time is to consider that people may intentionally try not to have other upcoming events interfere with what they are savoring. A husband and wife can deliberately not answer the telephone, if they are savoring a meal together and enjoying the conversation they are having. As we have suggested, savoring can be under considerable cognitive control. People can direct their attention to a savoring experience and avoid attending to other experiences. They can thereby stretch out an experience for a while, until something from the outside actively intrudes on their consciousness. Perhaps when people get "lost in a book," they are so attentive to what they are reading and their enjoyment of it that they don't hear or see stimuli to which they would ordinarily be sensitive. Thus, to some extent the duration of a savoring experience is a function of the attention we give more or less deliberately to the event.

In passing, we should again note the contrast between the experience of flow (Csikszentmihalyi, 1975, 1990, 2002) and the experience of savoring. Csikszentmihalyi has noted that in flow experiences, we are often amazed by the quick passage of time when we are immersed in doing something in which we are testing our competence with just the right level of challenge. Avid gardeners and other hobbyists can attest to this phenomenon. But this is quite different from sensing a stretching of time when we savor, however momentary that might be.

Does this differential experience of time make flow and savoring incompatible? In some sense, yes. As we noted earlier, as soon as we stop to savor a flow experience, we could very well interfere with the flow, at least temporarily. There is no reason, however, that we could not dovetail these experiences, although flow is less under conscious intentional control than is savoring. Although it has often been said, "Time flies when you're having fun," we suggest that time is less likely to fly when one is aware that one is having fun, that is, when one is savoring.

Stress Reduction

When people go from a period of stress in their lives to a time when the stress is minimized, gone, or forgotten, they are especially ripe for savoring something they enjoy that might be temporally associated with the stress reduction or accidentally paired with it. When people experience a savored pleasure that occurs right after they were stressed, the relief of stress becomes an add-on to the enjoyment they usually experience with that savored pleasure. This phenomenon may account for why such pleasurable experiences are so intensely enjoyed. At a simple level, for example, one is likely to appreciate having a warm shower after stress more than after a period of tranquility. There may even be physiological bases for this effect. The tensions in one's musculature after a period of stress relax with an especially pleasurable intensity when the warmth of the shower penetrates one's skin. People may savor eating and drinking more after a strenuous, unpleasant day at work than they do when all has gone well at the office. Moreover, when males are anxious or afraid, they find females more attractive (Dutton & Aron, 1974). Of course, this is not always the case. At other times, stress can be so pervasive that people are unable to stop thinking about it and as a consequence, cannot easily savor, no matter how positive the stimulus.

We are not suggesting that savoring would have been absent had the person experienced no stress. Having a shower, having something to eat or drink, or being with another person all could be pleasurable, *ipso facto;* and if one attended to any of those pleasures, then one might savor each experience. Instead, we are suggesting that if savoring occurs in connection with a reduction in stress, then the savoring is likely to be intensified.

Many men and women experience a heightened pleasure from sexual interaction in the wake of a stormy argument. For some couples, the tension is still so much with them that the sexual responses seem hollow. But for other couples, probably those who have satisfactorily resolved their tensions with one another, the sexual responses seem especially fulfilling. Of course, sexual responses often have the further meaning of giving and receiving love, and after a fight, a couple might be especially keen on reassuring themselves about each other's love. Thus, should pleasurable sexual activity occur in connection with stress reduction, we would expect that the activity might be savored with particular gusto.

In defining the basic conditions for the occurrence of savoring, we said earlier that a person had to be relatively free of social and esteem concerns because these issues can distract one's attention from savoring. Implied in that requirement is that savoring occurs best in the condition of reduced stress. Recall Joe's example of savoring a gourmet meal prepared for guests not when he served it to them, but rather the next day when alone with his wife eating the leftovers.

He was experiencing too much social tension to engage in a savoring mind-set during the lunch party, but could easily engage in such savoring when the social tension was absent.

Do we dare take the step of saying that the degree of savoring experienced might be a function of the degree of stress reduction, all other things being equal? It is certainly true that when there is some reduction in stress, but not complete reduction, a person might still be distracted by thoughts related to the residual stress. These distracting thoughts might interfere with attentional focus during savoring moments, producing "partial savoring," if you will. But whether relief from a terrifying stressor enhances savoring more than does relief from a mild stressor is hard to determine. As far as we know, there is no empirical research that addresses this question.

It would be potentially informative to conduct a randomized experiment comparing the enjoyment people experience in eating a favorite food after being released from a very noxious situation versus a much less noxious situation. It would also be interesting to use experience-sampling methods (Larson & Csikszentmihalyi, 1983) or have people keep a structured diary (DeLongis, Hemphill, & Lehman, 1992) about their meals; what they were doing just prior to each meal; how stressed they felt before, during, and after the meal; and how much they savored the meal. We could thereby test our hypothesis about the connection between savoring and the degree of stress reduction reported.

Another theoretical mechanism helps to explain why positive experiences that occur just after a time of stress or hardship are especially conducive to savoring. Somewhat different from the perspective of optimal-level theory, the notion of *hedonic contrast* (Brickman & Campbell, 1971) suggests that the more a particular stimulus departs from one's existing hedonic baseline, the more intensely that stimulus is experienced. A sustained period of stress effectively lowers one's hedonic baseline, so that pleasant experiences seem even more pleasant in contrast, compared to how these things would seem if one had instead been experiencing a sustained period of pleasurable good fortune. Little pleasures take on a special savor when they follow on the heels of difficulty. Wandering alone in a beautiful garden, sipping a cup of coffee in an easy chair, watching a butterfly sunning itself on a flower—such small pleasures people may well fail even to notice during times of struggle. However, people may find such micropleasures intensely enjoyable after the stress is over and they are able to savor them. Thus, hedonic contrast can amplify the intensity of the pleasure to be gained from savoring. As New England poet Anne Bradstreet observed in 1664 (cited in McElrath & Robb, 1981), "If we had no winter, the spring would not be so pleasant; if we did not taste of adversity, prosperity would not be so welcome."

Given the impact of hedonic baseline on the intensity of enjoyment, people may learn to actively manage their hedonic baseline, so as to optimize their positive experiences. This proactive approach to savoring entails purposefully lowering one's hedonic baseline before experiencing a positive event by working particularly hard, depriving oneself of luxuries, or abstaining from pleasure beforehand (Brickman, 1978). This intentional hedonic deprivation serves to intensify later positive feelings, thus making positive experiences more readily amenable to savoring processes. Given this contrast effect, we suggest that prolonged stress may well lower one's hedonic baseline, thus making positive experiences more easily savored.

Complexity

Situations that contain more complexity are likely to involve a greater variety of incentives. Consider first the multifaceted complexity of Fred's savoring experience on the summit of Snowmass Mountain: taking in the expansive alpine panorama; noticing and smelling the delicate wildflowers; taking photographs to capture the moment; connecting to the past and the future; sensing the bittersweet fleetingness of the moment; realizing that one has finally reached a long-sought goal; sharing the experience and one's feelings with cherished others; sensing connections to loved ones not present and to something greater than oneself; and giving thanks for the priceless blessings one is experiencing. Each of these various savoring facets is associated with its own positive value.

Contrast the simpler savoring experience of eating cheese—for example, closing one's eyes and focusing on the intensity and texture of the taste on one's palate. Yet, even this less complex savoring experience may take on additional facets when making associations to earlier experiences or places in the past; sharing one's feelings with close friends; trying to guess the type, ingredients, or recipe for the cheese; marveling at how the cheese was manufactured, packaged, and distributed; or giving thanks for the gift of taste. Obviously, there are likely to be individual differences in the tendency or ability to notice and process these various facets of the savoring experience.

Although it is tempting to assert that the intensity of the affective consequences of savoring directly corresponds to the number and the complexity of dimensions involved, we doubt that such a law of savoring exists, even if we had a reliable assessment of the complexity of the experience savored. The most critical factor that upends such an assertion is that different individuals differentially weight the importance of certain dimensions, compared to other dimensions. The simple pleasure of eating chocolates might be trivial for one person, but vital to another person's sense of enjoyment of life, either because the taste of chocolate was particularly pleasant to that person, or because the person had many pleasant contextual associations to eating chocolate, or both. For that same person, although he or she senses a whole host of pleasures, none of them might excite him or her as forcefully as the taste of chocolate.

Perhaps within a person's own hierarchy of joys, if you embedded a very important one with a set of other pleasures, then the assertion of a simple relation between level of complexity of the savoring experience and the degree of savoring would hold. For example, if a woman were passionate about chocolates, and you asked her to compare (a) eating chocolates while she listened to pleasant background music and sat in a comfortable stuffed chair in a room with a cheerful fire glowing in the fireplace, with (b) eating the same chocolates without the other accouterments of music, comfortable chair, and cheerful fire, then more than likely she would say that she savored (a) more intensely than (b). But that seems like such a simple-minded comparison that it gives us little insight into the general question of how complexity of experiences relates to the intensity of savoring.

Complexity of experience in savoring can have three very different meanings. The first meaning of "complexity of savoring" is the most straightforward: the *number of different perceptual elements that are being savored simultaneously.* The example we just gave of eating chocolates in a bland environment, as opposed to a situation in which one is also enjoying music, a comfortable chair, and an open fire, would contrast a relatively simple pleasure with a somewhat more complex situation regarding the number of elements being savored. In our experience of savoring, these elements can be attended to simultaneously or sequentially as long as the overall experience is perceived as a totality. However, if people divide their attentional resources too thinly in trying to savor many positive stimuli all at once, then they may not savor any of these separate experiences optimally (Linville & Fischer, 1991). Furthermore, if people have limited time in which to savor and must choose what to attend to versus ignore, then having more as opposed to fewer positive elements in a complex situation might increase regret and dampen savoring, especially among people who prefer to maximize rather than satisfice their hedonic experience (Schwartz, 2000; Schwartz, Ward, Monterosso, Lyubomirsky, White, et al., 2002).

A special case of complex savoring, which we call *intrasensory* or *synergistic savoring,* occurs when two or more senses involved in the context of one positive experience mutually enhance the pleasure of each of these senses. For example, the experience of listening to music while watching dancing occurs in the complex savoring of a ballet or Broadway musical. The auditory pleasure of the music and the visual pleasure of the dancing are expanded synergistically beyond the sum of the pleasure of either just listening or just watching. Likewise, some external objects are natural complements to one another, so that combining and savoring them together can actually heighten one's pleasure — for example, "Drinking a glass of wine may enhance the pleasure of a fine meal" (Linville & Fischer, 1991, p. 10); sharing a walk in a beautiful garden may enhance the pleasure of time spent with a close friend; and playing good music at a social gathering can make the party more enjoyable.

In the second meaning of "complexity of savoring," we speak of the *web of associations* that individuals might have in the context of an enjoyable experience that they are savoring. Memories, anticipations, connections with other people, or pleasurable thoughts about tangential or unrelated issues stimulated by the context of the savoring experience can expand the nature of the experience beyond the initial stimulus. These associations can be sparse and simple, or they can be plentiful and intricate. These associations can be quite personal, but can also be reinforced by one's culture.

Highly sentimental associations can emerge for whole groups of people who have been exposed to the same cultural information about such things as holiday events. For example, such shared associations occur for Americans gathered for a traditional Thanksgiving dinner. They enjoy the same rituals, the same images of the intergeneration connections, the same stories about the Pilgrims and the first Thanksgiving. There is no doubt that a savoring process like giving thanks at a Thanksgiving celebration entails common reactions across individuals. The particular associations people make in response to positive experiences are thus culturally and personally determined.

A third meaning of "complexity of savoring" reflects the *number and type of different savoring processes* that are involved in one context. Sitting at the Thanksgiving table, for example, people can enjoy the savory food and good fellowship with loved ones in a very direct way. But people can also bask in a sense of accomplishment in having prepared the meal or in response to others' compliments about the gathering, marvel at the wonders of life, give thanks for being able to share time with loved ones, and luxuriate in the pleasure of a full stomach after the meal. The quality of the savoring at Thanksgiving will vary depending on how many of these different savoring processes are co-occurring. In the same vein, we have already pointed out ways in which the processes of basking, marveling, thanksgiving, and luxuriating were all active in Fred's mountaintop savoring. Hence, we consider his savoring on the summit to be relatively complex, at least compared to the simple gustatory savoring process that many people described in large-scale surveys as one of their recurrent savoring experiences.

Degree of Attentional Focus

In discussing the general nature of savoring in chapter 2, we mentioned that savoring experiences emerge separately from mere pleasure when people can focus cognitively on the experience, and not just respond affectively while the event is occurring. Indeed, attending to an automatic, impulsive emotional reaction requires some degree of attending to one's affect as if it were an object separate from oneself. In this section, we suggest that the more closely and completely one focuses one's attention on a particular positive experience, the clearer and more vivid will be one's feelings, and hence the more easily and fully one will be able to savor the experience, remember it, and rekindle the feelings that one savored in the first place. Why would that be?

Let us start by contrasting two episodes of savoring. In the first savoring episode, there is little mindful focusing of attention and the savoring that results is minimal. Imagine you are driving a rental car through heavy traffic in a snow-storm in a city you have never visited before, and you turn on the car radio. You immediately hear the start of a brand-new recording by an unknown singer. As traffic signs get complicated and different lanes exit in different directions, you focus your attention closely on driving the unfamiliar rental car through the strange city on the slippery highway. As you drive in a state of hypervigilance, you barely notice the voice and the song on the radio. Your mind is concentrated on the driving, the traffic, and the road conditions, and you don't attend very closely to the song's lyrics. Occasionally you are aware of a pleasant musical phrase, a catchy rhythm, or the timbre of the singer's voice, and you attend to the song with some fleeting appreciation during these brief moments. Thus, you might say you experienced some momentary savoring while you listened to the song. Otherwise, hearing the song was mostly just pleasant sound in your ear without mindful savoring.

During the brief moments you mindfully attended to your pleasure in listening to the song, savoring did not last long because it is not easy to savor while you are intensely focused on driving. Your awareness of your feelings was not well focused, we say, because driving the car required most of your attentional resources and diverted your awareness elsewhere. Nevertheless, you intermittently attended to your pleasure in hearing the new song. The experience of savoring the song while driving involves very little attentional focus and is not very distinct from the immediate sensory experience itself.

Contrast this first savoring episode with a different musical experience. Imagine you are watching a PBS portrait of Leonard Bernstein, and near the end of the television broadcast, the camera focuses on Bernstein conducting the last movement of Beethoven's 9th Symphony at the site of the Berlin Wall as it was about to come down. The camera moves to him flailing his arms in his emotional gusto, then to the singers, then to the orchestra, then to the audiences on both sides of the wall, and back to Bernstein and members of the orchestra and chorus. The performance captures your attention, and your savoring is much more clearly focused compared to the occasional snippets of your own sensory intake that you momentarily savored while driving. Because you are not driving an unfamiliar car in a strange city under hazardous conditions, your attentional resources are free for you to direct more exclusively and clearly toward savoring the musical experience.

This second savoring episode is truly a complex experience, and one whose focus is easily maintained and is thus conducive to savoring processes that last longer. Indeed, one might well purposefully set aside several hours of time to have dinner with close friends, watch the PBS portrait of Bernstein, sip a glass of wine, and share feelings about the experience afterwards. In any event, the savoring in the two musical experiences is hardly the same.

Although you might have savored both musical experiences, the song on the car radio had less power for savoring than did the PBS film, we believe, because the driving diverted your attention so fully. Under the circumstances we described, most people would probably find it much harder to focus their full attention on the car-radio song than on the PBS film. We refer to this distinction as the degree of attentional focus involved in a savoring experience.

Savoring can be stimulated either by an external positive stimulus that captures one's attention (e.g., a majestic panorama) or by an internal thought or feeling to which one attends (e.g., an awareness that one is blessed with good health). In chapter 5, we present an integrative conceptual framework in which we argue that forces directing attention outward promote "world-focused" savoring, whereas forces directing attention inward promote "self-focused" savoring. We suggest that these two different focuses of attention (outward versus inward) evoke qualitatively different savoring experiences. Although it is possible to savor in ways that are primarily world-focused or self-focused, if an external stimulus were to capture attention completely, then it would be impossible for the individual to be aware of positive feelings during the encounter (as with flow experiences), and savoring as we define it could not occur. Far more common are positive experiences in which the perceiver savors by shifting attention back and forth between a positive stimulus and positive feelings in response to the stimulus. In any event, regardless of the target of attention, the more clearly focused one is on that target, the greater will be the potential to savor the experience.

Given these ways to conceptualize attentional focus in savoring, we return to the proposition that focused attending gives positive stimuli greater emotional power, gives people greater access to their feelings in response to these stimuli, and establishes a more reliable way to recall and relive a positive experience later. We suggest that focused attending makes a positive experience more distinctive, more vivid, and more easily and fully savored. Focused attending also enables the individual to make optimal use of available attentional resources when savoring a positive experience (Linville & Fischer, 1991).

In addition, we note that people can often more easily focus on a positive abstract feeling like love or awe when they "objectify" the feeling or stimulus in concrete terms. We can all visualize or hear or taste something better if it has some concrete "objective" point of reference, something on which we can more easily focus our attention.

Poets make use of this proposition. They construct emotionally moving poetry about joyful but personal experiences, by employing concrete "outside" images, sometimes called metaphors, rather than internal notions of feeling states. Because there has been relatively little systematic work on the nature of joy and savoring, there is for poets (as well as the rest of us) a much less vivid and rich vocabulary of feelings about joy and savoring as feelings in and of themselves, compared to the vocabulary of feelings about sorrow and coping. Ideas and words about objects and the way the world moves and changes thus help poets delineate these positive feelings. Consider this poem by E. E. Cummings (cited in Firmage, 1979, p. 367):

somewhere i have never travelled,gladly beyond
any experience,your eyes have their silence:
in your most frail gesture are things which enclose me,
or which i cannot touch because they are too near

your slightest look easily will unclose me
though i have closed myself as fingers,
you open always petal by petal myself as Spring opens
(touching skillfully,mysteriously)her first rose

or if your wish be to close me,i and
my life will shut very beautifully,suddenly,
as when the heart of this flower imagines
the snow carefully everywhere descending;

nothing which we are to perceive in this world equals
the power of your intense fragility:whose texture
compels me with the colour of its countries,
rendering death and forever with each breathing

(i do not know what it is about you that closes
and opens,only something in me understands
the voice of your eyes is deeper than all roses)
nobody,not even the rain,has such small hands

Notice how Cummings conveys his mysterious savoring of love for a woman in subtle metaphors of roses, petals opening and closing, and in other embedded figurative metaphors (e.g., rain) about his attentive adoration of her physicality. Feelings are there, but only indirectly through the poetic magic of *outside* referents that he weaves. Reading the words of the poem draws the reader's attention to things as well as feelings, thus more clearly focusing the experience and facilitating the process of savoring.

Also notice how Cummings alters the conventional capitalization of the first-person pronoun (i.e., "i") and omits the traditional typographical space following commas, colons, semicolons, and parentheses, to catch attention and force the reader to stop and slow down in reading the poem, to spend more time pondering the words and phrases than one would ordinarily. This clever grammatical device heightens attentional focus and thereby enhances savoring of the poem. As we noted earlier, such novelty evokes mindfulness (Langer, 1989), which in turn facilitates savoring.

Balanced Self-Monitoring

Thus far, we have discussed ways in which a greater focus on one's positive feelings can intensify savoring. However, we now wish to warn that sometimes too much cognitive focusing on one's feelings can interfere with savoring. Indeed, there is evidence that a highly introspective inward focus can actually dampen the subjective quality of positive experience.

Imagine three different musical experiences in which you listen to a recording of Stravinsky's *Rites of Spring*. In the first experience, you simply listen to *Rites of Spring*. In the second experience, while you listen to *Rites of Spring*, you try to make yourself feel as happy as possible. In the last experience, while you listen to *Rites of Spring*, you adjust a movable measurement scale to indicate your moment-by-moment level of happiness. In which scenario do you enjoy the music most?

According to a randomized experiment by Schooler et al. (2003), the answer is: the first musical scenario. Analyzing posttest ratings of enjoyment, Schooler et al. (2003) found that experimental participants who were instructed to try to make themselves as happy as possible or to provide real-time evaluations of how happy they were, actually enjoyed the musical recording less than did participants who simply listened to the music. Likewise, asking people to attend carefully to their own mirth responses while viewing humorous cartoons makes the cartoons seem less funny (Cupchik & Leventhal, 1974). Thus, too much focus on evaluating positive feelings, as opposed to just experiencing these feelings, may disrupt one's affective experience, thereby short-circuiting the process of savoring.

Clearly, excessive monitoring of one's reactions and emotions during a positive experience can weaken the underlying enjoyment of the moment. As John Stuart Mill noted in 1873, "Ask yourself whether you are happy, and you cease to be so." Yet, it is also necessary for one to be aware of one's own enjoyment, or else there can be no savoring by our definition of the term. As Samuel Johnson (1752/1999) asserted in 1750, "No man can enjoy happiness without thinking that he enjoys it."

Additional experimental evidence from Wilson, Lindsey, and Schooler (2000) suggests that forcing people to make rapid (i.e., 3-second) hedonic judgments restores their ability to access inner feelings and does not undermine overall enjoyment. Moreover, Schooler et al. (2003) found that allowing participants to see themselves in a mirror while going through a positive experience actually boosts enjoyment, by giving people the opportunity to observe and experience their own visceral hedonic responses. Evidently, the key to avoiding excessive monitoring of positive experiences is to focus mindfully on ongoing positive experiences, without worrying about or continually evaluating whether one is enjoying oneself as much as possible. Indeed, people who are consistently happy tend to be less introspective about why they behave or feel the way they do (Lyubomirsky & Lepper, 1999; Veenhoven, 1988). And there is even evidence that happy mood decreases self-focused attention (Green, Sedikides, Saltzberg, Wood, & Forzano, 2003).

Yet, there are undoubtedly times when cognitive reflection actually enhances enjoyment. Recall the example of Richard Feynman, noted earlier, as he reflected on the beauty of a flower through complex intellectual associations that enriched and inspired his savoring experience. Clearly, there may be ways to focus one's attention on one's feelings and make cognitive judgments about positive feelings that do not dampen or cut short enjoyment (e.g., engaging in brief intermittent self-monitoring rather than continual self-monitoring)—ways that intensify and prolong the savoring experience by broadening its scope and complexity (see Fredrickson, 1998, 2001). We return to these notions in chapter 4 when we discuss different types of savoring processes, and again in chapter 8 when we propose some cognitive and behavioral strategies that individuals can use to enhance their savoring experiences.

Social Connection: Interactive Consequences

In Chapter 2, we highlighted several issues concerning savoring experiences that involve social bases for savoring. Interacting with significant people in our lives during savoring moments—such as Joe's sharing his reactions to the chain letter with his wife, and Fred's reminiscing and being exultant with his climbing partners—are processes that inherently enhance the affective consequences of savoring. But why should that be? Why does one savor more intensely when other people's responses are part of the experience being savored?

We won't dwell on the fact that social interests are so important to human survival. One could argue that anything that emphasizes human interdependence, including the joy of human mutuality, would be an inherently powerful and vivid pleasure for all of us. As people savor some experience in the presence of other people, we suggest that the bonding that occurs in these savoring experiences may be especially and extraordinarily reinforcing of continued social connection with those people with whom savoring has occurred. This should be true even when people savor an everyday experience, let alone a peak experience of some sort. It should be clear, therefore, that bonding under conditions of savoring has greater positive consequences for the future well-being of the person than does savoring without a social component. The social consequences may not be consciously or rationally considered, but they form the underlying reason why social savoring may be especially strongly weighted and distinctively meaningful. One might say, "People who savor together, stay together."

In this way, savoring a tradition that has been part of a group identity can take on especially powerful meaning for a person. Savoring the joy of communing with others at a place of worship, savoring the pleasures of attending a sports event with other like-minded fans, and savoring a family reunion with close and distant relatives are all pleasures further charged by the identity-giving nature of the event. Added to the enjoyment of the pageantry of watching a local parade will often be the civic pride that accrues from just being present.

Even noticing ourselves savoring something in the same way that a stranger is savoring it may deepen our sense of connection with humanity in general. An instance of such stranger bonding occurs in Frances Mayes' paean to savoring life in Tuscany. In *Under The Tuscan Sun* (1996), she writes about an experience of coming upon the sight of rainbows around the dome of the local church, as she drives home in her car to the Tuscan home she renovated:

> Fog completely surrounds the church, and the dome floats above the clouds. Five intersecting rainbows dive and arch around the dome. I almost run off the road. At a curve I stop and get out, wishing everyone were with me. This is staggering. If it were the Middle Ages, I'd claim a miracle. Another car stops and a man dressed in fancy hunting clothes jumps out. Probably he is one of the murderers of sun birds but he, too, looks stunned. We both just stare. As the clouds shift, the rainbows disappear one by one, but the dome still drifts, ready for any sign that might be about to happen. I wave to the hunter. 'Auguri' [an Italian expression of goodwill, best wishes, and good luck], he calls. (pp. 218–219)

Not only did the author wish that "everyone [she loves]" were with her, but she also bonds with a stranger (someone whose interest in hunting she obviously dislikes) only because they are sharing this savored moment. There is an old adage, as John Ray noted in *English Proverbs* (1670): "Misery loves company." We could create an addendum: "and so does joy." And if people are alone in their joy, part of their savoring might even involve thinking about sharing the moment with others, one of the processes of savoring we highlight in chapter 4. The caption for a watercolor by the French artist Samivel embodies the essence of this notion. The painting portrays a solitary man gazing at a mountain sunset and thinking to himself, "How beautiful this would be if I could only share it with someone" (Waterman, 2002, p. 23).

Mutual sharing of savoring moments is often a powerful experience. In mutuality, people induce each other to maintain their attention to what they are savoring. Thus, mutuality can breed longevity of savoring. To be in a state of uncontrolled joyful amusement with another is hard to escape because the other person keeps reminding you of the pleasure you are having. This represents a kind of mutuality and a kind of modeling, if you will. Indeed, we have seen how modeling can get one into a savoring state in the first place. Good teachers, we said, do that. There is reason to think that such modeling can continue to help the student maintain a mindful orientation to what is being savored.

People may also react to and reflect on the positive experience differently when they are alone as opposed to sharing the experience with others. In the presence of strangers, on one hand, people may "clam up" and inhibit their outward facial and behavioral expressions in deference to social norms, as is common in eastern cultures (Lindberg, 2004; Matsumoto, Kudoh, Scherer, & Wallbott, 1988; Mesquita & Karasawa, 2002). In the presence of friends and loved ones, on the other hand, people may be more likely to express their feelings facially and behaviorally in sharing these feelings with close others. These facilitating factors suggest that sharing good times with others can enhance the

quality of people's savoring experiences. Consistent with this reasoning, correlational data indicate that the more college students share their feelings with
others while on vacation or in response to getting a good grade on a test or
paper, the more students report enjoying the vacation or good grade (Bryant,
2003, 2004). As noted earlier, longitudinal research also indicates that sharing
positive feelings with others helps people capitalize on positive experiences by
boosting the positive emotional impact of positive events (Gable, Reis, Impett,
& Asher, 2004; Langston, 1994).

It is no small wonder, therefore, that the English respondents in the Mass
Observation Study (Lowe, 2000) who reported on the pleasures that make up
their lives so often referred to family pleasures and love or sex. These intimate
moments are very important to people, not only for their present lives, but also
for the continued connection to the social world. Although respondents were
less likely to report group pleasures directly, such as the ones we mentioned
earlier, as identity-giving savoring moments, these group pleasures are often
tangentially related to other joys that were frequently mentioned: athletics, especially by men; and church, especially by women.

FACTORS AFFECTING ATTENTION TO THE
ENJOYMENT EXPERIENCED

Relative Strength of Other Tendencies

Earlier in this chapter, we introduced expectancy-value theory as a heuristic for
examining savoring when savoring reflects a choice among a set of tendencies
to act. In this section, we elaborate a bit on this perspective. We begin by considering the general case of how humans make choices. As Atkinson and Birch
(1970) do in *The Dynamics of Action* and as Veroff and Veroff (1980) do in *Social
Incentives*, we can consider a person at the moment of choice as having various
latent tendencies to act. We can say that these tendencies are vying with each
other for expression, and that people will choose to enact the strongest of these
competing tendencies.

Let's say the person is Fred, and his strongest tendency at this moment is to
read and savor the book he has been reading. The other tendencies he still has
latent in his repertoire and that compete with the savoring tendency to read
remain with him. An easy assumption to make about such competition is that
the degree of competition among these tendencies for expression will also affect
the degree of attention he can direct toward any one tendency, whether savoring
is involved in that tendency or not. If Fred's strongest tendency at a moment
in time is to read *and savor* the book to which he is attending, he might be
disrupted from his savoring experience if other tendencies he has while read-

ing become stronger over time, or if his tendency to read becomes weaker, or a combination of the two.

What other tendencies could get stronger? With the mere passage of time while savoring the book, his ongoing competing tendencies to eat, to check his e-mail, to sleep, or to do something else he was expected to do by a certain time, could get stronger. Furthermore, other new tendencies might also arise: answering the telephone, if the phone rings and he is alone; closing the windows, if he sees some lightning and hears a clap of thunder; speaking to his wife, if something he reads reminds him of her. These tendencies also compete and could disrupt savoring the book. Furthermore, his tendency to continue reading might get weaker if the book became boring. On the other hand, he might encounter some new engrossing elements in the book that make the savoring tendency even stronger. All these factors influence how easily or deeply Fred can focus on his book and savor reading it.

This analysis, while logically sound, leaves several questions unanswered. Just how do tendencies become stronger or weaker over time? Can a person control the surging of new tendencies? If so, when and how does that happen? Can savoring be so strong that one can avoid cues from other tendencies? If so, then under what conditions does that happen? We don't have the answers to all these questions, but we can begin to consider some of them.

In general, we have suggested that expectancies and incentives, which affect the strength of behavioral tendencies, can themselves become stronger or weaker over time. Attending to the joy of listening to a new CD may bring us into connection with more complex listening joys as the CD plays on. Incentives for savoring the experience of the CD thus get stronger. Or attending to the pleasure of companionship at a gathering of friends may provide us with more certainty that there would be continuing companionship with this group. Expectancies for savoring companionship may thus increase. With the increase in either incentives or expectancies, the strength of the tendencies they affect may get stronger. In the same way, experience with savoring can reduce the incentives and expectancies that support a given tendency over time, and reduce the resultant strength of that tendency.

Can people control the rising of new tendencies and maintain their attention to what they are savoring? This may again involve deliberate intentions either to hold the competing nonsavoring tendencies at bay, or to add new elements to what they are doing. People can purposely make an ongoing savored event more complex by inducing additional savoring processes, such as making connection with someone else who is savoring the same thing they are. We discuss such a technique of intensifying savoring, plus other specific savoring strategies, more fully in chapter 4. In other words, people can engage in various activities that enhance the strength of savoring. This could very well be deliberate, but people are not always aware of deliberately adopting a particular savoring strategy in the same way they might plan out a way to attain success. Yet there is no reason why they couldn't implement such strategies, if they were aware of them. In the final chapter devoted to enhancing savoring (chapter 8), we offer some cognitive and behavioral strategies for boosting the quality, intensity, and duration of savoring, and present some research findings to support the effectiveness of such strategies.

Can savoring be so strong that a person can ignore the cues from other tendencies? This question conjures up the image of the self-indulgent hedonist who perpetually avoids responsibility. That scenario can surely happen, although we would not wish to be strong advocates of thoughtless pleasure, especially if such pleasure occurs at the expense of one's own or someone else's health or well-being. We are simply analyzing the dynamics of maintaining long durations of savoring, in which the tendency to savor is so much stronger than other tendencies that the cues activating these other tendencies remain dormant.

What are some of these situations? We have touched on one. When a person is mutually savoring an event with another person, that mutuality tends to reinforce the pleasure in the event in a way that savoring it alone does not. Each person's feelings and ideas expressed can become stimuli for enhancing the other person's feelings and ideas. Shared savoring often dominates one's attentional focus, so much so that when they are savoring together, people easily forget other things they need or may even want to do. The phenomenon of "losing track of the time" may well be most applicable to mutual savoring.

Mindfulness

In her book, *Mindfulness,* Ellen Langer (1989) contrasted the characteristics of less conscious, more automatic cognition, which she called mindlessness, with the characteristics of actively processed thought, which she call mindfulness, in which people are open to new perspectives on their experience. We have assumed that positive experiences must include some degree of mindfulness for them to be savored. We can ask, therefore, what conditions reliably elicit active thought and attention? Langer provides some answers from empirical work about common settings for mindfulness: novel situations in which automatic thinking is diminished; high effort settings where people must focus to get something done; and highly uncertain situations. Let us look at each of these more closely.

Novel Situations. Joe speaks of a particular savoring experience he often has when he deliberately sets out to take photographs in black and white. Because people normally see in color, looking at the world through black and white glasses is a novel perceptual set to take for apprehending one's visual field. That novel mind-set forces people to pay attention to the distribution of light patterns they observe, something to which they normally do not attend. Joe reports a particularly engaging savoring that occurs when he looks at the world that way, one that he tries to convey in his photography, but one that even if he did not take pictures would offer him many savoring moments in experiencing the world around him. We can generalize somewhat from this phenomenon and posit that when people look for nuances in their experiences of pleasures, new facets to the elements that make up that experience, or novel sensory phenomena or associations, they are activating a mindful state. In being mindful, they can become aware of the very dynamism that we said underlies savoring—namely, shifts in optimal stimulation. In a certain sense, this premise provides a ratio-nale for what we noted earlier, that there may be more to our savoring if we are attending to a complex rather than a simple phenomenon.

Following the rules of curiosity motivation, however, all of us should be on the lookout for associations or ideas in our savoring that are so novel that they disrupt the pleasurable feedback and perhaps create anxiety or pain in its place. Books and films can have their jarring moments when they introduce something bizarre, and they break the savoring spell. People can also have peculiar self-created associations that have the same effect. One cannot control the author's odd moments in a book or the director's strange interludes in films, but to some extent men and women can control whether their own associations to an event are bizarre, however creative these thoughts may be. People who have trouble focusing and directing their thoughts are thus at a distinct disadvantage when it comes to avoiding disruptive cognitive associations that undermine savoring. Indeed, the reported frequency of automatic negative cognitions is strongly associated with lower levels of happiness (Bryant & Baxter, 1997).

Effortful Situations. Redoubling efforts to maintain savoring may not work, if we grant that savoring is a relatively immediate here and now experi-ence. And yet there may be something to the use of effort in mindful savoring. People put themselves in a highly focused state when they put forth their maxi-mum effort. They can also purposely try to block inroads into their savoring by denying or suppressing other demands for their attention. Earlier we mentioned adopting an inquiring mind-set as a way to maintain our attention to savor-ing. That attentional mind-set is what people would likely adopt in what Langer (1989) has called "effortful" situations.

The consequences of trying harder to savor a positive moment may well depend on how people go about being more effortful. As noted earlier, empirical evidence suggests that the process of continually evaluating one's level of enjoy-ment or explicitly trying to make oneself feel as happy as possible may actually reduce enjoyment over time (Schooler et al., 2003). In contrast, brief intermittent introspection may be structured so as to amplify enjoyment. Focusing attention outward on an external stimulus at times when feelings are particularly clear and strong might also be a powerful attentional strategy. This approach may facilitate longer and more intense savoring because it protects the ongoing flow of affective experience from disruptive cognitive interference. More importantly, people who seek to enhance the quality of their savoring would do well to direct their efforts toward increasing their level of mindful awareness during positive experiences.

This prescriptive notion is entirely consistent with long-standing religious traditions, such as Buddhism and Judaism, each of which teaches in its own way the value of being present in the moment. Buddhist philosophy emphasizes the infinite possibilities that exist in each moment and the deep inner peace and bliss that comes from being fully aware of the experience and no longer longing for what one does not have (Levine, 2000), from being here now (Dass, 1971), and from harnessing the power of the present (Tolle, 1999). Jewish tradition stresses that, "There is nothing better for a man than that he should eat and drink, and find enjoyment in his toil" (Ecclesiastes 2:24, Revised Standard Version). These convergent perspectives suggest that enlightenment lies in maintaining a mindful focus of attention on the present.

In contrast to a present focus, trying to find happiness by striving to obtain more possessions in the future may backfire. Indeed, a wealth of evidence indicates that the single-minded goal of achieving happiness through efforts to attain more material goods is self-defeating (Csikszentmihalyi, 1999; Easterbrook, 2003; Schooler et al., 2003). "If people strive for a certain level of affluence thinking that it will make them happy, they find that on reaching it, they become very quickly habituated, and at that point they start hankering for the next level of income, property, or good health ... studies have confirmed that goals keep getting pushed upward as soon as a lower level is reached" (Csikszentmihalyi, 1999, p. 823). In fact, people consistently underestimate their own tendency to adapt hedonically to continuing positive experiences (Gilbert, Pinel, Wilson, Blumberg, & Wheatley, 1998).

Yet, there is also evidence that people automatically engage in activities that maintain their mood when they are experiencing a happy feeling, even though they are not consciously aware of doing so. For example, the hedonic contingency model (HCM; Wegener & Petty, 1994) posits that people have learned to seek out positive activities while in a happy mood in order to maintain or elevate that mood. However, the situational context can influence whether or not people keep doing what they are doing when they feel good (Martin, 2001). For example, if people experiencing a positive mood evoke an "achievement rule," then they will infer that the positive mood signals task completion and will quit a task sooner. However, if people adopt an "enjoyment rule," then they will infer that the positive mood reflects task enjoyment and will persevere longer at the task (Handley, Lassiter, Nickell, & Herchenroeder, 2004; Martin, Ward, Achee, & Wyer, 1993). Extending the HCM model, Handley et al. (2004) have further proposed that, for people who are generally happy with their lives:

> The experience of a positive mood automatically evokes an implicit enjoyment rule given the context possesses no achievement demands. That is, happy individuals may, in general, automatically engage in mood-maintaining tasks and cease engagement in mood-depreciating tasks because of an automatically activated enjoyment rule." (p. 112)

Perhaps those who really know how to savor life have easily-activated enjoyment rules and have simply learned to trust their instincts.

Uncertain Situations. An awareness of uncertainty has been called "one of the most sophisticated cognitive capacities of humans" (Smith & Washburn, 2005, p. 19). Although Langer introduced the notion of uncertainty as a basis for mindfulness in connection with potentially anxiety-producing situations, we believe uncertainty can also enhance mindfulness in relation to savoring. Along these lines, Wilson, Centerbar, Kermer, and Gilbert (2005) have argued that uncertainty makes people more mindful of positive experience and thus actually prolongs their positive moods. However, the cognitive processes people use to make sense of positive events in order to eliminate uncertainty can also reduce the pleasure people obtain from these events—an effect Wilson et al. (2005) termed the *pleasure paradox.* As Wilson et al. (2005) put it: "People may be driven to understand the causes of positive events in order to make them more predictable and hence more replicable, but understanding them may also make them less enjoyable" (p. 5).

Indeed, experimental evidence supports this conclusion. In two experiments (Wilson et al., 2005, Studies 1B and 1C), receiving a free dollar prolonged people's positive moods more when they did not know who had given it to them or why they had received it, compared to when they knew who had given them the dollar and why. In a third experiment (Wilson et al., 2005, Study 3), college students described themselves to others in an on-line impression formation task, and then learned that three opposite-sex strangers from another university had selected them as their "best potential friend" based on their self-description. Although initial mood was equivalent regardless of uncertainty level, positive mood lasted longer when students did not know the identities of the opposite-sex strangers who had chosen them. Thus, being uncertain about some of the details of a positive event can prolong one's enjoyment of it.

But why does making sense of positive events make them less enjoyable? And what implications does this effect have for savoring? Concerning these issues, Wilson et al. (2005) noted:

> Sense making reduces the emotional power of events by turning extraordinary, attention-demanding events into ordinary ones that are no longer focal in people's thoughts and no longer trigger intense reactions. There are at least two mechanisms by which adaptation occurs. ... First, an emotional event becomes less cognitively accessible to people once it has been transformed from an unexpected, attention-grabbing one into an understandable, predictable one. Second, holding accessibility constant, unexpected, unexplained events trigger more intense emotional reactions than expected, explainable ones ... (p. 6)

Thus, preserving uncertainty about a positive event may increase the event's salience and make it easier for the event to capture people's attention, thereby enhancing mindfulness and facilitating the process of savoring.

However, Wilson et al. (2005) also emphasized that uncertainty prolongs people's positive moods only if people believe that the event in question is positive. In other words, uncertainty about the valence of the outcome does not contribute pleasure to the cognitive mix. Indeed, uncertainty is pleasurable only when people know that it will eventually be reduced (Loewenstein, 1994; Wilson et al., 2005).

Along these lines, after reviewing the literature on curiosity, Loewenstein (1994) concluded that curiosity is in fact an aversive state; instead it is the act of satisfying curiosity that is pleasurable. This reasoning suggests that people may find a positive event most pleasurable when they have yet to resolve it or make complete sense of it, but are certain that this uncertainty will eventually be eliminated. As Wilson et al. (2005) noted:

> If the odds of reducing uncertainty are too low, people will not choose to be curious. For example, few mystery lovers would want to read a novel in which the last chapter was torn out, because they would never be able to satisfy their curiosity about whether the murder was committed by the butler or the brother-in-law. (p. 19)

When it comes to savoring, elements of the unknown in the cause or meaning of the positive event may be most likely to add spice when the experience is clearly positive and people believe that it will all make sense to them eventually. Thus, preserving the joy of surprise may in some cases serve to prolong one's savoring of positive events.

Another uncertainty that people often consider when they are savoring something is whether they will ever be able to experience that event again. An awareness of the unique experience of visiting a distant place to which one may never return can force a person to attend to the glories of being there. Visiting a loved one who is on his or her deathbed often forces visitors to savor what they appreciate most about the person. A rare or unique reunion, concert, or astronomical positioning of planets will often create a savoring mind-set simply because those experiencing them are uncertain about whether they will have an opportunity to repeat such an event in the future. People can remind themselves of this uncertainty as a way to heighten mindfulness in savoring the event. Thus, bittersweet moments may be particularly amenable to savoring. We return to this notion shortly.

Can photographing an event enhance savoring in the same way? After all, people often take a picture because they think they will be unable to repeat an encounter with a beautiful landscape, a person, or a group of people, or they want to hold onto the experience of seeing their children doing something memorable or amusing. Certainly they will have the photographs to savor in the future. The question is, however, does photographing the event enhance the savoring while the particular positive event is unfolding? We are of two minds about that. The act of taking the picture can focus people even more closely on what they are savoring, but it can also detract from participating in the moment. In some ways, the event is no longer the same, but becomes a prop for taking pictures. Joe claims that he has lost the pleasure of going to family events like weddings, when asked to be the family photographer for the event.

Can people thus take advantage of these three factors in mindfulness — novelty, effort, and uncertainty — to enhance savoring? Yes, in all likelihood, if they look for novelty in their experiences, if they attend to the effort they are making to bring about the experience, and if they resist the urge to make sense of positive events all at once, or remind themselves of any uncertainties about ever reexperiencing the event. People are then likely to keep their attention focused on what they are savoring, and become more mindful in their savoring. We consider these strategies again in chapter 8, when we offer prescriptions for enhancing savoring.

Personality Differences

At least two different types of personality traits have implications for savoring: dispositional mindfulness and one's general orientation toward time.

Mindfulness. In addition to situational mindfulness, we should also recognize the importance of personality differences in mindfulness. Some individuals consistently attend to whatever they are experiencing, whether it is something to be savored or something to be dreaded (Bodner & Langer, 2001). They introspect easily, and they analyze the psychology of situations easily, perhaps sometimes to a fault. Whatever creates such a disposition, it enables them to adopt a mindful perceptual set when they encounter experiences that bring them joy. Such a disposition, however, could also lead them to become mindful of any interfering or distracting stimuli, including other responsibilities and problems in their life. Therefore, individuals who are characteristically mindful may not necessarily show an exceptional capacity for savoring. We might expect some correlation between dispositional mindfulness and the extent of savoring people experience in their lives, but the correlation is undoubtedly far from perfect.

Another way to think of the role of personality in mindfulness is to consider individual differences among people who either prefer to be in, or at least do not avoid, situations particularly conducive to mindfulness (Langer, 1989). In other words, people who prefer or do not shy away from situations that (a) involve novelty (i.e., who are high in sensation seeking; Zuckerman, 1979), (b) require effort (i.e., who are high in the achievement motive; McClelland, 1961), or (c) are uncertain rather than clear-cut (i.e., who are highly tolerant of ambiguity; Budner, 1962) might be more likely to experience situations that make them mindful. Thus, these personality traits might well predispose people to have more savoring experiences in their lives.

Time Orientation.   An additional personality characteristic that undoubt-edly influences the degree to which people attend to an ongoing positive experi-ence is their general orientation to time. Along these lines, Zimbardo and Boyd (1999) have discussed individual differences in temporal orientation and have linked such differences to reliable variations in affect, cognition, and behav-ior. Some people have a general here-and-now attitude toward life, a temporal perspective that would tend to direct attention toward what is to be savored in the moment. By contrast, other people are forever planning and thinking of the future consequences of what they are doing, so much so that they are unable to focus on the here and now and savor for very long. It is as if these latter individu-als have a short attention span for their ongoing experience and worry about what else they should be doing instead or about other upcoming concerns. That kind of future orientation may be just what one needs as a business manager or a social planner, but it can interfere with savoring, except where future dreams may be savored through anticipatory planning. Still other people are oriented to the past more than to any other time frame. Although these individuals may savor reminiscing, they often miss the chance to attend to what is happening in their current lives.

A related individual difference variable that influences people's perceptions of time is the Type A behavior pattern (Friedman & Rosenman, 1974; Glass, 1977). This coronary-prone style of behavior is characterized by time urgency, speed, impatience, and hostility and by a continual compulsion to achieve more and more in less and less time (Friedman & Rosenman, 1974; Friedman & Ulmer, 1985). Combined with hard-driving competitiveness, this "hurry sickness" may make it difficult for Type As to take the time to "stop and smell the roses" and savor their daily lives (Friedman & Ulmer, 1985). Although Type A behavior is associated with positive psychological outcomes in young adults (Bryant & Yar-nold, 1990), there is evidence that Type A behavior predisposes people toward dissatisfaction and depression in later years (Strube, Berry, Goza, & Fennimore, 1985). Thus, in rushing through life in pursuit of personal achievement, Type As may ultimately fail to find fulfillment along the way. Indeed, reviewing the literature on happiness, Myers (1992) concluded, "The essence of happiness is pausing to savor the gift of our present moments" (p. 203). Yet, there is evidence that Type As find leisurely relaxation to be stressful (Friedman & Ulmer, 1985). Clearly, it is hard to savor if one does not or cannot take the time to focus on positive moments as they are unfolding. You have to stop, if you want to smell the roses.

The particular context one is in can mirror some of these same issues. While on vacation, one can take a here-and-now mind-set more easily than one can in the middle of a work week. Weekends permit more savoring in the same way. Indeed, a common finding in the research literature on daily mood is that people's moods show a reliable upswing during the weekend (Watson, 2000). It seems that on weekends, most of us allow ourselves the room to attend to our own pleasures. Weekends may also foster a more exclusive present orientation by focusing one's thoughts more toward current activities and less toward pending future concerns.

Bittersweet Experiences

One type of experience that may be particularly powerful in eliciting savoring is what people commonly refer to as "bittersweet." Bittersweet experiences are pleasurable events in which people know the positive outcome they are enjoying will soon end. People may also know the pleasurable event (a) will not happen again for a long time (e.g., the last days of summer, a Christmas holiday), (b) may or may not ever happen again (e.g., childbirth, receiving an award), or (c) can never happen again in one's life (e.g., losing one's virginity, celebrating one's 50th wedding anniversary). This last type of bittersweet experience, which occurs only once in a lifetime, may be the most powerful.

Such bittersweet moments are tinged with both happiness and sadness, creating a heightened awareness of both present joy and impending loss. This greater awareness may override the normal habituation or adaptation process we discussed earlier, thereby enhancing one's capacity to appreciate the positive experience that is about to end. Because the bitterness enhances the perceived sweetness and vice versa, bittersweet experiences naturally create hedonic contrast effects. The awareness of the fleetingness of the moment may also motivate people to seize the day ("carpe diem"), helping them enjoy bittersweet moments more than if they expected these positive experiences to continue indefinitely. For example, one may savor the last night of a vacation with family or close friends with particular gusto, as one reflects on the fact that the time together soon will be only a happy memory. As the English essayist Charles Lamb observed in "Grace Before Meat," one of his *Essays of Elia* (1823): "The custom of saying grace at meals had, probably, its origin in the early times of the world, and the hunter-state of man, when dinners were precarious things, and a full meal was something more than a common blessing." One treasures bittersweet things that one does not take for granted.

Although it remains to be determined whether the savoring-enhancing effects of bittersweet experiences can be automatic, clearly it is possible to deliberately remind oneself of the transient nature of the positive experience to better seize the moment and enhance one's enjoyment of it. Indeed, authors of self-help books often advocate "living each day as if it were your last," in order to heighten awareness and appreciation of life's blessings (e.g., Lakein, 1974). Once again, however, we note that this cognitive reflection should not be overdone, so as to avoid short-circuiting the positive affective experience. Ruminating on the bitterness in the bittersweet experience might preclude savoring its sweetness, given that excessive self-evaluation can undermine enjoyment (Wilson et al., 2000).

We can speculate that the bitterness in bittersweet experiences increases in intensity as the positive event draws toward a close. The last few days of an annual vacation are a much stronger bittersweet experience than the first few days. Knowing an engrossing book will soon be over gives its last few pages an especially strong bittersweet flavor, compared to its first few pages. Although people generally know beforehand that good things must inevitably end, bittersweet feelings still naturally arise whenever people are aware they are about to finish a positive experience.

If awareness of bittersweet feelings facilitates savoring, then people should inherently be better able to savor endings, as opposed to beginnings, of bittersweet experiences. As the end of a positive event approaches, the poignancy of the fleeting moment may make people more mindfully aware of what they are about to lose and may amplify affective experience by drawing attention to positive feelings and to the positive experience that will soon end and by keeping attention mindfully in the present. Indeed, shifts from negative to positive can have the same effect — people sometimes find an experience that changes from bitter to sweet more pleasant than one that continually remains sweet (Aronson & Linder, 1965).

Nevertheless, some people may be unable or unwilling to accept that the sweetness of the moment must inevitably turn bitter, or that the sweetness of the memory may leave a bitter aftertaste. As a result, they may avoid looking back on happy times from the past. They may even hesitate to look forward to something good because they know it cannot last (Brickman, 1978). It's hard to anticipate sweetness if you know it will eventually sour. And the inexorable laws of hedonics are always in operation (Frijda, 1988). Unless one accepts the fact that "all good things must come to an end," the thought of an upcoming bittersweet experience, the ending of a once-in-a-lifetime positive event, or the remembrance of something cherished long ago may be too bitter to embrace.

Extending the notion of bittersweetness, we can also speculate that positive experiences are more easily savored when they represent positive outcomes that one had previously thought were lost forever. For example, people who have lost and later regained their ability to walk often report that they now enjoy the act of walking in ways they could never have imagined or appreciated if they had not been paralyzed. If one expects the results of diagnostic medical tests to be devastating, then the news that all is fine temporarily gives one an overwhelming appreciation of the blessing of good health; whereas this heightened appreciation would not occur, if one expected all along that the test results would be fine. As he savored the thrill of reaching the summit of Snowmass Mountain, recall that Fred reminded himself of an earlier time when a back injury had crippled him and cast doubt on whether he'd ever climb again. This downward temporal comparison to a bitter past heightened hedonic contrast and made the mountaintop moment all the sweeter.

SUMMARY

In this chapter, we outlined the initial scaffolding for a theory of savoring. Extending ideas introduced earlier about savoring as a process of attending mindfully to and appreciating positive experience, we reviewed three key premises of what savoring entails: the relatively weak activation of social and esteem needs; a here and now attitude toward what is being experienced; and some clear focusing on the positive experience. We proposed optimal-level theory and expectancy-value theory as background perspectives on how savoring tendencies surface and vanish in the stream of human activity and experience. Optimal-level thinking seems better suited for understanding apparently automatic surges in savoring, while expectancy-value thinking seems better suited for understanding strategic choices to savor or continue savoring. More middle-range theoretical schemes were considered, ones that could be more easily grappled with than the background perspectives.

We also considered conditions critical to an understanding of the intensity of feelings experienced in savoring: the duration of attention to the positive experience; whether stress reduction is involved in savoring; the level of complexity in the experience; the extent to which one focuses one's attention on the experience while one is savoring; and whether social connections are being made while savoring. In general, we propose that more intense positive feelings arise when the savoring experience lasts longer, involves more stress-reduction, is more complex, involves a clearer and more complete attentional focus, and includes more social connections.

We also formulated hypotheses about factors that influence the degree of attention to an ongoing savoring experience: the strength of competing tendencies; how mindful the person is in terms of being aware of novelty, open to effort, and attracted to uncertainty; and the person's time orientation. In addition, we discussed several personality differences (such as temporal orientation and Type A behavior), as well as situational characteristics (such as bittersweetness), that can affect one's focus of attention during savoring experiences.

4

Types of Savoring:
Some Empirical Inroads

By happy alchemy of mind
They turn to pleasure all they find.
—Matthew Green (1737/1804)

In the last chapter, we presented broad theoretical perspectives on what may be going on psychologically when people savor positive experiences, the conditions that affect the intensity of these experiences, and the degree of attention people give to these experiences when they occur. In this chapter, we distinguish several ways in which people savor positive events, thereby identifying the structure of savoring responses. Our rationale for undertaking the task of differentiating types of savoring strategies is our belief that it is difficult to formulate general theoretical propositions about the processes of savoring without specifying the kinds of savoring responses a person is demonstrating. It is our contention that more molecular theories of the specific conditions that affect savoring are needed in relation to the different ways of savoring we discuss. As we begin to distinguish one savoring process from another, we can begin to build minitheories of each process, which may give clearer insights into what occurs when people savor positive experiences.

We should perhaps ask, first of all, whether indeed there are distinguishable types of savoring processes that might follow their own particular, idiosyncratic rules. Despite the limitless number of events people can savor, we contend that there *is* a limited number of types of *processes* and *responses* involved in savoring. Although domains in which savoring occurs may vary considerably, we can narrow our perspective on what savoring is all about if we consider a small set of cognitive and behavioral savoring responses or strategies that people use across many different domains. As is true with respect to coping, these savoring strategies sometimes occur consciously, as we discussed in the previous chapter. But more often than not, they occur automatically, and people become aware of them only in hindsight.

Concerning strategies for amplifying enjoyment, Adler and Fagley (2005, p. 85) have distinguished between "triggers" (i.e., events that spontaneously and unintentionally evoke appreciation in people) and "strategies" (i.e., responses people intentionally employ in order to foster an attitude of appreciation). For example, seeing another person's misfortune may spontaneously trigger a feeling of thankfulness that one's own life is free from such adversity, whereas taking the time to count one's blessings and give thanks before a meal may be a deliberate, intentional strategy for appreciating (Adler & Fagley, 2005). We are concerned here with both spontaneous and deliberate savoring responses.

To begin, we first present the savoring strategies that emerged from initial research into what people say they do when they savor a positive experience. We then describe the development of a multidimensional self-report instrument to measure ways or dimensions of savoring (the Ways of Savoring Checklist), and we present evidence concerning the discriminant validity of this instrument. Based on our conceptualization of savoring, we test predictions about the pattern of relationships we should expect to find between ways of savoring positive experiences and savoring beliefs, and we examine personality and gender differences in ways of savoring that hold across positive events.

TYPES OF STRATEGIES USED
TO ENHANCE SAVORING

Dimensions of Savoring

Returning to the definition of savoring we provided at the outset — the capacity to attend to, appreciate, and enhance the positive experiences in one's life — we can further ask what humans do in carrying out that kind of capacity. When people like the way something feels or find something beautiful to look at or listen to, when people enjoy what they are experiencing or what just happened to them, what do they further do to enhance or attend to that experience? When people are not experiencing much joy in their lives, what do they do to bring it back in?

There are many strategies people use, even though they are not always directly conscious of employing these responses as strategies. They may stop whatever they are in the middle of doing and linger with whatever they have found so good in their lives. Sometimes people actively plan a change in what they are doing, in order to usher in what has been previously pleasurable but absent from their current lives. Sometimes they just go slower. They may reminisce about what has been happening or remind themselves of other such moments. Sometimes they force themselves to examine what they are experiencing in slow motion or in more detail. Sometimes they just banish other competing ideas from their minds and let the pleasurable moment they experience fully reign in the kingdom of their consciousness. Or they may adopt any number of these strategies simultaneously.

It would be illuminating to isolate in an objective way the various strategies that people use to help them savor their positive experience. With this goal in mind, Fred created a paper-and-pencil, self-report questionnaire that gives people the opportunity to check off the approaches they use in response to a specific positive event. This instrument is the Ways of Savoring Checklist (WOSC) that we briefly summarized in chapter 2. The results that emerged from this questionnaire have given us many insights into the ways people try to regulate their feelings in response to positive events.

The first step in the task of measuring savoring strategies was to ask respondents some very simple questions: What was the last good thing that happened to you? Are you aware of anything you thought or did when you were experiencing this positive event that might have influenced your enjoyment of it? If so, what were those thoughts or behaviors, and how did they influence your enjoyment? The initial data were very encouraging and helped to shape the eventual closed-ended instrument. To get a better sense of the richness and variety of people's savoring styles, consider some of the responses college students gave to these open-ended questions in the early pilot work.

The most commonly mentioned recent positive event was "going on a vacation." Here are some things that students reported thinking or doing while on vacation that they believe *increased* their enjoyment:

I talked about the vacation with my companions.

I took a lot of photographs.

I bought gifts to bring back for other people.

I thought about how much better it was than being at home.

I anticipated what the next day of the trip would be like.

I just went along with what was happening one day at a time.

I spent a lot of money.

I kept a travel journal.

I thought "your dream has come true," knowing I had planned on making this trip for years.

I tried to relive the events of the day while daydreaming.

I thought about telling my friends at home about it.

Now, here are some things that students reported thinking or doing while on vacation that they believe *decreased* their enjoyment:

I thought about coming home.

I thought about my girlfriend and got homesick.

I got drunk a few times.

I sometimes didn't stop to enjoy what I was doing in anticipation of the next thing.

I felt bad that I couldn't do everything I wanted to do.

I thought about how fast the days went by.

My heavy use of drugs by the end of the trip decreased my pleasure.

I worried about money.

I was disappointed when the trip wasn't as spectacular as I had hoped it would be.

I worried about little things.

Another common recent positive event was "a date with someone special." Here are some things that students reported thinking or doing while on their date that they believe *increased* their enjoyment:

I thought about how long it had taken me to ask her out.

I tried to carefully focus on what was happening and memorize the surroundings and my feelings.

I told him how much fun I was having.

I thought about how the date would end.

I thought about how good-looking she was.

I tried to stay calm and relaxed.

I noticed it when other guys looked at her and I felt good.

I took pictures.

I got together with a group of friends and tried to be nice to everyone.

I realized that the actual date was matching my predictions and felt happy.

I imagined that it would last forever.

And here are some things students reported thinking or doing while on their date with someone special that they believe *decreased* their enjoyment:

I worried about getting home on time.

I thought about a test I had to study for.

I realized that the date was going to have to come to an end.

I thought about how I could do things differently.

I thought about how I wasn't as attractive as his other dating partners.

I was self-conscious.

I agreed with him too much.

I realized that I had built him up to be Mr. Perfect, and when I saw he had faults I felt bad.

I drank too much.

I worried about *how* the date would end.

I got jealous and angry when other guys looked at her.

Notice several things about people's responses here. First, there are some *consistencies* in the perceived effects of savoring strategies across events. For example, for both the vacation and the date with someone special, some of the same strategies are reported to be effective in enhancing savoring: taking photographs to capture the moment; recalling an earlier time before the positive event had occurred; and sharing the experience with friends. And for both positive events, some of the same savoring strategies are reported as being ineffective: drinking too much, worrying, and comparing the experience to unrealistic expectations. These interevent consistencies are hints that some approaches to savoring may be effective or ineffective across situations. Later research supports this speculation.

In addition, notice that there are also some inconsistencies in the perceived effects of savoring strategies within events (for the vacation and the special date). Within either positive event, some of the same things that people mention as increasing enjoyment are mentioned by others as decreasing enjoyment of the same event. Considering the vacation, for example, some respondents felt that spending money and anticipating upcoming events enhanced their enjoyment, whereas other subjects felt that these savoring strategies inhibited their enjoyment. And considering the date with someone special, thinking about how the date would end and noticing others looking at one's partner seem to heighten enjoyment for some respondents, but seem to hinder enjoyment for others. These data suggest that the same approaches to savoring a particular event are not necessarily effective for all individuals.

To build a closed-ended questionnaire to measure individual differences in the use of savoring strategies, Fred selected the most frequently mentioned responses from the essays that people wrote about what they typically think or do when something good happens to them. He also consulted previous theories and findings on thoughts and emotions and how people try in one way or another to control them (e.g., Beck, 1976; Ellis & Greiger, 1977; Lazarus & Folkman, 1984; Meichenbaum, 1977; Tomkins, 1962). Following established procedures for checklist development (e.g., Hollon & Kendall, 1980; Ingram & Wisnicki, 1988), he ended up with a long list of ways of thinking or acting that he then refined through additional pilot testing. The final result was a core set of

60 thoughts and behaviors that describe how people may respond while going through a positive event. Of course, this list does not cover all possible thoughts and behaviors; nevertheless, it is reasonably comprehensive.

The final instrument, which Fred has called the Ways of Savoring Checklist (WOSC), requires a person to focus on a recent positive event (e.g., receiving a pay raise or celebrating a birthday), describe it in a few sentences, and then indicate the extent to which the person engaged in each of the 60 thoughts and behaviors in response to the particular event. In additional studies, respondents have been instructed to think back to a specific positive event (e.g., a vacation, a good grade on a test or paper, a date with someone special), and then to complete the WOSC in relation to this event. An initial set of 12 questions asks respondents to evaluate the positive event along a variety of different dimensions, including its desirability, foreseeability, frequency of occurrence, and one's degree of personal responsibility for the event's occurrence. These latter questions provide information about the specific cognitive appraisals that lead people to adopt one particular savoring approach or another. Two additional questions have often been included to measure retrospectively how much the respondent enjoyed the event and how long afterward they continued to enjoy the event (see Appendix D).

The WOSC was originally drafted during 1984–1985, and since then has been administered extensively over the years in college and older adult samples in the United States, and in college students in Canada, Australia, and Japan. Although the total number of data points gathered to date is well into the thousands, here we report results for a subset of 1,135 American college students who completed the WOSC in relation to either a vacation ($N = 488$) or a good grade ($N = 647$) between 2001 and 2003.

Based on prior theory and research, earlier pilot testing, and additional speculation, the WOSC was designed to reflect 10 basic dimensions of savoring, reflecting various combinations of different thoughts and behaviors. (For a list of the WOSC dimensions, along with their constituent items and reliabilities, see Table 2.3.) We describe these 10 ways of savoring next.

Sharing With Others   (e.g., seeking out others to share the experience with, telling others how much you value the moment). This savoring dimension parallels the use of social support as a coping strategy for handling stress. There is evidence that adolescents rely more on their social networks to help them savor positive experiences than they do to cope with negative experiences, and that social support enhances positive well-being more than it reduces subjective distress among high school students (Meehan, Durlak, & Bryant, 1993). Indeed, this social-behavioral approach to savoring is the single strongest predictor of level of enjoyment, and extraverts are more likely to use it than introverts. This reasoning suggests that shy people or those with impoverished social networks may be at a distinct disadvantage when it comes to savoring a positive experience. Sharing a positive experience with others who are clinically depressed or unable to enjoy (i.e., anhedonic) would be expected to result in lower levels of enjoyment, compared to sharing with others who are exuberant and outwardly expressive in sharing their joy.

However, note that these other people with whom one shares the experience need not be physically present when the positive event is happening—that is, merely thinking about sharing the memory of the ongoing positive experience later with other people is strongly reflective of Sharing With Others as a way of savoring. The 17th-century French playwright Molière (1666/1992) nicely summed up the transcendent power of friendship as a resource for savoring: "It is a wonderful seasoning of all enjoyments to think of those we love."

But why is this? Although we began to answer this question in chapter 3, we now address it in more detail. Why might sharing a pleasurable experience with others (or looking forward to doing so) make the experience more enjoyable? Although the empirical literature offers no definitive answers, there are several plausible possibilities:

• Watching one's friends or family enjoy themselves is itself an enjoyable activity, and this vicarious enjoyment may contribute to the pleasure of the moment. This suggests that the closer one is emotionally to others present who seem to be enjoying themselves, the more enjoyable one should find the particular positive experience.

• When others are present, they may point out pleasurable aspects of the experience that one may not have noticed on one's own, they may encourage one to make more extensive cognitive associations in relation to positive stimuli, and they may help to prolong the joy of happy moments by sharing and stimulating interpersonal reminiscence and directly encouraging one to laugh or smile.

• Other people may serve as behavioral models for savoring or may actively encourage one's cognitive and behavioral efforts to enjoy oneself by suggestion or direct instruction. Friends or family members may also actively plan social situations so that self-esteem concerns, future concerns, and distractions are at a minimum, thus facilitating the process of savoring an ongoing positive experience (e.g., as in organizing victory celebrations, throwing surprise parties, and hosting vacation visits).

• The desire to share the experience and one's reactions to it with one's friends may motivate a person to notice pleasurable details and feelings that he or she might otherwise miss. This effect might occur even when these friends are not physically present, if one anticipates retelling the event to them in the future.

• We may become more playful in the presence of others than when we are alone, and this increased playfulness make us more physically spontaneous, more creative, and more expressive of joy while we are savoring (Lieberman, 1977).

- In social settings, compared to solitary settings, people are more likely to smile (Kraut & Johnston, 1979), and they laugh about 30 times more often (Provine & Fischer, 1989). Thus, the mere presence of others may increase one's outward expression of positive affect, which would be expected to enhance positive emotion (Duclos et al., 1989; Kleinke, Peterson, & Rutledge, 1998; Laird, 1974, 1984; Strack, Martin, & Stepper, 1988).

- Focusing one's attention on others may decrease objective self-awareness (Duval & Wicklund, 1972), thereby increasing one's ability to become absorbed and lose oneself in the moment. If these other people are merely strangers, however, their presence may increase self-awareness and inhibit absorption in some situations.

- The actual or imagined presence of others may heighten one's level of autonomic arousal, which one may mislabel as positive affect in the form of elation, excitement, or titillation—a positive form of "excitation transfer" (Zillmann, 1988). If this explanation is correct, then the facilitating effect of other people should hold regardless of whether these others are friends or strangers. The example in chapter 3 of two strangers marveling at a beautiful Tuscan rainbow is consistent with the notion that the mere presence of others can enhance our ability to enjoy some kinds of positive experiences.

Memory Building   (e.g., actively storing images for future recall by taking "mental photographs," thinking of reminiscing about the event later with others). Fred discussed his use of this savoring approach in trying to capture the joy he felt on the summit of Snowmass Mountain. There is evidence that females (Bryant & Morgan, 1986) as well as Type Bs (Bryant et al., 1991) are more adept at encoding memories of positive experiences for later recall as these experiences unfold, compared to males and Type As, respectively.

We would also expect this greater capacity for memory building to be associated with a greater capacity to share these memories with others, so that active Memory Building should be at least moderately correlated with Sharing With Others—and the available data confirm this hypothesis. Active Memory Building is a way of savoring in which people search for, notice, and highlight those aspects of positive experiences they find most enjoyable. In the process, people not only pinpoint pleasurable situational features and accentuate the intensity of the positive experience as it is unfolding, but they also form clearer and more vivid memories that are more easily recalled and shared later with others. As we have noted, the desire to share a positive experience with another person who is absent may motivate one to appreciate the joy of the moment more fully.

Self-Congratulation   (e.g., telling yourself how proud you are or how impressed others must be, reminding yourself of how long you've waited for the event to happen). This style of savoring is a kind of "cognitive basking" in which the individual lavishes praise on the self and exalts in a warm glow of pride and self-satisfaction in response to a positive experience. Indeed, the Latin root word for "congratulate" is *congratulari,* which means "to wish joy."

One would expect this cognitive form of savoring to occur most often in response to personal achievements and successes. Although Self-Congratulation is primarily a cognitive activity, it can spill over into behavioral expressions of jubilant celebration in Western cultures under conducive social circumstances, as when professional football players dance, gesture, and shout, "I'm Number One," in the end zone after scoring a touchdown. Other forms of public self-congratulation, such as bragging and boasting, reflect excessive self-promotion that can antagonize and alienate others, shortening the duration of enjoyment in the short run and eroding the subjective quality of one's friendships in the long run.

Sensory-Perceptual Sharpening (e.g., intensifying pleasure by focusing on certain stimuli in the situation and blocking out others, trying to sharpen one's senses through effortful concentration). Joe has noted his use of this savoring approach in closing his eyes at certain times to heighten his appreciation of chamber music. Recall that Fred also closed his eyes on the summit of Snowmass Mountain to intensify the savoring as he marveled at the sound of the wind roaring up the mountainside from the valley below.

Competing sensory stimuli (e.g., peripheral sights or smells) may interrupt the flow of the positive affective experience and dampen savoring. Blocking out these distractions may enhance savoring by sharpening the focus of attention on the pleasurable experience itself. Thus, sensory-perceptual sharpening resembles the cognitive operation of *selective abstraction* (Beck, 1976; Larsen, Diener, & Cropanzano, 1987), whereby individuals think about certain aspects of the situation to the exclusion of others.

Comparing (e.g., contrasting your own feelings with what others seem to be feeling, comparing the present situation with similar times in the past or with what one imagined the event would be like). These cognitive comparisons can heighten enjoyment if they create a downward contrast; but they can also dampen enjoyment if they produce a sense of relative deprivation. Thus, comparing in and of itself might be expected to have little overall relationship with how much or how long people enjoy positive experiences. It is the specific target or type of comparison that one makes that determines affective reactions.

This reasoning suggests that if one wishes to enhance savoring, then one should be selective in making only downward rather than upward social (e.g., "I'm better off than others"), temporal (e.g., "I'm better off now than I was before"), or counterfactual (e.g., "Things might not have been this good") comparisons in response to positive events. To compare is to think not about what one has, but rather what one does not have; thus, excessive comparison would be expected to remove one from the flow of positive affect in the moment and undermine enjoyment.

Absorption   (e.g., trying not to think, but rather to get totally immersed or engrossed in the moment, relaxing and existing only in the present). This particular savoring style closely resembles Csikszentmihalyi's (1975, 1990, 2002) notion of optimal flow experience in its absence of conscious self-awareness and loss of a sense of person, place, and time. Savoring through absorption involves a deliberate avoidance of cognitive reflection and intellectual association in favor of a focus on simply experiencing the ongoing positive event as it is unfolding. Viewed from a Buddhist perspective, being in the moment does not involve judging what one is experiencing, but rather simply experiencing and being mindfully aware of what one is going through and feeling at the moment (Kabat-Zinn, 1990) so as to unleash "the power of now" and cultivate bliss (Dass, 1971; Tolle, 1999). This "experiential immersion" approach to savoring resembles the artist's approach to savoring the beauty of the flower, as opposed to Feynman's extensive use of cognitive elaboration.

Clearly, some people prefer not to think too much about what they are feeling during positive experiences, but just to feel their feelings, whereas other people prefer to reflect and make mental associations during positive experiences. Based on theory and research on individual differences in the need for cognition (Cacioppo, Petty, Feinstein, & Jarvis, 1996), we can speculate that people high in need for cognition might prefer to use an elaboration strategy, whereas people low in need for cognition might prefer to savor by absorption. However, the absence of cognitive reflection when savoring through absorption is not incompatible with a conscious awareness of the ongoing experience of being engrossed. As Lambie and Marcel (2002) noted: "Paradoxical though it seems, we are sometimes in states of both detached awareness and immersion, in which we are aware of our concurrently immersed phenomenology. Sometimes this is by an act of will; at other times, it is in states of heightened sensibility, such as during intense emotional experiences . . ." (p. 237).

Behavioral Expression   (e.g., laughing, giggling, jumping up and down, making verbal sounds of appreciation). In contrast to cognitive savoring strategies is a type of savoring response we refer to as *behavioral expression*. This purely behavioral response represents an outward physical manifestation of inner feelings in which one expresses an energetic response of exuberant joy, excitement, and enthusiasm by jumping up and down, dancing around, laughing out loud, or making verbal sounds of appreciation. Such responses or their inhibition may be purely reflexive and automatic, or may be deliberate.

Whereas people slow down their behavior when engaging in sensory-perceptual sharpening, they speed up their behavior when engaging in behavioral expression. Theory and research on self-perception theory and facial feedback support the notion that outwardly expressing positive feelings can intensify these feelings (Duclos et al., 1989; Kleinke et al., 1998; Laird, 1974, 1984; Strack et al., 1988; Tomkins, 1962). Thus, by "putting on a happy face," people may be able to make themselves feel more positive.

Temporal Awareness   (e.g., reminding oneself how transient and fleeting the moment is, wishing the moment could last forever, telling oneself that one must enjoy it now). Another purely cognitive style of savoring involves a heightened sense of "temporal awareness," or a conscious realization of the passage of time. With this type of savoring response, people remind themselves of the fleetingness of the moment, they think about a future time when the positive experience will be over, and they consciously wish the moment could last forever.

As we noted in chapter 3, certain types of positive experiences seem to evoke a powerful and deeply personal sense of the fleetingness and preciousness of time. These types of bittersweet experiences may well be especially conducive to savoring, as people naturally reflect on the positive experience that is about to end with a renewed sense of perspective and appreciation. The emergence of a savoring dimension reflecting heightened temporal awareness suggests that people do not necessarily have to wait for bittersweet moments to occur to be aware of the fleetingness of time, but can also deliberately remind themselves that their positive experiences are transitory and worthy of savoring in the here and now.

Counting Blessings   (e.g., reminding oneself of one's good fortune, thinking about how lucky one is). Counting blessings requires that one pinpoint what one is grateful for, identify the source of this particular blessing, and then link one's gratitude to this perceived source (Emmons & Shelton, 2002; McCullough, 2002; McCullough, Emmons, & Tsang, 2002). Thus, reflecting on one's blessings can enhance the affective quality of many savoring experiences, and we would therefore expect people to count blessings in relation to all sorts of positive outcomes.

However, just because one acknowledges a blessing to oneself does not mean that one necessarily outwardly expresses gratitude to someone for that blessing. Counting blessings and giving thanks for blessings are two related, but separate, activities. Some people express gratitude in prayers of thanksgiving; others in speech, poetry, song, or artwork; still others never express the gratitude they feel. Although counting one's blessings can promote subjective well-being (Emmons & McCullough, 2003), it is hard to feel gratitude if one sees nothing for which, or no one to whom, to be grateful. With concerted effort over time, however, one can cultivate an "attitude of gratitude" that can become habitual, thereby creating a trait known as the grateful disposition (McCullough et al., 2002). We return to this point in chapter 8, when we consider ways to enhance savoring.

Kill-Joy Thinking (e.g., reminding oneself of other places one should be and other things one should be doing, thinking of ways in which the positive event could have been better). In contrast to these nine ways of savoring is another way of thinking that actually decreases savoring. In developing the Ways of Savoring Checklist, Fred called this negative cognitive dimension *Kill-Joy Thinking*. It is a process that consists entirely of dampening cognitions, ways of interfering with savoring rather than promoting it, that diminishes and cut shorts enjoyment.

Viewed from a Western cultural perspective, it seems sad that people report this kind of joy-killing process when going through positive experiences. But in Eastern cultures, people may intentionally dampen enjoyment so as to conform to social customs or beliefs about the inevitable negative consequences of positive outcomes (Lindberg, 2004). Obviously, one would expect kill-joy thinking to be associated with lower levels of enjoyment. Beck (1976) highlighted kill-joy thinking as a hallmark of depressive cognition that intensifies and perpetuates depression. There is also evidence that people who are lower in self-esteem are more likely to engage in these dampening cognitions in response to positive outcomes, whereas people higher in self-esteem are more likely to engage in amplifying cognitions (Wood et al., 2003).

Certainly, we are not the first to highlight strategies people can use to enhance enjoyment. For example, the ways of savoring we have identified parallel some of the "eight aspects of appreciation" proposed by Adler and Fagley (2005). Specifically, Adler and Fagley (2005) argued that "appreciation" involves: (a) focusing on what one has rather than on what one lacks; (b) awe; (c) performing personal celebratory rituals; (d) focusing on the here and now; (e) making downward temporal or social comparisons; (f) gratitude; (g) finding benefits in loss or adversity; and (h) cherishing other people in our lives. Note the conceptual overlap here with the savoring dimensions of Comparing, Counting Blessings, and Sharing With Others. However, whereas "appreciation" is a broader concept that involves finding the good in both positive and negative experience (Adler & Fagley, 2005), savoring solely involves enjoying the positive.

Note that most of the WOSC strategies we have isolated are largely cognitive approaches to savoring. Six savoring dimensions seem to be primarily positive cognitive responses to positive events: Memory Building, Self-Congratulation, Sensory-Perceptual Sharpening, Comparing, Temporal Awareness, and Counting Blessings. These particular ways of savoring involve actively using one's mind to construct memories, admire the self, concentrate one's senses, evaluate comparative differences, reflect temporally, or identify cherished things in one's life, respectively. In addition, Kill-Joy Thinking is a seventh cognitive savoring dimension, but it is a negative response that interferes with the process of savoring.

Three other savoring dimensions—Behavioral Expression, Sharing With Others, and Absorption—are primarily behavioral in focus. These respective behavioral ways of savoring involve expressing positive feelings physically or interpersonally, or immersing oneself in an experience without cognitive reflection.

Savoring Responses as a Function of Cognitive Appraisals

Although these same 10 savoring dimensions surface in the WOSC data repeatedly across different samples and different positive events, the specific savoring strategies that people report using show some predictable variations as a function of their cognitive appraisals of the positive event. For instance, collapsing across events: (a) the more personally responsible people feel for a positive event, the more they report having engaged in Self-Congratulation; (b) the more people believe others were responsible for the positive event, the more they report Sharing With Other and Behavioral Expression; (c) the more rare the positive event is perceived to be, the more people report Memory Building and Temporal Awareness; (d) the longer the event lasted, the more people report engaging in Absorption and Sensory-Perceptual Sharpening; and (e) the more desirable the positive event and the more people report looking forward to it, the more they report Counting Blessings as a savoring response. Paralleling results found for ways of coping with negative events (Lazarus & Folkman, 1984), these findings suggest that people's cognitive appraisals of positive events may shape the ways they savor these events.

Profiles of Savoring

Examining simultaneously the 10 dimensions of savoring allows us to describe characteristic patterns of response to particular positive events. Figure 4.1 presents profiles of mean scores on the 10 savoring subscales for a sample of 1,146 college students who completed the WOSC during the years 2001–2003 in relation to either a vacation ($N = 624$) or a good grade on a test or paper ($N = 522$). Whereas a vacation is a pleasant leisure activity that unfolds continuously in real time over the course of sometimes a week or more, a good grade is a personal achievement in the form of discrete, written academic performance feedback.

To compare profiles of savoring between the two positive events, we used a mixed model repeated-measures analysis of variance, treating event as a between-groups factor and WOSC subscale as a within-subjects factor. This analysis revealed a statistically significant event × subscale interaction, $F(9,1126) = 214.19$, $p < .00001$, eta-squared = .16, indicating that WOSC profiles differed reliably as a function of event. Follow-up contrasts disclosed significant mean differences between the vacation and the good grade for each of the WOSC subscales (all $ps < .05$). As seen in Fig. 4.1, although there is more Self-Congratulation and greater Kill-Joy Thinking in response to the good grade than to the vacation,

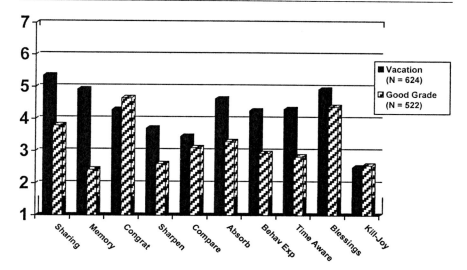

FIG. 4.1. Profile of Mean WOSC Subscale Scores in Relation to a Vacation and a Good Grade. Sharing = Sharing with Others. Memory = Memory-Building. Congrat = Self-Congratulation. Sharpen = Sensory-Perceptual Sharpening. Compare = Comparing. Absorb = Absorption. Behav Exp = Behavioral Expression. Time Aware = Temporal Awareness. Blessings = Counting Blessings. Kill-Joy = Kill-Joy Thinking. WOSC subscale scores are averages that range from 1 to 7, with a midpoint of 4. A mixed model repeated-measures analysis of variance revealed a statistically significant event × subscale interaction, $F(9,1126) = 214.19$, $p < .00001$, eta-squared = .16, indicating that WOSC profiles differed reliably as a function of event. Within each dimension of savoring, mean scores are significantly different for the two positive events at two-tailed $p < .05$, by independent-samples t test.

vacations involve more Sharing, Memory Building, Sensory-Perceptual Sharpening, Comparing, Absorption, Behavioral Expression, Temporal Awareness, and Counting Blessings. Clearly, students savor these two different types of positive experiences differently.

The relationships among the 10 savoring dimensions are also of interest. Table 4.1 presents the correlations among the 10 ways of savoring separately for vacation (tabled below the diagonal) and good grade (tabled above the diagonal). Several results are noteworthy and largely confirm our earlier arguments. For both vacation and good grade: (a) Sharing With Others is strongly to moderately correlated with Memory Building, Self-Congratulation, Behavioral Expression, Absorption, and Counting Blessings; (b) Memory Building is strongly to moderately correlated with all other WOSC subscales except Kill-Joy Thinking; (c) Kill-Joy Thinking is positively correlated with Comparing; and (d) Comparing is positively correlated with Temporal Awareness. This pattern of results

TABLE 4.1

Correlations Among the Ten WOSC Subscales
Separately for Vacation (Tabled Below the Diagonal)
and Good Grade (Tabled Above the Diagonal)

	SWO	MB	SC	SPS	C	A	BE	TA	CB	KJT
SWO		.55	.60	.41	.44	.42	.65	.33	.53	.03
MB	.61		.48	.65	.55	.61	.50	.59	.45	.26
SC	.63	.58		.39	.45	.44	.48	.34	.59	-.03
SPS	.21	.44	.33		.45	.62	.38	.50	.28	.31
C	.30	.41	.41	.36		.47	.34	.62	.47	.49
A	.44	.48	.45	.41	.25		.40	.47	.38	.18
BE	.63	.50	.51	.28	.27	.42		.30	.45	.09
TA	.33	.48	.34	.34	.52	.32	.26		.36	.42
CB	.63	.58	.64	.25	.28	.43	.43	.30		.10
KJT	-.22	-.06	-.09	.18	.48	-.14	-.10	.23	-.21	

Note.   Tabled *below* the diagonal are Pearson correlation coefficients for mean WOSC subscale scores in relation to a vacation ($N = 624$); tabled *above* the diagonal are Pearson correlation coefficients for mean WOSC subscale scores in relation to a good grade ($N = 522$). For the *vacation* (below the diagonal), $|rs| \geq .07$ are statistically significant at two-tailed $p < .05$. For the *good grade* (above the diagonal), $|rs| > .07$ are statistically significant at two-tailed $p < .05$. SWO = Sharing With Others. MB = Memory Building. SC = Self-Congratulation. SPS = Sensory-Perceptual Sharpening. C = Comparing. A = Absorption. BE = Behavioral Expression. TA = Temporal Awareness. CB = Counting Blessings. KJT = Kill-Joy Thinking.

generally supports the notion that certain ways of savoring tend to go together across both types of events.

Personality Differences in Ways of Savoring

Not only do different positive events produce distinct profiles of savoring, but differences in personality also exert an influence on how people savor positive experiences. Furthermore, these personality differences in savoring are evident even when collapsing across a wide variety of different positive events. As an illustration, we administered the WOSC to a sample of 280 undergraduates (105 males, 175 females), along with personality measures of affect intensity (the Affect Intensity Measure; Larsen & Diener, 1987), extraversion (the Eysenck Extraversion Scale; Eysenck & Eysenck, 1975), and dispositional optimism (the Life Orientation Test; Scheier & Carver, 1985). Respondents were instructed to think back to a recent positive event, describe it in writing, and then complete the WOSC with respect to this particular event. Respondents mentioned a wide variety of different positive events, including vacations, birthday celebrations, time spent with family, parties, musical concerts, romantic encounters, sports activities, job promotions, academic honors, and leisurely relaxation. For present purposes, we collapsed across all positive events before analyzing the data.

We constructed four different composite measures from the personality instruments. From the Affect Intensity Measure, we scored the Positive Affectivity subscale (α = .90), which reflects the characteristic strength with which people experience positive emotions (Bryant, Yarnold, & Grimm, 1996). From the Eysenck Extraversion Scale, we computed total score (α = .92). Finally, from the Life Orientation Test, we computed separate subscale scores for Optimism (α = .80) and Pessimism (α = .85), to assess generalized positive and negative expectations for future outcomes, respectively (Bryant & Cvengros, 2004).

Given our interpretation of the dimensions of savoring underlying the WOSC, we had clear-cut hypotheses about the pattern of relationships we expected to find between (a) positive affectivity, extraversion, optimism, and pessimism and (b) the 10 WOSC subscales. Based on the notion that the predisposition to feel strong positive affect should evoke savoring responses that enhance enjoyment, we expected that greater dispositional positive affectivity would be associated with higher scores on all of the WOSC subscales except for Kill-Joy Thinking. Based on the idea that extraversion involves greater sociability and exuberance, we expected that higher levels of extraversion would be associated with higher scores on Sharing With Others, Memory Building, and Behavioral Expression. And based on the notion that optimists tend to see the "bright side" whereas pessimists tend to harp on the negative, we expected that greater dispositional optimism would be associated with Counting Blessings, whereas greater dispositional pessimism would be associated with higher scores on Kill-Joy Thinking.

As seen in Table 4.2, the results of our correlational analyses strongly support these hypotheses. Consistent with predictions, positive affectivity was positively correlated with scores on every WOSC subscale except Kill-Joy Thinking. Further confirming hypotheses, extraversion was positively correlated with Sharing With Others, Memory Building, and Behavioral Expression. Unexpectedly, extraversion also showed reliable associations with Counting Blessings and Self-Congratulation, suggesting that the more outgoing one is, the more one tends to reflect on good fortune and personal accomplishment in response to positive experiences. Also supporting predictions, the higher one's level of optimism, the more one tended to count one's blessings in response to positive events; whereas the higher one's level of pessimism, the more one tended to engage in Kill-Joy Thinking in response to positive events. Unexpectedly, greater dispositional pessimism was also reliably associated with higher scores on Temporal Awareness, Sensory-Perceptual Sharpening, and Comparing. These latter findings suggest that the more one generally sees the future in negative terms, the more one tends to be aware of the fleetingness of positive events, the harder one tries to block out distractions when savoring, and the more time one spends comparing one's outcomes with social, temporal, or counterfactual standards in response to positive events.

These correlational results support our contention that cognitive and behavioral savoring responses reflect not only reactions to situational characteristics of

TABLE 4.2
Correlating the Ten WOSC Subscales
With Measures of Personality ($N = 280$)

WOSC Subscales	Personality Measures			
	Positive Affectivity	Extraversion	Optimism	Pessimism
SWO	.24	.25	.09	-.10
MB	.30	.24	.11	.02
SC	.27	.18	.11	-.01
SPS	.22	.13	.04	.17
C	.28	.13	.02	.15
A	.21	.10	.02	.08
BE	.36	.35	.10	-.04
TA	.17	.08	.02	.19
CB	.29	.20	.24	-.11
KJT	.07	.06	-.08	.29

Note. Tabled are Pearson product–moment correlation coefficients relating mean scores on the WOSC subscales to scores on personality measures. Respondents completed the WOSC in relation to any recent positive event of their choosing. $|rs| > .11$ are statistically significant at two-tailed $p < .05$. SWO = Sharing With Others. MB = Memory Building. SC = Self-Congratulation. SPS = Sensory-Perceptual Sharpening. C = Comparing. A = Absorption. BE = Behavioral Expression. TA = Temporal Awareness. CB = Counting Blessings. KJT = Kill-Joy Thinking.

positive experiences, but also stable personality traits that predispose people to think and act in certain ways when going through positive experiences. Our data clearly indicate that people who characteristically react to positive events with stronger positive affect tend to savor positive experiences differently, compared to people who characteristically react to positive events with weaker positive affect. In addition, the data show that extraversion and dispositional optimism or pessimism produce reliable differences in savoring responses across a diverse array of positive experiences. That each personality measure demonstrates a different pattern of associations with the savoring subscales strongly supports the discriminant validity of the WOSC. That these patterns largely conform to our a priori hypotheses further supports the construct validity of the WOSC.

Savoring Responses and Recalled Enjoyment

If savoring responses influence the intensity and duration of enjoyment, then how do scores on the WOSC subscales relate to how much and how long people report having enjoyed themselves? As we have argued, the answer to this question may well depend on the particular kind of positive events one experiences. For example, being aware of the fleetingness of time might enhance savoring of a vacation as it continuously unfolds. On the other hand, realizing that one's positive experience is transient might be less relevant in savoring a good grade, which occurs all at once as a discrete piece of performance feedback. Nevertheless, we might also expect some ways of savoring to both amplify and prolong enjoyment regardless of the positive experience involved. For example, being aware of one's good fortune might enhance savoring of both the vacation and the good grade.

To examine the relationship between savoring responses and recalled enjoyment, we asked a sample of undergraduates to complete the WOSC in relation to either a recent vacation ($N = 126$) or a good grade ($N = 125$), and then to indicate how much they enjoyed the particular event (1 = very little, 7 = very much) and how long their enjoyment lasted (1 = not for very long, 7 = for a very long time). Elapsed time since the event was uncorrelated with WOSC subscale scores and with the reported level and duration of enjoyment ($rs < .09$, $ps > .20$). Table 4.3 reports the correlations between (a) scores on the 10 WOSC subscales and (b) reported level and duration of enjoyment in response to each positive event.

The results are generally consistent with our expectations. Notice first that some ways of savoring show consistent relationships with both the recalled level and the duration of enjoyment across both positive events. In particular, Self-Congratulation, Absorption, and Counting Blessings all correlate strongly to moderately with both how much and how long people recall enjoying both the

TABLE 4.3
Correlations Between Scores on the Ten WOSC Subscales
and Self-Reported Level and Duration of Enjoyment
for Vacation ($N = 126$) and Good Grade ($N = 125$)

WOSC Subscales	Level of Enjoyment		Duration of Enjoyment	
	Vacation	Good Grade	Vacation	Good Grade
SWO	.61	.27	.54	.33
MB	.41	.16	.45	.45
SC	.28	.40	.45	.50
SPS	.13	.15	.19	.21
C	.15	.14	.08	.12
A	.41	.27	.39	.44
BE	.41	.13	.38	.19
TA	.32	.13	.13	.27
CB	.53	.31	.53	.42
KJT	-.49	-.20	-.40	-.13

Note. Tabled are Pearson product–moment correlation coefficients relating mean scores on the WOSC subscales to reported level and duration of enjoyment. SWO = Sharing With Others. MB = Memory Building. SC = Self-Congratulation. SPS = Sensory-Perceptual Sharpening. C = Comparing. A = Absorption. BE = Behavioral Expression. TA = Temporal Awareness. CB = Counting Blessings. KJT = Kill-Joy Thinking. $|rs| > .14$ are statistically significant at two-tailed $p < .05$.

vacation and the good grade. Thus, some types of savoring responses are associated with stronger and longer enjoyment across both positive events.

Other ways of savoring, in contrast, relate differently to the level or duration of enjoyment, depending on the particular positive event involved. For example, Sharing, Memory Building, and Temporal Awareness correlate more strongly with how much people report enjoying the vacation than with how much they report enjoying the good grade. And, perhaps not surprisingly, Self-Congratulation relates more strongly to how much people enjoyed the good grade than the vacation. This pattern of results supports our earlier speculation that people may savor a continuously unfolding positive event, such as a vacation, differently than they savor a brief, discrete outcome, such as a good grade.

Although these results are encouraging, we must also acknowledge their limitations. As with all correlational research, the associations we have found do not establish cause-and-effect relationships between savoring responses and positive affect (Cook & Campbell, 1979). Further work is required to demonstrate unequivocally that ways of savoring have a direct impact on the intensity and duration of people's positive emotions in response to positive experiences. In particular, experimental research is needed in which people are randomly assigned to engage in specific types of savoring strategies in response to specific positive events, with their emotional reactions measured during and after these events. In addition, longitudinal field studies are needed, using daily diaries (e.g., Duncan & Grazzani-Gavazzi, 2004) or experience-sampling techniques (e.g., Csikszentmihalyi & Hunter, 2003), to examine the short- and long-term emotional impact of thoughts and behaviors that spontaneously occur in relation to positive experiences.

Furthermore, additional psychometric work is needed to establish the construct validity of the WOSC. In this book, we present preliminary evidence to support the reliability and discriminant validity of the ten WOSC subscales. But to determine whether this instrument actually measures what we claim it does is a long-range task requiring multiple studies using multiple methods and samples across multiple settings (Bryant, 2000; Bryant, King, & Smart, in press). Clearly, we have just scratched the surface in this endeavor.

Relating Ways of Savoring to Savoring Beliefs

If these 10 dimensions of savoring actually measure what we think they do, then scores on the WOSC subscales should relate in theoretically meaningful ways to people's beliefs about their ability to savor positive experience (as assessed by the SBI). Such findings would not only advance our conceptual understanding of savoring, but also strengthen the divergent validity of the 10 WOSC subscales and the three SBI subscales in the process.

Along these lines, we would expect some ways of savoring—such as Sharing With Others, Self-Congratulation, Behavioral Expression, and Counting

Blessings — to be associated with a greater perceived ability to savor the moment across a wide variety of positive events. Some of these savoring dimensions (i.e., Sharing With Others and Behavioral Expression) focus attention on one's own positive feelings, whereas other savoring dimensions (i.e., Counting Blessings) focus attention on the positive features of the particular event. We would expect that the more people attend to and appreciate their positive feelings or positive features of the situation, the more aware they should be of their own enjoyment across a wide variety of different pleasant events, and the greater should be their perceived capacity to savor positive experiences in general.

However, there are also other ways of savoring — namely, Kill-Joy Thinking — that we believe make people less aware of positive feelings or positive environmental features. Because Kill-Joy Thinking focuses attention on negative aspects of the self or the situation, this particular cognitive savoring dimension dampens the intensity and duration of enjoyment. We assume that people who engage in this particular thought pattern are probably aware of the hedonic consequences and are therefore likely to perceive themselves as having less savoring ability. Because the generalized savoring response of Kill-Joy Thinking would presumably diminish the joy of *any* positive experience (Beck, 1976), we would expect the dampening effects of such thinking to hold across a wide range of different positive events.

On the other hand, we also expect other ways of savoring — such as Sensory-Perceptual Sharpening, Temporal Awareness, and Comparing — to enhance enjoyment only for certain kinds of positive experiences, and not for other kinds of positive experiences. For example, effortfully sharpening one's perceptual senses might heighten enjoyment of a virtuoso musical performance, but might not influence how much one enjoys receiving a compliment from a stranger. Likewise, reminding oneself of the fleetingness of time might enhance the savoring of rare "bittersweet" moments (e.g., a wedding or graduation), but might undermine the enjoyment of simple everyday pleasures (e.g., a quiet cup of tea alone, or a walk in a garden). Because the hedonic consequences of savoring strategies may depend on the particular positive events involved, we would not necessarily expect people who engage in these types of savoring responses to perceive themselves as having more or less savoring ability in general.

We have complicated the picture here by proposing that, in some cases, how strongly savoring beliefs relate to savoring responses may depend on the particular positive experience involved. For example, general savoring beliefs may be more predictive of actively building memories and becoming absorbed in the moment when one is on a leisurely vacation, but not when one has just received a good grade on a test or paper. In general, we can expect to see a complex and diverse pattern of relationships between: (a) general savoring beliefs with respect to the past, present, and future; and (b) ways of savoring in response to specific positive events. We use this predicted pattern of interrelationships (i.e., nomological net) to formulate and test a priori hypotheses, in order to gather further evidence concerning the discriminant validity of the SBI and WOSC subscales and advance our conceptual understanding of the construct of savoring.

To investigate the relationship between ways of savoring and savoring beliefs, we asked separate samples of college undergraduates to complete the WOSC in relation to either a vacation (N = 598) or a good grade (N = 502), along with the SBI. (These 1,100 respondents are a subsample of the data set we presented earlier in examining profiles of WOSC subscale scores.) We then inspected the pattern of correlations between ways of savoring and beliefs about savoring capacity, to see whether our conceptual hypotheses were confirmed or disconfirmed. Table 4.4 presents these intercorrelations.

The pattern of results in this table supports many of our a priori hypotheses about the relationship between ways of savoring ongoing positive experience and personal beliefs about savoring ability. As predicted, ways of savoring that focus attention on one's positive feelings (i.e., Sharing With Others and Behavioral Expression) or on positive features of events (i.e., Counting Blessings) are associated with greater beliefs in one's capacity to savor positive outcomes with respect to the past, present, and future. Also confirming predictions, Kill-Joy Thinking is associated with reporting less ability to savor outcomes with respect to all three time frames. And these relationships hold for both one's most recent vacation, as well as the last time one got a good grade on a test or paper.

But there are also some interesting differences in the pattern of relationships across the two positive events. In particular, use of Memory Building in savoring the vacation is positively correlated with beliefs about personal ability to savor the past, present, and future, whereas use of Memory Building in savoring the good grade is uncorrelated with general savoring beliefs. We suggest that a vacation provides more opportunity to systematically build memories over a greater length of time, compared to a good grade. Indeed, building a memory of a good grade would primarily involve memorizing one's surroundings or reactions when receiving the good grade; whereas building a memory of the vacation would unfold continuously in real time over the course of successive hours or days (or even weeks) and could be used to fuller advantage to commemorate and memorialize ongoing positive experience.

Along these same lines, becoming absorbed when savoring the vacation is positively associated with reported savoring capacity in all three temporal domains, but the tendency to become absorbed when savoring the good grade is unrelated to self-reported savoring capacity. We suggest that Absorption is a more viable strategy for savoring an ongoing continuous event as it is unfolding in actual time, as opposed to a discrete binary event (e.g., success–failure, victory–defeat).

Also as expected, for both positive events, Sensory-Perceptual Sharpening and Comparing are largely unrelated to global savoring beliefs. Although Comparing as a way of savoring a good grade is unrelated to beliefs about one's ability to savor the moment (r = -.06, p < .09), Comparing as a way of savoring a vacation does show a small negative association with reported capacity to savor the moment ($r = -.13$, two-tailed $p < .001$). By definition, the good grade is in comparison to other people who may or may not have done as well on the test or paper. However, the vacation is primarily a leisurely pursuit, the pleasure of which may well evaporate if one continually compares the experience to (a) the past, (b) imagined counterfactual alternatives, (c) what other people are experiencing, or (d) what one believes one is supposed to experience. It is hard to

TABLE 4.4

Correlations Between Scores on the Ten WOSC Subscales
and Scores on the Savoring Beliefs Inventory (SBI)

Ways of Savoring Subscales	Positive Event	Savoring Beliefs Inventory Scales			
		Anticipating	Savoring the Moment	Reminiscing	SBI Total Score
Sharing With Others	Vacation	.30	.35	.40	.40
	Good Grade	.19	.23	.17	.24
Memory Building	Vacation	.24	.25	.33	.31
	Good Grade	.05	.03	.03	.04
Self-Congratulation	Vacation	.20	.21	.25	.26
	Good Grade	.24	.21	.20	.25
Sensory-Perceptual Sharpening	Vacation	-.01	-.03	-.01	-.01
	Good Grade	.01	.01	-.05	-.01
Comparing	Vacation	-.03	-.13	-.01	-.06
	Good Grade	.04	-.06	-.02	-.01
Absorption	Vacation	.15	.20	.20	.21
	Good Grade	.08	.02	.03	.05
Behavioral Expression	Vacation	.18	.21	.21	.23
	Good Grade	.17	.20	.17	.22
Temporal Awareness	Vacation	.02	-.07	.03	-.01
	Good Grade	-.09	-.14	-.11	-.13
Counting Blessings	Vacation	.23	.33	.33	.34
	Good Grade	.23	.19	.20	.24
Kill-Joy Thinking	Vacation	-.27	-.40	-.38	-.39
	Good Grade	-.17	-.28	-.20	-.26

Note.   Tabled are Pearson product–moment correlation coefficients relating mean scores on the Ways of Savoring Checklist (WOSC) subscales to mean scores on the SBI scales. These results are for separate samples of college students who completed the WOSC in relation to either their most recent vacation ($N = 598$) or the last time they got a good grade on a test or paper ($N = 502$), and then also completed the Savoring Beliefs Inventory (SBI). For the *vacation*, $|rs| \geq .07$ are statistically significant at two-tailed $p < .05$; $|rs| > .09$ are statistically significant at two-tailed $p < .01$; and $|rs| > .12$ are statistically significant at two-tailed $p < .001$. For the *good grade*, $|rs| > .07$ are statistically significant at two-tailed $p < .05$; $|rs| > .10$ are statistically significant at two-tailed $p < .01$; and $|rs| > .13$ are statistically significant at two-tailed $p < .001$.

savor what one is experiencing in the moment when one is busy comparing it to what it is not.

We can speculate that there are other types of positive events for which Sensory-Perceptual Sharpening is associated with greater overall savoring beliefs. For example, a positive event in which a pleasurable stimulus is experienced primarily through one particular form of sensory perception (e.g., sound, taste, smell, touch, sight) would seem most conducive to Sensory-Perceptual Sharpening, in which one deliberately tries to heighten a specific sense by effortful concentration. Examples of such pleasurable events include listening to the sound of ocean waves while sitting on a beach, relishing the taste of a bite of food during a gourmet meal, smelling a rose while strolling through a garden, luxuriating in a relaxing massage, or marveling at the colors of the sky in a spectacular sunset.

Gender Differences in Ways of Savoring

Given that women compared to men tend to believe they are more capable of savoring, how does gender relate to the ways in which people savor positive experiences? A great deal of empirical evidence has accrued concerning differences in the ways males and females think about themselves and the world around them, experience and express emotions, and engage in social behavior in their everyday lives (e.g., Eagly & Wood, 1999; Maccoby & Jacklin, 1974). For example, we know that compared to men, women tend to have a richer and more complex inner life (Veroff, Douvan, & Kulka, 1981) and typically report more intense emotions (Diener, Sandvik, & Larsen, 1985). But how might these gender differences manifest themselves in the ways that men and women savor the same positive experiences?

To address this question, we evaluated possible gender differences in mean scores on the 10 WOSC subscales for an independent sample of college students in relation to a recent vacation, $N = 598$ (175 males, 423 females) or good grade on a test or paper, $N = 551$ (130 males, 421 females). Because women score higher on all three temporal subscales of the SBI (Bryant, 2003), we expected females to have higher scores than males on the WOSC subscales associated with greater reported enjoyment of the vacation and the good grade, and lower scores than males on the Kill-Joy Thinking subscale.

Confirming our hypotheses, there are some reliable differences in women's and men's savoring responses that hold across both positive events. As seen in Table 4.5, for both the vacation and the good grade, women reported a significantly greater use of Sharing With Others, Behavioral Expression, and Counting Blessings as savoring strategies, whereas men report a significantly greater use of Kill-Joy Thinking. However, there are no reliable gender differences in mean levels of Sensory-Perceptual Sharpening, Comparing, Absorption, or Temporal Awareness for either positive event. In addition, compared to males, females reported using Memory Building more in response to the vacation, and Self-

TABLE 4.5
Comparing Mean Scores of Males and Females
on WOSC Subscales for Vacation and Good Grade

| | Positive Event | | | | | | | |
| | Vacation | | | | Good Grade | | | |
WOSC Subscales	Males	Females	t	d	Males	Females	t	d
SWO	4.93 (1.43)	5.55 (1.19)	5.42**	0.49	3.52 (1.44)	3.88 (1.39)	2.50*	0.25
MB	4.60 (1.20)	5.07 (1.08)	4.68**	0.42	2.34 (1.05)	2.46 (1.14)	1.05	0.11
SC	4.22 (1.45)	4.32 (1.27)	0.83	0.07	4.40 (1.26)	4.73 (1.05)	3.00**	0.30
SPS	3.59 (1.18)	3.78 (1.22)	1.73	0.16	2.69 (1.28)	2.59 (1.26)	0.72	0.07
C	3.51 (1.09)	3.44 (1.06)	0.78	0.07	3.13 (1.13)	3.11 (1.11)	0.19	0.02
A	4.56 (1.22)	4.66 (1.21)	0.96	0.09	3.38 (1.37)	3.27 (1.26)	0.87	0.09
BE	4.06 (1.32)	4.36 (1.28)	2.65**	0.24	2.63 (1.25)	3.04 (1.35)	2.97**	0.30
TA	4.24 (1.38)	4.38 (1.38)	0.77	0.07	2.78 (1.37)	2.86 (1.29)	0.65	0.07
CB	4.69 (1.51)	5.05 (1.49)	2.64**	0.24	4.11 (1.61)	4.48 (1.55)	2.29*	0.23
KJT	2.64 (1.07)	2.45 (1.06)	1.99*	0.18	2.82 (0.97)	2.60 (0.96)	2.18*	0.22

Note. Tabled for males and females are mean scores on each WOSC subscale (along with standard deviations in parentheses). For Vacation, $N = 598$ (175 males, 423 females). For Good Grade, $N = 551$ (130 males, 421 females). WOSC subscale scores are averages that range from 1 to 7, with a midpoint of 4. t = observed value of the independent-samples t test (for vacation, $df = 596$; for good grade, $df = 549$). d = Cohen's d, a measure of effect size. A value of $d \leq 0.2$ is considered "small;" $d = 0.5$ is considered "medium;" and $d \geq 0.8$ is considered "large" (Cohen, 1988). SW = Sharing With Others. MB = Memory Building. SC = Self-Congratulation. SPS = Sensory-Perceptual Sharpening. C = Comparing. A = Absorption. BE = Behavioral Expression. TA = Temporal Awareness. CB = Counting Blessings. KJT = Kill-Joy Thinking.

*$p < .05$, two-tailed. **$p < .01$, two-tailed.

Congratulation more in response to the good grade. Estimates of effect size (d; Cohen, 1988) indicate that these gender differences are small to moderate in magnitude.

Our findings suggest that in response to positive events, women more than men (a) share their positive feelings with others; (b) outwardly express their feelings in terms of physical nonverbal behavior; (c) reflect on their good fortune; and (d) avoid negative thoughts that undermine savoring. Evidently, males have a harder time than females sharing and expressing their feelings, and spend less time counting blessings and more time thinking kill-joy thoughts in response to positive events. In addition, women more than men actively build a memory of their vacation, and congratulate themselves in response to their good grade. Women's greater reliance on these savoring strategies may help to explain why they consistently score higher than men on their perceived ability to derive joy through anticipating, savoring the moment, and reminiscing.

Research reveals that these sex differences in savoring beliefs emerge as early as fifth grade (Cafasso, Bryant, & Jose, 1994) and persist at least through age 65 (Bryant, 2003). And these same sex differences in savoring beliefs are found in data from Japan (Lindberg, 2004), Canada (Lindberg, 2004), and Australia (Macaulay, 2000). Relative to men, women seem to know how to enjoy themselves more, by using cognitive and behavioral approaches to savoring more effectively to enhance their enjoyment of positive experiences. We return to this point in chapter 8 when we consider ways to help people enhance their savoring.

SUMMARY

This chapter empirically differentiates types of savoring responses to positive experiences in order to provide researchers with the measurement tools necessary to advance our conceptual and empirical understanding of savoring. Ten different dimensions of savoring emerged from the Ways of Savoring Checklist (WOSC): Sharing With Others; Memory Building; Self-Congratulation; Sensory-Perceptual Sharpening; Comparing; Absorption; Behavioral Expression; Temporal Awareness; Counting Blessings; and Kill-Joy Thinking. This last savoring dimension reflects a cognitive style that dampens enjoyment of positive experiences. Whereas most ways of savoring are primarily cognitive (i.e., Memory Building, Self-Congratulation, Sensory-Perceptual Sharpening, Comparing, Temporal Awareness, Counting Blessings, Kill-Joy Thinking), others are primarily behavioral (i.e., Behavioral Expression, Sharing With Others, Absorption). These particular dimensions of savoring do not represent the universe of all possible ways of savoring positive events, but rather are an initial starting point intended to stimulate further research on how people go about trying to enjoy the positive experiences in their lives. Supporting the construct validity of the WOSC subscales, we presented data indicating that different positive events produce different profiles of savoring across the 10 WOSC subscales; personality influences the ways people savor across a wide variety of positive experiences; specific savoring strategies are associated with a greater reported level and duration of enjoyment; beliefs about one's ability to savor positive outcomes relate in predictable ways to the use of different savoring strategies; and females more than males use savoring strategies associated with greater enjoyment of positive experiences.

5

Types of Savoring: An Integrative Conceptual View

There is more difference in the quality
of our pleasures than in the amount.
—Ralph Waldo Emerson (1841/1906)

In the last chapter, we presented research developing a measurement instrument for assessing 10 ways in which people savor positive experiences, and we considered the instrument's construct validity in relation to a variety of critical personality, situational, and emotional variables. We did not distinguish different types of savoring processes as such, except to say that different savoring processes involve different savoring responses, and that some savoring responses arise rather automatically, whereas others are often strategic choices that individuals make in response to a particular positive experience.

We now develop an integrative conceptual framework for understanding and distinguishing different types of savoring processes in more depth. We begin by considering different types of savoring responses more generally in terms of their basic functions. We then distinguish savoring experiences, and their underlying savoring processes, in terms of whether they are primarily world-focused or self-focused in their general directedness, and whether they primarily entail cognitive reflection or experiential absorption. Combining these two conceptual distinctions, we derive a 2 × 2 typology of four main types of savoring processes — basking, thanksgiving, marveling, and luxuriating — each of which involves (a) a different mixture of world- versus self-focus and reflection versus absorption, (b) a specific motivational orientation to positive experience, and (c) a distinct subjective phenomenology. We further propose that each of these four basic savoring processes has an opposite counterpart in negative experience that can monopolize a person's attentional resources, thereby making it particularly difficult for the person to attend to the related form of savoring.

A BROADER CONCEPTUAL VIEW: THREE BASIC FUNCTIONS OF SAVORING

With the initial classification of savoring dimensions through the Ways of Savoring Checklist, we were encouraged to explicate the finite pool of savoring resources people could use in initiating or enhancing savoring experiences in their lives. Adopting a more general conceptual view not only of the savoring dimensions underlying the WOSC, but also of other savoring dimensions or responses that were not included in this instrument, we have synthesized potential savoring responses under three basic functions of savoring: *prolonging* the experience, *intensifying* the experience, and *shifting gears to savoring*. A closer look at these basic functions provides promising leads into how people manage their emotional life to bring more joy into it, and suggests concrete approaches for enhancing an appreciation of life's bounties.

Prolonging the Moment: Extension of Savoring Over Time

Positive events or moments that are discrete and of short duration are more challenging for savoring than are events or experiences of long duration. Discrete positive events — such as being paid a compliment, getting a raise or promotion, catching a fish, sinking a hole-in-one, receiving a first kiss from a beloved — are so brief that, on the face of it, they defy prolonged savoring. And yet we know most people employ simple strategies to extend the impact of these short-lived events in their awareness. Indeed, there is a paradoxical difference between the natural duration of good and bad events: if unchanged, the latter more often continue on their own, whereas the former more often end on their own. Here are some ways that people prolong their savoring of positive events.

Reminiscence and Recall. Generalizing from the Ways of Savoring Checklist subscale of Memory Building, we first consider reminiscence and recall as strategies to prolong savoring. People can resurrect a savored event far after its immediate emotional impact has evaporated, by reminiscing or attempting to recall what was special for them when it happened. One may not use these specific savoring strategies for *all* positive events of short duration, but they are often employed for notable "milestone" positive events, such as "the first time we made love," "the day I finished my first marathon," or "the moment my child was born." People can relive the positive event by reminding themselves of what it was like, talking about it with others, or reviewing memorabilia such as photographs or souvenirs to help them relive the event. In chapter 6, we highlight the strong connection between savoring and storytelling. Indeed, people's tendency to prolong savoring by sharing through reminiscence helps promote storytelling. It is easiest to remember a special moment in the context of a story that has some buildup to that particular moment and perhaps some denouement resulting from that moment.

Chaining.   The brief positive events we encounter, whether or not they are notable milestones, can be prolonged psychologically by considering a web of associations that spin off from the initial encounter. Thus, people can cognitively chain other considerations to the original experience. Fred has spoken of the exhilaration he feels in his climbing adventures when he reaches the top of a mountain. Technically, that feeling can be experienced only momentarily, and yet while on the mountaintop he can absorb other sensory phenomena—the 360° panorama, the sound of the wind or the hushed silence, the smell of the mountain air—and he can contemplate the meaning of the event as a sense of accomplishment, as well as a sense of connection to his fellow climbers and to the vastness of the universe. These add-ons to the more limited discrete event of reaching the summit are links in the chain that now make up the positive experience. Some of this chaining can be automatic, and some can be under deliberate conscious control. In either case, a brief encounter with savoring has been prolonged.

Chaining can be even further elaborated when people reminisce. In recounting a story about the past, people often add associations that were not necessarily there originally, as we think back through the events associated with our memory. To tell a coherent story, especially when retelling the event to someone else, people often mention details they might have passed over in the original encounter. Whether these embellishments actually happened is irrelevant because they become part of the web of associations that operate to prolong the original savoring moment well into the future.

Sharing After the Moment.   As noted earlier, the process of sharing a positive experience with others is a dominant savoring response in the Ways of Savoring Checklist. Sharing is obviously a direct way to prolong savoring, not only while a positive event is happening, but also after it has ended. People often purposely reminisce about past joy in the presence of others, most often with loved ones and friends, but sometimes with strangers. They tell stories about their good fortune, past joys, and happy times. Sometimes these stories are bragging, if they reflect excessive self-congratulation in publicly extolling personal virtue or competence. But usually such storytelling is more than conceited boasting.

Consider two brief examples. When Fred's wife, Linda, views photographs she just had developed, she often insists that he view them with her a second time. When they look at the pictures together and he also enjoys them, she vicariously extends her own savoring of the images. As another illustration, Fred learns that a paper he has submitted to a prestigious journal has finally been accepted for publication, and so he immediately calls a colleague to extend the joy of receiving that news. When observing his colleague's pleasure in hearing the news, Fred is extending his own savoring experience. Linda and Fred are each prolonging the original savored moment by sharing it afterwards with others.

As we noted earlier with respect to Sharing With Others as a style of savoring, if people are savoring something when alone or when separated from others for whom the savoring experience is also relevant, they can enhance savoring if they merely imagine sharing the moment with these relevant others sometime in the future. Like many positive anticipations, thinking about later sharing becomes part of the savoring and hence prolongs the experience. How often have you told yourself, "I can't wait to tell _____ about what happened," and then looked forward to that sharing with great glee? Fred noted his use of this prolongation strategy on the summit of Snowmass Mountain. In addition, most of us like to go to movies with someone else, in part because talking about our experience after we leave the theatre prolongs the original experience. If we savored the film, such talk enables us to prolong our enjoyment.

We have already noted that telling the story of a savored moment is a way to chain more details into savoring and prolong the experience. We must keep in mind that in most instances, a person tells a story to an audience, and hence also shares the experience, which is another way to prolong savoring. In fact, telling a story to a receptive audience can often be the means by which a person combines all three prolonging processes we have been discussing — *reminiscing* by talking of something past, *chaining* by integrating the experience in story form, and *sharing* by telling the story to someone else.

Celebration. In all world cultures, a well-established mechanism for extending the duration of positive events is to commemorate them through formal celebration (Isambert, 1969; Turner, 1982). Typically, festive celebration is a planned social response to a positive event bringing together friends, food, drink, and often entertainment in a way that sustains the good feelings associated with the event. As a prolonging process, celebration can be a form of synergistic savoring in which people and situational elements are combined in a way that magnifies the whole savoring experience beyond the sum of its parts.

People seem most likely to engage in commemorative celebration on the occasion of discrete positive events, such as receiving an honor or award, getting a raise or promotion, graduating from high school or college, or reaching a birthday or anniversary—events that would otherwise be of only brief duration. Celebration not only prolongs savoring of positive events in the present, but also helps to memorialize these events for later past-focused savoring. Indeed, the urge to photograph, videotape, or somehow preserve a record of ongoing celebrations reflects the desire to capture the fleeting joy of the moment in order to facilitate later reminiscence.

Intensifying the Moment: Amplification of Savoring

There are other strategies people use to strengthen the savoring experienced at the very moment the outcome or event is occurring. We discuss two such general strategies next and also note specific forms these strategies may take. These two types of strategies for enhancing savoring, which are closely related to one another, are blocking out interfering stimuli and enhancing attention to the stimuli eliciting the savoring. These strategies are clearly interrelated because as we block out interfering stimuli, we often pay more attention to other stimuli we wish to savor, and vice versa. Blocking extraneous distractions and attending to positive features are related to the savoring strategies of Sensory-Perceptual Sharpening and Absorption, respectively, which emerged in the Ways of Savoring Checklist.

Blocking Out Interfering Stimuli. Many people set the mood for a particular type of savoring experience by establishing an ambience that will not distract them from what they wish to savor. This is most easily recognized with regard to enjoying a meal or immersing oneself in erotic play. A booming radio program simultaneously heard while eating or making love could distract one from savoring the moment, especially if the program concerns a topic that is of interest. Under such conditions, the person usually would be unable to savor the food or sex, and it might be better to turn off the radio.

In more subtle ways, people can psychologically block out things that are currently on their mind, especially things about which they may be worried, and concentrate more exclusively on the positive stimuli they are savoring. Some people are especially good at using such denial in order to engage in a temporary indulgence. Indeed, people sometimes escape into a savoring experience as a means of blocking out something that is troubling them. At an extreme level, savoring food or sex could become a means of escape from something hard to face, and could thus become an "addictive" savoring activity on which one grows dependent for managing affective experience. We hesitate to call such "addiction" a savoring intensification strategy, but it would be hard to distinguish people who are psychologically dependent in this way from people who intentionally deny worrisome aspects of their life as a way to intensify their savoring of food or sex.

Heightened Focus on the Savoring Moment. By definition, savoring requires some degree of attention to a pleasurable experience, although one could be more or less in an attentive frame of mind while savoring. When people consciously tell themselves to focus on the savoring stimuli to the exclusion of all other stimuli, then they are using the strategy we are considering here. One way to sharpen focus of attention on the present moment is to structure the situation in ways that make it conducive to the savoring experience. Earlier we talked about a radio program as a distraction from savoring a meal or savoring sex. Suppose what was playing on the radio was music that the diners thought befitted dining, let's say a softly played string serenade by Tschaikovsky, or music that the lovers thought befitted their lovemaking, let's say Ella Fitzgerald tenderly singing Cole Porter songs. Then the music could, in fact, enhance the attention to eating in the first instance, or to being sexual in the second instance. Thus, a person can use strategies to establish a savoring atmosphere that will intensify his or her pleasure.

This analysis is not, of course, limited to food and sex. We have presented these domains first because they are simpler to discuss. We can also apply this analysis to more intellectual savoring experiences as well. Consider savoring the reading of a book. To help you attend more to your savoring, you might ask others not to interrupt you. You might position yourself in a chair so as to be totally relaxed, with no need to shift around to avoid discomfort. You might prepare a cup of tea and wrap a blanket around yourself to stay warm. As you are reading, the experience is savored more because you have prevented yourself from being distracted from the pleasures you are deriving from reading. This approach can be quite deliberate, in which case it could be considered a strategy of increasing attention to what is being savored.

On the other hand, we have all had the opposite experience of reading a passage and suddenly realizing that for an undetermined time we have been thinking about something else while mindlessly moving our eyes from one word to the next, and we have no idea of what we have just read. Clearly, there has been no in-depth savoring of the written words in this case. As Schooler et al. (2003) noted:

> What is so striking about this experience is that although one consciously experiences the contents of the mind-wandering episode, one fails to notice that one's mind has wandered. Otherwise, one would have either stopped reading or stopped daydreaming. The fact that both activities continue demonstrates the absence of awareness that one is daydreaming even though this is precisely what is occupying one's mind at the time. (p. 65)

In mindfully savoring the reading of a book, in contrast, people might linger over written passages they find particularly enjoyable, reading and rereading them over and over, deliberately stopping to contemplate certain implications in more depth and detail, and allowing themselves time to experience the emotions associated with each word as they slowly read it. Savoring involves a mindful processing of one's own positive affective experience. Mindless processing simply does not allow one to savor.

In the following paragraphs, we wish the reader to try out a brief experiment of sorts. Begin by reading the following block quotation as quickly as you can, making sure to keep your mind from lingering on any one word or phrase as you read. Refrain from letting your thoughts wander, and finish reading the passage as fast as you possibly can:

> Below my feet the foot-hills nestle, brown with flecks of green;
>> and lower down the flat brown plain, the floor of earth,
>> stretches away to blue infinity.
> Beside me in this airy space the temple roofs cut their slow
>> curves
>> against the sky.
> And one black bird circles above the void.
>
> Space and the twelve lean winds are here;
> And with them broods eternity — a swift, white peace, a presence
>> manifest . . .
> But I shall go down from this airy space, this swift white peace,
>> this stinging exultation;
> And time will close about me, and my soul stir to the rhythm
>> of the daily round.
> Yet, having known, life will not press so close, and always
>> I shall feel time ravel thin about me;
> For once I stood
> in the white windy presence of eternity. (Tietjens, 1919, pp. 95–96)

Now try a different approach. Imagine you are standing with good friends atop a high mountain you had longed to climb for many years, and suddenly you realize the fleetingness of the moment. You remind yourself that you will probably never be there together in that special place again, you feel a bittersweet sense of the preciousness of the moment, and you desperately try to hold onto the feeling. With this scenario in mind, now go back and reread the poem, this time slowly savoring every word and line deliberately and carefully, letting your mind pause, linger, and wander as you read, even reading a line over and over to let the feelings sink in, if you choose. Take your time, be aware of the feelings that the words evoke, and savor the experience. When you are finished, return to the paragraph after this one.

The difference between these two ways of reading the poem demonstrates the emotional power of savoring. Merely reading the words mindlessly and rushing quickly through the passage creates none of the thoughts or feelings that occur when you deliberately slow down and savor the poem. To savor the poem (excerpted from *The Most Sacred Mountain* by Eunice Tietjens) is to take time to swish its essence around in your mind as expert tasters do a fine wine on their palate, to let yourself experience and express the various feelings the poem evokes, to linger on a word or phrase, to reflect and make other associations, to be mindfully aware of the positive experience as it unfolds. Which way of reading the poem did you enjoy more?

By slowing down and lingering over the words as you read them, you allowed time for your feelings to develop in response to the passage, time to experience these positive emotions, to make cognitive associations, and to be mindfully aware of the entire experience. But when rushing through the passage, in contrast, you had no time to experience mindfully the positive feelings and mental elaborations associated with the words you were reading. As we noted earlier, slowing down heightens one's attentional focus, induces a mindful orientation, and promotes savoring.

Naturalists often look at a scene not in a full sweep of a panorama, but in short focused bursts of attention on small parts of what they are observing (Schaller, 1980). In chapter 2, Fred spoke of his search for small details in a summit vista as a form of "mental movie making," as if his mind were a camera focusing on the panorama. Likewise, birders use binoculars, which not only permit them to see at a distance, but also block out peripheral stimuli and permit them to concentrate their attention more narrowly on a single bird to observe its coloring and habits in some detail. These examples are all instances of psychological strategies for heightening one's focus of attention on what is to be savored.

One method of enhancing attention to an event is to etch it deliberately into one's memory. Fred often uses this strategy in his mountain climbing. He reports that this deliberate memory building not only expands his exhilaration at the moment, but also enables him to relive the event later with greater feeling. Indeed, memories of savored moments that are stored in this active way may well be more easily retrieved and more vividly relived after the fact than memories that are formed more passively. In other words, the ways in which people build memories of the present may not only influence their enjoyment of the moment, but may also shape their ability to savor the memory when they reminisce about it later.

Sharing the Moment.   Just as sharing a savoring moment (or thinking about sharing it) can prolong savoring after the experience ends, so too can sharing the moment while it is occurring intensify the experience. This is especially true if the other person is a close friend or loved one. When people witness, with someone to whom they are close, an extraordinary event that transports them into bliss — such as an unusually moving concert or theater production, a dramatic come-from-behind victory by a favorite team, or a blazing explosion of northern lights in the night sky — these people experience especially intense savoring. Their feelings are enhanced because the bonding that occurs from witnessing something extraordinary together is itself an experience to be savored, quite separate from what was witnessed. Thus, it is not surprising that Sharing With Others is the single, most dominant savoring dimension in the Ways of Savoring Checklist.

Adopting a Flexible Temporal Perspective. Before shifting gears, we note that adopting a flexible temporal perspective in relation to positive experiences can be an effective strategy for increasing both the intensity and the duration of savoring. In particular, both reminiscence and anticipation can be used to either intensify or prolong savoring of ongoing positive experiences. While a positive moment is unfolding, for example, one can intensify savoring by looking back (in recalled anticipation) or looking forward (in anticipated recall), both of which intensify the joy of the moment. Thus, anticipation lays the groundwork for its later recall. And remembering similar experiences from the past while enjoying a positive experience can also intensify one's enjoyment of the moment. Clearly, when it comes to savoring, it pays to be open with respect to one's temporal orientation.

Shifting Gears to Savoring

Thus far, we have considered savoring strategies that prolong or intensify savoring experiences as these experiences occur. Now we consider strategies for eliciting savoring when people are not experiencing positive feelings but wish to do so. In these instances, they want to bring savoring into their lives; they want to shift gears from no savoring to savoring.

Planning and Anticipating. When Fred spoke of the multifaceted savoring experience he had in mountain climbing, one aspect of this experience was the joy he savored in anticipating and planning the ascent. Planning not only lets him successfully carry out a complex mission, the pleasure of which he would never experience without adequate preparation in advance, but also lets him experience some of the future pleasure in anticipation right then and there. Planning for a positive event is often a strategy to maximize the likelihood of an event occurring. Indeed, many a vacation that had been pleasantly anticipated has turned into a disaster because of inadequate planning about travel or accommodations. Planning is not a strategy that guarantees that a future event will be savored, but it helps.

More important in understanding how people use planning to shift gears into a savoring mode, we should note that the act of planning can be pleasurable and savored for its own sake. This is because planning is not only connected to a positive future event, but also provides a sense of perceived control over positive outcomes (Bryant, 1989; Flaherty, 2003; Lakein, 1974; White, 1959). A planning strategy can thus engage savoring in at least two ways: through connection with future pleasure and through a sense of personal control over that pleasure.

Anticipating is a similar strategy for shifting gears to savoring. When we feel sad, we can stop and think about a future visit from a friend or loved one, a visit we look forward to with great pleasure. Just thinking about it can make us shift from feeling blue to a momentary sense of savoring. Anticipation of a future savored moment thus can help people shift into a savoring mode, in which they enjoy in the present the pleasant feeling they imagine they will experience in the future, or enjoy at least a partial version of that future experience.

Nevertheless, it is not unusual for people who savor a future event through anticipation to find themselves unable to enjoy the actual event when it finally occurs. As a little girl, Fred's older daughter, Hilary, looked forward to her birthday parties with great relish, but they never matched her expectations. In some instances, the act of anticipating might interfere with the actual experience, if one expects too much. An anticipatory strategy thus has to include expectations that are within the bounds of reality to avoid the experience of being let down, although such bounds may be difficult to establish. This analysis implies much more rational conscious deliberation than what is usually involved in anticipatory savoring.

What about the anticipatory strategy used to concoct something unrealistic, in the realm of pure fantasy? Can we not still savor these fantasies? Many novels or plays focus on such themes. Tennessee Williams' plays are replete with characters savoring their fantasized anticipations of the good life. Williams' perspective communicates considerable tragedy in unrealistic anticipatory savoring, and yet the characters indulging in savored fantasies are sympathetically drawn as if they were just doing what anyone would in similar circumstances.

Concerning unrealistic anticipation, the role of anticipation in savoring might differ for familiar as opposed to unfamiliar situations. Consider three different scenarios, in each of which you hold in your hand an envelope that you are about to open. Inside the envelope are free roundtrip airline tickets to a vacation spot that you will be visiting. In the first scenario, you are not told what the vacation spot is or where it is located. In the second scenario, you are told only that the location is the south-sea island of Rimatara, a place you've never heard of before. In the third scenario, you are told that the location is your favorite vacation spot. Before opening the envelope, you are given some time to look forward to your upcoming vacation. How might your experiences of anticipation differ in the three scenarios?

In the first scenario, because you have no idea exactly where you'll be traveling, you cannot anticipate specific details of your upcoming vacation. You could, however, fantasize about possible destinations and what your time there might be like. But this would not be anticipation in the purest sense of the word. Rather, it would be imagining hypothetical possibilities, fabricating a range of potential vacations in different places involving different experiences, each of which is of unknown likelihood.

In the second scenario, you know a little more about what your upcoming vacation will be like, that it will be in a warm tropical climate on an ocean island. You could fantasize about your time on tropical Rimatara, imagining yourself relaxing in a hammock strung between palm trees, sipping a cool lemonade in the shade, or strolling along a deserted beach, for example. These anticipated experiences would be based on either your own previous experiences in similar settings or your stereotype of tropical islands. But in either case, your anticipation would not be based on actual, previous experiences on Rimatara. Here your anticipation is likely to be more concrete and specific than in the first scenario, but you would still be uncertain about whether or not your fantasies are an accurate picture of reality. Rimatara may be so noisy and crowded that you'll be unable to relax. Or, it may be so primitive and underdeveloped that it lacks even the basic amenities of civilization. For all you know, Rimatara may be a wilderness covered by an impenetrable jungle swarming with poisonous snakes and insects. As in the first scenario, you simply cannot know how realistic your anticipated experiences are.

In the third scenario, you know exactly what your vacation experience is likely to involve. In fact, because of your familiarity with your destination, you would probably spend some of your time planning and anticipating specific activities that you'll want to do. Here you can be much more concrete and specific in actively imagining what you will see, hear, smell, taste, and feel. Your anticipation would be based on your own memories of previous experiences in the same setting, and you could be reasonably certain that your fantasies are accurate and realistic. It is this latter type of scenario that is most conducive to intense, vivid savoring via anticipation.

It's hard to look forward in an emotionally involving way to something that you cannot imagine concretely. If a person has nothing specific to anticipate, then he or she must conjure up an expectation from scratch. Having previous experiences with an upcoming positive event, on the other hand, provides the person with a storehouse of tangible memories from which to create a mental image of the upcoming event. This suggests that the most vivid forms of anticipation involve a projection of the memory of similar past experiences into the future. Clearly, there seems to be a close connection between the ability to look forward to an experience and the ability to look back on the same experience. Indeed, the correlation between scores on the SBI subscales of Anticipating and Reminiscing was .56 (31% shared variance) in a sample of 415 college students (Bryant, 2003).

Advertisers sometimes take advantage of elements of assumed familiarity with their products to induce anticipated savoring. Fred recalls a TV commercial that featured a close-up view of a partially tilted bottle, from which a trickle of ketchup slowly crept toward a waiting hamburger. The sound track for the commercial was the Carly Simon song, "Anticipation." Watching this commercial when he was particularly hungry, he remembers feeling his mouth begin to water in anticipation. Had he never tasted a hamburger with ketchup before, watching this television commercial would have been a very different experience. The more people know about what the upcoming experience will be like, the more vividly they can create the feelings and sensations of the experience beforehand.

Refocusing by Comparison.   A commonly used strategy for switching gears to initiate savoring is highlighted in the Ways of Coping Checklist (Folkman & Lazarus, 1980). This strategy tends to be a highly moralistic one. If people are feeling low or unsatisfied, they can force themselves (or another person may remind them) to think of other people who are worse off than they are. Note that this tactic entails a downward social comparison aimed at creating positive hedonic contrast with one's current state. This comparative strategy attempts to get people to stop complaining and enjoy the pleasures they are able to have that others do not have. We spoke briefly about such matters earlier in the context of thanksgiving — namely, other people's difficulties can stimulate thankfulness for one's own good fortune. In the context of shifting gears to savoring, downward social comparison is a deliberate strategy to evoke savoring when none is being felt.

However, in helping people initiate savoring, the target of comparison need not be other people. A comparison to a time in one's past experience when life was falling apart, or when one was particularly distressed or worried, can also be strategically used to get oneself into a savoring mode. Reviewing one's own history of adversity can help put some perspective on the here and now that fosters genuine savoring. As the poet Robert Pollok put it in 1828: "Sorrows remembered sweeten present joy."

For example, Fred's wife, Linda, and older daughter, Hilary, often play a game together in which they playfully savor the present by reminding each other of past obstacles they have surmounted and how far they have come. One of them will pretend to complain about something stressful or difficult she is facing, while each knows full well that this particular problem lies in the past and has already been resolved. This counterfactual game of make-believe intensifies savoring of present blessings by refocusing on past stressors, savoring the sense of relief and gratitude, and accentuating progress.

DISTINGUISHING WORLD-FOCUSED AND SELF-FOCUSED TYPES OF SAVORING

So far, we have highlighted distinct types of savoring processes that reflect different strategies for regulating positive experience. However, we can also differentiate general orientations to savoring in terms of whether one's dominant focus of attention when savoring is either outside or inside oneself. That is, when one is savoring, one's attention can be primarily world-focused or self-focused. Most savoring experiences are not wholly one or the other type, but when they approach being that way, important new forms of savoring can be discerned.

Savoring that is world-focused often involves transcendent feelings people experience when participating in overwhelming aesthetic moments, such as the first time one enters a magnificent building like the cathedral at Chartres, or one's first view of a majestic natural wonder like the Grand Canyon. We high-light this important type of savoring shortly. It is certainly dramatically different from the self-focused savoring a person might experience when basking in the warm self-congratulatory glow of success.

By the nature of their personality, some people may be predisposed to savor positive experience with either a world-focused or self-focused orientation. We can speculate that individuals with an external generalized locus of control (Rotter, 1966) tend to savor positive outcomes in world-focused ways, whereas individuals with an internal generalized locus of control (Rotter, 1966) tend to savor positive outcomes in self-focused ways. In addition, people whose personality predisposes them to feelings of guilt and shame may find it easier to adopt a world-focused as opposed to self-focused savoring orientation. We also suggest that narcissism may make people more prone to engage in self-focused savoring, whereas low self-esteem may make it hard for people to engage in self-focused savoring.

In understanding the nature of subjective experience, it is important to consider the general directedness of the focus of attention — that is, whether one focuses inwardly on the self or outwardly on the world (Lambie & Marcel, 2002) — because different focuses of attention permit alternative perceptual orientations to positive experience. This distinction between self (internal) versus world (external) is a common component of many theoretical models of human experience, including work on consciousness (Crook, 1980), personality (Rotter, 1966), motivation (Deci, 1975), causal attribution (Weiner et al., 1971), perceived control (Rothbaum, Weisz, & Snyder, 1982), subjective well-being (Bryant & Veroff, 1984), as well as in the field of philosophy (Sartre, 1939/1962). For example, Rothbaum et al. (1982) have distinguished between attempts to change the world (i.e., primary control) and attempts to change oneself in response to the world (i.e., secondary control).

Research on the construct of inspiration supports this world–self distinction. In particular, Thrash and Elliot (2004) have reported empirical evidence that the feelings of being inspired "by" something or someone (which we would term a world-focused experience) versus being inspired "to" do something (which we would term a self-focused experience) are distinctly different phenomena. Just as we would predict based on this world–self distinction, reported *transcendence* (i.e., spirituality, meaning, and insight) was positively correlated with being inspired "by," but negatively correlated with being inspired "to," whereas reported *responsibility* (i.e., volitional control, self-responsibility, and perceived controllability) was positively correlated with being inspired "to," but negatively correlated with being inspired "by" (Thrash & Elliot, 2004). Thus, self-focused inspiration entails a greater sense of personal responsibility and motivation to act than does world-focused inspiration.

In synthesizing theoretical work on awareness and emotion, Lambie and Marcel (2002) distinguished between self-focused and world-focused attention in relation to emotional experience:

Our present distinction between self-focused and world-focused experience is one of content, but it relies particularly on experienced location and locational directedness. With regard to conscious thought, we distinguish between thoughts of which the focal content is the self and thoughts of which the focal content is the world . . . the self or world can be either figure or ground. Experientially, which one is figure is a matter of attentional focus. A preeminent way of focusing on the self is to attend to (among other information) perceptual modalities or information concerning one's bodily state. Therefore, with regard to self-focused experience, the self is a spatial object defined by focus of attention. In world-focused experience, the self is the ground present but perceptually recessive. In experience, self and world are always in some particular relation. (pp. 235–236)

Adopting Lambie and Marcel's framework, we use the term *world* to denote "either a portion of the world, for example, a person, animal, thing, or group of them, or the whole of what is 'not self'" (Lambie & Marcel, 2002, p. 223). In addition, we consider the experience of self to include not only thoughts, feelings, and behaviors, but also bodily sensations (Bermudez, Marcel, & Eilan, 1995; Lambie & Marcel, 2002).

World-Focused Savoring

World-focused savoring involves an awareness of positive feelings in which people surrender much of their sense of self to something experienced as being outside them or in the world. Because these experiences transcend the usual experience of self, we call this world-focused savoring. There is a sense of communication or merging with something more compelling than our own individual person, such as a work of art, the natural world, another person, or even a supernatural force or being. The critical feature in these transcendent feelings is that during the experience, the source of the positive feelings is primarily identified with something or someone outside the self.

As an example of world-focused savoring, consider the following passage, written by Hudson Stuck (1914/2004), describing his experience of descending from the summit of the highest mountain in North America, during the first complete ascent of Denali (Mount McKinley; 20,320 ft.):

> Only those who have for long years cherished a great and almost inordinate desire, and have had that desire gratified to the limit of their expectation, can enter into the deep thankfulness and content that filled the heart upon the descent of this mountain. There was no pride of conquest, no trace of that exultation of victory some enjoy upon first ascent of a lofty peak, no gloating over good fortune that had hoisted us a few hundred feet higher than others who had struggled and been discomfited. Rather [it] was the feeling that a privileged communion with the high places of the earth had been granted; that not only had we been permitted to lift up eager eyes to these summits, secret and solitary since the world began, but to enter boldly upon them, to take place, as it were, domestically in their hitherto sealed

chambers, to inhabit them, and to cast our eyes down from them, seeing all things as they spread out from the windows of heaven itself. (p. 72)

In this passage, notice the climber's external focus in savoring. In particular, he denies self-focused pride in his accomplishment and instead reports a profound sense of indebtedness to the "high places of the earth," and of being connected to the world and others in communion through a sacred blessing. This type of savoring focuses more on the external world than on oneself. Yet also notice the element of self-focused savoring that opens the passage, when Stuck relishes the feeling of "content that filled the heart" when the "great and almost inordinate desire" to climb the mountain was "gratified to the limit of their expectation." As we noted earlier, most savoring experiences are neither purely world-focused nor purely self-focused, but rather a blend of both.

In its purest form, world-focused savoring involves a sense that a positive figural object outside oneself is irresistibly drawing one toward it — an experience Lambie and Marcel (2002) termed *gerundival perception,* or "an experience a subject has of an object whereby the object strongly implies or 'impels' an action that should be performed with regard to itself" (p. 239). Action-oriented examples of this type of world-focused perception in savoring include "awareness of a 'cake-to-be-eaten,' 'a kitten-to-be-stroked . . . 'a woman-to-be-kissed'" (Lambie & Marcel, 2002, pp. 239–240). As additional examples, we add "a person-to-be-thanked," "a God-to-be-praised," "a wonder-to-behold," "a sight-to-be-marveled-at," "a leader-to-be-followed," and "a person-to-whom-to-surrender-oneself."

In such cases, the positive stimulus object may seem to possess an almost magnetic power to attract the perceiver, as when we describe a person, place, or thing we enjoy as being alluring, charming, tempting, enticing, tantalizing, captivating, mesmerizing, spellbinding, bewitching, bedazzling, enchanting, enthralling, or entrancing. Indeed, to be "entranced" means literally to be in a trance — which the Oxford English Dictionary (Simpson & Weiner, 1989) defines as either (a) "a state of extreme apprehension or dread," (b) "a swoon, a faint;" or (c) "a state of mental abstraction from external things; absorption, rapture, ecstasy" — and to lose one's sense of self in the process.

When adopting a pure world-focus, people experience savoring as primarily an involuntary, uncontrollable positive emotional response to an external stimulus, as when one feels something "tugging at one's heartstrings" or when one craves or feels "addicted" to the positive aspects of such things as chocolate (Hetherington & MacDiarmid, 1993), sex (Griffin-Shelley, 1994), arcade games (Griffiths, 1992), the Internet (Young, 1998), gambling (Mobilia, 1993), tanning (Warthan, Uchida, & Wagner, 2005), running (Chapman & De Castro, 1990), or even mountain climbing (Wickwire & Bullitt, 1998). With an extreme world-focus, the locus of control for the savoring experience resides in the external stimulus rather than in the self — a perception that might direct people's attentional resources toward features of the world around them, and away from efforts to regulate or change the self in order to enhance savoring.

Analyzing world-focused experiences of transcendence, Haidt (2003) termed these phenomena experiences of elevation, in which people feel uplifted, open to experience, and optimistic about the world and humanity, in contrast to experiences of disgust, in which people feel downtrodden, shut off from experience, and cynical toward the world and others. We examine three forms of transcendent feelings in world-focused savoring: thanksgiving, marveling, and surrendering oneself to a person or group.

Thanksgiving. Sometimes people are overwhelmed with gratitude for their blessings, gifts, or achievements, and they outwardly express their appreciation to others or to fate; and often, in our culture, they end up in reverent reflection or prayer to God. People think of their good fortune and attribute it to something or someone external and find themselves overcome with feelings of gratitude to that particular agent. We refer to this savoring process as thanksgiving.

The process of thanksgiving may occur following stressful events, such as near-accidents or recovery from potentially fatal diseases, in which downward counterfactual alternatives are highly salient. It may also occur immediately after an extremely rare positive event, such as winning a lottery; or when one nearly fails to succeed, as when winning an Olympic bronze medal (Medvec, Madey, & Gilovich, 1995). Thanksgiving may occur after much more mundane realizations, such as being aware of good health, a loving spouse, a happy home life, or a job free from stress. These more commonplace experiences of thanksgiving become especially salient when friends or acquaintances encounter health problems, indicate they have tortured conflicts at home, or speak of their gnawing hassles at work.

In the transcendence of thanksgiving, one may have a sense of powerlessness or indebtedness, but neither of these potentially negative feelings mitigates the positive feelings that the person attends to when he or she savors life in a thanksgiving mode. Such feelings of gratitude, in which one is grateful to the gift-giver or source of the outcome, are clearly distinct from feelings of gladness, in which one is simply happy, pleased, or satisfied with a particular outcome (Lindsay-Hartz, 1981). In chapter 7, we argue that the savoring process of thanksgiving can broaden and build spiritual relationships.

Marveling. With marveling, as with thanksgiving, people transcend some of their own sense of self in the savoring moment and concentrate on something outside themselves; but, unlike thanksgiving, the experienced state is not gratitude, but rather awe or wonder in the presence of what is viewed as marvelous. For Fred, it is being on a mountaintop after a challenging climb. For Joe, it is listening to a string quartet playing Beethoven's Rosamousky Quartets. For many of our professional colleagues, it is the beauty of scientific understanding when they ponder discoveries that unlock the mysteries of nature. For the devout, it is sometimes being in the presence of what they view as divine. Marveling as a form of savoring is a type of absorption in the sublime grandeur of something external. It involves an intense, often fleeting experience of awe. Such experiences are more likely to occur when people perceive that the phenomenon to which they are attending is rare or beyond their ability to comprehend (Keltner & Haidt, 2003).

A feeling frequently accompanying awe is a sense of one's own insignificance, which in many other circumstances is an uncomfortable feeling, but which in the context of being overwhelmed with awe is part of the positive transcendence. Indeed, too much refocusing on the self during a world-focused marveling experience could undo the feelings of awe either partially or entirely. Intense self-consciousness and marveling do not go hand in hand.

Surrendering Oneself to Another Person or Group.   Most social joy comes in full awareness of the interactive pleasure of being with another person or a group of other people. People are aware of their own good feelings, the good feelings they are inspiring in others, and the feelings of communion in being together. The pleasure of dancing with another person or a group of others is a good example of this kind of interactive pleasure. And one can savor the moment if the social interaction is attended to as something slightly removed from the self.

But what happens when the self becomes totally immersed in or surrendered to the social connection? We can call that an experience of self-surrender. When we speak of surrendering oneself to another person or group, we deemphasize the interactive quality of the feeling and instead emphasize a focus almost exclusively on the other person or people involved. This experience involves an unbalanced attention to the other. Some religious peak experiences can reflect such surrender, as when one is overwhelmed by the presence of God or by the presence of a sanctified person who one believes is a special ambassador of God. Some sexual loving can also reflect such surrender, as when one actively or passively submits to the seductive overtures and compelling desires of the other without any attention to one's own personal needs. Total obeisance through absorption in a charismatic leader can be similar. So can one's loss of self in a crowd of supporters for a sports team or a political cause.

In each of these instances, we can ask: Is there actual savoring, when in fact the attention is focused totally away from the self? True, there can be joy in that surrender and enjoyment of the merging with the other person or the group. These can be moments of special ecstasy. Such surrender can lead people to do things they normally would not do. For example, after surrendering her life to Christ, Mother Teresa devoted most of her adult life to providing health care for the poorest of the poor in India.

In a sense, with absolute self-surrender people are far away from attending to themselves as parties to any savoring. And as a result, we would say from our theoretical viewpoint that little savoring is going on when there is such ecstasy. In such cases, there is too much absorption in the other person to permit an awareness of one's own experience. People need to draw back into themselves somewhat for savoring to occur. It is hard to know what draws people back into attending to themselves when they are experiencing self-surrender. Perhaps the charismatic person begins to move away. Perhaps the group experience becomes less focused, and people are left with their usual selves to consider. Or perhaps people simply become habituated to the positive experience. At any rate, only something less than total surrender can elicit a savoring mode. Savoring through marveling, thanksgiving, or social connection requires some reemergence of a separate self that can attend to what is being experienced.

Self-Focused Savoring

In chapter 2, we explicated the meaning of the term savoring and asserted that there has to be some mindful focus on what we savor, or "meta-awareness." In self-focused savoring, some aspect of a person (e.g., one's talents, hard work, personality, behavior, or physical body) can become an object of savoring in its own right; and the feelings savored are perceived as originating within the self. In self-focused savoring, on one hand, people might savor the warm kiss of the sun on their bare skin while sunbathing, savor the way their whole body feels during sexual arousal, or relish the sense of recognition they have gotten after receiving an award. All of these positive experiences would involve self-focused savoring, with the person's primary focus of attention being on himself or herself. On the other hand, world-focused counterparts to these same savoring experiences are being awestruck by the sun's awesome power while sunbathing, enjoying the pleasure one gives to a sexual partner, or being overwhelmed by gratitude toward others when receiving an award.

Society often tends to label self-focused savoring as "self-indulgent" or narcissistic because such experiences sometimes seem to be a form of self-glorification. We hesitate to consider all self-focused savoring self-indulgent, because this term has a pejorative meaning, which we do not wish to convey. Indeed, the Latin root of the word indulge is *indulgere*, which means "to be complaisant" (Simpson & Weiner, 1989). Sometimes self-focused savoring *is* self-indulgent, especially when it interferes with a more responsible attitude toward others. However, as often as not, self-focused savoring is not so self-indulgent, but rather reflects simple human pleasure in sensory experience or in appreciation of the way we are or what we have done.

As an example of self-focused savoring, here is a description of the joy of solo scuba diving, written by Philippe Diole (1953), one of the first people ever to use the aqualung underwater:

I continue to go down, slipping over rays of sunlight half strangled by shadow. A silky silence broken by the rhythm of my breathing: a comic gurgling, like pipe bubbles, accompanies my exploration of this endless blue silk. I roll over on my side for the pleasure of lying on a bed made of water. At the same time I bask in my loneliness: the sea surface seems so far away. Someone overhead is throwing pearls into the sea. No, I am wrong, these pearls are born of my breath. (p. 161)

In this passage, notice the diver's focus on himself while savoring. In particular, he finds joy in reveling in the pleasure of motion, cherishing his underwater solitude, and discovering his own breath forming "pearls" in the water overhead. This type of savoring tends to focus, from the outset, more on one's feelings, thoughts, actions, or bodily sensations than on the external world. Yet also notice the element of world-focused "gerundival" savoring that coexists in the passage, when Diole also finds humor in the "comic gurgling" of the "pipe bubbles." Once again, it is rare to find savoring experiences that are exclusively self-focused or world-focused.

In its purest form, self-focused savoring involves a sense of the self as a figural object with the external world in the background. Self-focused savoring experiences can focus on (a) personal thoughts (e.g., happy memories, creative insights, a sense of personal uniqueness); (b) feelings (e.g., pride, pleasure, joy); (c) psychophysical sensations (e.g., goose bumps, chills, racing heart); or (d) behavioral urges (e.g., smiling, laughing, shouting), rather than external stimuli that elicit positive emotional responses. When savoring, an example of self-focused perceptual awareness is the thought, "I am fulfilled," whereas an example of world-focused perceptual awareness is the thought, "The world is fulfilling" (Lambie & Marcel, 2002, p. 239).

There is a sense in which *all* savoring requires a self-focus. Indeed, one must be aware of one's positive feelings while one is feeling them, in order for savoring to occur. Occasionally, however, a savoring experience is entirely focused on the self, with no outward focus on the external world at all, as when one ponders the joy of one's train of thought — this type of experience is what we mean by self-focused savoring. But at other times, an external stimulus can dominate attentional focus in savoring because of its power to evoke strong positive emotions, as when one ponders the mind of a creative genius such as Einstein, although there must still be at least some awareness of one's positive feelings during the experience for savoring to occur — this is what we mean by world-focused savoring.

One can adopt a self- or world-focus with respect to each temporal form of savoring. In savoring through anticipation, self-focused perceptual awareness is of the form, "I will enjoy that," whereas world-focused perceptual awareness is of the form, "That will be enjoyable." In savoring the moment, self-focused perceptual awareness is of the form, "I am enjoying this," whereas world-focused perceptual awareness is of the form, "This is enjoyable." And, in savoring through reminiscence, self-focused perceptual awareness is of the form, "I enjoyed that," whereas world-focused perceptual awareness is of the form, "That was enjoyable."

Viewed with a pure self-focus, one's positive emotional responses may well appear to emanate primarily from inside oneself, as with the personality trait of *exuberance* (Jamison, 2004), in which one describes oneself as feeling alive, ablaze, radiant, bursting with joy, beaming with satisfaction, overflowing with gratitude, bubbling with enthusiasm, filled with zest, gusto, or joie de vivre. With a pure self-focus, the locus of control for the savoring experience resides within the self rather than the outside world—a perception that might direct people's attentional resources toward efforts to regulate or change the self, and away from efforts to change features of the external object in order to enhance savoring.

Self-focused savoring naturally brings with it a self-evaluative frame of mind. According to objective self-awareness theory (Duval & Wicklund, 1972; Silvia & Duval, 2004), when people focus their attention on themselves, they also tend to evaluate themselves, primarily in relation to relevant standards. When people perceive a gap between who they are (actual self) and who they would like to become (ideal self), they experience dejection and depression; whereas when they perceive a gap between who they are (actual self) and who they think they should become (ought self), they experience agitation and anxiety (Higgins, 1987; Higgins, Klein, & Strauman, 1985). This negative affect motivates people to change the self, change the standard, or change the situation (Phillips & Silvia, 2005). A perceived match between the self and the standard of comparison produces positive affect, which rewards the behavior that established the self-standard match (Duval & Silvia, 2002; Duval, Silvia, & Lalwani, 2001).

An objective self-awareness perspective suggests several interesting hypotheses concerning self-focused savoring. For example, because of the heightened emphasis on self-evaluation, people may be more likely to ask themselves, "Am I enjoying myself as much as I should be?" when they are engaged in self-focused savoring, as opposed to world-focused savoring. This suggests that the enjoyment of self-focused savoring experiences may be particularly susceptible to the dampening effects of excessive self-reflection (Schooler et al., 2003). In addition, research reveals that people more closely align their behavior with relevant standards when self-focused (Carver, 1975; Gibbons, 1978; Hormuth, 1982). This evidence suggests that people are more likely to behave in ways that accurately reflect their internal standards about how to experience or express their positive emotions when they are engaged in self- as opposed to world-focused savoring.

Next we examine two forms of self-focused savoring: basking and luxuriating.

Basking. Here we are using the term *basking* metaphorically. "Bask" comes from the Old Norse word, "bathask," which means "to bathe oneself," and generally conjures up images of bathing in the warmth of the sun. For our analysis of self-focused savoring, we wish it to convey the enjoyment of the warmth of reflected accomplishment when one has done something that meets with recognition, admiration, or congratulation from others or from oneself. Along these lines, Cialdini et al. (1976) have studied the phenomenon of "basking in reflected glory," as when football fans derive a sense of pride in celebrating the victories of their favorite team. One of the dimensions emerging from the Ways of Savoring Checklist was a similar savoring strategy that we termed Self-Congratulation. We previously referred to this as a kind of cognitive basking. Basking can occur at the moment of reaching an achievement goal, but it can also occur beforehand in fantasy or anticipation, and can continue afterwards in reminiscence. Basking focuses on a personal victory or achievement, for which responsibility is attributed to oneself. Humans sense their own pride of accomplishment and feel gratified by the personal tributes that others may pay. Indeed, the regulation of pride through the process of basking is inherently linked to the maintenance of self-esteem (see Tracy & Robins, 2004).

Extended public displays of such basking, however, may carry an interpersonal price. Prolonged public basking can disrupt ordinary social interactions, if other people see the person as arrogant, conceited, or flaunting their basking in an obvious way. The threat of such accusations can lead people cursed with overdoses of guilt or modesty to avoid basking as a form of savoring altogether, however justified their feelings of pride may be. In fact, people sometimes prefer private rather than public recognition of their achievements because of concerns about the envious hostility of others (Exline, Single, Lobel, & Geyer, 2004). Indeed, prideful feelings are sometimes considered self-centered hubris in a traditional moralistic society—pride being the first of the seven Deadly Sins. As the Bible puts it, "Pride goes before destruction, and a haughty spirit before a fall" (Proverbs 16:18, Revised Standard Version).

The savoring process of basking has its own discrete form of emotional expression. As Tracy and Robins (2004) demonstrated, prideful basking typically involves "a small smile, with head tilted slightly back, visibly expanded posture, and arms raised above the head or hands on hips" (p. 194). Indeed, independent observers can reliably distinguish the expression of pride from the expression of other positive emotions, such as happiness or excitement, as well as from the expression of negative emotions, such as contempt or boredom (Tracy & Robins, 2004).

Luxuriating.   Another form of self-focused savoring involves delighting or indulging the self in physical pleasure, or what we call *luxuriating*. With this type of savoring experience, people luxuriate in the way their bodies feel. Joe's wife, Jody, spoke of that experience when she mentioned swimming as a savored activity in her life. People think of bodily feelings as being luxuriant when they can extend these sensations for some period of time. Many ordinary savoring moments can produce luxuriant feelings, if people linger with their bodily sensation for a period of time. Men and women deliberately luxuriate in sexual embraces at times when they slow down in lovemaking. Wine tasters luxuriate in the taste of wine when they slow down and sip very slowly and carefully. Most of us can luxuriate in the pleasure of a song, if we listen to it repeatedly.

People can also luxuriate in doing nothing at all as a way to relax, escape, or recharge for a while. Indeed, many people see luxuriant feelings as somehow deserved after a period of stress or hard work, and think of luxuriating as something they owe themselves or to which they are now entitled. As we have noted, luxuriating may be most intense when it follows a period of hard work or physical tension, which can increase hedonic contrast and accentuate pleasure. Relaxation techniques sometimes take advantage of this effect by instructing practitioners to tense their muscles before trying to relax, so as to make the difference between tension and relaxation more obvious.

Yet, such self-focused pleasure is often seen as self-indulgent. Indeed, another term for such luxuriating is "pampering oneself" — a phrase that sometimes has a negative, narcissistic connotation. Indeed, "pamper" is a variant of the Dutch word *pampelen*, meaning to cram voraciously or eat greedily; and its primary and secondary meanings are to (a) indulge oneself with food and feast luxuriously and (b) spoil with luxury or excessively indulge. Nevertheless, people often pamper themselves or others when they believe they need or deserve such special treatment. In extreme luxuriance, people sometimes engage in episodes of bingeing or splurging, in which they lavish excessive amounts of pleasure on themselves. Because the pleasure from these luxuriant feelings is often short-lived, however, the person savoring in this way often feels guilty afterwards. Hence, people who splurge often feel a need to justify their extravagant behavior by saying they deserve it or have earned it. Indeed, the link between self-indulgence and guilt in luxuriating is evident in the root Latin word for "luxuriate," *luxus*, which means "excess." Thus, self-recrimination is the natural enemy of pleasurable luxuriating.

Optimal World- and Self-Focused Savoring

Extending work on gain-savoring (Linville & Fischer, 1991), we suggest that people are motivated to direct their attentional resources toward the world or toward the self in ways that optimize their savoring opportunities and experiences. Although people may find it hard to give their exclusive undivided attention to both the self and the world at exactly the same moment in time, they can nonetheless experience both self and world within the same positive experience at different points in time, or simultaneously in relation to different aspects of the same experience (Lambie & Marcel, 2002). When people adopt a world-focus, however, they may attend more to positive features of stimulus objects than to their own emotional responses, especially at the beginning and at the end of the savoring experience, as they seek to stimulate or sustain their emotional responses, respectively — for example, the first and last sight of a loved one; the first and last bites of a piece of chocolate; the start and close of a symphonic concert; the first and last days of a vacation.

It is often the case that we do not know beforehand when such world-focused savoring experiences will begin or end, as when we stumble upon an unexpected natural sight, such as a rainbow or vista, that adds the joys of discovery and surprise to the pleasurable image. These world-focused experiences are typically not under our own direct personal control, but rather change or remain the same independent of us (although sometimes in a predictable way, as with the sun, moon, or stars). Any cues that suggest a world-focused savoring experience is about to end tends to increase our attentional focus on positive features of the stimulus — we gaze with special intensity at the sunset's last rays; we savor with special relish the last bite of dessert or the last days of summer. This thinking echoes the notion that bittersweet experiences (in which one is about to lose a good thing) possess a unique poignancy and power to evoke savoring. It is easier to savor something when you are more intensely aware of it.

With self-focused savoring experiences, on the other hand, people direct their attentional resources inward when they attempt to intensify or sustain their positive emotions optimally. Because self-focused savoring experiences are often under more direct personal control, there is typically less emphasis on manipulating elements of the immediate environment and more emphasis on cognitive effort in attempting to optimize self-focused savoring.

Deficits in World- and Self-Focused Savoring

Although attentional focus (on self or world) can be induced, the perceiver can also freely choose attentional focus. Nevertheless, "Voluntary control of attentional directedness to self or world requires that these alternative foci must be able to figure in intentions. For this to be the case, there must be distinct representations in some form of self and world" (Lambie & Marcel, 2002, p. 236). This logic suggests that people with blurred or fragmented representations of their inner self or of the outer world may experience problems in savoring. In particular, people who dislike themselves may find self-focused savoring harder, whereas people who distrust the world or others may find world-focused savoring harder.

In addition, over the course of the life span, separation, loss, and trauma may change people's perceptions of themselves or the world around them. For example, people in grief often experience their loss as an injury to the self that a cruel world has inflicted (Parkes, 1996). This loss may alter one's representation of the world, as when people in grief provide "reports of experiencing the world as devoid of objects of interest and of the feeling that the world is a dangerous, insecure place" (Lambie & Marcel, 2002, p. 222). Believing in a maleficent world that threatens the self might make it particularly hard to engage in world-focused savoring. But the sense of loss in grief can also alter one's representation of the self, by shattering one's sense of identity, lowering self-worth, and taking away one's ability to feel pleasure, purpose, hope, or meaning in life (Parkes, 1996). Given the importance of accepting loss in working through grief (Kübler-Ross, 1969), adjusting to disability (Fitzpatrick, 1999), and adapting to older age (Brandtstadter & Wentura, 1995), we suggest that successful resolution of these life challenges may also involve relearning how to find pleasure in a broken world or a wounded self by discovering and creating new ways to engage in world-focused or self-focused savoring.

Day-to-Day Savoring Experiences

As we have emphasized, most day-to-day experiences of savoring are neither as purely world-focused nor as purely self-focused as those we have discussed thus far. Such ordinary "garden variety" savoring involves positive feelings that have elements of both world and self, with neither sphere especially emphasized as the source of the feelings. World-focused savoring has the self as a participant in the feelings to some extent, but the world as the greater source of positive feelings. The opposite is true of self-focused savoring, in which the participation of the world is considered to some extent, but the self is the greater source of positive feelings.

With ordinary savoring experiences, which are neither entirely world-focused nor entirely self-focused, there is the perception that both the world and the self are relatively equal coparticipants. When people savor a meal, they enjoy the taste in their mouths and are aware of the food as the source of the taste at the same time. When people are savoring an outing with friends in a park, they may be simultaneously aware of the fellowship they see residing in the group and their own sense of good feelings of affiliation. Most of us don't concentrate on only one aspect or the other of the experience, as we do in the more extraordinary forms of savoring we have previously discussed. It is important to realize that these ordinary savoring experiences are impossible to differentiate further except by domain and by the strategies people use to prolong or intensify them.

DISTINGUISHING COGNITIVE REFLECTION AND EXPERIENTIAL ABSORPTION

We have distinguished world-focused and self-focused savoring as endpoints on a continuum describing people's orientation toward positive experience. And we have noted that most everyday savoring involves a mixture of both world- and self-focus.

Following Brickman (1978), we now also distinguish two other types of attentional orientations to positive experience: *cognitive reflection* (in which one introspects about one's subjective experience) and *experiential absorption* (in which one minimizes introspection in favor of perceptual engrossment). Concerning this latter distinction, Lambie and Marcel (2002) similarly noted that states of behavioral immersion are distinct from second-order states of analytic cognitive elaboration. We thus allow for two broad classes of savoring experiences involving either mental elaboration (e.g., the WOSC savoring response of Counting Blessings) or behavioral engrossment without cognitive reflection (e.g., the WOSC savoring response of Absorption).

As with all forms of savoring, there must be at least some level of meta-awareness or metacognition (Nelson, 1992) in relation to ongoing positive feelings for reflective or absorptive savoring to occur. When savoring involves cognitive reflection, such meta-awareness is part and parcel of the savoring experience as one fully contemplates and elaborates on one's positive affect. When savoring involves experiential absorption, on the other hand, meta-awareness may be more sporadic and fleeting as one tries to avoid thinking too much about what one is feeling. Nevertheless, in both reflective and absorptive savoring, people are aware they are experiencing positive feelings, although they do not dote on this realization as much when trying to immerse themselves in the experience as when trying to reflect on it.

DIFFERENTIATING FOUR PRIMARY SAVORING PROCESSES

We can combine the distinctions between (a) attentional focus on the world versus on the self and (b) cognitive reflection versus experiential absorption to obtain a potentially useful 2 × 2 classification model of savoring (see Table 5.1). As portrayed in Table 5.1, the savoring processes of thanksgiving and basking primarily involve cognitive reflection, whereas the savoring processes of marveling and luxuriating primarily involve experiential absorption. In addition, focus of attention is primarily outside the self in thanksgiving and marveling, but primarily on the self in basking and luxuriating. We can thus use this classification framework to differentiate four primary savoring processes and their associated positive emotional states.

It is instructive to consider the conceptual and practical benefits of differentiating these four different types of savoring processes—what does this fourfold typology tell us about savoring that we would not know otherwise? And what are the implications of these insights for people's lives? Table 5.2 summarizes some of the main points of similarity and dissimilarity among these four primary types of savoring processes: thanksgiving, basking, marveling, and luxuriating.

As we noted in Table 5.2, the four primary savoring processes differ in terms of the ease with which they can be sustained over time. Note that it may be easier to prolong cognitive reflection than to extend experiential absorption through

TABLE 5.1
Differentiating Four Primary Savoring Processes
and Their Associated Positive Feelings

	Focus of Attention	
Type of Experience	External World	Internal Self
Cognitive Reflection	Thanksgiving (gratitude)	Basking (pride)
Experiential Absorption	Marveling (awe)	Luxuriating (physical pleasure)

one's own conscious effort, due to perceptual and physical habituation. Thus, people may be better able to prolong basking and thanksgiving, as opposed to luxuriating and marveling.

The timing of the affective experience in relation to the positive stimulus also varies across the four savoring processes. Marveling and luxuriating are focused on the present and are rooted in the positive stimulus or event as it is unfolding, whereas people typically engage in basking and thanksgiving after a discrete positive outcome has occurred.

It is also useful to consider factors that enhance each of these four savoring processes. Social interaction augments all four types of savoring processes. For example, other people may facilitate (a) basking by flattering one with praise or making favorable social comparisons, (b) thanksgiving by eliciting or reinforcing one's expressions of gratitude, (c) marveling simply by sharing an awe-inspiring experience, and (d) luxuriating by reminding us how much we deserve to indulge ourselves.

Downward hedonic contrast also enhances all four processes. For example, people can enhance basking by reminding themselves of an earlier time when their personal achievement was only a dream. They can enhance thanksgiving by imagining what it would be like not to have received the blessings or gifts for which they are so grateful. They can enhance marveling by reminding themselves how precious and rare the awe-inspiring external stimulus is. And they can enhance luxuriating by accentuating the difference between the presence and absence of physical pleasure. In addition, sensory-perceptual sharpening, in which one attempts to block out extraneous sensory feedback, may be a more effective strategy for enhancing the sensations that embody experiential absorption (marveling and luxuriating) than for enhancing the thoughts that embody cognitive reflection (basking and thanksgiving).

Consider also the personal and situational factors that inhibit the four main forms of savoring. Some factors would seem to dampen all forms of savoring, as with guilt, low self-esteem, depression, social concerns, time urgency, mindlessness, fatigue, and distraction. Yet other factors are uniquely inhibiting with

TABLE 5.2

Comparing the Four Main Types of Savoring Processes

Criteria	Thanksgiving	Marveling	Basking	Luxuriating
Conceptual definition	acknowledging or expressing gratitude for blessings, gifts, or favors	being struck with awe by an external stimulus, losing sense of self & time	receiving praise or congratulations from self or others	indulging oneself in pleasurable physical sensations
Perceptual stimulus	good fortune or gifts received	great majesty, power, rarity, or mystery in an external stimulus	personal victory or accomplishment	deservingness of pleasure or need for restoration
Focus of attention	world (others, fate, or a deity)	world (external stimulus)	self	self
Type of experience	reverent reflection (outward expressions of appreciation)	reverent absorption in sublime grandeur	cognitive self-reflection (self-praise or self-admiration)	experiential absorption in physical delight
Dominant feeling	gratitude (can be reverent)	awe (can be reverent)	pride	physical pleasure
Real-world examples	victorious athletes crediting God or others, grateful survivors of accidents or disasters, telling others you cherish them	one's first view of the Grand Canyon, viewing an art exhibit, listening to a virtuoso musician, watching a sunset	social compliments, award ceremonies, celebration (which can also include both thanksgiving & luxuriating)	soaking in a Jacuzzi, treating oneself to special luxury, gourmet dining, massage, sexual behavior
Time of experience	before, during, or after a positive event (reactive), or at will (proactive)	during a positive event (in reaction to an unfolding stimulus)	after achievement (reactive) or at will (proactive)	after stress or hard work
Outward expression	head bowed, eyes closed, physically still with serious demeanor	wide-eyed, open-mouthed, immobilized, with goose bumps, chills	self-satisfied smile, head slightly tilted back, expanded posture, with arms raised	eyes closed, satisfied smile, expressive sounds ("mmm" or "ahh")

138

Locus of control for positive outcome	external (though one can also give thanks for internalized personal achievements)	external	internal	internal
Temporal duration of savoring experience	can be prolonged, less subject to habituation	intense, fleeting, harder to prolong, habituation also occurs	can be prolonged, less subject to habituation	harder to prolong, habituation also occurs
Enhancers	downward comparison (social, temporal, or counterfactual)	curiosity, spirituality, mindfulness	internalizing; high self-esteem, downward comparison (social, temporal, or counterfactual); flattery from others	perceived entitlement ("I owe it to myself"); downward hedonic contrast
Inhibitors	upward comparison (social, temporal, or counterfactual), guilt, mindlessness	self-awareness, external distraction, time pressure, mindlessness	externalizing, guilt, depression, low self-esteem, perfectionism, excessive modesty or punitive criticism, upward comparison	guilt or belief in the Protestant Ethic, mindlessness
Potential benefits	thankful gratitude, feelings of self-worth	awe, wonderment, astonishment, amazement, the roots of spirituality	esteem of self or others, self-confidence, ego enhancement	soothing pleasure, physical ecstasy
Potential costs	sense of indebtedness or powerlessness	sense of personal insignificance or existential angst	egocentrism, narcissism, bragging	narcissistic hedonism
Opposite feeling	resentment	horror	shame	pain
Opponent process	holding a grudge	being horrified or traumatized	self-blame	suffering

respect to the particular savoring process involved. For example, excessive modesty and humility dampen basking, and excessive self-consciousness inhibits marveling.

The potential benefits and costs of each form of savoring also shed light on the motives, rewards, and pitfalls of the savoring process. Basking promotes a sense of self-esteem, but at the potential risk of arrogant egocentrism or appearing boastful to others as with bragging. Thanksgiving enhances one's appreciation of positive outcomes, but at the potential risk of resentment for one's subsequent indebtedness to the gift-giver (McWilliams & Lependorf, 1990). Marveling engenders awe and wonder, but can also lead to a sense of powerlessness, insignificance, and existential angst in the face of an overwhelmingly awesome experience. Luxuriating soothes and replenishes the weary body, mind, and soul with self-indulgent pleasure, but can give rise to destructive narcissistic hedonism if pursued single-mindedly.

Negative Opponent Counterparts of the Four Primary Savoring Processes

We propose that each of the four primary savoring processes has its own opposite counterpart in the form of a corresponding opponent process that regulates negative experience (cf. Solomon, 1980). The more attentional resources people devote to one type of process, either positive or negative, the fewer attentional resources they have to devote to the other type of process. Once they are activated, lower order negative concerns tend to block out higher order savoring processes, making it difficult to engage in world- or self-focused savoring via cognitive reflection or experiential absorption. Thus, each negative opponent process impairs people's ability either to give thanks to others, bask in pride, marvel in wonder at the world, or luxuriate in self-focused pleasure. Next we consider the four primary savoring processes, their respective negative opponent processes, and the affects accompanying each.

Gratitude Versus Resentment. The negative counterpart of *thanksgiving,* in which one experiences and expresses gratitude to others for their perceived favors or blessings toward oneself, is harboring a grudge, in which one experiences and expresses resentment or hostile ill-will toward others for their perceived wrongs or transgressions against oneself (Smith, 1759/2000). The Oxford English Dictionary (Simpson & Weiner, 1989) defines resentment as, "A strong feeling of ill-will or anger against the author or authors of a wrong or affront." Concerning the essential oppositional nature of the "moral sentiments" of gratitude and resentment, the philosopher Adam Smith (1759/2000) noted:

> The causes of pain and pleasure, whatever they are, or however they operate, seem
> to be the objects, which, in all animals, immediately excite those two passions of

gratitude and resentment. They are excited by inanimated, as well as by animated objects. We are angry, for a moment, even at the stone that hurts us. A child beats it, a dog barks at it, a choleric man is apt to curse it. The least reflection, indeed, corrects this sentiment, and we soon become sensible, that what has no feeling is a very improper object of revenge. When the mischief, however, is very great, the object which caused it becomes disagreeable to us ever after, and we take pleasure to burn or destroy it. We should treat, in this manner, the instrument which had accidentally been the cause of the death of a friend, and we should often think ourselves guilty of a sort of inhumanity, if we neglected to vent this absurd sort of vengeance upon it. We conceive, in the same manner, a sort of gratitude for those inanimated objects, which have been the causes of great, or frequent pleasure to us. The sailor, who, as soon as he got ashore, should mend [build] his fire with the plank upon which he had just escaped from a shipwreck, would seem to be guilty of an unnatural action. We should expect that he would rather preserve it with care and affection, as a monument that was . . . dear to him. (p. 94)

Thus, hostile resentment is the opposite of loving gratitude, and the process of harboring a grudge is the natural opponent of the savoring process of thanksgiving.

Awe Versus Horror. The negative counterpart of *marveling,* in which one approaches something wonderful, inspiring, or sublime in a state of awe or reverence, is the experience of being horrified or traumatized, in which one recoils from something terrible, threatening, or disgusting in a state of fear or dread. Concerning the essential connection between awe and fear, the English journalist Harriet Martineau (1833) observed, "It is possible to conceive of terribleness, without being in a position obnoxious to the danger of it, and so without fear; and the feeling arising from this contemplation of dreadfulness, ourselves being in safety, as of a stormy sea from the shore, is properly called awe." Indeed, when the hedonic tone of one's focal experience suddenly changes from positive to negative, being amazed and inspired by something awesome quickly shifts to being shocked and horrified by something awful. In the movie *King Kong,* for example, the giant gorilla is displayed in chains onstage in a theater before a live audience, who first marvel in awe as Kong becomes increasingly agitated, then suddenly recoil in horror as he breaks loose and begins to ransack the theater. Thus, horror is the opposite of awe, and the process of being traumatized by something horrifying is the natural opponent to the savoring process of marveling at something awe-inspiring.

Pride Versus Shame. The negative counterpart of *basking,* in which one cognitively congratulates oneself for personal accomplishments or virtues and feels pride, is self-blame, in which one cognitively criticizes oneself for perceived failures or shortcomings and feels shame (Beck, 1976). Indeed, a great deal of theory and research supports the notion that a self-focused locus of causality underlies pride in response to success and shame in response to failure (Weiner et al., 1971). Research indicates that the balance between the frequency of self-affirming and self-critical cognitions — that is, the balance between self-focused basking and shaming — predicts not only overall level of psychological functioning (Schwartz, 1992; Schwartz & Garamoni, 1989), but also level of response to cognitive-behavioral therapy (Garamoni, Reynolds, Thase, Frank, & Fasiczka, 1992). Thus, shame is the opposite of pride, and the negative process of self-blame is the natural opponent of the savoring process of basking.

Pleasure Versus Pain. The negative counterpart of *luxuriating,* in which one enjoys physical pleasure or comfort, is suffering, in which one endures physical pain or discomfort. The pleasure–pain distinction is fundamental to many philosophical and psychological traditions (Higgins, 1997), including those of Aristotle, Buddha, and Freud. Indeed, the English philosopher John Locke (1690/1995) suggested that, "Things are good and evil only in reference to pleasure and pain" (p. 160). At one hedonic extreme is the negative experience of writhing in the agony of physical pain; at the other extreme the positive experience of writhing in the ecstasy of physical pleasure. Thus, pain is the opposite of pleasure, and the process of physical suffering is the natural opponent of the savoring process of luxuriating.

We theorize that when a particular negative opponent process dominates a person's attentional resources, then the person has fewer attentional resources available to devote to the corresponding savoring process. As is well documented, negative experience has a special power to capture and command our attention when the need arises, to the exclusion of other attentional processes (Lambie & Marcel, 2002). Indeed, recent brain-imaging studies indicate that unpleasant stimuli activate an older, more primitive part of the human brain, whereas pleasant stimuli activate a younger, higher order part of the human brain of more recent evolutionary origin (Hamann, Ely, Hoffman, & Kilts, 2002; Paradiso et al., 1999). Consistent with these findings, MacLean (1990) suggested that negative experience primarily engages the older, primitive "reptilian brain," whereas positive experience primarily engages the younger, executive functioning "mammalian brain." We suggest that in order for people to maximize savoring in each of its primary forms, lower order negative opponent processes must be deactivated, so that attentional resources can be freed up for use in relation to the respective higher order savoring processes.

Given this opponent-process model, we can speculate that (a) depressed individuals prone to self-blame and shaming the self may find it particularly difficult to savor via self-focused basking; (b) angry individuals who hold resentful grudges and find it hard to forgive others may have deficits in world-focused thanksgiving; (c) traumatized individuals prone to feelings of fear and vulnerability may have trouble savoring via world-focused marveling; and (d) individuals suffering from pain or agony may have particular difficulty luxuriating in self-focused pleasure. These speculations have important clinical implications for helping people learn to enjoy their lives more fully. Successful treatment for depression, anger-related disorders, trauma, and chronic pain may require not only providing effective coping tools, but also helping people relearn how to activate the specific savoring processes that are blocked by the respective negative opponent processes, in order to bring savoring back more fully into their lives.

SUMMARY

This chapter conceptually differentiates types of savoring processes to set the stage for minitheories adapted to each type. Seven different savoring processes emerged when we considered processes that fulfill the three main functions of savoring (i.e., prolonging, intensifying, or shifting gears to savoring). Concerning processes for prolonging the moment, we considered *reminiscing, chaining,* and *celebration.* Concerning processes for intensifying the moment, we considered *blocking out interfering stimuli* and *heightened focusing on the savoring experience.* We also discussed *sharing the moment* and *adopting a flexible temporal perspective* as processes that both prolong and intensify positive experiences. Concerning processes for shifting gears, we considered *anticipatory planning* and *refocusing by comparison.*

Four primary savoring processes emerged when examining positive experiences that involve primarily either cognitive reflection or experiential absorption in relation to either the self or the world: thanksgiving (world-focused cognitive reflection), marveling (world-focused experiential absorption), basking (self-focused cognitive reflection), and luxuriating (self-focused experiential absorption). We also highlighted another type of world-focused savoring process that primarily involves experiential absorption: *surrendering oneself to another person or group.*

We distinguished among the four primary savoring processes (i.e., thanksgiving, marveling, basking, and luxuriating) in terms of their dominant positive feeling, outward expression, locus of control, temporal duration, potential costs and benefits, and the personal and situational factors that enhance or inhibit savoring. Extending the clinical implications of this conceptual model, we proposed that each of the four primary savoring processes has a lower order negative counterpart or "opponent process" that, when activated, captures attentional resources and precludes that particular type of higher order savoring experience. Hostile resentment prevents thanksgiving. Trauma and feelings of vulnerability impair marveling. Depressive self-blame interferes with basking. Finally, pain and suffering prevent luxuriating.

6

Savoring and Time Orientation

*The present is the ever moving shadow
that divides yesterday from tomorrow.*
—Frank Lloyd Wright (1958)

Time plays a profound role in many aspects of savoring. Indeed, we have touched on temporal concepts throughout our discussions of savoring. In chapter 2, we emphasized that, although savoring was a process for the here and now, there are savoring experiences that partake of the past and savoring experiences that partake of the future. When people actively invoke positive feelings in reminiscing, they may be using savoring processes to examine the past. When people actively invoke positive feelings in anticipating what might or will happen in the future, they may be using savoring processes to consider the future. In chapter 3, we discussed ways in which time can turn positive experiences bittersweet, sometimes enabling people to savor them more fully. In chapter 4, some of the savoring strategies we discussed (e.g., memory building, comparing, temporal awareness, and more generally, prolonging the moment) reflected potential reminiscence or anticipation that might contribute to various savoring processes. We also pointed out, however, that people who have too strong a future orientation to what they are doing might find it hard to savor their ongoing lives.

In this chapter, we explicitly adopt a temporal perspective on the process of savoring to expand on these essential points. All of the types of savoring responses we identified in chapter 4 will potentially come into play here, although they may be components of a recalled or anticipated event. To bolster the points we make, we draw on relevant research findings, including our own studies.

SAVORING THE PAST

For he lives twice who can at once employ
The present well, and ev'n the past enjoy.
(Alexander Pope, 1730/1879)

When the future begins to shut down on older people as they advance in years, there is a common tendency for them to turn to the past as a source of gratification. When in their 60s and 70s and beyond, people often have more opportunity to savor their past, the life they have lived, the places they have been, the things they have done, and the lives of people they have touched or who have touched them. Older adults can enjoy reminiscing as a way to see their lives in perspective (Sedikides et al., 2004). They often use reminiscence as a common style of engaging with life, with perhaps some of this reminiscence being savoring of what once was. Reminiscence can also provide a source of positive experience for the elderly, either by bolstering self-esteem (Lewis, 1971; McMahon & Rhudick, 1967) or by generating pleasure and enjoyment for its own sake (Hughston & Merriam, 1982; Thornton & Brotchie, 1987). There is even evidence that reviewing one's life retrospectively promotes well-being among the elderly (Coleman, 1974; Fallot, 1979–1980; Lewis & Butler, 1974). We highlight these findings in chapter 7 when we discuss the positive health implications of savoring processes. We suggest that people of any age can profitably spend time reviewing their lives and savoring past memories, and we present data from college students that highlight the value of savoring the past for this younger age group.

Thinking about the past, especially when men and women are able to recharge memories with rich sensory overlays, can occupy attention for long periods. These memories can be of past experiences that occurred seconds ago or they can be experiences that go back many years. When they savor through reminiscence, people are not necessarily remembering savoring experiences from the past. Rather, they are savoring the way they feel when they remember the past. They may experience traces of some original savoring events, but that's not always the point in savoring the past.

Many people can, like a camera, go over specific details about the way a room or house from childhood looked. Thus, remembering details can be part and parcel of what is being savored. If one views reminiscence not as a highly sentimental or simple nostalgia trip, but as a process for establishing deep reconnections with persons and places of the past, it can be conceived as identity-giving. In reminiscence, humans can remember who they are, where they came from, and who and what has been important in their lives. Often one can have new insights about these connections, especially if such savoring is in the company of others who can offer some missing pieces to the memory puzzle.

Two Studies of Reminiscence and Savoring in Young Adults

In this section, we differentiate savoring processes within reminiscences that are strongly felt and often partake in identity-giving functions from savoring processes that are weakly felt and have little connection to self-affirmation. We begin with some research Fred has done with two of his graduate students, Scott King and Colette Smart, exploring the connection of positive reminiscence (i.e., recalling pleasant memories) to savoring (Bryant, Smart, & King, 2005). This research had three main goals: (a) to determine why people reminisce about positive memories, and what function it serves in their lives; (b) to discover the strategies people use to stimulate and intensify their recall of the past, and whether some styles of reminiscing are associated with greater levels of happiness; and (c) to explore possible gender differences in reminiscence in terms of whether men and women differ in how often they reminisce, what they reminisce about, how they go about reminiscing, and the consequences of their reminiscence. All three research goals are relevant to savoring the past.

In the first of two studies, Bryant et al. (2005) asked a sample of 180 volunteers a variety of different questions about reminiscing and about happiness. This sample consisted of students from Loyola University Chicago and from the University of Illinois at Chicago, as well as middle-aged and older Loyola alumni. The participants filled out a 10-page paper-and-pencil questionnaire that included questions about what, how, when, and why they typically reminisced (see Bryant & Morgan, 1986). Respondents also indicated how capable they felt of enjoying their life, as measured by the Perceived Ability to Savor Positive Outcome scale (PASPO; Bryant, 1989).

So, what did the data reveal? First, the situation in which people were most likely to reminisce about positive memories was when they were feeling sad or blue. More than three times as many people (36% vs. 10%) said they typically reminisce when they feel bad as said they typically reminisce when they feel good. This finding suggests that reminiscing about positive memories, a process we identify as savoring the past, can serve as a coping strategy aimed at reducing or eliminating emotional distress of the present. There is no clear evidence, however, that recalling happy memories when one feels sad is savored for its own sake, or gives the person much in the way of positive self-affirmation.

Consistent with the view of savoring the past as a coping strategy, the most commonly mentioned reason for reminiscing was to gain new perspective and self-insight toward present problems. Roughly a third (29%) of the participants indicated that they reminisced about positive memories to help them handle problems better. The next most common reasons for reminiscing were to make oneself feel good (19%) and to escape from the present (18%).

There were also some interesting gender differences in the antecedents and consequences of positive reminiscence. Women reported a greater capacity than men to enjoy life based on their scores on the PASPO scale. In addition, women more than men said they reminisced in order to gain insight and perspective, which was associated with feeling better able to savor life. Men more than women reported that they reminisced to escape the present, which Bryant et al. (2005) found to be negatively related to perceived savoring ability.

And what about people's styles of reminiscing? When asked if they consciously did or thought anything to help them intensify their recall of pleasant memories, 7 out of 10 people (71%) responded "yes." These results support the view that savoring past memories can be part of a planned strategy. Among participants who reported using a recall strategy, nearly two thirds (61%) mentioned that they primarily relied on behavioral strategies to intensify recall. These behavioral strategies for reminiscing included looking at memorabilia (23%), sharing memories with others (14%), playing music associated with the pleasant memory (13%), and trying to reenact behaviorally the events associated with the pleasant memory (13%). About one third (39%) of the sample, in contrast, mentioned that they primarily used cognitive imagery to intensify their recall of pleasant memories. Using cognitive imagery involves creating a picture of the past event in one's mind. Another third of the sample said that they thought or did nothing in particular to try to intensify their reminiscing.

But what about the relationship between savoring beliefs and reminiscence? How does reminiscing relate to one's perceived ability to savor life? Are certain styles of reminiscing associated with greater levels of happiness? First, the more time people reported reminiscing about positive memories, the stronger their savoring beliefs. In other words, the more often people reminisced about pleasant memories, the more they felt they could savor life. Again, this provides further support for the notion that reminiscing about past positive events can serve an adaptive function in people's lives.

However, the benefits of reminiscence also depended both on one's reasons for reminiscing and on the way in which one went about reminiscing. First, those who said they used reminiscence primarily to gain perspective and self-insight reported a greater capacity to savor life than did those who used reminiscence primarily to escape from the present. This result suggests that the greater adaptive value of reminiscence is not so much as a form of escape from present problems, but rather as a constructive tool for increasing awareness and providing a sense of perspective in the present, perhaps even a sense of self-affirmation.

To give the reader a better feel for these different uses of reminiscence, here are some responses that typify what participants told Bryant et al. (2005). First, here is the response of a male participant, who reminisced primarily for escape:

I reminisce when I'm bored or really stressed-out. I think about when I was a kid and had no problems or worries. . . . This helps me stop worrying for a while, but then I've always got to come back to the here and now. And when I do, I feel worse. I end up asking myself why it has to be like this, why it can't be like it was when I was a kid, and I get angry and depressed.

Here, on the other hand, is the response of a female participant, who reminisced primarily to gain perspective and self-insight:

Thinking of good times from the past makes me feel better about the present. It helps me appreciate things more. It gives me an idea of where I was then, where I am now, and where I ultimately want to be. It helps me understand the present and deal with it. . . . These memories also give me a sense of confidence—kind of a "you did it before, you can do it again" type of thing. If things are bad, I use my memories to start thinking of ways to make it better rather than thinking about how bad it is.

Reminiscing about pleasant memories in order to escape present problems in the long run may be maladaptive because it makes one's current situation seem even worse in contrast to the pleasant past. Savoring the past to escape the present creates an upward hedonic contrast between present problems and the more pleasant past, further eroding current happiness. Reminiscing in order to gain motivation, perspective, or self-insight, on the other hand, may be more adaptive because it provides something constructive that one can bring back to the present to help solve ongoing problems. Earlier we suggested that savoring can be adaptive or maladaptive depending on the consequences, and that savoring was not automatically adaptive. The different orientations to savoring memories featured here are good examples of both maladaptive and adaptive savoring.

The benefits of reminiscence, however, also depend on how people go about recalling the past. Specifically, Bryant et al. (2005) found that people who consciously used some particular strategy to intensify memory recall felt better able to enjoy life than did those who lacked a specific strategy for intensifying memory recall. Furthermore, those who relied primarily on mental imagery to intensify their reminiscence had stronger savoring beliefs than those who relied primarily on behavioral strategies, such as looking at memorabilia, to intensify reminiscence. In other words, cognitive imagery seems more effective in intensifying reminiscence than behavioral approaches, such as looking at souvenirs and photographs.

To explain this finding, Fred and his students speculated that when people use a photograph of an event or place to trigger a memory, they're somewhat confined by the limits of the photograph. We see what the picture contains, but do not see the details that it omits. If thoughts are used to trigger the memory, on the other hand, then we can embellish the mental picture and add as many details as we might like. Also, thoughts are always available, stored away in the mind and connected to many aspects of the self. A picture, in contrast, must be physically present to trigger the memory.

In their second study, Bryant et al. (2005) tested some of these ideas in a randomized field experiment, in which students thought about their lives in one of three different ways for 10 minutes twice a day for a week. In an initial pretest, participants listed all of the personal mementos (e.g., memorabilia, photographs, gifts, awards, and souvenirs) of happy times from the past that they readily had physical access to each day, and they then briefly described the specific positive memory associated with each particular cherished object.

After each 10-minute "thinking session," participants completed an open-ended form describing the session, and answered closed-ended questions about the experience. Both before and after the weeklong experiment, participants completed a questionnaire assessing the frequency of happy feelings during the past week (Fordyce, 1988).

According to a random schedule, participants received one of three different sets of experimental instructions for how to think about their lives. They were asked to review these instructions before each thinking session. In the cognitive imagery condition, participants were instructed as follows:

> First, turn to your list of positive memories and choose one to reflect upon. Then sit down, take a deep breath, relax, close your eyes, and begin to think about the memory. Allow images related to the memory to come to mind. Try to picture the events associated with this memory in your mind. Use your mind to imagine the memory. Let your mind wander freely through the details of the memory, while you are imagining the memory.

In the memorabilia condition, participants were instructed for each thinking session to turn to the initial inventory of memorabilia and associated positive memories and choose one of these pieces of memorabilia to reflect on. Participants in both experimental groups were told they could either choose the same or a different object (or memory) for each thinking session. For each thinking session, participants in the memorabilia condition were instructed as follows:

> First, turn to your list of mementos and choose one to reflect upon. Next, retrieve this object from where you keep it. Then sit down with it, take a deep breath, and relax while holding the object in front of you. Begin to think about the memory associated with the memento. Allow images related to the memory to come to mind. Try to keep focusing on the object. Let your mind wander freely through the details of the memory, while you are looking at the memento.

Note that both the cognitive imagery and memorabilia groups reminisced about memories associated with personal mementos in their thinking sessions. However, the former group relied on mental imagery in reminiscing, whereas the latter group relied on the personal memento itself in reminiscing. This procedure equated the two experimental groups in terms of the recency, content, and richness of the particular memories they recalled.

In the control condition, participants were instructed as follows:

> First, think about any event, circumstance, or issue that is of interest or concern to you these days. Then sit down, take a deep breath, relax, close your eyes, and begin to think about the event, circumstance, or issue that you've chosen to focus on. Allow any thoughts to come to mind while you think about the topic you've chosen to focus on. Let your mind wander freely through the details of the topic, while you are thinking about your chosen topic.

This control condition was added to the design so as to include a group of participants who spent an equivalent amount of time sitting quietly by themselves, relaxing, and thinking about life events in general, compared to the two reminiscence groups.

Confirming hypotheses, participants who reminisced showed greater increases in the reported percentage of time they felt happy during the past week, compared to participants in the control group. This result is consistent with the positive correlation between happiness and frequency of positive reminiscence found in Study 1, and it demonstrates that positive reminiscence can boost happiness.

But the strength of the affective benefit gained from reminiscing also varied depending on whether one used cognitive imagery or memorabilia to stimulate recall. Specifically, participants who reminisced using cognitive imagery showed a stronger increase in reported levels of happiness over the week-long period than did those who reviewed memorabilia to stimulate reminiscence. Consistent with earlier interpretations, those who relied on cognitive imagery reported that their reminiscing was more vivid and detailed than did those who relied on memorabilia. Supporting prior research (Strack, Schwarz, & Gschneidinger, 1985), additional analyses revealed that the perceived vividness of recalled memories, but not the amount of detail in memories, partially mediated the relationship between reminiscing with cognitive imagery and greater increases in happiness. These results support the notion that mental imagery enhances people's ability to reminisce in vivid, actively involving ways that promote an adaptive savoring of the past.

Savoring and Storytelling

Some reminiscences take the form of a story. People often impose some dramatic form on their memories, and when they do, the memories can give rise to savoring processes. In a story, people can recast their lives and make them more interesting. Along these lines, sometimes people actively write stories about their past, either as slightly disguised fiction or as autobiography. Sometimes they just orally recount past experiences to another person or group, perhaps in an everyday conversation. Indeed, it has been argued that people's personal identity is based on the particular stories they tell about themselves (McAdams, 1993).

Whether in writing or face to face, stories can be savored by both the person telling the story and the audience who receives it. If storytellers attend a great deal to the reactions or potential reactions of the audience, they may distract themselves from the feelings involved in the experiences they are recounting. The best story-tellers may not necessarily be those who are actively savoring their experience while they are retelling it, although there is often a communication of strong savoring when the story is told by a person well known as a raconteur.

Narrative truth does not have to conform completely to historical truth, especially when people are savoring their past. The storyteller often has some poetic license. Men and women often tell their personal stories to friends, lovers, children, and grandchildren. Somehow, savoring a story about oneself told to a loved one, who also seems to be savoring what is being told, can be one of the most gratifying social exchanges people experience. Joe reports that he and his wife have noticed that they occasionally retell each other the same story they had told a number of times in the past, but they don't tell each other that they have heard it before. It is not mere politeness. The story is enjoyable the 34th time around because there are nuances to the new way of telling the same general story that comes from the specific new context in which it is being told, nuances that add facets to the old story that were never conceived or heard before. Thus, interest is maintained. Unless a person is suffering from considerable dementia and is constantly repeating the identical story within moments of having just told it, most of us still savor hearing the "same" story retold, and the storyteller savors retelling it. By such means our lives are constantly refreshed, even without dramatic changes in life circumstances.

Further expanding on retelling stories with his wife, Joe noted the following about an important story in their lives that they tell themselves and others — how they met:

We met in the library. She [Jody] needed a book that I had for a course we were both taking. We were sitting at the same table and she asked to borrow the book. I had had my eyes on her from afar, but being a bit shy about these matters smiling at her from a distance was about the most I could muster. To be helpful to this lovely woman without a book gave me the necessary courage to ask her to join me in coffee when the closing time in the reading room was upon us. She did join me and we haven't stopped talking to each other since. We soon became an item and remained so through some rather difficult times, especially my coming down with polio in our second year of study. There were a couple of periods of separation. Our families were not supportive, mine because Jody was not Jewish, hers because I was Jewish, and disabled besides. We were married without their blessings, but with full support from our fellow graduate students, after our third year. Our first child was born in our fourth year of graduate study.

Joe reports that this story gets told and retold. Sometimes the emphasis is on how they met, sometimes on the misgivings that came up, sometimes on family battles, sometimes on coping with health problems, sometimes on how to do a wedding, sometimes on becoming parents so quickly into a marriage. Joe reports further that he and his wife tend to overlook the times of separation before they were married, which they interpret as an indicator of the happiness that exists in their married life.

Undoubtedly, the social context for retelling a story promotes one emphasis or another. If Joe or Jody told their story to a couple about to be married, then this context would probably evoke more details about the wedding than if they told the story to someone who was mostly interested in how Joe and Jody became a couple in the first place. In any case, people can savor their past in new ways as they retell a story. The past can become part of a person's life, as if the past were part of the present.

Some research Joe conducted with Holmberg (reported in Holmberg & Holmes, 1994) focuses on how such courtship stories are retold. They found that some couples who told the story of their courtship a few months into their first year of marriage and then again 2 years later showed some interesting changes in the affectivity of the courtship stories. Among 13 couples whose first year of marriage was equally happy, those whose levels of happiness decreased from year 1 to year 3 recalled in the third year more negative feelings and ambivalence during the courtship than did couples whose levels of happiness did not decline over time. Thus, the savoring of memories from courtship may remain prominent in couples who remain happily married.

Like many general conclusions in the study of marital relationships over time, however, further analyses made the picture more complicated. Holmberg, Orbuch, and Veroff (2004) examined a broader sample of 144 couples who remained married after 7 years and told their courtship story not only in the first and third year of marriage but also in the seventh year. The researchers' analyses discovered a different effect than Holmberg and Veroff found earlier. In particular, they found that many couples who were savoring positive reports of their courtship were couples whose marriages were in trouble. The savoring of past memories was therefore seen as a contrast to what married life was currently like for them. Thus savoring the past might reflect regrets about the present. The researchers were unable to determine when savored memories about courtship reflected ongoing well-being, as opposed to a contrast to ongoing difficulties in marriage. It would be important to isolate factors that moderate this effect.

Reminiscence as a Substitute for Living in the Present.   As soon as we acknowledge that savoring the past may reflect some kind of unhappiness with the present, we can ask the question of whether savoring through reminiscence can potentially interfere with savoring the ongoing present. Indeed, reminiscence can have a connotation of escape. We have already suggested that a masculine stereotype for reminiscing is that it is a retreat from the present and the future. It could also be the case that older people who lack an active current life can turn to what has been, as a way to revisit a time when they had an active ongoing life. This may occur especially after a reluctant retirement or after an important person in their life, such as a spouse or child, has died. When one's reminiscences take that turn, we argue, they function mainly as a substitute for life as it is and represent a form of living in the past.

For example, Joe's grandmother arrived in the United States from Eastern Europe in her middle years and never did accommodate to living in the new country. She was forever telling Joe and others about her past life in the old country, not necessarily because she savored it so, we might say, but because it was the only real life with which she ever felt comfortable. Her new life was always as a stranger in the new land. This may be another instance where savoring might be maladaptive because the savoring prevented her from coping with her present life.

We might also say that Joe's grandmother's absorption in the past was not necessarily savoring. She seemed to lack any conscious appreciation of her past and the positive feelings it evoked. Too much of her identity depended on the reminiscences.

Although enjoying an unfolding positive moment is the essence of savoring, some writers have suggested that we are never really able to appreciate a good thing fully until it passes. In other words, we don't know what we've got till it's gone. As Shakespeare observed in *Much Ado About Nothing:*

> For it so falls out
> That what we have we prize not to the worth
> Whiles we enjoy it, but being lacked and lost,
> Why then we rack the value, then we find
> The virtue that possession would not show us
> Whiles it was ours.   (Shakespeare, 2002)

Clearly, life may seem more positive in retrospect than people experience it in the present.

SAVORING THE FUTURE

It has been a thousand times observed, and I must observe it once more, that the hours we pass with happy prospects in view are more pleasing than those crowned with fruition.   —Oliver Goldsmith (1766/1982)

Although we have claimed that the prototypical savoring experience occurs when we are appreciating something positive that is unfolding right at the moment, we have also acknowledged that people can savor ideas and images of things that they are striving to make happen in the future (their plans or goals in life), are hoping will happen in the future (their dreams for their lives), or are merely wishing would happen in the future or even right at the moment (their fantasies). These imaginings cannot be discounted in the list of things people savor. Although some of these images of the future can be ephemeral and rather vague, so that people mostly savor the feelings they will have if they obtain their goals or fulfill their dreams, other images of the future are quite concrete.

For example, we have talked to some students who have a clear notion of what their experiences at a graduation exercise would be, proudly surrounded by their happy family. Some never-married people can imagine their wedding—what everyone would be wearing and what they would look like. Some people can imagine the floor plan of their first home. Such fantasies can be wildly imaginative and delicious in their specific detail. James Thurber's *The Secret Life of Walter Mitty*, a short story about a meek young man's adventures through his bold and exciting alter egos, was easy to adapt to the screen because Thurber was rich on the details about these other imaginary lives.

Remember, we are speaking of savoring the future, not just considering the future. Most Americans are quick to take the future into account in their planning and dreaming, but whether they savor these plans or dreams is another matter. Although people may be mindful about the future, they usually have few enjoyable feelings explicitly attached to that mindfulness, particularly in comparison to the wider range of positive feelings associated with the past. In fact, we have stated in a number of places that being overly attentive to the future often stands in the way of savoring the present.

SAVORING THE PRESENT
BY ANTICIPATING THE FUTURE

Before a pleasurable moment occurs, it is often possible to look forward to it, to imagine what it will be like, and to savor it through the joy of anticipation. What is required in this future-focused form of savoring, in contrast to the present-focused savoring of the moment, is an ability to actively fantasize about a pleasurable moment that has not yet occurred.

Anticipation is a very special form of savoring because it demands that one transcend the here and now, and construct a pleasurable moment in one's mind entirely from scratch. Unlike savoring the moment, there is no ongoing experience from which to derive joy. And unlike reminiscence, there are no memories of the future moment to get one started (that is, unless one is anticipating the repetition of an early positive experience). With anticipation, individuals must create the experience purely by fantasy, by imagining how it might unfold, or perhaps by projecting a future like the circumstances they have already encountered. Perhaps this explains why people typically report they are least able to savor their lives through anticipation, compared to the other two time frames (Bryant, 2003).

In the Holmberg et al. (2004) study of newlyweds mentioned earlier, many husbands and wives who told their thoughts about the future spoke about topics with which they were already familiar—for example, what their jobs or housing might be like. Many newlyweds, on the other hand, spoke about having children in the future. Although some of these newlyweds entered marriage with children, most did not, and so for these people their anticipation of future parenthood was without precedence. Given their lack of certainty about the future, we expect the savoring in these newlyweds' accounts of the future, especially about becoming a parent, to be minimal. Supporting this prediction, only 12% of the future stories told by the newlyweds had any affective content at all, unlike the much higher percentage of stores with affective content that they told about the past and present state of their relationship. Thus, people may encounter certain obstacles to initiating the capacity to savor when considering unknown future prospects. If people focus on a more certain future, on the other hand, one they can concretely imagine, then it should be easier for them to experience savoring when adopting this future perspective.

While being thoughtful and mindful about the future can, under the right circumstance, enhance a person's savoring of the present, it can sometimes have a negative effect. On one hand lies the person's joy of looking forward, the warm, savoring preglow of the upcoming moment. One can literally wallow in this delectable anticipatory joy, envisioning the future event in any form imaginable. People can fantasize that the upcoming event will be overwhelming in its splendor, that it will be the happiest moment of their life, and that it will magically transform them in some special way. They can embellish the future event in any way they want, adding tantalizing details, elaborating and refining the fantasy to heighten the imaginary relish. All these mental reconfigurations of the experience provide people with joy before the experience has even happened, and as a consequence they end up feeling positive about the present as well.

On the other hand, in anticipation lies the potential specter of disappointment. As Argyle (1987) put it, ". . . if someone has high hopes for an event, and these are not realized, he or she will be less pleased than if nothing was expected" (p. 146). The more people idealize an upcoming event, the more they may exaggerate its positive qualities. The more perfect they imagine the future event will be, then the more likely the actual event may be to fall short of what they anticipated, and the more disappointed they are likely to feel as a consequence (Wilson, Lisle, Kraft, & Wetzel, 1989). It's hard for something to live up to expectations that are sky-high. Mitchell and Thompson (1994) speak of a similar phenomenon. In particular, they have identified a process that involves the *dampening* of positive current experiences compared to both anticipated and remembered ones. We discuss this effect in the next section on rosy prospection and rosy retrospection.

But when it comes to anticipating and savoring the moment, it may be possible to have your cake and eat it, too. The way to prevent anticipation from dampening present affect is to strike a balance between what we savored in anticipation and what we savor in the present. This balance can be achieved by avoiding direct comparisons between prior expectations and present reality. In other words, people may be able to have the best of both worlds (i.e., both anticipatory savoring and on-the-spot savoring) if they look forward with delight before the upcoming event, but then forget about their expectations (especially comparisons with what they thought their pleasures would be) once the event actually occurs.

But anticipation also has another downside. Looking forward to something positive not only runs the risk of future disappointment, but also tends to diminish the joy of surprise. To anticipate an upcoming positive experience, one must know beforehand that it is about to occur; but to be surprised by joy, there can be no forewarning, no prior knowledge, no expectation. Indeed, the surprisingness of events makes people notice them and become more mindful of these events, whereas anticipation may decrease uncertainty and thereby reduce mindfulness. Although surprise might enhance the intensity of people's initial enjoyment of positive events, however, anticipation might enrich the sense of meaning people find in positive events over time, as they realize they are now experiencing something once only hoped for.

There are other potential drawbacks to future-focused savoring. In our survey research with college students and older adults, respondents have mentioned various additional reasons why they prefer not to spend time anticipating a positive event before it happens. Some people equate anticipating with "counting your chickens before they've hatched" or "putting the cart before the horse," which they believe is arrogant and presumptuous. Others superstitiously believe that to anticipate good fortune tempts Fate and may jinx the future by sabotaging the outcome. Still others believe that time and attention spent daydreaming about the future are better devoted to working in the present to make the desired outcome actually happen. Finally, other people report that imagining what an upcoming pleasure will feel like makes it harder to get back to more mundane everyday work and makes it more painful to endure having to wait for the upcoming pleasure, which remains tantalizingly out of reach.

Indeed, the word "tantalize" comes from the ancient Greek myth of King Tantalus of Sipylus, whom Zeus invited to dine with the gods, but who stole ambrosia and shared it and the gods' secrets with humans (Zimmerman, 1964). As punishment, Zeus banished Tantalus to the underworld, forever imprisoned up to his chin in water, which receded whenever he tried to drink it. Suspended above his head were delicious fruits, which the wind blew out of his reach whenever he tried to touch them. And, as if that weren't enough, above Tantalus' head Zeus also placed a delicately balanced boulder, poised to fall at any moment. Zeus really knew how to put a damper on savoring. Clearly, it's hard to look forward to something good that always seems just out of reach (especially when a big problem is hanging over you).

Nevertheless, there can be no doubt that, by anticipating a pleasant future event, people often enhance their savoring of the present moment as they anticipate the future. As we have noted, this phenomenon can be especially powerful when people find themselves anticipating telling others about a pleasurable moment they are currently experiencing. The idea that thinking about sharing the moment later can enhance savoring now is similar to the notion that expressing our feelings to others may intensify these feelings.

The joy of looking forward to sharing the memory of the present moment in the future illustrates the amazing richness and complexity of time in relation to savoring. On the mountaintop, Fred was anticipating — that is, enjoying beforehand — the pleasure of reminiscing about the present in the future. In other words, he was looking forward to looking back on the here and now (or what we term *anticipated recall*). Similarly, when he was on the summit, he reminisced with his friends about how much they had looked forward to sharing the moment (or what we term *recalled anticipation*). In other words, they looked back on when they had looked forward to the here and now. This uniquely human capacity to time-travel in our minds holds one of the important keys to savoring.

THE PHENOMENA OF ROSY PROSPECTION AND RETROSPECTION

Basing their ideas on cognitive information processing theory, Mitchell and Thompson (1994) spelled out the conditions under which a person may evaluate a current positive event as being either less positive than what he or she had expected to experience (*rosy prospection*), or less positive than what he or she later remembers experiencing (*rosy retrospection*). In explaining these effects, Mitchell and Thompson (1994) suggest that such phenomena are most likely to occur when the events themselves are: clearly positive and not negative; clearly ego-involving and not ego-distancing (e.g., visiting a close friend as opposed to visiting an unknown dignitary); self-contained as opposed to having many further connections to other events; and not weighty in their implications. In addition, they posit that the phenomena occur only when the person experiencing the event has some personal control over the outcome and also realizes that the event is not determined by external circumstances. Thus, their theory does not apply to all positive events. Nevertheless, the theory is intriguing, and the results supporting it are exciting and quite relevant to our discussion of savoring the past or future.

Adopting a cognitive perspective, Mitchell and Thompson (1994) argue that any given event is evaluated overall by taking into consideration various aspects of that particular event. Which aspects are considered and how much weight is given to each of these can help explain why overall evaluations of that particular positive event (as it is experienced, as it is remembered, or as it is anticipated) may be different in different time periods. Rosy prospection or rosy retrospection can occur under any one of the following conditions: (a) if certain negative features of the event are omitted either before or after the event; (b) if certain positive features that actually never occurred are injected before or after the event; or (c) if positive features are weighted more favorably either before or after the event than during the event. Any one of these conditions by themselves can produce the rosy phenomena, but if they operate together the rosy effects are even more likely to occur.

There are many reasons why these conditions differentiate affective reactions to current events from affective forecasts or recollections. Table 6.1 lists the various processes that Mitchell and Thompson (1994) discussed as giving rise to the conditions just enumerated.

By themselves, these are exciting propositions about how, under certain conditions, people may savor the future or past more than they would the present. They are all the more exciting when one realizes that some of them have been demonstrated experimentally. In particular, Mitchell et al. (1997) described three studies, each encompassing different positive events: a 12-day tour of Europe, a Thanksgiving vacation, and a 3-week bicycle trip across California. Assessing college students' enjoyment prospectively, concurrently, and retrospectively, they found evidence of rosy phenomena in all three studies.

TABLE 6.1
Processes Effecting Rosy Prospection
and Rosy Retrospection

---

1. *Ambiguity effects:* Enhanced positive regard can occur when there is ambiguity about the event, and generally there is more ambiguity about the past and future than the present.

2. *Availability effects:* In general, positive aspects of the past or future more readily come to a person's mind than do positive aspects of the present.

3. *Effect of constructing a story:* A consistent positive constellation of ideas about an event is more likely to emerge when people construct a story about an event, and people are more likely to construct a story before or after an event occurs than while an event is occurring.

4. *Effect of distraction:* More negatively distracting aspects of events can occur in experiencing the present compared to anticipating it or remembering it.

5. *Environmental interferences:* Negative environmental factors take greater precedence in appraising the present compared to the past or future.

6. *Effects of regret and disappointment:* Both the phenomena of regret and disappointment elicit more salient negative feelings about the present than they do about anticipatory or remembered feelings.

Note. See Mitchell and Thompson (1994).

In the European Tour Study, for example, Mitchell et al. (1997) asked questions assessing overall enjoyment of the event (worded "I will enjoy the trip" before the tour, "I am enjoying this trip" during the tour, and "I enjoyed this trip" after the tour); and found that overall enjoyment was lower during the tour than before and after. Parallel results emerged in the Thanksgiving Break Study in which students filled out questionnaires the Monday before the break (the "before "condition), the Monday at the end of the break (the "during" condition), and two Mondays after the break (the "after" condition). And the same pattern of findings also emerged in the California Bicycle Study, in which there were 12 assessment points over time — 3 weeks and 2 days before the trip began, eight different days during the trip, and 1 week and 1 month after the trip. In this latter study, the rosy effects on the measures of overall enjoyment were apparent in a significant curvilinear pattern over time, with greater reported enjoyment on the "before" and "after" days than on the "during" days.

Rosy phenomena also surfaced in participants' narrative descriptions of their subjective experience. In both the Thanksgiving Break Study and the California Bicycle Study, students wrote narrative accounts about the trip on blank pages, with general instructions to write about what they were doing, what was going on around them, and what they were thinking and feeling. In the before conditions, these were imagined responses, and in the after condition these were recalled responses. In both studies, responses were more negative during the event than before or after, confirming in these open-ended responses what was found using closed-ended items.

This dampening of present feelings in contrast to prospective and retrospective feelings operated not only in terms of changes in enjoyment, but also in terms of changes in disappointment. In both the Thanksgiving Break and California Bicycle studies, Mitchell et al. (1997) assessed specific reactions to the events at different time periods of the study. In both studies, students during the event reported, on a scale measuring *disappointment*, that the positive event tended not to meet their expectations. In the California Bicycle Study, only 5% of the preevent narratives mentioned the possibility of disappointment, whereas 50% of during-the-event narratives mentioned disappointment. However, this disappointment was softened in the postevent narratives, where only 11% of students mentioned any disappointment in retrospect.

These fascinating results demonstrate that anticipation and reminiscence may be savored much more readily than an actual positive event as it is unfolding. We should note, however, that experiences for which the rosy phenomena occur are limited to clearly positive events that are circumscribed and not critical to people's self-involvements. The rosy phenomena would thus hardly apply to events that are critical to one's interpersonal relationships or personal achievements in the world.

Rosy phenomena may also reflect the trouble people often have being aware of their joy in the present, that is, the difficulty of capturing the joy of the moment as it is unfolding. Perhaps if people could learn to savor the present more fully, then rosy effects would disappear. If this reasoning is correct, then it's not that we don't enjoy positive events when we go through them, but rather that we're more aware of our joy beforehand and afterwards than we are during the moment.

In any event, Mitchell et al.'s (1994) results are provocative and raise questions about when rosy phenomena extend to other circumstances and about the ways in which more personal outcomes or events are differentially savored when they are part of ongoing positive experiences, compared to when they are anticipated or remembered. When it comes to rosy retrospection, the 20th-century American social critic, Oscar Levant, may have said it best when he cynically quipped, "Happiness is not something you experience, it's something you remember" (Winokur, 1987, p. 133). However, happiness is also something you look forward to (in rosy prospection), we might add.

TEMPORAL CONSTRUAL THEORY

As we have just described, how much people think they will enjoy an upcoming positive event and how much they recall enjoying it tend to exceed how much they actually enjoy the positive event when it occurs. In other words, positive events can seem better in the "rosy glow" of anticipation or reminiscence than in the "harsh glare" of the moment. But there is also reason to believe that people look forward to upcoming positive events differently over time, as these events shift from the distant future to the near future.

Concerning the psychological consequences of temporal distance from future events, Trope and Liberman (2003) proposed a theory of temporal construal, whereby:

> Individuals form more abstract representations, or higher-level construals, of distant-future events than near-future events. High-level construals consist of general, decontextualized features that convey the essence of information about future events, whereas low-level construals include more concrete, contextual, and incidental details. (p. 403)

In other words, when a positive event is in the distant future, people conceive of it in general abstract terms that lack a specific context. But when the positive event is in the near future, on the other hand, people conceive of it in concrete, context-specific terms. Thus, distant future events are construed in simpler terms that involve a few broad categories conceived in terms of a prototypical ideal case that has greater cognitive value, whereas near future events are construed in more complex terms that involve a larger number of narrow categories that have greater affective value (Trope & Liberman, 2003). Broadening the scope of their model, Trope and Liberman (2003) noted that:

> The construal process we propose may apply not only to temporal changes in value but also to temporal changes in reasoning, planning, and prediction. Temporal changes in these judgments may be mediated by the same representational mechanism that mediates temporal changes in value. Furthermore, a similar mechanism may also underlie the psychological consequences of other dimensions of psychological distance from events, including temporal distance from past events. (p. 404)

Thus, according to temporal construal theory, people tend to see positive events differently in foresight or hindsight depending on how far away these events are in time.

Extending this analysis to temporal forms of savoring, we suggest that dynamically unfolding positive events appear "rosier" the farther away they are in time, or the greater their "psychological distance" (Lewin, 1951). Thus, the passage of time may have opposite effects on rosy prospection versus retrospection. Based on temporal construal theory, we can speculate that the strength of rosy prospection should *decrease* as time passes and the upcoming positive event approaches, whereas the strength of rosy retrospection should *increase* as time passes and the positive event recedes in time. Clearly, many unanswered questions remain for future researchers to explore.

IMAGINARY RELISH
AND EXQUISITE TORTURE

Although we consider anticipation to be a future-focused form of savoring, anticipating a positive experience in not always entirely pleasurable. Previous theorists have noted that delaying a positive outcome may appear to increase its value because anticipating a positive event can itself be a pleasant experience (Elster & Loewenstein, 1992; Loewenstein, 1987; Lovallo & Kahneman, 2000). But surely anticipating a positive experience is sometimes unpleasant, as when intrusive thoughts monopolize attention in "elaborative rumination" (Kavanagh, Andrade, & May, 2005, p. 448).

Have you ever found yourself craving something pleasurable to the point where you just couldn't think of anything else? Consider the following example from Kavanagh et al. (2005):

> Here you are, innocently reading a psychology journal [or a book about savoring]. And an article [or quotation] suddenly mentions someone drinking a cup of excellent coffee at a sidewalk café on a sunny Sunday morning. Chances are that you immediately imagine how good it would be to have a cup yourself. Maybe you imagine the smell of the freshly ground coffee beans, the smell and taste of the coffee, and perhaps even the sound of the grinder and the bubble and steam of the espresso machine. If you do not especially enjoy coffee or have just finished a cup, this image may have little appeal. But if you would really enjoy a cup of coffee

right now, the image has a pleasurable piquancy — a tantalizing enchantment that like a tickle to your foot, moves easily to a sense of torture if the desire cannot be fulfilled. From its conception, the thought captures your attention. It has strong emotive power, and there is a sense that it triggers action. You may even feel unable to continue to read this article [or book] until you get a cup. What are the essential elements of this subjective experience? Our impression is that they include the intrusive and often unexpected nature of the initial thought, the imagery of the coffee and of drinking it, and the pleasure and torture that image brings. Once begun, it is difficult to stop thinking about it — in fact, it is difficult to think about anything else. (p. 446)

If right now you feel you simply cannot continue reading until you get a cup of coffee, then you have just experienced elaborative rumination. And the more vivid the mental images you have constructed relating to coffee, the stronger should be both the relish you are imagining and the discomfort you are enduring. Once activated, "progressive elaboration of the target-related thoughts, particularly in the form of imagery, is the key process underlying the persistence of desires during craving episodes" (Kavanagh et al., 2005, p. 448). Based on this reasoning, Kavanagh et al. (2005) proposed "an elaborated intrusion (EI) theory of desires," in which ruminative cognitive elaboration along with vivid sensory images fuels appetitive urges and creates both "imaginary relish" and "exquisite torture" (p. 446).

Clearly, anticipation can be either delightful or tortuous, depending on the accessibility of the desired object. As Kavanagh et al. (2005) noted:

Desires are pleasurable when consumption is imminent. Just thinking about prospective consumption clearly is pleasurable when there is no significant delay before consumption and there are no immediate concerns about negative effects from it. . . . Desires are particularly aversive in extended deprivation or attempted control. When consumption has to be substantially delayed or there is potent current motivation not to consume the substance, the predominant emotional response to craving is negative. (p. 457)

Thus, it is enjoyable to imagine the delicious taste of one's favorite meal while one is sitting at a restaurant watching the waiter prepare to serve the food. But it is excruciating to imagine this same savory taste while one is backpacking deep in the wilderness and has only freeze-dried rations to eat. Anticipation can be delightful when the desired object is near and consumption is imminent, but agonizing when the desired object is distant and consumption is impractical.

With respect to future-focused savoring, the foregoing discussion suggests that the sooner one believes a particular positive event is about to occur, the more one will enjoy anticipating that event. Note that this conclusion matches Jevons' (1905) hypothesis (as quoted in chapter 1) that, "The nearer the date fixed for leaving home approaches, the greater does the intensity of anticipal pleasure become" (p. 64).

A LIFE SPAN PERSPECTIVE ON SAVORING

Another way to think of temporal issues in relation to savoring processes is to think about savoring across the life span. The capacity for reminiscence and anticipation changes as we go through various transitions in life. It is a truism to say that the elderly have more to reminisce about, or that young adults have more to consider about their future, or that very young people might have little capacity to anticipate. Nevertheless, temporal issues must play a role in the way a person at a given stage of life uses the past or the future in accentuating savoring processes. We consider these issues, among others, next.

Savoring in Children

Reminiscence During Childhood.   Clearly, even very young children are capable of remembering the past. Children as young as 3 can accurately describe details of events that occurred several months earlier. Indeed, experimental evidence indicates that 3-year-olds whose mothers engage them in "elaborative" verbal participation during a structured positive experience show better memory for details of the experience, compared to children whose mothers do not actively promote verbal elaboration (Haden, Haine, & Fivush, 1997; Haden, Ornstein, Eckerman, & Didow, 2001; Reese, Haden, & Fivush, 1993). By the end of the preschool years, children are capable of narrating their own past experiences to others, regardless of whether or not their audience has shared those experiences (see Fivush, Haden, & Reese, 1996, and Fivush & Haden, 1997, for reviews). Attesting to the importance of past-focused reflection in children's lives, theorists have suggested that verbal reminiscence provides an adaptive function in helping children develop skills, define identity, learn social norms, and find mastery and meaning in the world (Fivush & Haden, 2003).

But do children truly *savor* the process of positive reminiscence, that is, do they mindfully attend to and appreciate their positive feelings in relation to the past? We suspect that children at least sometimes enjoy the process of storytelling, as when other people react with joy, laughter, awe, gratitude, or praise in response to their stories. However, exactly when children begin to engage in positive reminiscing in their own minds as a means of cherishing the past remains undetermined. To our knowledge, there has been no research on when children first develop the metacognitive skills necessary to appreciate mindfully their own positive feelings in relation to the past.

We must keep in mind that savoring the past is a higher order process than simply recalling the past. Clearly, the mental capacity to savor by reflecting on feelings associated with pleasant memories requires that one be aware of one's own inner life and be able to think abstractly about that experience. Thus, the higher order cognitive functions necessary to engage in this type of past-focused self-reflection may not fully develop until late childhood or early adolescence

(Inhelder & Piaget, 1958; McAdams, 1985). For this reason, we suggest that children gradually learn through socialization to articulate their inner experience in relation to the past, first mastering the art of retelling and reliving positive memories in the presence of others, and then later learning how to savor positive memories in their mind when they are developmentally capable of such abstractions. Although even very young children can accurately recall the past, they must first practice recalling memories in more complex, coherent, and evaluative ways with parents and peers, and then develop the prerequisite cognitive abilities to appreciate positive memories mindfully, before they can truly be said to *savor* the past.

Anticipation and the Delay of Gratification. Although the joy of anticipation can be delightful, obtaining "imaginary relish" requires tolerating the immediate discomfort of self-denial by temporarily delaying the gratification of one's consummatory desires (Frederick, Loewenstein, & O'Donoghue, 2002). With respect to anticipation in children, "The emergence of the self-concept is critical for the development of time sense" (Arlow, 1990, p. 136). As early as age 2, children show awareness of the future in their speech and behavior (Atance & O'Neill, 2001), and the ability to delay gratification dramatically increases between 3 and 4 years of age (Thompson, Barresi, & Moore, 1997). However, children typically do not develop the cognitive resources and perspective-taking skills necessary to delay gratification until age 4 or 5 (Mischel, Shoda, & Rodriguez, 1989). Not surprisingly, this lack of impulse control makes it hard for young children to savor upcoming positive experiences through anticipation. Tell a 2-year-old child that he or she is going to receive a wonderful present tomorrow, and the child will typically respond, "I want it now." The need for instant gratification banishes the joy of anticipation.

In studying delay of gratification, a common research paradigm in developmental psychology (Mischel, 1974, 1981) involves giving preschoolers a choice between a small but immediate reward (e.g., one marshmallow now) and a larger delayed reward (e.g., several marshmallows in 15 minutes). Typically, children who attend to the desirable features of the delayed reward cannot wait as long as children who are distracted from these thoughts (Mischel & Ebbeson, 1970; Mischel, Ebbeson, & Raskoff-Zeiss, 1972; Rodriguez, Mischel, & Shoda, 1989). Keeping the rewards in sight makes it harder for children to delay gratification; they are able to wait nearly twice as long when desired objects are hidden (Mischel, 1974, 1981).

Successfully delaying gratification involves "willpower" (Metcalfe & Mischel, 1999), or cognitive processes that shift attention away from the "hot" consummatory features of the desired object (e.g., how delicious the food would taste) toward "cool" distracting thoughts (e.g., how comfortable the room is) or abstract thoughts about the treat (e.g., how many different ingredients the food contains). Mothers of 2½-year-olds who could refrain from touching a forbidden toy were more likely to use distraction as a technique to help their children regulate behavior during the waiting period (Putnam, Spritz, & Stifter, 2002). Analyzing contingent behaviors, Putnam et al. (2002) found that mothers and children effectively coregulated child behavior by following one another's lead in allocating attention away from the taboo object. In other words, children whose mothers were proactive in helping them delay gratification were better able to resist the temptation of the smaller immediate reward, compared to children whose mothers were exclusively reactive.

Preschoolers who can tolerate having to wait for something wonderful are quite different from their less patient counterparts. Indeed, youngsters who can delay gratification are calmer, more tolerant of frustration, less irritable, less aggressive, more capable of concentrating, and tend to get higher grades in school (Funder & Block, 1989; Funder, Block, & Block, 1983). There is even prospective longitudinal evidence that preschoolers who can control themselves are better able to deal with stress later as adolescents and have higher SAT scores when they apply to college (Shoda, Mischel, & Peake, 1990). Clearly, the ability to delay gratification is linked to many adaptive tendencies in early adolescence.

Furthermore, being unable to delay gratification may be a specific risk factor for externalizing disorders. For example, young adolescent males who display externalizing symptoms (i.e., aggression and delinquency) are more likely to seek immediate gratification during the delay paradigm than are boys who show either internalizing symptoms (i.e., anxiety and depression) or no symptoms at all (Krueger, Caspi, Moffitt, White, & Stouthamer-Loeber, 1996). Considered together, this evidence converges on the conclusion that learning to delay gratification — a necessary precondition for savoring through anticipation — is healthy and adaptive.

A comparable ability to delay gratification has even been observed in non-human animals. For example, rats (Killeen, Smith, & Hanson, 1981) and pigeons (Grosch & Neuringer, 1981) can inhibit responses for a fixed interval to attain a preferred outcome. In addition, chimpanzees will delay pressing a button (which delivers a less preferred reward) during a delay interval, in order to obtain a more preferred reward (Beran, Savage-Rumbaugh, Pate, & Rumbaugh, 1999).

Being able to savor the imaginary relish of anticipation requires that you also be able to endure the exquisite torture of having to wait for what you would rather have right now. However, the mere capacity to delay gratification does not necessarily bring with it the joy of anticipation. On the contrary, the joy of anticipation requires not that one revel in distracting thoughts while delaying gratification, but rather that one derive pleasure while focusing precisely on the positive outcome one is awaiting. In fact, the more vivid and actively engaging the mental imagery associated with the desired object, the sweeter should be the imaginary relish (and the greater the potential for exquisite torture in self-denial). Note, however, that preschoolers learn to avoid thinking about the upcoming positive outcome as a strategy for enduring their discomfort while having to wait. Yet this is hardly future-focused savoring.

The joy of anticipation gets more complicated when the desired object is a consumable good, such as a bottle of fine wine, a free airline ticket, or one's life savings. For example, if people can control their consumption of the desired object, then they can prolong the pleasure of anticipation by postponing or delaying consumption repeatedly, each time deciding at the last minute not to consume the object if they so choose (Frederick et al., 2002). Obviously, however, this self-regulatory skill requires the ability to delay gratification in anticipation of later consumption not only when the situation calls for it, but also when one freely chooses. We suspect that most preadolescents, indeed many adults, would have trouble deliberately engaging in the process of perpetual postponement when it comes to a desirable consumable outcome. Thus, anticipation is hardly child's play.

Nevertheless, there may be special occasions or cultural rituals in children's lives that foster their ability to look forward to positive events in ways that engender joy. For example, parents or teachers who work together with a child to plan a vacation, holiday, birthday celebration, school project, or outing engage the child's attention positively toward the desired future outcome and help the child learn how to savor future positive events in anticipation. In this way, parents and educators may teach children how to manage the positive side of emotional life in relation to the future. With respect to disappointment, for example, through socialization children learn the effortful control required not only to handle disappointment (Spinrad, Stifter, Donelan-McCall, & Turner, 2004), but also to hide it when receiving an undesirable gift (Kieras, Tobin, Graziano, & Rothbart, 2005) — with children typically adopting the latter display rule between ages 6 and 10 (Saarni, 1984).

Savoring the Moment Among Young Children.   Children enjoy many things about their lives, but do they use savoring processes that enhance their enjoyment of good things in the present? Do they pay mindful attention to and appreciate their pleasures? Because there was nowhere to turn for answers in the psychological literature, we decided to take the question into our own hands and ask some children about savoring. This is what we discovered.

We asked children of different ages, the youngest being 5, the oldest 10, about the things they enjoy. Our instructions were as follows: "Think of the last time you really liked doing something or liked something that was happening to you. Tell me about what it was, when it happened, what were you thinking about, and what were you feeling."

No child with whom we spoke had any trouble identifying something they enjoyed. One child mentioned a vacation, another playing sports, a third swimming, another eating a sundae. The hitch was that it was a hard task for them to label what they were thinking about without simply saying they just liked the experience. And it is true that this can be a difficult task for adults as well. Adults, too, sometimes say they liked a particular event because they enjoyed it or because it was enjoyable. The more elaborated verbal thinking that we had hoped to see as evidence of mindfulness in children just did not emerge, except for a 7-year-old who said that his body felt calmed when he swam a lot. But we were able to obtain this particular response only after insistent probing. We were struck with the fact that we must rely on much more indirect evidence of savoring in young children.

Beyond children's own say-so, can we make other observations that implicate a robust savoring capacity at least in some children? We think so, but we would emphasize that these observations are of only some children who may be unusual. Most young children do not behave in a way that would lead us to believe they are savoring. There is no better way to captivate little children, even age 3 or younger, than to tell them a story that connects with their wishes or fears. You may have to prime them a little by asking such questions as, "Do you know what happened next?," or by asking them about their experience with respect to a particular feature of a story that came up. But most young children will listen intently.

However, does that mean they are savoring what they are hearing? Not necessarily — but certain responses, if they also occur, do suggest that children might be savoring the story. Such responses as smiling, nodding, asking questions spontaneously, forgetting other desires, or assuming statuesque postures could lead an observer to think that children are not only enthralled by what they are hearing, but are also thinking hard about what they hearing. But you can still ask, are these children thinking hard about their own pleasures in being enthralled? There's the rub. Although we know no more than we do when we observe an adult, being adults ourselves, it is easier to empathize and imagine an adult in the same situation adopting an ongoing savoring mode.

It is apparent that we need something more explicit to infer savoring in children as they react to stories because they won't or can't tell us directly. One possible criterion is to check whether children are eager to have the story repeated. Another is whether the story ideas linger in children's thoughts. How many parents are asked by their children to read the same books to them repeatedly? How many children watch a videotape over and over again, even if the video is scary, perhaps especially if it is scary? The Disney ploy of getting a main character in a dangerous situation is an age-old trick of tellers of fairy tales. The Brothers Grimm and Walt Disney have much in common in that respect. Whether scary or not, a story or video repeatedly sought out by children is reasonable evidence to infer anticipatory pleasure. It suggests that the children have some mental image of an enjoyable encounter with the story or video in which they would like to engage.

Is the evidence that a child has an image of a past pleasant event sufficient evidence of savoring? It is indeed very primitive savoring, if savoring at all. The fact that the child actively asks for the return of the image is one step above classical conditioning of a positive experience, a process that can be observed in infants. The sight of the bottle soon becomes a reliable way to get savoring-like smiles and excitement in a 5-month-old. How mindful infants are about what is exciting them is another matter entirely.

There may be an even more solid inference of savoring in children when the children themselves are the source of the repetition of the image or the story. A crude version of this effect occurs when very young children obviously enjoy repeating jokes that they have heard. When they catch on to the double entendre in knock-knock jokes, children may incessantly bombard a willing listener with countless repetitions. As the child retells the joke, the adult does not savor repeatedly hearing the joke, but rather savors the child's savoring of retelling the joke.

An incident that occurred when Fred's younger daughter, Erica, was 4 years old provides anecdotal evidence that young children can learn strategies to prolong savoring. The family had enjoyed a fun day of climbing sand dunes in a state park. As they were in the car driving home, Erica sat in the backseat giggling with her older sister, and still enjoying the day, pronounced, "Let's laugh all the way home!" Obviously, she wanted to prolong the joy of the moment, and she knew that shared laughter can keep positive feelings alive.

Savoring Beliefs Among Preadolescents.   To date, the most ambitious investigation of savoring among preadolescent children has been the master's thesis research of Lynda Cafasso (1994; Cafasso, Bryant, & Jose, 1994), a former graduate student in developmental psychology at Loyola University Chicago. Her sample of school-aged children consisted of 365 students (151 boys and 201 girls, with 13 students missing information about gender). The sample included 90 fifth-graders (41 boys, 49 girls), 92 sixth-graders (36 boys, 56 girls), 81 seventh-graders (36 boys, 45 girls) and 88 eighth-graders (37 boys, 51 girls). The children were enrolled in one of five parochial Catholic schools—a Chicago urban school and four Chicago suburban schools. Of the total sample, 57% were Caucasian, 21% were African-American, 9% were Asian-American, 7% were Hispanic-American, and 6% were of other heritage.

To begin her research, Cafasso modified the 24-item Savoring Beliefs Inventory (Bryant, 2003) originally developed using college students, so that grade-school children could understand the meaning of the items. Item readability analyses revealed that her revised scale, the Children's Savoring Beliefs Inventory (CSBI), is appropriate for respondents with at least a fifth-grade reading level (Cafasso, 1994; Cafasso et al., 1994). A copy of the CSBI is included in Appendix F, and Appendix G provides detailed instructions on how to score the CSBI.

What do the CSBI data reveal about children's savoring beliefs? Preliminary structural analyses of responses to the CSBI indicated that, unlike college students, children in Grades 5 through 8 do not make distinctions among their abilities to savor in anticipation, in the moment, or in reminiscence, but instead hold global beliefs about their overall capacity to savor positive experience. Providing an acceptable measurement model, a one-factor confirmatory solution with positive and negative "method" factors explained over 90% of the variance in children's responses to the CSBI (Cafasso, 1994; Cafasso et al., 1994). Indeed, CSBI total score was a reliable indicator of savoring beliefs for males and females in all four grade levels (Cronbach's αs = .84 - .93). These findings suggest that savoring beliefs are unitary in preadolescents, reflecting a single underlying capacity to savor, in contrast to the multidimensional savoring beliefs of adults in relation to the past, present, and future.

As criteria for construct validation, Cafasso selected several well-validated measures of subjective adjustment. To assess *positive subjective adjustment,* she used the Well-Being Scale (Schlosser, 1990); the Positive Affect subscale of the Index of Psychological Well-Being (Berkman, 1971); and the Self-Perception [self-esteem] Profile for Children (Harter, 1985). To tap *negative subjective adjustment,* she used: the Children's Depression Inventory (Kovacs, 1985); the Negative Affect subscale of the Index of Psychological Well-Being (Berkman, 1971); and the State-Trait Anxiety Inventory for Children (Spielberger, 1973). Supporting discriminant validity, CSBI scores had significantly stronger correlations with measures of positive adjustment (well-being, positive affect, and self-esteem) than with measures of negative adjustment (depression, negative affect, and anxiety), in three of the four grade-levels for boys and girls. This pattern of findings supports the conclusion that the CSBI is a valid measure of savoring beliefs in preadolescent children.

Cross-validating research with older populations, girls had higher CSBI total scores than did boys when collapsing across the four grade levels. In other words, compared to boys, girls generally perceived themselves as better able to enjoy positive experience. Thus, gender differences in perceived savoring ability appear to emerge as early as fifth grade. Considered together, the data suggest that children do make judgments of their capacity to savor their lives, but that these evaluations are less differentiated with respect to time than are adults' evaluations.

Yet, it may not be until the stage of "formal operations" in early adolescence that young people truly develop the capacity to reflect deliberately on their inner experience (Inhelder & Piaget, 1958). Before adolescence, children may certainly be aware of specific instances in which they are enjoying themselves, and they may also be fully capable of becoming absorbed in positive experience. But children are typically less aware than adults of their own subjective experience as occurs in savoring. Indeed, young children think primarily in terms of concrete operations in relation to the physical world, and until adolescence, typically lack the necessary cognitive resources to engage in deeper high-order abstraction (McAdams, 1985). Thus, preadolescents may lack the cognitive ability to engage in elaborative savoring, in which they reflect on their positive feelings and make mental associations to their own enjoyment.

Children's earliest experiences of savoring in relation to the past, present, and future may well occur in structured social rituals such as birthday or holiday celebrations with family and friends. We propose that it is through these shared positive events that children learn how to apply and refine their emerging meta-cognitive skills in savoring. We further speculate that the ability to savor interpersonally in the context of social activity develops before the ability to savor intrapersonally in one's own mind.

Regardless, the data clearly indicate that preadolescent children are aware of their own capacity to savor positive experience. The fact that preadolescent girls, compared to boys, perceived themselves to be more capable of enjoying life mirrors the gender difference consistently found in older samples (Bryant, 2003; Lindberg, 2004). And it supports the notion that females develop a capacity for self-reflection earlier in their lives than males do.

Savoring in Adolescents

We have thus far been tenuous in our answer to the question of whether young children can truly savor. Is adolescence a transition time for full-blown savoring? We think so. Indeed, there is a strong theoretical basis for the argument that savoring first becomes prominent as a process in adolescence.

Following Erikson's (1959, 1968) early insights about the special nature of adolescent development, many theorists have spoken of adolescence as a time of identity formation, when the person begins to consolidate a perspective on himself or herself as a continuing integrated person with a past, present, and future. Theorists reason that until adolescence, children may have integrated slices of themselves into a sense of self that is more context-specific than continuous over time.

In the process of identity formation, adolescents become absorbed in thinking about the self in relation and in comparison to other people. Preadolescents rarely think of themselves in such a way. Adolescence is often a time for deliberate choice of friends and peers. It is a time for falling in love and discovering sexual passions and pleasures. It is a time for commitment to styles of life and ways of being. The processes underlying these phenomena all involve deep self-reflection. The adolescent begins to ask, "What do I like or enjoy or love? What do I not like or not enjoy or hate?" It is in the midst of such thinking about feelings that insights about savoring can occur, whether it be about a crush on a girlfriend, a movie idol, a new hobby, a new kind of music, or a new way of dressing or talking. Although they may decline, these processes do not disappear as people enter adulthood.

Indeed, the possible ways of savoring positive experience would seem to expand exponentially as adolescents enter the stage of formal operations. As McAdams (1985) cogently argued:

... as one's ways of knowing become more and more abstract in formal operations, one comes to focus introspectively upon one's own thought processes. Thus, the adolescent may take his or her own thought as an object to reflect upon. ... With respect to identity, then, the adolescent or young adult who has entered Piaget's stage of formal operations comes to reflect upon his or her past and present and how they may or may not connect to a host of hypothetical futures. Further, he or she comes to reflect upon the process of reflecting. Approaching the reflection from the perspective of the knower who is able to understand the nature of things both real and hypothetical, the individual may strive to bind together, in reflection, the reality of the past and present with an imagined hypothetical future. (p. 10)

These cognitive developmental changes also enable adolescents for the first time to adopt a variety of different temporal orientations in savoring positive experience. For example, as abstract cognitive capabilities evolve during adolescence, people can experience the joys of anticipated recall (i.e., looking forward to looking back) and recalled anticipation (i.e., looking back on having looked forward). Furthermore, adolescents in the formal operational stage are capable of the abstract reasoning required to engage in active memory building as a means of facilitating later reminiscence; to prospectively plan and anticipate happy times; to retrospectively reinterpret positive outcomes as blessings; to compare their own experience with what others are experiencing, what they expected, or what might have been; to congratulate themselves for their achievements; and to marvel at the exquisite wonders of the universe.

This conceptual analysis further suggests that the special power of bittersweet experiences to evoke strong savoring may first emerge in adolescence, as individuals develop an abstract awareness of time. Savoring a bittersweet moment requires that one is aware the experience is about to end and that it will not recur for some time, if at all — an awareness only possible once one has reached the stage of formal cognitive operations. Indeed, without this a priori temporal awareness, one does not experience bitterness until after the positive experience has actually ended.

Adolescents' expanded awareness and higher levels of abstract reasoning are also associated with a heightened interest in forming social relationships and in defining the self in relation to others (Flavell, 1977; Harter, 1998; McAdams, 1985). Along these lines, Harter (1998) argued that young adolescents first begin to differentiate the self as a function of social contexts. This greater social awakening is perhaps most clearly seen in adolescents' strong need to share positive experiences with their friends. Indeed, it is during adolescence that males and females first learn to manage their social resources to help them optimize positive experiences. As Vaux (1988) noted, "Social support can alter the experience of positive events: by promoting their occurrence, facilitating their recognition, promoting their management, and enhancing their enjoyment" (p. 154). Clearly, we would expect Sharing With Others to emerge as a dominant strategy for savoring positive outcomes during adolescence.

Savoring Beliefs Among High School Students.   Results from an empirical investigation of savoring in an adolescent sample (Meehan et al., 1993) support this hypothesis. The work in question was the master's thesis research of Michael Meehan, a graduate student in clinical psychology at Loyola University Chicago. The primary goal of this research was to answer the following questions: Do adolescents distinguish between their abilities to cope and savor? And is the size and quality of their social network more strongly tied to their beliefs about savoring than to their beliefs about coping?

To explore savoring among adolescents, Meehan et al. (1993) focused on a sample of 82 high school juniors and seniors, ages 16 to 18, attending a Midwest suburban school serving primarily middle-class families, most of whom were White. Respondents completed measures of social support (Sarason, Levine, Basham, & Sarason, 1983); subjective mental health (Bryant & Veroff, 1984); and beliefs about avoiding, coping, obtaining, and savoring (Bryant, 1989). Preliminary analyses indicated that the key composite measures had reasonable reliabilities for the adolescent sample.

What do these data reveal about adolescents' perceptions of their abilities to cope with negative outcomes and savor positive outcomes? The results essentially replicate earlier findings with college students (Bryant, 1989). Whereas there were strong correlations between beliefs about obtaining and savoring ($r = .52$, $p < .0001$) and about avoiding and coping ($r = .62, p < .0001$), beliefs about savoring and coping were uncorrelated ($r = .02, p < .43$). Thus, high school students clearly considered their capacity to savor positive outcomes to be distinct from their capacity to cope with negative outcomes.

And what do the data tell us about the relationship of social support to savoring and coping among adolescents? Both the reported quality ($r = .41$) and quantity ($r = .45$) of social support were significantly correlated with perceived capacity to savor positive outcomes ($ps < .0001$ with Bonferroni correction). However, neither quality ($r = .25$) nor quantity ($r = .01$) of social support was significantly correlated with perceived capacity to cope with negative outcomes ($ps > .05$ with Bonferroni correction). In other words, social support was more strongly related to young adolescents' beliefs about savoring than to their beliefs about coping. This pattern of results suggests that social support serves primarily as a resource for enhancing young adolescents' enjoyment of positive experiences, rather than as a tool for helping them cope with stress or adversity. Thus, not only is savoring a relevant concern for young adolescents, but relationships with others are strongly linked to savoring in their lives. And longitudinal data indicate that sharing one's feelings with others actually amplifies the impact of positive events on positive emotions among young adults (Gable et al., 2004; Langston, 1994).

Savoring in Adulthood

We thus feel that savoring first fully emerges in adolescence. Indeed, one could argue that there is more savoring during adolescence than during early adulthood, when people are busier enacting choices than considering preferences. Certainly adults can experience the savoring processes we highlighted in the last chapter, but as we have noted, they often do not have or take the time to savor. Only when people are older and step away from many life responsibilities can they reconsider savoring as they did when they were adolescents. Because adolescence is often characterized as a period of great upset as well, it is not that savoring characterizes what adolescents do in general, but simply that the capacity to savor blossoms at that time. However, savoring may not reach its full power in people's lives until they are much older.

Data support this reasoning. In particular, Bryant (2003, Study 6) administered the SBI to 36 older adults (14 males, 22 females; mean age = 65.4, SD = 6.8) along with measures of happiness (Fordyce, 1988). Confirming the SBI's psychometric properties in this older sample, the three temporal subscales showed strong reliabilities (αs = .83–.89) and substantial positive correlations with both intensity and frequency of happiness (rs = .46–.60). Of particular interest are mean scores on the three SBI subscales for this older sample compared to younger samples. For purposes of comparison, we pooled the data of the five college-aged samples reported in Bryant (2003). Reanalyses of these data reveal that the older sample scored significantly higher than the pooled college sample on Anticipating, $t(473)$ = 2.84, two-tailed p < .005, Savoring the Moment, $t(464)$ = 3.15, two-tailed p < .002, and Reminiscing, $t(472)$ = 3.43, two-tailed p < .0007. Thus, compared to college students, older adults reported a higher capacity to savor positive experience in relation to the past, present, and future.

In their later years, people realize that they have confronted many difficult exigencies in their lives, along with the pleasures they have enjoyed. It is perhaps that realization that puts the possibility for savoring into a new bright light. Older people can now orient themselves toward making the most of the time they have left to live. Why merely endure the mechanics of living? Why not focus mostly on what there is to enjoy, including the pleasures of everyday life? Such is part of the wisdom of being an experienced older person who has perspective on the meaning and richness of life. But it may well take a heap of living to get there. As an old German proverb puts it: "We grow too soon old and too late smart."

There are many other facets to what we call wisdom in the elderly—a certain tolerant judiciousness about what is important, a direct open reasoning style, an acceptance of life's difficulties, seeing things as more gray than black and white. In fact, Orwoll and Achenbaum (1993) have identified nine facets to being wise that exist in psychological views on wisdom. Three facets concern the ways in which individuals with wisdom approach their own views of themselves (they permit themselves to grow, they know what they are like, and they have integrated the values they hold). Three facets concern the ways in which wise individuals relate to other people (they are empathic, they understand other people's views, and they deal with others in a mature way). And three facets concern the ways in which wise individuals make sense of the universe and find meaning in life (they are self-transcendent, they recognize the limits of knowledge, and they develop commitments to the spiritual side of life).

And yet behind all of those characteristics may be the capacity to savor what is good about living and being human, not only about oneself, but about others and in light of the difficulties generally facing the world. Indeed, in thinking about wisdom across the life span, Baltes, Gluck, and Kunzmann (2002) argued that a crucial balance between self-regard and social responsibility in one's values and incentives may be at the heart of what we mean by wisdom. This critical balance may be a phenomenon that particularly emerges among some elderly people, who confront the realization that, in the limited time remaining in their lives, they wish to savor what they currently experience and have experienced.

SUMMARY

In this chapter, we outlined issues that arise when savoring is considered in relation to time. With respect to savoring the past through reminiscence, we reviewed two studies that suggest savoring pleasant memories can boost happiness, particularly when one uses vivid mental imagery to enhance recall (Bryant et al., 2005). We also noted that people often reminisce by telling stories to others that may reflect either current joys one wants to share or current problems one wants to resolve. In some cases, people may retreat into the past as a substitute for living in the present, and may only enjoy their lives retrospectively.

With respect to savoring the future through anticipation, we noted that people can derive joy by looking forward to upcoming positive events, even though prospective savoring precludes the joy of surprise and produces the possibility of disappointment. People may avoid anticipating due to humility, instrumentality, superstition, or affective self-defense. Illustrating the rich complexity of time perspective in relation to savoring, people can enhance current joy by looking forward to looking back on the present (*anticipated recall*) or looking back on having looked forward to the present (*recalled anticipation*).

We also identified conditions that produce temporal differences in perceived enjoyment (Mitchell & Thompson, 1994; Mitchell et al., 1997), whereby people enjoy a positive event less while experiencing it, compared to how much they expected to enjoy it beforehand (i.e., *rosy prospection*) or how much they later recall having enjoyed it (i.e., *rosy retrospection*). These rosy effects are most likely to occur when an outcome is clearly positive, ego-involving, personally controllable, and self-contained in its implications.

To understand how time influences perceptions of events more generally, we drew on temporal construal theory (Trope & Liberman, 2003), which assumes people construct more abstract, decontextualized cognitive representations of *distant* past or future events, and more concrete, contextualized cognitive representations of *near* past or future events. Based on this theory, we hypothesized that the strength of rosy prospection *decreases* over time, as an upcoming positive event approaches and becomes more contextualized; whereas the strength of rosy retrospection *increases* over time, as a positive event recedes into past and becomes more decontextualized. Extending the conceptual analysis of anticipation, we considered the "imaginary relish" of anticipatory craving, in which one endures the "exquisite torture" of fantasizing about enjoying a desired object (Kavanagh et al., 2005) — an experience that produces either agony or ecstasy, depending on the accessibility of the desired object.

We concluded by outlining a life span developmental perspective on savoring. With respect to savoring in children, we noted that preschoolers can recall the past and delay gratification long enough to tolerate the discomfort of self-denial required for anticipation. However, we argued that children typically do not develop the cognitive skills necessary to mindfully savor positive experience retrospectively or prospectively until late childhood or early adolescence. We also reviewed research validating a children's version (CSBI) of Bryant's (2003) Savoring Beliefs Inventory (Cafasso, 1994; Cafasso et al., 1994) that suggests preadolescents have not yet fully developed the capacity to savor in all three temporal domains. With respect to savoring during adolescence, we noted a dramatic rise in savoring during this critical stage of human development, in which abstract thinking and formal cognitive operations first emerge (Inhelder & Piaget, 1958), the very skills necessary to support the higher order self-reflection crucial for savoring. Finally, with respect to savoring in adulthood, we noted that growing older often involves a return to issues concerning enjoyment, when one has fewer life responsibilities (as in retirement) and an opportunity to develop wisdom in balancing self-regard and social responsibility in one's values and incentives. Thus, the concept of time is inextricably linked to savoring.

7

Savoring and Human Concerns

The aim of life is appreciation.
—G. K. Chesterton (1936)

In this chapter, we present the case for considering the process of savoring as crucial in relation to a number of important human concerns. We concentrate only on those human concerns upon which we think savoring processes might have an impact. We will hypothesize not only that savoring processes engage experiential states that directly enrich every person's life, but also that these same processes can become resources for adding strength to the development of life goals. We first discuss ways in which savoring can boost romantic relationships and friendships, and then move on to four other large-scale concerns people have in their lives—health, creativity, meaning, and spirituality. In all of these domains, we suggest that savoring processes play a substantial role in broadening and building positive experiences.

First, let's consider the relationship of savoring to loving relationships. What has savoring got to do with love?

SAVORING AND LOVE

Romantic Love

Consider a man and a woman in love with each other, Jack and Jill. Each of them may act in various ways to show their love for the other. Jack may help Jill with her chores, and Jill may bake Jack's favorite pie. They may give presents to one another, they may touch and embrace each other, they may be passionate with one another. But nothing so deeply conveys to Jill Jack's joy in loving her as when he communicates to her how much he savors the joy of having her in his life, and vice versa. And we dare to say that, in general, when such savoring spontaneously takes place in the presence of a person's beloved, and the person communicates that event to his or her partner, nothing could be more powerful in reassuring that partner about being loved. A comparable effect occurs in close friendships when one friend says to another, "It doesn't get any better than this" — the quintessential affirmation of optimal savoring.

When a person is savoring a beloved, by definition, several features of that experience are operative. Let's consider Jack savoring his love for Jill and letting her know about it. First, our definition of savoring tells us that Jack's other social needs are not dominant. He is not concerned about whether loving Jill is acceptable by other peoples' standards, whether loving Jill makes him feel powerful or a man of world, or whether or not Jill loves him. Second, if Jack is savoring his love for Jill, according to our presentation of savoring, then his attentional focus is on the here and now, and this orientation enhances the intensity of his savoring. And finally, if Jack is savoring his love for Jill, we have suggested in our general discussions of savoring that it's something of which he is explicitly and mindfully aware. This quality of being clearly focused with undivided attention in savoring means that when Jack communicates to Jill how much he savors the joy of loving her, he clearly lets Jill know that he is attending to her. Different from the pro forma giving of gifts, as with valentines, birthday, or anniversary presents, savoring the beloved in the presence of the beloved is a profound communication of caring.

What does Jill realize and understand when Jack savors his love for her and communicates that love to her? We suggest it is a special kind of love that effectively affirms Jill with caring and respect. Along these lines, Joe and his colleagues (Veroff, Douvan, & Hatchett, 1995) have created an instrument to measure "affective affirmation" that reflects the savoring of love one can communicate to one's partner. Four items constitute the Affective Affirmation measure:

Now let us talk about the pleasures and good feelings that come from being married. For each one of the feelings on this list, mark an "x" in the box telling how often in the past month or so you have had such feelings — often, sometimes, rarely, or never. During the past month how often did you:

1. Feel that your (husband/wife) felt especially caring toward you?
2. Feel that your (husband/wife) made your life especially interesting or exciting?
3. Feel that your (husband/wife) made you feel good about having your own ideas and ways of doing things?
4. Feel that your (husband/wife) made you feel good about the kind of person you are?

Note that all four items assess how often spouses are aware of their partner communicating a savoring orientation toward the beloved. The spouse communicated caring and, at the same time, an excitement about the moment, without any approval and esteem issues, just a mindful appreciation of the kind of person the beloved is.

In a longitudinal analysis of married couples using this measure, Joe has found that spouses who feel particularly affirmed by their partners have marriages that are in good shape. This study was based on a representative urban sample located through public records of marriage licenses. Couples in the Detroit area were interviewed in the first, third, and seventh years of their marriages. Controlling for income and education, men who felt affirmed by their wives in this way during the first year of marriage (as reflected in husbands' responses to the Affective Affirmation measure) were more likely to remain in stable marriages over time (Veroff et al., 1995). Furthermore, women in all income and education groups who felt affirmed by their husbands in this way during the first year of their marriage felt the strongest commitment in the seventh year to maintaining their marriages (Veroff, 1999). These are powerful results that hold for both African-American and White couples. Thus, the study supports our contention that the communication of the savoring of love to a spouse has a powerful effect on the quality and resilience of the marital relationship.

How does this kind of savoring of a lover actually get communicated? Next we discuss several answers to this question.

Appreciative Sharing and Mutuality.   Significantly correlated with measures of affective affirmation were measures of how much spouses think they share each others' interests, as well as measures of how collaborative the couples are on a shared task. These results speak to the likelihood of affective affirmation occurring when couples are in tune with each other's interests and activities, and have a rich mutuality in what they do. Out of mutuality develops a trust in the other person and a capacity to read each other's loving feelings that would likely emanate when partners are savoring their love for their beloved.

An instance of such loving mutuality can be seen in another study of marriage in which spouses told an interviewer an oral history of their relationship (Buehlman, Gottman, & Katz, 1992). Couples answered many open-ended questions about such matters as how they met, how they decided to get married, as well as some good and bad times in their marriage. Buehlman et al. (1992) found that couples who were not forthcoming — in particular, not very expansive in the memories that they shared during the interview — had unstable marriages that eventually dissolved. This finding suggests that a couple's unwillingness to discuss openly the story of their courtship and to savor the feelings that this memory evokes is a telltale sign of a lack of intimacy in the marriage.

Self-Disclosure.   From what we have just said, it would be reasonable to hypothesize that willingness to disclose personal information to another person

can be a basis for mutual intimacy, which can in turn lead to savoring the relationship. Tannen (1991) suggested that women are more likely than men to share
memories about their past, especially ones that reveal vulnerabilities. Women
may coax men into self-disclosure of this kind in everyday conversation, but men
often resist and in so doing turn down opportunities for intimacy. Thus, women
more than men may savor memories of their feelings of the past, and men may
not even recognize such opportunities for a reciprocal loving exchange. Women
often express disappointment in men's unwillingness to be communicative in
this way. Tannen (1991) also noted that although men may not directly disclose
their memories about feelings to women, they still indirectly reveal their feelings
about their lives when they recall such events as a job promotion, a camping trip
with friends, or a sporting event they attended. Women have to be particularly
adroit at reading the feelings involved, in order to recognize and understand
men's self-disclosure.

   Minding.   In the process of savoring a loved one, we attend to details about
that particular person that we might otherwise miss during ordinary experiences in everyday life. As an attentional process, savoring gives us clues about
the likes and dislikes of our beloved. Harvey, Pauwels, and Zickmund (2002)
called this the process of *minding,* or a conscious attention to the beloved and
what he or she is like. Over time, this attentiveness alerts lovers to the characteristics of their beloved and in so many ways help preserve the relationship. In
minding, a person might even adopt idealized illusions about what the beloved
is like, in order to maintain connections with the person (Murray, Holmes, &
Griffin, 1996). Thus, through the process of minding, savoring might ultimately
communicate one's desire to respect and care for the beloved, whether or not
one's perceptions of the beloved are totally accurate.

   Collaboration.   Working in synchrony with someone you love on a shared
task can induce feelings of well-being that are mutually shared. To the extent that
such collaboration is part of savoring time spent together, it is bound to lead to
savoring each other as well. A synchronous moment can be a rather heady experience. Such collaboration implies dovetailing of activities where neither lover is
more dominant than the other or is seeking approval or respect from the other.
Rather, true collaboration occurs when people work together in synchrony on
the task at hand. These synchronous moments are hard to manufacture, but
when they happen, the communication of savoring of the beloved is powerful.
   As might be expected, in the Detroit married couples study cited earlier, Joe
and his colleagues found a significant correlation between levels of affective
affirmation and the amount of collaboration that the couple showed on a joint
task. The task was to tell the story of their relationship together from the time
they first met until the present and into the future. All interactions between the
couple were coded in terms of whether or not they were collaborative. Being collaborative meant incorporating the partner's previous response in a cooperative

way, such as finishing each other's thoughts or adding to what the person just said. Some spouses disagreed with each other, which certainly is not collaboration. Some just merely laughed or agreed. Nor is that collaborative. Only those responses that built cooperatively on what the spouse previously said were considered collaborative. It was that type of collaboration in storytelling that characterized spouses who felt affirmed affectively. We suggest that these couples were savoring each other during their collaborative storytelling. Couples that savor together, affirm each other.

Sexual Empathy. In the Detroit study, there were significant correlations between (a) the measures of affective affirmations in both men and women and (b) measures of their enjoyment of sex, which included an appraisal of how much their partner enjoyed sexual relationships with them (Henderson-King & Veroff, 1994). These findings are consistent with the notion that in the process of mutual sexual satisfaction, there is a communication of savoring each other. Indeed, mutual enjoyment of sex implies an empathy with the partners' feelings as well as an awareness of one's own feelings, both of which would be strong indicators of savoring the relationship in general. It is no wonder that a satisfying sexual relationship often underlies a deeply loving relationship. The crucial link may not be the passion per se, but rather the communication of a savoring affirmation of each other.

In sum, we have highlighted five processes through which one's savoring of a beloved can communicate love—namely, appreciative sharing and mutuality, self-disclosure, minding, collaboration, and sexual empathy. Clearly, these processes are interrelated. For example, collaboration can give rise to appreciative sharing, self-disclosure can stimulate minding, and sexual empathy can involve each of the other four processes. This set of processes is a starting point for future work on savoring in romantic relationships.

Savoring and Romantic Poetry

We cannot leave the topic of savoring and romantic love without noting that this topic has inspired some of the most important poetry ever written. As we mentioned in the previous chapter, the metaphors used in poetry can help convey the mindfully focused attention that occurs in savoring, the translation of one's positive feelings into images of the beloved, in situations either near or far from the beloved. Indeed, absence from the beloved can be filled with savoring thoughts about the individual.

Consider Sonnet 61 from Shakespeare:

> Is it thy will, thy image should keep open
> My heavy eyelids to the weary night?
> Dost thou desire my slumber to be broken,
> While shadows like to thee do mock my sight?

> Is it thy spirit that thou send'st from thee
> So far from home into my deed to pry,
> To find out shames and idle hours in me,
> The scope and tenor of thy jealousy?
> O, no! thy love, though much, is not so great:
> It is my love that keeps mine eye awake,
> Mine own true love that doth my rest defeat,
> To play the watch-man ever for thy sake:
> For thee watch I, whilst thou dost wake elsewhere,
> From me far off, with others all too near.
>   (Shakespeare, 1996)

Here, the lover portrays his love as attention directed toward his distant beloved that keeps him awake. Note the sense of involuntary savoring, of being compelled by the outside force of one's love for the beloved in a powerful kind of world-focused romantic savoring experience that one is powerless to resist.

Or consider another 20th-century poem, *Part of Plenty,* by Bernard Spencer, found in a recent anthology of love poetry (Abse, 2005). In this poem, Spencer refers to simple activities in which his beloved engages in ordinary life, such as carrying a meal from the table and placing flowers in a vase. Spencer sees these images and others as "part of plenty" in the way he encounters love—he savors his beloved in the simple activities of everyday life, we would say.

Even the curmudgeon Henry Higgins, reflecting on his feelings for Eliza Doolittle in the song "I've Grown Accustomed to Her Face" from the musical *My Fair Lady,* communicates his reluctant savoring of his beloved. Had Eliza heard Higgins' song, she would have been bowled over with pleasure in his back-handed loving communication of her being "second nature" to him, like his own breathing. Clearly, poetic savoring of love takes many forms.

Savoring and Other Kinds of Personal Love

Although we have focused on romantic love, we should also consider other kinds of love. After all, people are in many different kinds of relationships with each other in which we can speak of love or caring for a person in a deep way. Filial love, paternal love, platonic love, love between siblings, certain strong friendships—all are common experiences in our social lifespace. We can also use savoring processes to understand such love.

It is also possible to consider a concept closely related to love, namely, the feeling that sometimes emerges when people are in a group and feel a strong bond with it. We call this collective feeling camaraderie, or a strong sense of belonging and identification. In the same way, Csikszentmihalyi (2002) has discussed the concept of "shared flow" that happens in groups convened for a common purpose, as in jam sessions when musicians lose their self-focus and become engrossed in the music they are performing together.

As with all psychological processes, we must distinguish savoring from the direct experience of the positive feelings involved. Becoming aware and attending to the pleasures people find in their important social relationships (i.e., savoring) is not the same as directly feeling the joys of camaraderie, shared flow, or family closeness. These latter experiences make a person feel accepted, provide a sense of belonging, and are instrumental in directing social goals one may have for affiliation, acceptance, or caring, but they are not what we mean by savoring.

Nonetheless, in the process of experiencing these social feelings, one can savor. One can stop what one is doing and revel in these feelings, reminisce about past times with that person or group, or anticipate future plans with these same people. All of these responses would be savoring strategies, if they were meant to prolong the experience of the positive goal or the pleasures one may be experiencing in the company of one or more family members or close friends. Just as savoring a beloved can broaden and build romantic love, we suggest savoring relationships with a group or family can likewise broaden and build the sense of interconnection or camaraderie. People can directly or indirectly communicate their savoring of a relationship to their family, friends, or other groups, who, in turn, will often reciprocate that love. In other words, the mutuality of the shared savoring experience can create a special bond among coparticipants that is itself a pleasure to be savored.

Recall our example from chapter 3 of the two strangers drawn closer while marveling together at the five rainbows in *Under the Tuscan Sun* (Mayes, 1996). The savoring of camaraderie strengthens one's feeling of connection with one's companions, enhances the quality of friendship, and provides meaning. Indeed, among the strongest motivations in seeking adventure is the bond of comradeship (Noyce, 1958). As the French poet and aviator Saint-Exupéry (1942) noted:

> Happiness! It is useless to seek it elsewhere than in this warmth of human relations. Our sordid interests imprison us within their walls. Only a comrade can grasp us by the hand and haul us free. And these human relations must be created. One must go through an apprenticeship to learn the job. Games and risk are a help here. When we exchange manly handshakes, compete in races, join together to save one of us who is in trouble, cry aloud for help in the hour of danger — only then do we learn that we are not alone on earth. (p. 28)

Along these lines, Emmons and McCullough (2003) argued that "the experience of gratitude, and the actions stimulated by it, build and strengthen social bonds and friendships" (p. 388). Extending this reasoning, we propose that savoring provides a mechanism for building, broadening, and deepening human friendships.

Imagine two different interpersonal relationships, each of which involves two friends. In the first friendship, the two individuals enjoy each other's company, but never directly or explicitly express to each other how much they appreciate their sense of interconnection. In the second friendship, in contrast, the two individuals not only enjoy each other's company, but also openly express to each other their sense of interconnection and how much they cherish it. We hypothesize that the mutual savoring of camaraderie will accelerate the growth and enrich the perceived quality of the friendship in the second relationship, relative to the first. Along these same lines, Isen (1987) presented evidence that positive affect enhances relationship formation. From an evolutionary perspective, the ability to find joy under harsh conditions, especially with one's peers, would be highly adaptive in forming the strong social bonds necessary to fuel and sustain the human instinct to engage in exploratory adventure (Noyce, 1958). Savoring and friendship go together hand in glove. As King (2000) noted:

> The experience of pleasure converges with the experience of attachment. The experience of positive emotion during social interactions is the glue that bonds human beings. One could undoubtedly argue that shared joy is more bonding than shared tragedy . . . and the amount of fun experienced by married couples during shared activities is a strong correlate of commitment. (paragraph 5)

Clearly, savoring is an adhesive process that bonds human beings. Sharing the joy of camaraderie brings people closer together, enhances the quality, depth, resilience, and longevity of their friendships, and promotes the selfless *agape* love of close friendship. Thus, savoring processes are integral in the development and maintenance of friendship.

SAVORING AND HEALTH

We now turn to the role that savoring plays in health concerns. To savor an experience is to be consciously aware of enjoying it. Savoring is clearly a positive process through which people feel good about their lives. As such, it can play the same role that Fredrickson (2002) claims positive emotions in general play in fostering health and well-being. She contends people should cultivate positive emotions because such feelings broaden personal resources, which in turn transform people in "upward spirals toward enhanced emotional well-being" (Fredrickson & Joiner, 2002, p. 174). In the same way, we can argue that savoring helps broaden the individual's life repertoire and build personal resources. The more you savor, the more you find ways to enjoy life. It would not be a big leap to suggest that savoring can facilitate "upward spirals" toward greater physical and mental health.

As Fredrickson and Joiner (2002) noted, the impact of positive emotion on well-being is in stark contrast to the downward spirals of negativity associated with dysphoria and depression. Whereas joy and depression both create the cognitive, behavioral, and emotional conditions that tend to perpetuate these affects, the latter cultivates a closed pessimistic perspective, the former an open optimistic perspective. A field experiment that Fred conducted supports such a proposition, at least on a small scale. This study was simple and straightforward, but the results clearly demonstrate the benefits of savoring for general psychological well-being.

A Field Experiment on Savoring

Fred began with the reasonable assumption that effective savoring strategies intensify or prolong the joy experienced in a happy moment. In that sense, savoring has direct implications for expanding and extending a positive emotion. He then assumed that over time, finding greater joy in the moment might not only boost momentary positive emotion, but also increase one's overall level of happiness. He also assumed that a simple but potentially effective approach to savoring is merely to notice and explicitly acknowledge to oneself the things one finds pleasurable in one's immediate environment. The research hypothesis was that people might better appreciate simple things that they would otherwise miss or take for granted, if they paid more attention to those aspects of their surroundings they find pleasing. And over time, this heightened attentional focus on positive features might well boost overall happiness.

To test this idea, Fred conducted a field experiment in which he asked college students, on their own, to take a 20-minute walk once a day for a week. Students were randomly assigned to receive one of three different sets of instructions for their walk. The "positive focus" group ($n = 25$) was instructed to try to notice as many positive things around them as they could (e.g., flowers, sunshine, music), to acknowledge each of these things in their mind when they noticed it, and to identify what it was about each thing that made it pleasurable to them. The "negative focus" group ($n = 23$) was instructed to try to notice as many negative things around them as they could (e.g., litter, graffiti, noise), to acknowledge each of these things in their mind when they noticed it, and to identify what it was about each thing that made it aversive to them. The "normal focus" control group ($n = 22$) was instructed simply to "go for a walk," with no specific instructions about what to do or think while they were walking. All students filled out measures of their overall level of happiness (Fordyce, 1988), both before their first walk and after their last walk at the end of the week.

As hypothesized, the strategy of noting and explicitly acknowledging pleasurable stimuli boosted happiness over the course of the week more than did focusing on the negative or simply going about business as usual. Specifically, the students who noticed positive environmental features and focused on what they liked about these things during their walk reported a significantly greater 1-week increase in overall level of happiness, compared both to the students who focused on negative environmental features during their walk, $t(46) = 2.93$, one-tailed $p < .003$, and to the students who simply went for a walk, $t(45) = 3.12$, one-tailed $p < .002$. These results suggest that making a conscious effort to notice and explicitly acknowledge the various sources of joy around us can make us happier.

Responses to open-ended questions about experiences related to the experiment further support this interpretation. Specifically, nearly two thirds of the participants in the "positive focus" condition spontaneously mentioned they felt a greater sense of appreciation for the world around them (e.g., nature, flowers, architecture) as a result of participating in the study, whereas none of the participants in the "negative focus" condition or "no instruction" control group reported such feelings. Thus, we suggest that practicing the art of savoring may actually help people become better at savoring, to extend what Fredrickson (2001) called "broadening" the positive emotions experienced. Hence, we speculate that the more one savors in one context, the greater one's overall well-being will be in other contexts as well.

Savoring and Physical Health

Being able to savor positive experiences can boost the frequency, intensity, and duration of positive emotions. That's what savoring is all about—becoming more mindful of joy in one's life. And over time, this enhanced experience of joy in turn may promote physical health. As the wise King Solomon put it: "A cheerful heart is a good medicine" (Proverbs 17:22, Revised Standard Version).

Such a proposition is more than mere idle speculation. Consistent with the notion that savoring has health benefits, Norman Cousins' (1979) provocative *Anatomy of an Illness* outlined the success of a personal intervention aimed at combating his own physical illness by increasing laughter and enhancing positive feelings. Supporting the link between savoring and physical health, there is experimental evidence that positive affect in general (Levy, Herberman, Maluish, Schlein, & Lippman, 1985) and humor in particular (Dillon, Minchoff, & Baker, 1985–1986) can boost human immunological functioning. And there is prospective evidence that positive emotions improve short-term physical health (Dua, 1994; Middleton & Byrd, 1996; Pettit, Kline, Gencoz, Gencoz, & Joiner, 2001). Reviewing the literature on emotional states and physical health, Salovey, Rothman, Detweiler, and Steward (2000) concluded that positive emotions and health outcomes are linked through a variety of different pathways, including immunology, psychological resilience, and health-relevant behaviors. Thus, the process of savoring would seem to have positive health consequences.

To extend this viewpoint, Fredrickson's (2001) broaden-and-build theory is grounded on the assumption that "positive emotions accumulate and compound" (Fredrickson & Joiner, 2002, p. 175), thereby maximally benefiting the individual in the long run. Based on this reasoning and on the available empirical evidence, we propose that savoring is a protective health factor that provides individuals with both short-term and long-term physical benefits.

Over the course of a lifetime, a rich and varied history of savoring should be predictive of not only a higher quality of life, but also a higher quantity of life. Clearly, because of their heightened immunocompetence, we might expect people who savor life to have fewer illnesses and live longer than those who have a hard time savoring. Supporting this conclusion, there is prospective evidence that positive emotions not only protect individuals from physical decline in old age (Ostir, Markides, Black, & Goodwin, 2000), but also increase longevity (Danner, Snowdon, & Friesen, 2001). Enhancing people's ability to savor might even lower their health-care costs in the long run (cf. Pettit et al., 2001). The instruments we have developed for studying savoring provide the measurement tools necessary to investigate prospectively the potential links between savoring and physical health.

These links between present-focused savoring of the moment and physical health have their temporal parallels in the adaptive health benefits of past-focused reminiscence and future-focused anticipation. With respect to the *past,* for example, there is experimental evidence that the process of reviewing one's life retrospectively promotes well-being among older adults (Butler, 1963; Butler & Lewis, 1982; Lewis & Butler, 1974); and that positive reminiscing increases happiness among younger adults (Bryant et al., 2005). With respect to the *future,* the capacity to derive joy by looking forward expectantly requires an optimistic orientation (i.e., a generalized positive expectancy toward the future), which has been strongly tied to positive health outcomes in numerous studies (for reviews of this research, see Scheier & Carver, 1985, 1992). There is even prospective evidence that optimism protects against the development of coronary heart disease (Kubzansky, Sparrow, Vokonas, & Kawachi, 2001). As reported in chapter 2 (see Table 2.2), the Anticipating subscale of the SBI strongly correlates with dispositional optimism, $r = .56$, $p < .0001$ (Bryant, 2003). Thus, we can speculate that positive affect from reminiscence and anticipation may well enhance human immunology through the same mechanisms that present-focused positive affect does. In other words, savoring may bring identical physical benefits, regardless of its temporal focus.

Savoring as a Dimension of Mental Health

For researchers and practitioners who wish to consider not just the ways in which people experience distress in terms of anxiety, depression, or immobilization, but also the ways in which people experience well-being in terms of happiness, satisfaction, and fulfillment, savoring life could be on top of the list as an experience to consider. One can ask, however, is savoring like feeling happy, feeling competent, or feeling satisfied? These are the major positive self-evaluations that psychologists have considered. Is savoring nothing more than part of these experiences?

As we briefly noted in the preface and in chapter 1, we have examined the many positive and negative dimensions that can be considered in staking out the parameters of subjective mental health (Bryant & Veroff, 1984). In noting the ways that various measures of people's reactions to their own well-being cluster together, we were able to isolate six somewhat independent factors: happiness, gratification in life, self-confidence, perceived vulnerability, psychophysical strain, and uncertainty. None of these six factors seems to encompass the meaning of savoring.

Aside from isolating these six dimensions of subjective well-being, we also introduced four theoretical dimensions that underlie ways of conceptualizing not only the six factors that emerged in our analyses, but also other factors that might be part of people's self-evaluations (Bryant & Veroff, 1984). These four conceptual dimensions are: (a) the positive versus negative anchoring of self-evaluation (happiness and gratification are positive; vulnerability and strain are negative); (b) time orientation (gratification, vulnerability, and strain are past-focused; self-confidence is present-focused; uncertainty is future-focused); (c) self-focused versus world-focused orientation (gratification and self-confidence are self-focused; vulnerability and uncertainty are world-focused); and (d) spontaneous versus reflective appraisal (happiness and vulnerability are spontaneous; gratification and self-confidence are reflective).

How does savoring fit into this four-dimensional scheme? First, savoring is clearly a positive rather than a negative experience. Second, the orientation of savoring is mostly present, but can also include the past and future. Third, as we noted in chapter 5, savoring can be about sensing the world, sensing the self, or some blend of the two, depending on the specific focus of attention involved. Last, savoring is both spontaneous in its power to boost enjoyment, as well as reflective in the mindful state of awareness that lies at its very heart; and savoring experiences can be categorized as involving either reflection or absorption, as we previously noted (see chapter 5).

Thus, savoring does seem to be a dimension of subjective mental health that, at least in Bryant and Veroff's (1984) scheme, is untapped by standard questions posed about peoples' life experiences. It is perhaps time that researchers include a measure of savoring in their battery of mental health assessments (Bryant, 2003). Not only is it meaningful to talk of the positive mental health of people who savor their lives, but also one can easily talk of some deficiencies in the psychological well-being of those among us who do not or cannot savor their lives.

In chapter 2, we presented evidence from Bryant (2003) linking people's levels of savoring beliefs to standard measures of subjective adjustment (see Table 2.2). These data reveal moderate to strong negative correlations between the perceived capacity to savor the moment and neuroticism, physical anhedonia, social anhedonia, depression, and psychophysical symptoms of strain. Scores on the Savoring the Moment subscale of the SBI also show moderate positive correlations with happiness, self-esteem, and gratification, but are unrelated to measures of socially desirable responding. Clearly, savoring is associated with higher levels of subjective mental health and seems to reflect positive adaptive functioning (Ryff, 1989). Extending this perspective, we suggest that psycho-therapy in general has much to gain in using savoring as a protective factor and in helping clients learn how better to savor their lives effectively (cf. Duckworth, Steen, & Seligman, 2005; Seligman, 2002b; Seligman & Peterson, 2003).

There is another way to think of the process of savoring as a dimension of mental health, and that is as a basic style of approaching experience. This per-spective is similar to what Watson (2002) has done with the concept of "positive affectivity," or the dispositional tendency to experience positive feelings. Watson and his colleagues have shown considerable independence in three self-report measures of dispositional affectivities: joviality, self-assurance, and attentiveness. And these three measures correlate highly with the extraversion scale of the "Big Five" personality trait assessment (Goldberg, 1993). Correlational studies of the positive affectivity scales suggest that such personality dispositions, although negatively linked to a variety of psychopathological states (e.g., phobias, schizo-phrenia, posttraumatic stress syndromes), show their greatest negative connec-tion to the mood disorders. Although only correlational, these studies suggest that positive affectivity protects people from experiencing those negative syn-dromes involved in psychiatric diagnoses. Of course, we should always be alert to the reverse causal direction, that is, disturbed people can find it hard to savor. Dwelling on one's depression and savoring life are mutually exclusive processes.

SAVORING AND CREATIVITY

A third human concern in which we think savoring plays a role is in enhancing human creativity. Indeed, there is evidence that positive affect can boost creativ-ity (Carnevale & Isen, 1986; Isen, Daubman, & Nowicki, 1987). The flow that is likely to occur for many people who are following creative urges may be in some ways similar to the flow people experience when they are swept away in savoring the moment. As people savor an experience and attend mindfully to their ongo-ing sensory and cognitive experiences, they can feel propelled by a vital energy that stems from their positive feelings. This energy can be the grist for injecting those positive feelings into a work of art or into a new solution to a problem.

Many novelists and poets take notes about their life experiences while they are savoring these experiences. Artists often sketch ideas as they are experienc-ing a new landscape and enjoying it with a mindful eye. These notes or ideas may be relatively random while savoring an experience in a freely associative way, but an artist can later use this material in producing something creative. It is almost as if a period in which one savors one's observation is critical to artistic produc-tion, even when this work concerns a difficult or painful subject.

Might this same phenomenon be characteristic of scientific creativity as well? As psychologists, we might savor a family reunion, attend to the details of that experience, and in a quieter moment use those savored observations to help us develop theories of the nature of family ties. It is very hard to pinpoint how this occurs, but there is no doubt that it does. Savored observations of the social world may be more amenable to translation into legitimate social science theory than observations made more dispassionately. The same might be said for the physical and natural scientist as well.

In his biography of Benjamin Franklin, Morgan (2002) described how Franklin's omnivorous curiosity led Franklin to scrutinize the intricacies of natural phenomena. Once as a young man, Franklin hung a glass of oil and water on the ceiling as a reading lamp during a voyage home from England, and found himself staring and pondering the repulsion of the oil and water. In his diary, he wrote about his fascination with this experience in what could easily be viewed as the savoring of an observation. His thoughts about this experience never left him, and he found himself experimenting with oil and water even to the advanced age of 67, when he conducted an experiment on the seashore. The savoring first stemming from his enormous curiosity led to creative ways to explore and understand the problem.

One reason why savored experiences may enhance creativity is that in the process of savoring, people are more fully exposed to the complexities of the situation they are in. In their open mindfulness, they are free to roam in any direction that the stimulus they are considering takes them. Guilford (1950) called this a capacity to engage in "divergent thinking." In that sense, savoring resembles mindful meditation. Boundaries are loosened; complexity is expanded. Once a person is in a savoring frame of mind, repetition of the very same stimulus becomes boring. He or she needs to move on, as we have suggested in hypothesizing that an optimal level of stimulation is a critical motivating factor in inducing savoring. Savoring is thus a dynamic process tuned to expanding a person's own curiosities.

In addition, there is a playfulness in savoring, a willingness to combine unusual stimuli, to perceive more deeply, to explore unique contrasts and comparisons. Savoring has to occur playfully or else it becomes purely an instrumental task to be completed, or a problem to be solved. Then it is no longer savoring, but something else. But once the playfulness in our savoring occurs, then reassessing what has been savored often unveils creative insights, scientific discoveries, or fresh works of art. Thus, savoring cultivates new capacities for complex associations and thoughts, as well as a degree of playfulness about these associations and thoughts. In this way, savoring may be a major root of human creativity.

Some psychologists who have spent their lives studying creativity have concluded that intrinsic motivation is an essential ingredient in making something judged to be creative. Amabile and her colleagues (Amabile, 1983) examined the motivations underlying creativity in a controlled setting. She asked children and adults to perform various open-ended tasks (e.g., drawing, finding solutions to problems) and generally found that the tasks performed under intrinsic incentive conditions (e.g., relying on the person's own interests) are judged by evaluators blind to the motivational conditions as being far more creative than the same tasks performed for explicit rewards (e.g., recognition, money). Such intrinsic motivation may be most important during stages of the creative process in which novelty is vital, such as when it is crucial to generate new ideas (Amabile, 1996). In a different style of research, Torrance (1969) examined the psychological makeup of well-known creative individuals and found that the one common feature in their descriptions of their work was that they were in love with what they were doing. For example, Torrance discussed the life and work of Roger Tory Peterson, the eminent, highly productive ornithologist, who in many ways indicated that from a very early age he was joyfully passionate about his search for birds in the wild.

Following Torrance's style of research, Csikszentmihalyi (1996) interviewed 91 well-known artists, scientists, and scholars, all over age 60 but still actively engaged in their fields, in search of the aspects of their lives that enabled them to become innovators during the 20th century and the factors underpinning the creative process. In many ways, Csikszentmihalyi's (1996) insights about the creative process overlap with our views on how savoring is important to creative work. We cannot do full justice to Csikszentmihalyi's brilliant book, *Creativity*, but through the many chapters devoted to the motivational basis for creativity runs the theme that creative people show genuine joy and fulfillment in what they do and show little evidence for the stereotype of the "tortured genius." In their responses to Csikszentmihalyi's questions, these creative individuals emphasized their curiosity about particular problems and their joy in finding answers, not unlike what Roger Tory Peterson told Torrance. For example, a group of physicists claimed that what inspired them to find out about the movement of atoms and stars was their own exhilaration from the sights they experienced viewing tall peaks and the night sky. It is an upbeat and positive picture of the life of creative men and women in our current society, a picture congruent with our linkage of savoring to the creative process.

We should also note, however, that Csikszentmihalyi was dealing with recognized creative people, for whose work there was already public acclaim. It is thus not surprising that issues of energy, being smart, or being disciplined enter into the picture, inasmuch as a successful product is at stake in their work. In pure savoring, we have argued, people stand back from issues of recognition and the creation of something important to the world. So while savoring seems highly relevant to creativity for these famous innovators, they would never have "arrived" and done what they did based on savoring alone. Work, ambition, being rooted in reality, and being objective about what one is doing had to be central in the lives of these creative people. Thus, we can say that savoring is a necessary but not sufficient condition for becoming and remaining a well-recognized creative individual.

According to Csikszentmihalyi (1996), flow characterizes the experience of many innovators during the actual creative process. However, we reiterate the point we made at the outset of this book — flow is similar to savoring, but is also different in some important respects (see chapter 1). We believe savoring involves more present-focused mindfulness and has less connection with problem solving and task challenges than Csikszentmihalyi implies is present in flow experiences. Nevertheless, we could very well use an example Csikszentmihalyi (1996) gave of the poet Mark Strand's flow experience of being "right in the work," to illustrate the poet savoring his own cognitive processing during creativity:

> Well you're right in the work, you lose your sense of time, you're completely enraptured, you're completely caught up in what you're doing, and you're sorta swayed by the possibilities you see in this work. If that becomes too powerful, then you get up because the excitement is too great. You can't continue to work or continue to see the end of the work because you're jumping ahead of yourself all the time. The idea is to be so . . . saturated with it, that there's no future or past, it's just an extended present in what you're, uh, making meaning. And dismantling meaning, and remaking it . . . (p. 121)

One might ask Strand whether he goes through a similar savoring (flow) experience when he is considering a painful topic, either from his own or others' experience. Poetry, after all, deals directly with the problems of life as much as or even more than its joys. Indeed, there is sometimes great anguish to consider in creativity. What sense does it make to call on the process of savoring as an integral part of such moments? To answer our own question: only to the degree that mindful attention to anguish and working through it to reach some understanding represents a kind of heartfelt enlightenment after going through the engaged flow that Strand describes. Afterwards, there is some positive feeling, perhaps the catharsis Aristotle noted regarding the nature of an aesthetically meaningful tragedy, that results from the energy of such a process, especially if the creative person has experienced a release from the anguish he or she was considering. It would be difficult to call that savoring per se, but it could be an offshoot of it.

Indirectly we all experience a similar process when we read a beautifully written tragic novel, or hear a mournful piece of music, or contemplate a horrific photograph about a terrible event, and find any one of these experiences compelling and moving. In a way, we are savoring our aesthetic reaction to these upsetting works of art. We can be gripped by a suspenseful drama and then be brought back to a resolved state. As observers, we are reacting creatively to what we have experienced. Either creating the work of art or observing it unfold permits us to have an emotional resolution that we can savor.

SAVORING AND SPIRITUALITY

The last human concern we consider in relation to savoring is the human quest for a spiritual life. With few notable exceptions (e.g., James, 1902/1985),

20th-century psychology eschewed the spiritual side of human experience. Only as we have begun the next century have serious-minded psychologists entertained ideas that reflect spiritual concerns, despite the fact that these phenomena are difficult to pin down using rigorous scientific methods (Miller & Thoresen, 2003). To make this task especially hard, problems abound in conceptually defining spirituality (see Pargament & Mahoney, 2002). Nevertheless, it is clear that the concept of spirituality has deep roots in human experience. Some theorists have even proposed a genetic basis for these profound human concerns: "In short, we posit that tens of thousands of years of evolution have deeply planted sociality, spirituality, and meaning making in our genome and in our societies" (Cacioppo, Hawkley, Rickett, & Masi, 2005, p. 145). Although "spiritual" and "spirituality" have diverse meanings, these various meanings all assume there is something important about the nonphysical person, some metaphysical aspect of experience that is sacred to the individual.

Savoring and Making Meaning

To study spirituality, however, most psychologists make a more general assumption that people try to find meaning in their lives on a larger scale (e.g., Allport, 1961; Frankl, 1963). Wong and Fry (1998) argued that "personal meaning is important not only for survival but also for health and well-being" (p. xvii). Indeed, Zika and Chamberlain (1992) found that having a sense of meaning in life was a more consistent predictor of college students' psychological well-being than the personality variables of assertiveness and locus of control. And personal meaning has been found to correlate positively with well-being across nearly every stage of life (Reker, Peacock, & Wong, 1987; Zika & Chamberlain, 1992).

Sometimes this meaning comes from one's belief in an organizing sacred force loosely identified as God. Sometimes this meaning is found in some overall biological purpose. And sometimes meaning resides in abstract values (e.g., love, justice, universality) people find in their own or others' appraisals of the world. Although we can assume the desire to make meaning in life is a given for humans who have such well-developed brains, the direction that this meaning making takes obviously depends on many personal, social, and cultural factors. These factors reside in both the general historical circumstances in one's life and the specific contexts that affect the world in which one is embedded. For some thinkers, these factors can also reflect genetic propensities that guide the way people think in general. It is no small wonder that spirituality means different things to different people.

How should we define "spiritual" and "spirituality" in thinking about the ways in which savoring might connect to spirituality? We stick to the general idea that spirituality is a process of "meaning making," without specifying what type of meaning that is, beyond the fact that the meaning rests on something outside the self. In finding meaning, the person seeks some value, some "good," some sense of a moral, social, or natural force that exists in an important way independent of one's material being. In the simplest of terms, therefore, we argue that savoring facilitates the process of making meaning in life by connecting people with what they see as the larger enduring forces outside their physical worlds.

In previous chapters, we hinted at the link between savoring and spirituality. In chapter 5, we discussed three types of savoring that we called "world-focused" — thanksgiving, marveling, and surrendering oneself to a person or group. Each of these types of savoring has the potential to engage spiritual connections to something outside oneself. People intentionally or unintentionally operate as spiritual beings whenever they are: in awe of the grandeur of nature; overwhelmed by the magnificence of a symphonic performance; astonished by the elegant order of a brilliant scientific theory; moved by the communion experienced during important patriotic, political, or religious events; swept up in the love of another person; moved by the goodness or grace of another; or overcome by a deep sense of gratitude for the good fortune that life or a religious deity has bestowed on them. The important thing in all these world-focused instances of savoring, we argue, is that people lose most of the constraints on their physical existence, for the moment at least, and under these conditions encounter a force larger than themselves. In other words, they experience spiritual connections.

We have noted that special savoring often occurs when people are under particular uncertainties about what they are experiencing. For example, soldiers sometimes experience intense awe when marveling at their experiences during the hazards of wartime. Authors especially savor something they have written that was extremely difficult to create. It is not that people automatically have spiritual experiences under circumstances of uncertainty. However, these circumstances often produce spiritual reactions, especially if the circumstances involve uncertainties in life that are especially momentous, rather than mundane everyday concerns, such as what one should eat or where one should go on a walk.

Consider some uncertainties in life that are of great consequence: for example, what people should do with their lives, whether a woman should commit herself to a lifelong relationship, how parents should prepare their children for life, how one should think about a pessimistic medical diagnosis for oneself or a loved one. How might savoring come into play during those far-reaching uncertainties, those times when people pose and ponder pivotal questions about meaning and confront spiritual answers to these questions? We assert that these weighty situations are ripe for powerful savoring experiences that may be inherently attached to a search for meaning. It is as if individuals savor what they observe *especially* when they need to make meaning in an uncertain life situation. For example, ecstatic religious experiences often occur when people are confused about what is happening to them, when people are in search of meaning because of some grave illness or impending tragedy that makes no sense to them.

Another bridge between spirituality and savoring that we discussed earlier is in the similarity of meditation and savoring processes. Many spiritual quests have involved meditation. The secret to most meditative states is that one should block out stimulation that feeds the senses and loosely focus on nothing of an evaluative or problem-solving nature. Zen teachings advocate repeating a mantra to attain a fluid state that transports one outside the usual way of thinking about the world and the self and become more in touch with one's inner self, sometimes losing a sense of the self altogether to reach a unique state of consciousness of being. These meditative processes depend on attuning the self to its connections with larger forces that are believed to exist. Is this not a special kind of mindful savoring, the savoring of one's inner awareness of self to become more aware of larger forces of existence?

Savoring, Positive Affect, and the Perception of Meaning

Besides its links with spirituality and religion, however, savoring has another connection with the human quest for meaning in life. Not only does a sense of meaning typically promote positive affect (Reker & Wong, 1988), but also positive affect can promote a sense of meaning. In particular, King, Hicks, Krull, and Del Gaiso (2006) have demonstrated that positive moods can predispose people to find life more meaningful. Across six studies, King et al. (2006) found that: (a) positive affect is a stronger predictor of meaning in life than is one's level of conflict and confusion about personal goals; (b) positive mood is a stronger predictor of perceived meaning in a given day than are goal-related thoughts and activities; (c) and experimentally manipulating positive mood produces higher ratings of meaning in life and increases people's sensitivity to the difference between meaningless and meaningful tasks. Thus, positive moods may actually help people find meaning in life.

This conclusion suggests that savoring processes facilitate people's quest for personal meaning. Being able to mindfully appreciate the moment — to rejoice, surrender oneself to something larger than oneself, give thanks for blessings, bask in personal accomplishments, marvel at the wonders in the world, or luxuriate in pleasure — increases the likelihood that one can find purpose, fulfillment, and meaning in one's life. In other words, savoring provides more than just feelings of joy, gratitude, pride, awe, or pleasure. It also enriches a sense of connection with other people, with the world, and with existence at a deeper metaphysical level, compared to ordinary, everyday experiences.

Savoring and Religious Experience

Three savoring processes we have discussed — namely, marveling, giving thanks, and self-surrender — dovetail with common ideas about spiritual processes, particularly in the context of religion. Concerning the distinction between spirituality and religion, Miller and Thoresen (2003) noted:

> In one sense, religion is an institutional (and thus primarily material) phenomenon. Though often centrally concerned with spirituality, religions are social entities or institutions, and unlike spirituality, they are defined by their boundaries. Religions are differentiated by particular beliefs and practices, requirements of membership, and modes of social organization. What is spiritual or transcendent may be a central interest and focus, but religions are also characterized by other nonspiritual concerns and goals (e.g., cultural, economic, political, social). Thus, religion can be seen as fundamentally a social phenomenon, whereas spirituality (like health and personality) is usually understood at the level of the individual without specific contexts (Thoresen, 1998). Viewed in this way, the field of religion is to spirituality as the field of medicine is to health. (pp. 27–28)

As with spirituality, there are also individual differences in the experience and expression of religiousness. For some people, religiousness and spirituality are strongly interconnected, whereas for other people, even within the same religion, there may be very little overlap (Miller & Thoresen, 2003). There are also both public and private forms of religiousness, whereas spirituality has traditionally been conceptualized as a more private concern (Thoresen, 1998).

Marveling.   Savoring permeates religion most clearly in the religious practices of prayer and worship. When encountering the divine, most organized religions espouse a reverent sense of awe and wonder in the face of infinite power, wisdom, and holiness. The Book of Psalms, for example, tells us, "Let all the earth fear the Lord: let all the inhabitants of the world stand in awe of Him!" (Psalm 33:8, Revised Standard Version). Indeed, the Jewish Torah is filled with stories recounting God's awesome might, at which believers have marveled for centuries. Thus, most traditional religions encourage followers to marvel reverently and experience humble awe in the presence of a supreme deity. This reverent marveling may take place either privately in prayer or meditation, or publicly in organized corporate worship. Among believers, a mindful awareness of a divine presence naturally produces awe, as one ponders the far-reaching implications.

Thanksgiving.   Many formal religious systems also involve some form of thanksgiving in which the worshipper expresses gratitude for providence, sustenance, support, guidance, love, or protection to the perceived source of these blessings. For example, traditional Christian worship services typically include time not only for intercessory prayer asking God's help for oneself or others, but also for praising and giving thanks to God for blessings one has received. And in Judaism, formal worship often involves outward expressions of gratitude, as when King David exhorts the faithful to "Make a joyful noise to the Lord, all the lands! Serve the Lord with gladness! Come into his presence with singing!

... Enter his gates with thanksgiving, and his courts with praise! Give thanks to him, bless his name!" (Psalm 100: 1, 2, 4, Revised Standard Version). Clearly, the savoring response of counting blessings, and the expressive savoring process of thanksgiving, are closely tied to these forms of religious worship.

Concerning the role of thanksgiving in religious experience, the 19th-century Christian devotional writer E. M. Bounds (1925/1991) observed in *The Essentials of Prayer:*

> Gratitude is an inward emotion of the soul, involuntarily arising therein, while thanksgiving is the voluntary expression of gratitude. ... Thanksgiving is ... the giving of ... something to God in words which we feel at heart for blessings received. ... As we think of mercies past, the heart is inwardly moved to gratitude. Love is the child of gratitude. Love grows as gratitude is felt, and then breaks out into praise and thanksgiving to God. ... Gratitude and love move to larger and increased praying. ... Consideration of God's mercies not only begets gratitude, but induces a large consecration to God of all we have and are. So that prayer, giving, and consecration are all linked together inseparably. (pp. 31–32)

Paralleling Fredrickson's (2001; Fredrickson & Joiner, 2002) theoretical model, over the long term these powerful transcendent feelings might well produce upward spirals of spiritual well-being (see Moberg & Brusek, 1978), in which gratitude induces love, thanksgiving, and praise, which in turn produce stronger transcendent feelings.

Rejoicing. As Bounds' observations clearly suggest, besides the savoring processes of marveling and thanksgiving, religious experience can also involve the process of *rejoicing,* or expressing joy, gladness, elation, or delight in meditation, prayer, or worship. Paralleling the savoring response of behavioral expression, to rejoice is to outwardly express one's positive feelings, to give visible expression to inner experience. Underscoring the central importance of expressing one's positive emotions in the context of religious practice, the 150 Psalms of the Bible include 35 references to the words "joy" or "joyful," and 67 references to the words "rejoice" or "rejoicing." Noting the jubilant expressiveness that permeates the Psalms, Peterson (1997) termed this form of religious experience "an earthy spirituality that's exuberantly holy" (p. 10).

Surrendering Oneself. In the course of expressing such deep feelings, people may also experience a sense of being transported beyond themselves and of merging with something larger and more profound—a metaphysical experience often associated with rapturous feelings of serenity, ecstasy, or bliss. Relevant here is the savoring process of surrendering oneself to something greater than the self, as when Christian believers turn their lives over to Jesus and are said to be "born again."

Extending the implications of savoring in religious experience, we suggest that over time, the process of mindfully appreciating one's relationship with a religious deity and of continually marveling and giving thanks in prayer and worship for counted blessings broadens and builds spirituality, thereby promoting feelings of love, devotion, and commitment toward the religious deity. These loving feelings, in turn, deepen one's sense of connection with the deity, which further deepens love, gradually spiraling upward. Viewed from this perspective, it is perhaps not surprising that religious practice is correlated not only with greater happiness and satisfaction with life (Poloma & Pendelton, 1990), but also with greater physical health and longevity (Koenig, Smiley, & Gonzales, 1988; Levin & Schiller, 1987). Clearly, savoring is an integral part of religious experience and practice.

SUMMARY

In this chapter, we considered ways in which savoring processes relate to important life experiences that most people greatly value — romantic love, marriage, friendship, physical and mental health, creativity, making meaning, spirituality, and religious experience. In discussing love, we noted how people's own savoring of their beloved or their family or friends can induce a reciprocal savoring in these loved ones, creating a "snowball effect" on their interconnections. In the same manner, the savoring of camaraderie is also itself a source of joy in friendship, which broadens and builds interpersonal relationships. In discussing health, we suggested that the emotional glow during savoring strengthens human immunology and evokes positive physical responses within our bodies and psychological responses within our psyches. In discussing creativity, we asserted that there is a spin-off from the attentional focus during the savoring process that heightens people's awareness of new images, ideas, and insights. Finally, in discussing spirituality, we recognized that savoring often leads people to search for special meaning in their savoring moments, and we noted how the savoring processes of marveling, thanksgiving, surrendering oneself, and rejoicing are integral parts of many traditional religious systems.

When it comes to connections between savoring and human concerns, however, these topics are merely the tip of the conceptual iceberg. We could also have examined savoring in relation to family, work, leisure, adventure, education, sports, loss, and rehabilitation. Our point is simply to demonstrate that savoring is an adaptive, integral part of human life and a phenomenon worthy of further study. Although much of our thinking is speculative, we have also drawn on the research literature to support our general contentions that savoring broadens and builds interpersonal and spiritual relationships, promotes mental and physical health, boosts creativity, and facilitates the process of finding connection and meaning in life.

8

Enhancing Savoring

No day comes twice.
Each moment savored more precious
than a span of jade.
— Zen tradition

How can people promote savoring experiences in their lives, as so many would like to do? How can people cultivate the capacity to appreciate the wonders of life, to cherish precious memories from the past, to anticipate good things the future may hold, to capture the joy of the moment? Are there simply people who can or cannot savor — that is, "savorers" and "nonsavorers," the way we speak of extraverts and introverts, or optimists and pessimists? Or is it possible for people to learn to think and act in ways that enhance the quality of the savoring experiences in their lives? If it is possible to become more adept at savoring, then what specific approaches or orientations should people adopt if they want to enhance savoring? And how can people learn these approaches to savoring?

This final chapter sets out some guiding principles that could enhance savoring for everyone, regardless of whether or not they easily or customarily savor positive experiences. Our deeply ingrained training as social psychologists makes us believe that under carefully crafted conditions, it would be possible to elicit savoring experiences in almost anyone, regardless of the individual's starting point. Accordingly, we consider this chapter a sort of beginner's guide to savoring. To add to our hubris, from time to time we suggest exercises one can do that embody some of the generalizations we make. These exercises are based on our earlier discussions of savoring, as well as on techniques borrowed from the literature on meditation, psychotherapy, and affect management. We close by suggesting that true happiness lies not just in knowing how to savor, but also having the wisdom to savor in ways that provide meaning and purpose.

CAN PEOPLE ALTER THEIR OVERALL LEVEL OF HAPPINESS?

Happiness Set-Point and Savoring

To what extent is the capacity to savor determined by nature versus nurture? There is evidence that some people, compared to others, are genetically predisposed to feel positive feelings more strongly. Along these lines, theorists have proposed that people's long-term levels of happiness are largely stable and fluctuate only slightly around a genetically determined "set point" (Diener & Diener, 1996; Heady & Wearing, 1992; Lykken, 1999). In the same vein, Watson (2000) proposed that positive affect is a relatively stable trait or temperament measurable by a dispositional personality scale assessing what he calls "positive affectivity." But what does it mean to have a set point for positive affect that is genetically determined, and what are the implications of this notion for enhancing savoring?

Using a wonderfully insightful metaphor, Lykken (2000) suggested that all of us are born with a certain baseline level of happiness that he likens to a lake on which our ship is sailing — the higher the level of the lake, the better we feel. The baseline level (or set point) of the lake varies from person to person for genetic reasons. But given this baseline, the level of the lake also fluctuates within each person over time depending on one's energy level, stress, and recent events.

These latter transient influences temporarily alter the level of the lake, so that it is almost never completely calm. Although life events cannot permanently change the lake's baseline level, positive events create waves that temporarily raise our boat, whereas negative events create troughs that temporarily lower our boat. Big waves from particularly wonderful events, and big troughs from particularly terrible events, take longer to subside than their smaller counterparts. But eventually the level of the lake always returns to its baseline.

In its most extreme form, set-point theory maintains that it is useless to try to raise the level of one's lake permanently. Viewed from this perspective, "trying to be happier is as futile as trying to be taller" (Lykken & Tellegen, 1996, p. 189). Yet, a more accurate way of thinking about baseline levels of positive affect may be to conceive of them not as set "points" but rather as set "ranges." Indeed, Seligman (2002a) suggested that, "A set range is a more optimistic notion than a set point ... since you could live at the upper level of such a happiness range rather than the lower level" (p. 279).

Regulating one's level of positive affect within one's "set range" is the essence of savoring. To extend Lykken's (2000) lake metaphor, we suggest *coping* involves sailing one's boat so as to avoid troughs and steer out of troughs that one cannot avoid, whereas *savoring* involves sailing one's boat so as to find the waves one wants to encounter and make them bigger and longer lasting, if one so chooses.

Prior Work on Boosting Happiness

What does the empirical literature suggest concerning the notion that people's positive affect has a flexible set-range rather than a rigid set-point? Reviewing research on the pursuit of happiness, Lyubomirsky, Sheldon, and Schkade (2005) concluded that "emerging sources of optimism exist regarding the possibility of permanent increases in happiness" (p. 111). For this reason, it would seem all the more important for people with chronically low levels of enjoyment to "pay greater attention to the 'hedonic book keeping' of their activities" (Meehl, 1975, p. 305).

Many writers have offered recommendations aimed at helping people find greater joy in life. Indeed, there is no shortage of "pop psychology" self-help books and "how to" magazine articles offering tips for achieving happiness. Although much of this advice has been based on little more than intuition, some recommendations have been solidly grounded in theory and research.

In one of the earliest systematic investigations aimed at boosting happiness, Fordyce (1977, 1983) experimentally demonstrated the effectiveness of a semester-long educational intervention, consisting of 14 components designed to increase personal happiness. Fordyce's intervention involved teaching people to become more active, spend more time socializing, be productive at meaningful work, become better organized, stop worrying, lower expectations, increase positive thinking, become present-oriented, develop a healthy personality, become more extraverted, be themselves, eliminate negative feelings, strengthen close relationships, and place more value on happiness. Although one cannot be sure which particular aspects of the multifaceted treatment were responsible for increasing happiness, we note that at least half of the components of this intervention are variables we have linked to enhanced savoring—namely, socializing, avoiding worrying, thinking positively, being present-oriented, avoiding negative feelings, strengthening close relationships, and valuing happiness.

In a similar vein, Lichter, Haye, and Kammann (1980) experimentally demonstrated that people can raise overall levels of happiness either by replacing negative self-relevant beliefs and attitudes with more positive ones (through eight 2-hour sessions during one month), or by rehearsing positive feeling statements (10 minutes daily for 2 weeks). In addition, Lyubomirsky et al. (2005) reported several experiments in which increasing the frequency of people's positive activities boosted happiness. Furthermore, across three experiments, Emmons and McCullough (2003) showed that increasing the frequency with which people experience gratitude can increase levels of well-being.

Reviewing the research on happiness, Myers (1992) offered 10 suggestions for achieving a happier life: (a) realize that enduring happiness does not come from success; (b) take control of your time; (c) act happy; (d) seek activities that engage your skills; (e) become more physically active; (f) get an adequate amount of sleep; (g) give priority to close relationships; (h) reach out to other people; (i) give thanks each day for the positive aspects of your life; and (j) nurture your spirituality. Again, notice that many of these suggestions are also relevant for enhancing savoring.

And yet, despite what positive psychology has discovered about the roots of happiness, it is not easy or necessarily effective to provide universal "rules" for finding joy in the moment. As Csikszentmihalyi (1990) argued, "A joyful life is an individual creation that cannot be copied from a recipe" (p. xi). As with the process of coping, there is no one general prescription that will optimally enhance savoring for everyone across all situations. What we offer instead are "steps toward enhancing the quality of life," to borrow a phrase from the dust jacket of Csikszentmihalyi's (1990) popular book, *Flow: The Psychology of Optimal Experience.*

Six Factors That Enhance Both Coping and Savoring

Although coping and savoring involve separate sets of concerns that are only modestly correlated (Bryant, 1989, 2003; Meehan et al., 1993), some variables serve to facilitate both types of processes. Before highlighting guiding principles specifically aimed at enhancing savoring, we first briefly note six cognitive-behavioral constructs that serve to enhance both coping with negative experience, as well as savoring of positive experience: (a) social support; (b) writing about life experiences; (c) downward hedonic contrast; (d) humor; (e) spirituality and religion; and (f) awareness of the fleetingness of experience. These factors are particularly valuable tools for managing affect because of their widely applicable versatility in helping people not only handle bad things, but also savor good things.

Social Support. Across most forms of adversity, one of the most adaptive forms of coping with stress and misfortune is social support, in which one shares one's feelings with significant others in one's social network (Bloom, 1990; House, 1981; Lazarus & Folkman, 1984). A great deal of research has demonstrated that social support buffers the negative effects of stress on individuals, thereby ameliorating distress (Cohen & Wills, 1985; Vaux, 1988). And as we have noted repeatedly throughout this book, sharing one's positive feelings with other people also enhances savoring. Sharing feelings with others can boost the emotional impact of positive outcomes (Gable et al., 2004; Langston, 1994), and our own data show strong and consistent relationships between expressing positive feelings to others and greater enjoyment of positive events (see chapter 4). Thus, people with larger and more accessible social networks may not only cope better, but may also savor more fully.

Writing About Life Experiences.   A great deal of research supports the notion that writing about negative life experiences has beneficial effects on physical health. For example, writing about traumatic life events enhances immune functioning (Esterling, Antoni, Fletcher, & Margulies, 1994; Pennebaker, Kiecolt-Glaser, & Glaser, 1988) and decreases symptoms of asthma and rheumatoid arthritis (Smyth, Stone, Hurewitz, & Kaell, 1999). To explain these effects, Pennebaker and Seagal (1999) suggested that writing about trauma helps people make sense of negative life experiences. In other words, the health benefits of writing about trauma seem to stem from the creation of a logical narrative that helps people gain insights into the meaning of their personal suffering (Niederhoffer & Pennebaker, 2002).

This type of narrative construction can also be useful in boosting the benefits of positive experiences. For example, compared to students randomly assigned to write about a neutral topic, students assigned to write about their best possible "future selves" showed greater physical health benefits and psychological well-being after writing (King, 2001); and students assigned to write about intensely positive peak experiences showed greater positive mood at the posttest and fewer health center visits for illness 3 months later (Burton & King, 2004). Other data suggest that simply talking about positive experiences with others, explaining the details and meaning of one's joys, can provide the same benefits as writing about these experiences (Niederhoffer & Pennebaker, 2002). Thus, people who tell stories or write diary entries, letters, poetry, or songs describing and interpreting their life experiences may not only work through negative experiences more effectively, but may also enhance savoring and gain greater physical and psychological benefits from positive experiences.

Downward Hedonic Contrast.   Another strategy that enhances both coping and savoring is the creation of downward hedonic contrast, through cognitive evaluations that make one's current state seem better in relation to relevant comparative standards. One way to create downward contrast is through counterfactual thinking (Markman, Gavanski, Sherman, & McMullen, 1993; Roese, 1994, 1997), or thoughts about the way things might have been. For example, imagining how a negative outcome could have been worse dampens its emotional impact (Roese, 1994; White & Lehman, 2005), whereas imagining how a positive outcome might not have happened boosts its emotional impact (Roese, 1994). With respect to downward counterfactuals in savoring, Frijda (1988) proposed:

> Adaptation to satisfaction can be counteracted by constantly being aware of how fortunate one's condition is and of how it could have been otherwise, or actually

was otherwise before—by rekindling impact through recollection and imagination. Enduring happiness seems possible, and it can be understood theoretically. However, note that it does not come naturally, by itself. It takes effort. (p. 354)

Along these same lines, the Greek philosopher Epicurus (341–270 B.C.) offered the following advice: "Do not spoil what you have by desiring what you have not; but remember that what you now have was once among the things only hoped for." Note that Item 3 of the Ways of Savoring Checklist (WOSC) captures precisely this sentiment: "I reminded myself how long I had waited for this to happen."

Downward *social* comparison, on the other hand, may not always boost enjoyment of positive events (Buunk, Collins, Taylor, VanYperen, & Dakof, 1990). Sometimes one may feel guilty when comparing oneself to others who are worse off. In the fall of 2005, for instance, some people found it hard to celebrate the Labor Day weekend because of guilt, when so many others were suffering in the aftermath of Hurricane Katrina (Associated Press, September 3, 2005). Thus, it may be a more effective savoring strategy to compare one's current state to worse possible outcomes than to others who are worse off.

Humor. Another response that enhances both coping and savoring is the use of humor. With respect to *coping,* humor not only relieves tension and anxiety (Kuiper & Martin, 1993; Moran & Massam, 1999; Yovetich, Dale, & Hudak, 1990), but also buffers people from the affective and physical consequences of stress (Lefcourt & Martin, 1986; Martin & Dobbin, 1988; Martin & Lefcourt, 1983). With respect to *savoring,* injecting humor into: (a) the classroom makes learning more enjoyable (Bryant & Zillmann, 1988; LoShiavo & Shatz, 2005); (b) television commercials enhances enjoyment of the programs containing these ads (Cantor, Bryant, & Zillmann, 1974; Perry, 2001); and (c) video material increases levels of hopefulness toward the future (Vilaythong, Arnau, Rosen, & Mascaro, 2003). Furthermore, laughter not only helps maintain perspective in the midst of adversity, but also increases the outward expression of joy, which can enhance savoring. Thus, humor enhances the capacity to cope with negative experience and derive benefits from positive experience.

Spirituality and Religion. Spirituality and religion not only provide a source of strength, comfort, hope, and meaning in facing and overcoming adversity (Hood, Spilka, Hunsberger, & Gorsuch, 2003; Pargament, 1997), but also are linked to higher levels of happiness (Myers, 1992; Myers & Diener, 1995). With respect to coping, mothers with a disabled child are less likely to be depressed if they have a strong religious faith as opposed to little or no religious faith (Friedrich, Cohen, & Wilturner, 1988). Moreover, a meta-analysis of 29 research studies found that religious involvement is associated with lower mortality—specifically, odds of survival are 29% higher among highly religious individuals, compared to their less religious counterparts (McCullough, Hoyt, Larson, Koenig, & Thoresen, 2000). And with respect to savoring, people who say their religious faith is the most important influence in their life are twice as likely as people low in spiritual commitment to report being "very happy" (Gallup, 1984). Thus, spirituality and religious involvement not only serve as a coping resource, but may also help people savor positive experiences and find joy in life.

Awareness of the Fleetingness of Experience. Realizing that one's current experience will not last forever can both reduce stress and heighten enjoyment. During stressful periods, imagining a future time when one's troubles will be over can help put problems in perspective, thus engendering hope and boosting morale (Folkman & Lazarus, 1980). And as we noted in chapter 4, an awareness of the fleetingness of one's current joy can enhance the bittersweetness of the moment and motivate people to enjoy themselves while they can. For example, parents of 2-year-olds often remind themselves that their child will be grown up before they know it—a thought that not only increases their ability to cope with the stresses of childrearing, but also helps them savor time spent with their child. Along these lines, Jewish legend has it that King Solomon, renowned for his exceptional wisdom, had an inscription engraved on his ring, at which he would glance whenever he experienced something positive or negative. The Hebrew inscription supposedly read, "Gam zeh ya'avor"—"This too shall pass." The saying reminds one that misfortune will fade with time, thereby helping one endure hardship. But it also adds bittersweetness to positive experiences and reminds us to capture the joy now while it is still present.

Clearly, these six affect management strategies—sharing feelings with others, finding meaning in life events, creating downward hedonic contrast, being humorous, being spiritual or religious, and being aware of the fleetingness of experience—are uniquely versatile tools for both adapting to hardship and enjoying life. And they are skills well worth cultivating.

ESTABLISHING THE THREE ESSENTIAL PRECONDITIONS FOR SAVORING

In our general definition of savoring, we contend that three critical preconditions must exist in order for savoring to occur. First, people must be relatively free of pressing social and esteem needs. Second, people must be focused on attending to their present experience. And third, people must have some degree of awareness of the positive feelings they are experiencing.

For people who savor their lives easily, these preconditions arise quite automatically. But what about people who find it hard to savor, who have trouble breaking free of distracting thoughts, staying present-focused, or being mindfully aware of positive feelings? What can these individuals do to foster these three preconditions for savoring?

Becoming Relatively Free of Social and Esteem Concerns

We first suggest some basic aids to set the stage for savoring. With the demands and rewards of most people's everyday life, it may be a tall order to forego thinking about the responsibilities and social incentives that compose the world we inhabit. It is not as if people have internal switches that allow them to turn off their ordinary pursuits. Nor is it necessarily easy to stop oneself from worrying about problems and concerns in one's life. But if people have a finite amount of attentional resources they can use to optimize their emotional experience (Linville & Fischer, 1991), then worrying and thinking about pressing problems deplete these attentional resources and reduce people's ability to savor.

One strategy to short-circuit worrying is literally to pull the plug on it. Here we take a tip from concentrative meditation training, in which a person is asked to focus on a single stimulus (e.g., a repeated word or one's own breathing) and thereby blot out other stimuli from attentional focus. This strategy is a form of sensory-perceptual sharpening, a savoring response we discussed in chapter 4. Needless to say, this approach might not work if a person were in the grips of severe pain, thirst, or other extreme discomforts. Nevertheless, some pain therapists teach chronic pain patients ways to relax that resemble what we advocate. For example, although the data are not entirely consistent (Seers & Carroll, 1998), relaxation training has been found to decrease pain, improve functioning, and reduce anxiety, compared to receiving standard pain medication (Good, 1996; Kessler, Patterson, & Dane, 2003; Mandle, Jacobs, Arcari, & Domar, 1996; Syrjala, Donaldson, Davis, Kippes, & Carr, 1995).

Assuming people are not overwhelmed by any physical discomforts, how then might they ignore social and esteem needs simply by using concentrative meditation methods? First, one should have a willful intention to relax and divert attention from ongoing esteem or social concerns. Given this requirement, one should focus attention as narrowly as possible on the repeated word or mantra without stopping to consider any competing thoughts that might arise. For example, Benson (1975) advocated that people repeat in their mind the word "one" or "relax" as a mantra, in order to evoke what he termed the "relaxation response." Evidence indicates that this form of meditation reduces metabolic rate, decreases heart rate, lowers blood pressure, and decelerates breathing (Benson, 1975, 1984).

When people meditate in this way, at first they often find it difficult to block out thoughts about present concerns, worries, and ways to solve their problems. The mind tends to wander quickly from focusing on the meditative mantra toward these other interfering thoughts. According to Benson (1975), however, when these distracting thoughts occur, one should simply try to disregard them and redirect attention toward repeating the mantra. Nor should one worry about how well one is performing the meditative technique, as this too inhibits the relaxation response. Instead, one should adopt a passive, receptive attitude and "just let it happen." This orientation is a form of experiential absorption that we distinguished from cognitive reflection in chapter 5.

This meditative process resembles the mind-set one must take in falling asleep. Many people, when getting into bed and watching television to relax, experience the unintended phenomenon of falling asleep when repetitive advertising or highly irrelevant material is discussed or presented. At least for a moment, a person could adopt this same kind of relaxed mind-set in connection with any stimulus field, and attempt to make the flow of stimuli irrelevant to one's interests or goals and devoid of any practical meaning. We contend that, besides promoting sleep, this technique could also provide a ripe context for the development of savoring by helping one ignore competing stimuli.

We are not simply suggesting that people who wish to savor try not to worry. Rather, we are instead advocating that people actively discount any thoughts or external stimuli that might interfere with savoring by reinterpreting these distractions as being temporarily irrelevant. Along these lines, research suggests that the particular set of "stopping rules" people adopt when worrying can determine how long they persist in ruminating. Individuals who worry until they no longer feel like continuing stop worrying sooner than those who worry until they feel they have generated as many potential solutions as possible (Davey, Startup, MacDonald, Jenkins, & Patterson, 2005; Martin et al., 1993). One implication of this finding is that the more strongly one believes worrying can help solve problems, the harder it may be to savor. This reasoning suggests that rather than trying to generate as many potential solutions to their problems as possible, when people worry they should set aside a fixed amount of time in which to do so constructively, and then stop worrying afterwards (cf. Borkovec, 1985). Adopting this time-limited approach to worrying would help free up attentional resources to use for savoring, if people so choose.

Other theorists have recommended rational, cognitive-behavioral strategies to reduce worrying. For example, Fordyce (1983) suggested that people keep a daily record of worries, analyze the amount of time spent worrying, determine how many worries actually come true, and use thought-substitution techniques to change their worried thoughts. Adopting a rational-emotive approach, Ellis (1999) encouraged people to make a rational choice: If one wants to experience happiness, then one should devote one's attention to pursuing it, and not to fruitless worrying about possible catastrophes that worrying cannot prevent. Again, the long-range goal of all of these self-change interventions is to take one's attention away from negative thoughts and feelings associated with ruminative worrying, thereby providing more attentional resources for use in savoring positive experience. Returning to the notion of opponent processes that we proposed in chapter 7, guilt and worrying (or kill-joy thinking) may well be the primary negative counterpart process to savoring—worrying makes it hard to find the attentional resources required to savor. If you want to savor, then you need to check your worries at the door.

Focusing on the Present

What interventions can we suggest to help people attend to their present flow of experience in the moment, and not dwell on the past or future? People can also use the meditative strategy we advocated for silencing worries to cease focusing on the future or the past. But we extend this meditative technique a step further. To help one attend more fully to what is happening in the present, we use ideas derived from intentional mindfulness techniques of meditation, in which all internal and external stimuli become possible targets of attention during a state of relaxed openness to experience.

At first blush, mindfulness meditation may seem at odds with the concentrative techniques we have just described for shutting out pressing needs. However, mindfulness meditation is not contradictory when it occurs *after* a concentrative meditative technique has already been implemented. Once a person is ready to adopt a savoring orientation, intentional mindfulness techniques can enable the person to let consciousness flow more easily (Kabat-Zinn, 1990). Having relinquished distracting thoughts or blocked out irrelevant stimuli, people are then free to focus their attention mindfully on their present experience as it is unfolding.

What we suggest here about ways of getting into a mindful savoring orientation is much like some of the "intentional mindfulness qualities" that Kabat-Zinn (1990) and Shapiro et al. (2002) list as being conducive to meditation. We particularly highlight the qualities of: (a) nonjudgmental orientation (i.e., "impartial witnessing" or not concerning oneself with evaluation); (b) openness (i.e., seeing things as if for the first time; Shapiro et al., 2002, p. 640); and (c) acceptance (i.e., being focused on things as they are in the present).

How people become nonjudgmental, open to novelty, and present-focused must be cast in idiosyncratic terms. For example, becoming nonjudgmental might require consciously reminding oneself not to evaluate one's ongoing experience. Becoming open to novelty might require purposefully doing or trying something different for a change. Becoming more present-focused might require putting away one's appointment book and removing one's wristwatch. Shortly, we will present a few exercises aimed at helping people foster these critical qualities during positive experiences.

Enhancing Attentional Focus on Positive Experience

We have suggested that the third condition necessary to establish a savoring context is the capacity to enhance attentional focus on pleasurable aspects of one's ongoing experience. How do we suggest that people learn to enhance their attentional focus on the positive stimuli and feelings they experience, as one does when savoring? Generally speaking, people can use the same meditative process we suggested for focusing on the present to focus more mindfully on ongoing positive experiences. We have suggested from the very beginning that savoring is not simply experiencing pleasure or enjoyment. On the contrary, savoring involves taking the perspective of an inquiring journalist toward one's own pleasurable experiences and then reporting these inquiries to oneself.

One suggestion that can help people focus more intensely on the present is to avoid multitasking, or what has been termed *polyphasic activity* (Friedman & Ulmer, 1985). Polyphasic activities involve "trying to think about or to do two or more things simultaneously" (Friedman & Ulmer, 1985, p. 40). A hallmark of Type A behavior, these frenetic, time-urgent pursuits divide one's attention among multiple targets, thereby making it harder to attend to the joy of a happy moment as it is unfolding (Friedman & Ulmer, 1985). It is hard for people to focus closely on the joy they feel if they are also thinking about or trying to do other things at the same time. Thus, people can enhance savoring by devoting their attentional resources more exclusively to those aspects of ongoing positive experience that they find enjoyable.

Being meta-aware of one's ongoing positive experience often dovetails with the elimination of social and esteem needs and a focus on the present. Therefore, strategies for enhancing savoring are often relevant to two or more of these contextual preconditions. For example, we can suggest a "trick" to enhance the poignancy and power of the moment that increases attentional focus on both the present and its pleasurable aspects. Specifically, we recommend an extension of one of Lakein's (1974) "lifetime goals questions" to intensify savoring. In particular, Lakein (1974) suggested that people ask themselves, "If I knew I would be struck dead by lightning six months from today, how would I live until then? (This means you would have only six months to live and would have to squeeze whatever you consider important into your dramatically reduced time on earth . . .)" (p. 33).

Slightly modifying this perspective, we suggest that when people encounter a positive experience, they imagine that this is the last time they will ever go through the particular experience, be it a beautiful sunset, a conversation with a friend, sipping a warm cup of tea, or a stroll on the beach. Imagining the positive moment to be a last-of-a-lifetime experience produces an extremely intense bittersweetness, making the present much more vivid and salient; and imagining one will never again experience the particular moment (i.e., downward counterfactual thinking) dramatically accentuates the positive features and feelings involved through hedonic contrast, making it easier to notice and appreciate those aspects of the moment that are most readily savored.

Another strategy to enhance savoring is to become more aware of one's positive feelings. Just as people vary in their baseline levels or ranges of positive affect, people also vary in the degree to which they are consciously aware of their own feelings. In particular, there are individual differences in the personality trait of mood attention (Salovey et al., 1995) or mood awareness (Swinkels & Giuliano, 1995), which includes both mood monitoring and mood labeling. These personality differences may well predispose some people to be more capable than others of recognizing and interpreting their positive feelings while they are experiencing them and of telling themselves how they feel. As noted in chapter 1, we expect higher levels of both mood monitoring and mood labeling to facilitate savoring. Along these lines, we suggest that people practice noticing and explicitly labeling their positive moods, so as to enhance their ability to savor. Indeed, one reason why women are typically more adept at savoring than men is that they tend to be more consciously aware of their feelings (cf. Gohm, 2003).

For example, the next time you find yourself going through a positive experience, take a moment to try to identify the specific positive feelings you are experiencing. First, find words to describe your pleasant feelings. Are they affectionate, mellow, awesome, energizing, uplifting, exciting, or empowering? Are they fun, fulfilling, comforting, inspiring, heartwarming, prideful, or grateful? Are they happy, pleased, satisfied, content, glad, relieved, or elated? Try first to put your finger on exactly what it is you are feeling. You may well be experiencing more than one positive feeling. Once you have put your positive feelings in words, tell yourself explicitly at that moment that you are feeling this way right now. Then return your attentional focus to the stimuli or event from which you are deriving these feelings in the first place. Practicing this process of attending mindfully to positive feelings, and explicitly labeling them, can help one become more aware of positive feelings and thereby enhance one's ability to savor.

Strategies for Enhancing Contexts for Savoring

Throughout this book, we have highlighted various ways in which people can generate, intensify, or prolong savoring experiences. These savoring strategies include: sharing with others; active memory building; self-congratulation; sensory-perceptual sharpening; downward social, temporal, and counterfactual contrast; experiential absorption; behavioral expression; heightened temporal awareness; counting blessings; and avoiding kill-joy thinking. Next we offer three general suggestions that people often find helpful to enhance the situational conditions that are ripe for savoring experiences, and for each of these suggestions, we provide specific exercises designed to induce savoring.

Taking Time Out From Everyday Activity. A basic strategy that enhances opportunities to savor is to purposely take "time outs" from ordinary ongoing life. The momentum American men and women establish for accomplishing what needs to be done for their lives often requires a 48-hour day. By and large, Americans are earnest workers, trying hard to earn enough for a comfortable standard of living. And the time they spend doing nonwork tasks such as shopping, cooking, cleaning, and fulfilling required social functions is endless. There are no siestas for most Americans. Indeed, they often indulge in recreation with the same earnestness. They get tired, and sometimes find that collapsing in front of the TV set is the most satisfying respite from the pace. Mindless TV viewing — what's to savor, if people work, play, and carry out their routines so earnestly and so breathlessly that time does not stop long enough for them to appreciate the good things around them?

A remedy for this pace of existence clearly is to take some time off to let life pass more slowly. Anything that makes people step off life's daily treadmill without discomfiting them or arousing their guilt or concern about falling behind in their work could be part of such a remedy. Vacations sometimes are meant to do just that. And yet there are people who pursue vacations in the same pell-mell pace that characterizes their daily schedules. For these people, the pursuit of leisure becomes a job rather than a joy. However, if vacations really bring a shift in the pace of life, then vacation time might be an ideal time for savoring, or a time to try out some of the other exercises we propose to invigorate savoring. In fact, the word "vacation" comes from the Latin word *vacare,* which means to be free or exempt, as from stress, burdens, or obligations. For most people, however, vacations come but once or twice a year. A remedy for these people is to build daily or weekly "minivacations" into their lives or regular routines.

Indeed, minivacations are sometimes easier to arrange than longer holidays. A weekend getaway, a day off from work, time away from having to cook, or freedom from other types of everyday responsibilities in one way or another — at these moments of escape from the daily grind, deliberate strategies for savoring can be applied, if savoring processes are not automatically activated.

One tip for enhancing savoring is to become more *proactive* rather than purely *reactive* in finding enjoyment. Note that there is a natural asymmetry between coping and savoring. On one hand, the sorrows in life inevitably find us and force us to feel them despite our best efforts to avoid them, and they require us to actively cope to reduce their negative emotional impact. On the other hand, the pleasures in life more often require us to hunt for them or else they will not happen despite our best hopes, and they require us to actively savor to enhance their positive emotional impact. These facts suggest that people should make savoring a priority if they wish to enjoy themselves (cf. Fordyce, 1977, 1983). Along these lines, it is important to recognize that the frequency and intensity of positive affect are largely independent (Diener, Larsen, Levine, & Emmons, 1985), and the frequency of one's positive affect is a stronger predictor of overall level of happiness than is the intensity of one's positive affect (Diener, Sandvik, & Pavot, 1991). These findings suggest that increasing the total number of savoring episodes one has will boost overall happiness more than simply intensifying enjoyment while one is in a savoring episode. Indeed, increasing the number of pleasurable activities in which people engage has been shown to increase subjective well-being and decrease subjective distress (Reich & Zautra, 1981). Here we present a semistructured activity, *The Daily Vacation Exercise,* that helps people practice savoring proactively in the context of everyday life.

The Daily Vacation Exercise

1. Each day for one week, plan and participate in a formal "daily vacation" during which you spend time doing something you find enjoyable for at least 20 minutes. This activity might be going for a walk, sitting quietly in a garden, reading a book, treating yourself to a cup of coffee, going out to eat, visiting a museum or art gallery, taking a shower or soaking in a bathtub, spending time with a friend, or watching a sunset. Be creative in finding sources of enjoyment that you can look forward to and savor. This exercise works best if you do not use the same activity every day, but instead seek a variety of experiences in your daily vacations.

2. Before starting each daily vacation, make sure to set aside worries and concerns, pressing responsibilities, and sources of stress for at least 20 minutes, and do your best to structure the situation so as to prevent distractions while you are savoring. Remind yourself not to be judgmental, but rather to see things as if for the first or last time, and to focus on what is happening and what you are feeling as it unfolds in the present.

3. While you are on your daily vacation, try to notice and explicitly acknowledge to yourself each stimulus or sensation that you find pleasurable. Identify your positive feelings and explicitly label them in your mind. Actively build a memory of the feeling and the stimuli associated with it, close your eyes, swish the feeling around in your mind, and outwardly express the positive feeling in some way.

4. At the end of your daily vacation, plan your daily vacation for tomorrow and begin to look forward to it. At the end of the day, look back on your daily vacation, and recall and rekindle the positive feelings you savored.

5. At the end of the week, take a few minutes to recall all seven of your daily vacations. Look back on the activities you enjoyed doing and try to reexperience the positive feelings you felt during each daily vacation. Compare the way you have felt over the past week and the way you feel right now to the way you usually feel during a typical week. People typically report having felt happier a greater percentage of the time during their week of daily vacations and report feeling happier at the end of the week, compared to the way they usually feel.

The purpose of The Daily Vacation Exercise is to give people direct experience with proactive savoring, to give them the opportunity to bring savoring into their lives on a regular basis, and to help them practice the art of savoring daily life. After engaging in this exercise, some people may want to make daily vacations part of their everyday routine.

Becoming More Open to Experience. Once there is time to experience life in a savoring mode, a person has to be open to and aware of the varieties of experience that are there to be savored. People have to relax sufficiently to undo the restraints on their views of the world and themselves if they are to let savorable stimulation enter. In chapter 4, we spoke of a general way of extending the duration of savoring as chaining together one's positive experiences. One kind of chaining is a set of free-associative linkages that one creates, sometimes haphazardly, other times intentionally. Next is an exercise, *The Life Review Exercise,* that can facilitate this kind of associative chaining in contemplating one's life.

The Life Review Exercise

1. Identify an activity or experience that you currently savor in the way we have defined savoring in this book.

2. Think of the last time you had such a savoring experience, and write down in as much detail as you can the situation you were in, the people who were there, the place you were, the time of day, the time of year, and so on.

3. Do the same for one other time that is similar to what you report in Step 2, including all the accompanying data.

4. Do the same as in Step 3 for the very first time you remember savoring something in the way we have defined savoring in this book.

The purpose of The Life Review Exercise is to give people direct experience with the cognitive savoring process of chaining, in which one links positive associations together in one's mind, thereby broadening and prolonging an ongoing savoring experience. In this way, people may eventually make what at first requires deliberate effort into a habitual pattern of thinking.

Narrowing One's Focus. In the next exercise, *The Camera Exercise,* we recommend what appear to be two paradoxical processes that always seem to be involved in savoring. The exercise requires people to narrow their focus of attention on a small, given target, and yet be wide open to any stimuli that may come their way when attending to the target with this narrow focus. We know of no better way to practice this orientation than to take photographs without an explicit goal concerning the subject or target.

The Camera Exercise

1. Get access to a camera, your own or one you can borrow for a day. The simpler the camera, the better. This exercise works best if you do not have to think too much about the functions and settings on the camera. If you are unfamiliar with the camera, spend some time first getting acquainted with the simplest settings. Get a roll of color film for prints, not slides; or better yet, use a digital camera.

2. Select a sunny day, if you can. Having an active play of light on your visual field enhances this exercise. Go to a relatively quiet location near where you live. It could be nearby, if you live in the country or on a quiet street in a town or city. It could be in a park, if you live in a noisy town or city. Find a comfortable place to sit or stand for a period of time, and simply wait there while you scan what is in your immediate field of vision.

3. Find an object close by. It could be a building or part of a building. It could be a tree, or other vegetation. It could be a machine or parked vehicle. It could be

anything that will remain relatively still while you gaze at it. Now take the mind-set of seeing the abstract patterns in the object that you have selected. These could be contrasts in color, light, or shading. Or these could be variations in texture.

4. Start taking pictures from different angles that represent alternative perspectives you can take in relationship to the object. Move a bit in one direction, then in another; hold the camera higher, then lower; tilt the camera to one side, then the other. Vary your stance and the angle with which you hold the camera in relation to the object. Snap any shot that appeals to you. Don't worry about a shot being totally balanced and symmetrical. Just shoot those images you find interesting or pleasing. Remember, this exercise is not a photo contest. Rather, it is designed to help you develop your savoring skills.

5. Find another object, and repeat the procedures in Steps 3 and 4 until all of the film has been exposed, or until you have taken 30 to 40 digital shots.

6. Develop the film (the quicker, the better—perhaps in a 1-hour photo shop) or download the digital photos, and carefully study the pictures for patterns that please you.

7. Repeat Steps 2 through 6 another day as soon as you can, photographing the same or similar objects.

The Camera Exercise forces one to attend closely and mindfully to ways in which an ordinary object can have pleasant visual effects. The photographer scrutinizes the object in the field of vision and takes time to compose an image. Often the photographic results are illuminating and reinforce the experience of enjoyment in examining objects and taking pictures. Reviewing the photos returns one's eyes to images that hold memory traces of what had previously been felt in the initial visual scanning.

Savoring, Wisdom, and the Good Life

In his classic treatise on ethics, Aristotle (350 B.C./1925) argued that there are two distinct forms of happiness: *hedonia,* or the pleasures inherent in life, as when one fully savors a positive experience; and *eudaimonia,* or the life well-lived, as when one lives a virtuous, meaningful, or purpose-driven life. Aristotle considered this latter form of happiness to be "the highest of all goods achievable by human action" (Ryff, 1989, p. 1070). Others have suggested eudaimonia is more accurately defined as "the feelings accompanying behavior in the direction of, and consistent with, one's true potential" (Waterman, 1984, p. 16). In any event, it is important not to confuse these two different positive subjective states.

Whereas hedonia is the "life of pleasure," eudaimonia is the "life of purpose." Explicating the latter term, Seligman (2002a) cogently argued:

> The good life consists in deriving happiness by using your signature strengths every day in the main realms of living. The meaningful life adds one more component: using these same strengths to forward knowledge, power, or goodness. A

life that does this is pregnant with meaning, and if God comes at the end, such a life is sacred. (p. 260)

In encouraging people to find ways to enhance savoring in their lives, it is not our intention to promote selfish hedonism or to suggest that pursuing the joy of the moment should be one's primary goal in life. On the contrary, the single-minded pursuit of hedonia and nothing else would be a vacuous existence aimed solely at maximizing personal hedonic gain with no higher purpose. The life of pleasure devoid of eudaimonia would be empty and meaningless indeed. Yet, the "good life" filled with virtue and meaning would be stolid and sterile, if it achieved eudaimonia at the price of never being able to savor one's life. The Greek philosopher Epicurus (300 B.C./1993) made precisely this point in arguing, "It is impossible to live pleasantly without living prudently, well, and justly, nor is it possible to live prudently, well, and justly, without living pleasantly" (p. 70).

We suggest that true wisdom lies in learning to savor in ways that achieve both hedonia and eudaimonia, without trading one form of happiness for the other. Indiscriminate savoring pursues the empty pleasures to be gained in satisfying "wrong desires" (Adler, 1991). Along these lines, Adler (1991) argued that there are three basic types of wrong desires:

> . . . either (a) the wrong desire is for something that, while really good and needed, is only a partial good . . . yet is desired inordinately as if it were the only good, the whole good; or (b) something that, while good as a means, is a limitless good for those who desire it as an ultimate end; or (c) something that, though it may appear to be good when actually desired, is an apparent good that is noxious rather than innocuous. The prime examples of this threefold classification of the objects of wrong desire are (a) pleasure, (b) money, and (c) fame and power . . . pleasure, much more frequently than these other partial goods, is the object of wrong desire when it is desired as the only good, and as the ultimate goal of one's striving. (pp. 37–38)

As Adler (1991) noted, "In sharp contrast, persons motivated by right desire, while differing in minor traits, are all of the same moral character. Moral virtue is the same in all of them" (p. 55). Thus, wisdom and virtue go hand in hand to guide one toward pursuing those things that provide meaning and fulfill purpose in life, which include those positive experiences that are truly worth savoring for the right reasons. And these moral traits help insure that people savor their lives in ways that bring joy, awe, gratitude, pride, and pleasure, without harming oneself or others and without sacrificing eudaimonia in the process.

Conclusion

Although we have argued that savoring is a crucial process in the regulation of positive emotion and is vital to a wide variety of human concerns, we hasten to add that savoring is certainly not the only important process in positive psychology. On the contrary, there are many other constructs and processes that play a role in this growing field. These concepts include flourishing, thriving, transcendence, elevation, inspiration, hope, optimism, virtue, wisdom, forgiveness, compassion, altruism, self-actualization, spirituality, and love, to name just a few. Savoring processes are, in turn, related to each of these other constructs of positive experience. Savoring may be a missing link in understanding how people transform many of these positive experiences into emotions. It is our fondest hope that this book will encourage others to pursue savoring as a topic worthy of further scientific study.

SUMMARY

In this final chapter, we noted that although people may have a genetically determined range within which they experience positive affect, they can learn to regulate positive emotions in ways that keep them in the upper level of this hedonic range. After reviewing prior research on boosting happiness, we considered six factors that enhance both coping and savoring: social support, writing about life experiences, downward hedonic contrast, humor, spirituality and religion, and awareness of the fleetingness of experience. We then offered specific strategies that people can use to establish the preconditions necessary for savoring. To set the stage for savoring, we suggested that people free themselves from social and esteem concerns through concentrative meditation, cognitive reinterpretation, adopting a rational-emotive perspective, or using cognitive-behavioral techniques to extinguish worrying. To focus more exclusively on the present, we suggested that people use mindfulness meditation to foster a nonjudgmental orientation, openness to ongoing experience, and acceptance of the present. To increase attentional focus on positive feelings, we suggested that people avoid multitasking and polyphasic activity, imagine their savoring opportunities to be last-of-a-lifetime positive experiences, and practice noticing and explicitly labeling their positive moods. To enhance contexts for savoring, we suggested that people intentionally take time out from everyday activities to savor, and we provided three hands-on exercises designed to help people practice (a) savoring their daily lives (The Daily Vacation Exercise), (b) chaining together positive thoughts associated with ongoing positive events (The Life Review Exercise); and (c) narrowing their attentional focus in savoring (The Camera Exercise). Finally, we considered the vital role of virtue and wisdom in guiding people's choices in savoring so as to avoid narcissistic hedonism and facilitate growth toward eudaimonia, or the "life of purpose."

Epilogue

We close this book with a brief account of a very special positive moment in one person's life. The person is Swiss physician Bertrand Piccard, who, in March 1999 with British copilot Brian Jones, became the first person to fly nonstop around the world in a balloon. On the last night of their historic voyage, when he realized that he had now finally achieved his lifelong goal, Piccard wrote the following passage in his diary while floating silently 36,000 feet above the earth. As you read this passage, note the various elements of savoring that flow throughout it:

> During the last night, I savor once more the intimate relationship we have established with our planet. Shivering in the pilot's seat, I have the feeling I have left the capsule to fly under the stars that have swallowed our balloon. I feel so privileged that I want to enjoy every second of this air world. During our three weeks of flight, protected by our high-tech cocoon, we have flown over millions of people suffering on this earth. . . . Why are we so lucky? . . . Very shortly after daybreak, [our balloon] will land in the Egyptian sand, Brian and I will be lifted away from the desert by helicopter, and we will immediately need to find words to satisfy the public's curiosity. But right now, muffled in my down jacket, I let the cold bite of the night remind me that I have not yet landed, that I am still living one of the most beautiful moments of my life. The only way I can make this instant last will be to share it with others. . . . (Piccard, 1999, p. 44)

Piccard and his colleague were savoring a unique, once-in-a-lifetime positive experience. All of us, however, also savor more mundane positive experiences. Anyone can try to prolong the joy of a particular moment, look forward to a special joy that may happen in the future, and remember joyful times from the past. As we have argued in this book, any one of these processes could contribute to savoring, even without a once-in-a-lifetime, around-the-world balloon flight.

References

Abse, D. (2005). *Homage to eros: 100 great poems of love and lust.* London: Robson Books.

Ackerman, D. (1990). *A natural history of the senses.* New York: Random House.

Adler, M. G., & Fagley, N. S. (2005). Appreciation: Individual differences in finding value and meaning as a unique predictor of subjective well-being. *Journal of Personality, 73,* 79–114.

Adler, M. J. (1991). *Desires, right & wrong: The ethics of enough.* New York: Macmillan.

Allport, G. W. (1961). *Pattern and growth in personality.* New York: Holt, Rinehart & Winston.

Amabile, T. M. (1983). *The social psychology of creativity.* New York: Springer-Verlag.

Amabile, T. M. (1996). *Creativity in context.* Boulder, CO: Westview Press.

Andrews, F. M., & Withey, S. B. (1976). *Social indicators of well-being: Americans' perception of life quality.* New York: Plenum.

Argyle, M. (1987). *The psychology of happiness.* London: Methuen.

Aristotle (1925). *The Nichomachean ethics* (W. D. Ross, Trans.). London: Oxford University Press. (Original work published 350 B.C.)

Arkes, H. R., & Garske, J. P. (1982). *Psychological theories of motivation.* Monterey, CA: Brooks Cole.

Arlow, J. A. (1990). Emotion, time, and the self. In R. Plutchik & H. Kellerman (Eds.), *Emotion: Theory, research, and experience* (Vol. 5, pp. 133–146). San Diego, CA: Academic Press.

Aronson, E., & Linder, D. (1965). Gain and loss of esteem as determinants of interpersonal attractiveness. *Journal of Experimental Social Psychology, 1,* 156–171.

Associated Press (2005, September 3). Gas prices, hurricane guilt keeps many at home. Retrieved September 5, 2005, from http://www.kirotv.com/automotive/4933109/detail.html

Atance, C. M., & O'Neill, D. K. (2001). Episodic future thinking. *Trends in Cognitive Sciences, 5,* 533–539.

Atkinson, J. W., & Birch, D. (1970). *The dynamics of action.* New York: John Wiley & Sons.

Baltes, P. B., Gluck, J., & Kunzmann, U. (2002). Wisdom: Its structure and function in regulating successful life span development. In C. R. Snyder & S. J. Lopez (Eds.), *Handbook of positive psychology* (pp. 327–347). New York: Oxford University Press.

Barrett, L. F., Gross, J., Christensen, T. C., & Benvenuto, M. (2001). Knowing what you're feeling and knowing what to do about it: Mapping the relation between emotion differentiation and emotion regulation. *Cognition & Emotion, 15,* 713–724.

Beck, A. T. (1976). *Cognitive therapy and the emotional disorders.* New York: International Universities Press.

Benson, H. (1975). *The relaxation response.* New York: William Morrow and Company.

Benson, H. (1984). *Beyond the relaxation response.* New York: Times Books.

Bentham, J. (1970). An introduction to the principles of morals and legislation. London: Athlone. (Original work published in 1781)

Bentham, J. (1948). *An introduction to the principles and morals of legislation.* New York: Hafner. (Original work published in 1789)

Beran, M. J., Savage-Rumbaugh, E. S., Pate, J. L., & Rumbaugh, D. M. (1999). Delay of gratification in chimpanzees (Pan troglodytes). *Developmental Psychobiology, 34,* 119–127.

Berenbaum, H. (2002). Varieties of joy-related pleasurable activities and feelings. *Cognition & Emotion, 16,* 473–494.

Berkman, P. L. (1971). Measurement of mental health in a general population survey. *American Journal of Epidemiology, 94,* 105–111.

Berlyne, D. E. (1960). *Conflict, arousal, and curiosity.* New York: McGraw-Hill.

Berlyne, D. E. (1966). Curiosity and exploration. *Science, 153,* 25–33.

Bermudez, J. L., Marcel, A., & Eilan, N. (Eds.). (1995). *The body and the self.* Cambridge, MA: MIT Press.

Bloom, J. R. (1990). The relationship of social support and health. *Social Science & Medicine, 30,* 635–637.

Bloomfield, H. H., Cain, M. P., & Jaffe, D. T. (1975). *T.M.: Discovering inner energy and overcoming stress.* New York: Delacorte Press.

Bodner, T. E., & Langer, E. J. (2001, August). *Individual differences in mindfulness: The Langer mindfulness scale.* Paper presented at the 13th annual American Psychological Society convention, Toronto, Ontario, Canada.

Bounds, E. M. (1991). *The essentials of prayer* (Revised ed.). Grand Rapids, MI: Baker Book House. (Original work published 1925)

Borkovec, T. D. (1985). Worry: A potentially valuable concept. *Behaviour Research and Therapy, 23,* 481–483.

Brandtstadter, J., & Wentura, D. (1995). Adjustment to shifting possibility frontiers in later life: Complementary adaptive modes. In R. A. Dixon & L. Backman (Eds.), *Compensating for psychological deficits and declines: Managing losses and promoting gains* (pp. 83–106). Hillsdale, NJ: Lawrence Erlbaum Associates.

Brickman, P. (1978). *Happiness: Can we make it last?* Unpublished manuscript, Northwestern University, Evanston, IL.

Brickman, P., & Campbell. D. T. (1971). Hedonic relativism and planning the good society. In M. H. Appley (Ed.), *Adaptation level theory: A symposium* (pp. 287–302). New York: Academic Press.

Brickman, P., Coates, D., & Janoff-Bulman, R. (1978). Lottery winners and accident victims: Is happiness relative? *Journal of Personality and Social Psychology, 36,* 917–927.

Brown, K. W., & Ryan, R. M. (2003). The benefits of being present: Mindfulness and its role in psychological well-being. *Journal of Personality and Social Psychology, 84,* 822–848.

Bryant, F. B. (1989). A four-factor model of perceived control: Avoiding, coping, obtaining, and savoring. *Journal of Personality, 57,* 773–797.

Bryant, F. B. (2000). Assessing the validity of measurement. In L. G. Grimm & P. R. Yarnold (Eds.), *Reading and understanding more multivariate statistics* (pp. 99–146). Washington, DC: American Psychological Association.

Bryant, F. B. (2003). Savoring Beliefs Inventory (SBI): A scale for measuring beliefs about savouring. *Journal of Mental Health, 12,* 175–196.

Bryant, F. B. (2004, May). *Capturing the joy of the moment: Savoring as a process in positive psychology.* Invited address presented at the 76th annual meeting of the Midwestern Psychological Association, Chicago, IL.

Bryant, F. B., & Baxter, W. J. (1997). The structure of positive and negative automatic cognition. *Cognition & Emotion, 11,* 225–258.

Bryant, F. B., & Cvengros, J. A. (2004). Distinguishing hope and optimism: Two sides of a coin, or two separate coins? *Journal of Social and Clinical Psychology, 23,* 273–302.

Bryant, F. B., King, S. P., & Smart, C. M. (in press). Multivariate statistical strategies for construct validation in positive psychology. In A. G. Ong & M. van Dulmen (Eds.), *Handbook of methods in positive psychology.* New York: Oxford University Press.

Bryant, F. B., & Morgan, L. (1986, August). *The role of reminiscence in everyday life.* Paper presented at the 94th annual American Psychological Association convention, Washington, DC.

Bryant, F. B., Smart, C. M., & King, S. P. (2005). Using the past to enhance the present: Boosting happiness through positive reminiscence. *Journal of Happiness Studies, 6,* 227–260.

Bryant, F. B., & Veroff, J. (1984). Dimensions of subjective mental health in American men and women. *Journal of Health and Social Behavior, 25,* 116–135.

Bryant, F. B., & Yarnold, P. R. (1990). The impact of Type A behavior on subjective life quality: Bad for the heart, good for the soul? *Journal of Social Behavior and Personality, 5,* 369–404.

Bryant, F. B., Yarnold, P. R., & Grimm, L. G. (1996). Toward a measurement model of the Affect Intensity Measure: A three-factor structure. *Journal of Research in Personality, 30,* 223–247.

Bryant, F. B., Yarnold, P. R., & Morgan, L. (1991). Type A behavior and reminiscence in college undergraduates. *Journal of Research in Personality, 25,* 418–433.

Bryant, J., & Zillmann, D. (1988). Using humor to promote learning in the classroom. *Journal of Children in Contemporary Society, 20,* 49–78.

Budner, S. (1962). Intolerance of ambiguity as a personality variable. *Journal of Personality, 30,* 29–50.

Buehlman, K. T., Gottman, J. M., & Katz, L. F. (1992). How a couple views their past predicts their future: Predicting divorce from an oral history interview. *Journal of Family Psychology, 5,* 295–318.

Burton, C. M., & King, L. A. (2004). The health benefits of writing about intensely positive experiences. *Journal of Research in Personality, 38,* 150–163.

Butler, R. N. (1963). The life review: An interpretation of reminiscence in the aged. *Psychiatry, 26,* 65–76.

Butler, R. N., & Lewis, M. I. (1982). *Aging and mental health: Positive psychosocial and biomedical approaches.* St. Louis, MO: C. V. Mosby.

Buunk, B. P., Collins, R. L., Taylor, S. E., VanYperen, N. W., & Dakof, G. A. (1990). The affective consequences of social comparison: Either direction has its ups and downs. *Journal of Personality and Social Psychology, 59,* 1238–1249.

Cabanac, M. (1992). Pleasure: The common currency. *Journal of Theoretical Biology, 155,* 173–200.

Cacioppo, J. T., Hawkley, L. C., Rickett, E. M., & Masi, C. M. (2005). Sociality, spirituality, and meaning making: Chicago health, aging, and social relations study. *Review of General Psychology, 9,* 143–155.

Cacioppo, J. T., Petty, R. E., Feinstein, J. A., & Jarvis, W. B. G. (1996). Dispositional differences in cognitive motivation: The life and times of individuals varying in need for cognition. *Psychological Bulletin, 119,* 197–253.

Cafasso, L. L. (1994). *Uplifts and hassles in the lives of young adolescents.* Unpublished master's thesis, Loyola University Chicago, Chicago, IL.

Cafasso, L. L., Bryant, F. B., & Jose, P. R. (1994, August). *A scale for measuring children's savoring beliefs.* Paper presented at the 102nd annual American Psychological Association convention, Los Angeles, CA.

Campbell, A., Converse, P. E., & Rodgers, W. L. (1976). *The quality of American life: Perceptions, evaluations and satisfactions.* New York: Russell Sage Foundation.

Cantor, J. R., Bryant, J., & Zillmann, D. (1974). Enhancement of humor appreciation by transferred excitation. *Journal of Personality and Social Psychology, 30,* 812–821.

Carnevale, P. J., & Isen, A. M. (1986). The influence of positive affect and visual access on the discovery of integrative solutions in bilateral negotiation. *Organizational Behavior and Human Decision Processes, 37,* 1–13.

Carver, C. S. (1975). Physical aggression as a function of objective self-awareness and attitudes toward punishment. *Journal of Experimental Social Psychology, 11,* 510–519.

Carver, C. S. (2003). Pleasure as a sign you can attend to something else: Placing positive feelings within a general model of affect. *Cognition & Emotion, 17,* 241–261.

Chapman, C. L., & De Castro, J. M. (1990). Running addiction: Measurement and associated psychological characteristics. *Journal of Sports Medicine and Physical Fitness, 30,* 283–290.

Chesterton, G. K. (1936). *Autobiography of G. K. Chesterton.* New York: Sheed & Ward.

Cialdini, R. B., Borden, R. J., Thorne, A., Walker, M. R., Freeman, S., & Sloan, L. R. (1976). Basking in reflected glory: Three (football) field studies. *Journal of Personality and Social Psychology, 34,* 366–375.

Cohen, J. (1988). *Statistical power analysis for the behavioral sciences* (2nd ed.). Hillsdale, NJ: Lawrence Erlbaum Associates.

Cohen, S., & Wills, T. A. (1985). Stress, social support, and the buffering hypothesis. *Psychological Bulletin, 98,* 310–357.

Coleman, P. G. (1974). Measuring reminiscence characteristics from conversation as adaptive features of old age. *International Journal of Aging & Human Development, 5,* 281–294.

Compas, B. E., Connor, J., Osowiecki, D., & Welch, A. (1997). Effortful and involuntary responses to stress: Implications for coping with chronic stress. In B. H. Gottlieb (Ed.), *Coping with chronic stress.* (pp. 105–130). New York: Plenum.

Cook, J. (1997). *The book of positive quotations.* Minneapolis, MN: Fairview Press.

Cook, T. D., & Campbell, D. T. (1979). *Quasi-experimentation: Design and analysis issues for field settings.* Chicago: Rand McNally.

Cousins, N. (1979). *Anatomy of an illness as perceived by the patient: Reflections on healing and regeneration.* New York: W. W. Norton.

Crook, J. H. (1980). *The evolution of human consciousness.* New York: Oxford University Press.

Csikszentmihalyi, M. (1975). *Beyond boredom and anxiety: The experience of play in work and games.* San Francisco: Jossey-Bass.

Csikszentmihalyi, M. (1990). *Flow: The psychology of optimal experience.* New York: Harper & Row.

Csikszentmihalyi, M. (1996). *Creativity: Flow and the psychology of discovery and invention.* New York: HarperCollins.

Csikszentmihalyi, M. (1999). If we are so rich, why aren't we happy? *American Psychologist, 54,* 821–827.

Csikszentmihalyi, M. (2002). The concept of flow. In C. R. Snyder & S. J. Lopez (Eds.), *Handbook of positive psychology* (pp. 89–105). New York: Oxford University Press.

Csikszentmihalyi, M., & Hunter, J. (2003). Happiness in everyday life: The uses of experience sampling. *Journal of Happiness Studies, 4,* 185–199.

Cupchik, G. C., & Leventhal, H. (1974). Consistency between expressive behavior and the evaluation of humorous stimuli: The role of sex and self-observation. *Journal of Personality and Social Psychology, 30,* 429–442.

Danner, D. D., Snowdon, D. A., & Friesen, W. V. (2001). Positive emotions in early life and longevity: Findings from the nun study. *Journal of Personality and Social Psychology, 80,* 804–813.

Dass, R. (1971). *Be here now.* New York: Crown.

Davey, G. C. L., Startup, H. M., MacDonald, C. B., Jenkins, D., & Patterson, K. (2005). The use of "as many as can" versus "feel like continuing" stop rules during worrying. *Cognitive Therapy and Research, 29,* 155–169.

de La Rochefoucauld, F. (1694/1930). *Moral maxims and reflections.* London: M. Gillyflower & J. Everingham.

Deci, E. (1975). *Intrinsic motivation.* New York: Plenum.

Deikman, A. J. (1982). *The observing self: Mysticism and psychotherapy.* Boston: Beacon Press.

DeLongis, A., Hemphill, K. J., & Lehman, D. R. (1992). A structured diary methodology for the study of daily events. In F. B. Bryant, J. Edwards, R. S. Tindale, E. J. Posavac, L. Heath, E. Henderson-King, et al. (Eds.), *Methodological issues in applied social psychology* (pp. 83–109). New York: Plenum Press.

Diener, E. (1984). Subjective well-being. *Psychological Bulletin, 95,* 542–575.

Diener, E. (1994). Assessing subjective well-being: Progress and opportunities. *Social Indicators Research, 31,* 103–157.

Diener, E., & Diener, M. (1995). Cross-cultural correlates of life-satisfaction and self-esteem. *Journal of Personality and Social Psychology, 68,* 653–663.

Diener, E., & Diener, C. (1996). Most people are happy. *Psychological Science, 7,* 181–185.

Diener, E., Larsen, R. J., Levine, S., & Emmons, R. A. (1985). Intensity and frequency: Dimensions underlying positive and negative affect. *Journal of Personality and Social Psychology, 48,* 1253–1265.

Diener, E., Sandvik, E., & Larsen, R. J. (1985). Age and sex effects for emotional intensity. *Developmental Psychology, 21,* 542–546.

Diener, E., Sandvik, E., & Pavot, W. (1991). Happiness is the frequency, not the intensity, of positive versus negative affect. In F. Strack, M. Argyle, & N. Schwarz (Eds.), *Subjective well-being: An interdisciplinary perspective* (pp. 119–139). New York: Pergamon.

Dillon, K. M., Minchoff, B., & Baker, K. H. (1985–1986). Positive emotional states and enhancement of the immune system. *International Journal of Psychiatry in Medicine, 15,* 13–18.

Diole, P. (1953). *The undersea adventure.* New York: Julian Messner.

Dobb, E. (1998, August 30). Lives. The swimmer. *The New York Times Magazine,* Late Edition — Final, Section 6, p. 64, Column 1.

Dua, J. K. (1994). Comparative predictive value of attributional style, negative affect, and positive affect in predicting self-reported physical health and psychological health. *Journal of Psychosomatic Research, 38,* 669–680.

Dube, L., & Le Bel, J. L. (2003). The content and structure of laypeople's concept of pleasure. *Cognition & Emotion, 17,* 263–295.

Duckworth, A. L., Steen, T. A., & Seligman, M. E. P. (2005). Positive psychology in clinical practice. *Annual Review of Clinical Psychology, 1,* 629–651.

Duclos, S. E., Laird, J. D., Schneider, E., Sexter, M., Stern, L., & Van Lighten, O. (1989). Emotion-specific effects of facial expressions and postures on emotional experience. *Journal of Personality and Social Psychology, 57,* 100–108.

Duncan, E., & Grazzani-Gavazzi, I. (2004). Positive emotional experiences in Scottish and Italian young adults: A diary study. *Journal of Happiness Studies, 5,* 359–384.

Duncker, K. (1941). On pleasure, emotion, and striving. *Philosophy & Phenomenological Research, 1,* 391–430.

Dutton, D. G., & Aron, A. P. (1974). Some evidence for heightened sexual attraction under conditions of high anxiety. *Journal of Personality and Social Psychology, 30,* 510–517.

Duval, T. S., & Silvia, P. J. (2002). Self-awareness, probability of improvement, and the self-serving bias. *Journal of Personality and Social Psychology, 82,* 49–61.

Duval, T. S., Silvia, P. J., & Lalwani, N. (2001). *Self-awareness and causal attribution: A dual systems theory.* New York: Kluwer Academic.

Duval, S., & Wicklund, R. A. (1972). *A theory of objective self-awareness.* New York: Academic Press.

Eagly, A. H., & Wood, W. (1999). The origins of sex differences in human behavior: Evolved dispositions versus social roles. *American Psychologist, 54,* 408–423.

Easterbrook, G. (2003). *The progress paradox: How life gets better while people feel worse.* New York: Random House.

Ellis, A. (1999). *How to make yourself happy and remarkably less disturbable.* Atascadero, CA: Impact Press.

Ellis, A., & Greiger, R. (Eds.). (1977). *Handbook of rational-emotive therapy, Vol. 1.* New York: Springer.

Elster, J., & Loewenstein, G. (1992). Utility from memory and anticipation. In G. Loewenstein & J. Elster (Eds.), *Choice over time* (pp. 213–234). New York: Russell Sage Foundation.

Emerson, R. W. (1906). Prudence. *Essays, first series.* New York: Morgan Shepard Co. (Original work published 1841)

Emmons, R. A., & McCullough, M. E. (2003). Counting blessings versus burdens: An experimental investigation of gratitude and subjective well-being in daily life. *Journal of Personality and Social Psychology, 84,* 377–389.

Emmons, R. A., & Shelton, C. M. (2002). Gratitude and the science of positive psychology. In C. R. Snyder and S. J. Lopez (Eds.), *Handbook of positive psychology* (pp. 459–471). New York: Oxford University Press.

Epicurus. (1993). *The essential Epicurus: Letters, principal doctrines, Vatican sayings, and fragments* (E. O'Connor, Trans.). Amherst, NY: Prometheus Books. (Original work published 300 B.C.)

Erber, R., Wegner, D. M., & Therriault, N. (1996). On being cool and collected: Mood regulation in anticipation of social interaction. *Journal of Personality and Social Psychology, 70,* 757–766.

Erickson, E. H. (1959). Identity and the life cycle: Selected papers. *Psychological Issues, 1,* 1–171.

Erickson, E. H. (1968). *Identity: Youth and crisis.* New York: W. W. Norton.

Esterling, B. A., Antoni, M. H., Fletcher, M. A., & Margulies, S. (1994). Emotional disclosure through writing or speaking modulates latent Epstein-Barr virus antibody titers. *Journal of Consulting and Clinical Psychology, 62,* 130–140.

Exline, J. J., Single, P. B., Lobel, M., & Geyer, A. L. (2004). Glowing praise and the envious gaze: Social dilemmas surrounding the public recognition of achievement. *Basic and Applied Social Psychology, 26,* 119–130.

Eysenck, H. J., & Eysenck, S. B. G. (1975). *Manual of the Eysenck Personality Questionnaire.* London: Hodder and Stoughton.

Fallot, R. D. (1979–1980). The impact on mood of verbal reminiscing in later adulthood. *International Journal of Aging & Human Development, 10,* 385–400.

Firmage, G. J. (Ed.). (1979). *The complete poems of E.E. Cummings, 1904–1962.* New York: Liveright.

Fitzpatrick, M. C. (1999). The psychologic assessment and psychosocial recovery of the patient with an amputation. *Clinical Orthopaedics and Related Research, 361,* 98–107.

Fivush, R., & Haden, C. A. (1997). Narrating and representing experience: Preschoolers' developing autobiographical recounts. In P. W. van den Broek, P. J. Bauer, & T. Bourg (Eds.), *Developmental spans in event comprehension and representation: Bridging fictional and actual events* (pp. 169–198). Hillsdale, NJ: Lawrence Erlbaum Associates.

Fivush, R. & Haden, C. A. (2003). Introduction: Autobiographical memory, narrative, and self. In R. Fivush & C. A. Haden (Eds.), *Autobiographical memory and the construction of a narrative self: Developmental and cultural perspectives* (pp. vii–xiv). Mahwah, NJ: Lawrence Erlbaum Associates.

Fivush, R., Haden, C. A., & Reese, E. (1996). Remembering, recounting, and reminiscing: The development of autobiographical memory in social context. In D. C. Rubin (Ed.), *Remembering our past: Studies in autobiographical memory* (pp. 341–359). New York: Cambridge University Press.

Flaherty, M. G. (1999). *A watched pot: How we experience time.* New York: New York University Press.

Flaherty, M. G. (2003). Time work: Customizing temporal experience. *Social Psychology Quarterly, 66,* 17–33.

Flavell, J. H. (1977). *Cognitive development*. Englewood Cliffs, NJ: Prentice-Hall.

Folkman, S., & Lazarus, R. S. (1980). An analysis of coping in a middle-aged community sample. *Journal of Health and Social Behavior, 21,* 219–239.

Folkman, S., & Lazarus, R. S. (1985). If it changes, it must be a process: Study of emotion and coping during three stages of a college examination. *Journal of Personality and Social Psychology, 48,* 150–170.

Fordyce, M. W. (1977). Development of a program to increase personal happiness. *Journal of Counseling Psychology, 24,* 511–520.

Fordyce, M. W. (1983). A program to increase happiness: Further studies. *Journal of Counseling Psychology, 30,* 483–498.

Fordyce, M. W. (1988). A review of research on the happiness measures: A sixty-second index of happiness and mental health. *Social Indicators Research, 20,* 355–381.

Frankl, V. E. (1963). *Man's search for meaning: An introduction to logotherapy*. New York: Washington Square Press.

Frederick, S., Loewenstein, G., & O'Donoghue, T. (2002). Time discounting and time preference: A critical review. *Journal of Economic Literature, 40,* 351–401.

Fredrickson, B. L. (1998). What good are positive emotions? *Review of General Psychology, 2,* 300–319.

Fredrickson, B. L. (2001). The role of positive emotions in positive psychology: The broaden-and-build theory of positive emotions. *American Psychologist, 56,* 218–226.

Fredrickson, B. L. (2002). Positive emotions. In C. R. Snyder & S. J. Lopez (Eds.), *Handbook of positive psychology* (pp. 120–134). New York: Oxford University Press.

Fredrickson, B. L., & Joiner, T. (2002). Positive emotions trigger upward spirals toward emotional well-being. *Psychological Science, 13,* 172–175.

Freedman, J. L. (1978). *Happy people: What happiness is, who has it, and why*. New York: Harcourt, Brace, Jovanovich.

Friedman, M., & Rosenman, R. H. (1974). *Type A behavior and your heart*. New York: Alfred Knopf.

Friedman, M., & Ulmer, D. (1985). *Treating Type A behavior and your heart*. New York: Ballantine Books.

Friedrich, W. N., Cohen, D. S., & Wilturner, L. T. (1988). Specific beliefs as moderator variables in maternal coping with mental retardation. *Children's Health Care, 17,* 40–44.

Frijda, N. H. (1988). The laws of emotion. *American Psychologist, 43,* 349–358.

Funder, D. C., & Block, J. (1989). The role of ego-control, ego-resiliency, and IQ in delay of gratification in adolescence. *Journal of Personality and Social Psychology, 57,* 1041–1050.

Funder, D. C., Block, J. H., & Block, J. (1983). Delay of gratification: Some longitudinal personality correlates. *Journal of Personality and Social Psychology, 44,* 1198–1213.

Gable, S. L., Reis, H. T., Impett, E. A., & Asher, E. R (2004). What do you do when things go right? The intrapersonal and interpersonal benefits of sharing positive events. *Journal of Personality and Social Psychology, 87,* 228–245.

Gallup, G., Jr. (1984, March). *Religion in America. Gallup Report*. Washington, DC: Gallup.

Garamoni, G. L., Reynolds, C. F., Thase, M. E., Frank, E., & Fasiczka, A. L. (1992). Shifts in affective balance during cognitive therapy of major depression. *Journal of Consulting and Clinical Psychology, 60,* 260–266.

Garfinkel, H. (1967). *Studies in ethnomethodology*. Englewood Cliffs, NJ: Prentice-Hall.

Gibbons, F. X. (1978). Sexual standards and reactions to pornography: Enhancing behavioral consistency through self-focused attention. *Journal of Personality and Social Psychology, 36,* 976–987.

Gilbert, D. T., Pinel, E. C., Wilson, T. D., Blumberg, S. J., & Wheatley, T. P. (1998). Immune neglect: A source of durability bias in affective forecasting. *Journal of Personality and Social Psychology, 75,* 617–638.

Glass, D. C. (1977). *Behavior patterns, stress, and coronary disease.* Hillsdale, NJ: Lawrence Erlbaum Associates.

Gohm, C. L. (2003). Mood regulation and emotional intelligence: Individual differences. *Journal of Personality and Social Psychology, 84,* 595–607.

Goldberg, L. R. (1993). The structure of phenotypic personality traits. *American Psychologist, 48,* 26–34.

Goldsmith, O. (1982). *The vicar of Wakefield.* New York: Oxford University Press. (Original work published 1766)

Goleman, D. (1995). *Emotional intelligence: Why it can matter more than IQ.* New York: Bantam.

Good, M. (1996). Effects of relaxation and music on postoperative pain: A review. *Journal of Advanced Nursing, 24,* 905–914.

Goodman, R. B. (1990). *American philosophy and the romantic tradition.* New York: Cambridge University Press.

Green, M. (1804). *The spleen and other poems.* Philadelphia, PA: B. Johnson & J. Johnson & R. Johnson. (Original work published 1737)

Green, J. D., Sedikides, C., Saltzberg, J. A., Wood, J. V., & Forzano, L. B. (2003). Happy mood decreases self-focused attention. *British Journal of Social Psychology, 42,* 147–157.

Griffin-Shelley, E. (1994). *Adolescent sex and love addicts.* Westport, CT: Praeger.

Griffiths, M. D. (1992). Pinball wizard: The case of a pinball machine addict. *Psychological Reports, 71,* 160–162.

Grosch, J., & Neuringer, A. (1981). Self-control in pigeons under the Mischel paradigm. *Journal of the Experimental Analysis of Behavior, 35,* 3–21.

Gross, J. J. (1999). Emotion regulation: Past, present, future. *Cognition & Emotion, 13,* 551–573.

Guilford, J. P. (1950). Creativity. *American Psychologist, 5,* 444–454.

Haden, C. A., Haine, R. A., & Fivush, R. (1997). Developing narrative structure in parent–child reminiscing across the preschool years. *Developmental Psychology, 33,* 295–307.

Haden, C. A., Ornstein, P. A., Eckerman, C. O., & Didow, S. M. (2001). Mother-child conversational interactions as events unfold: Linkages to subsequent remembering. *Child Development, 72,* 1016–1031.

Haidt, J. (2003). Elevation and the positive psychology of morality. In C. L. Keyes & J. Haidt (Eds.), *Flourishing: Positive psychology and the life well-lived* (pp. 275–289). Washington, DC: American Psychological Association.

Hamann, S. B., Ely, T. D., Hoffman, J. M., & Kilts, C. D. (2002). Ecstasy and agony: Activation of the human amygdala in positive and negative emotion. *Psychological Science, 13,* 135–141.

Handley, I. M., Lassiter, G. D., Nickell, E. F., & Herchenroeder, L. M. (2004). Affect and automatic mood maintenance. *Journal of Experimental Social Psychology, 40,* 106–112.

Harter, S. (1985). *Manual for the Self-Perception Profile for Children.* Denver, CO: University of Denver.

Harter, S. (1998). The development of self-representations. In W. Damon & N. Eisenberg (Eds.), *Handbook of child psychology: Social, emotional, and personality development* (Vol. 3, pp. 553–617). New York: Wiley.

Harvey, J. H., Pauwels, B. G., & Zickmund, S. (2002). Relationship connection: The role of minding in the enhancement of closeness. In C. R. Snyder & S. J. Lopez (Eds.), *Handbook of positive psychology* (pp. 423–433). New York: Oxford University Press.

Headey, B., & Wearing, A. (1992). *Understanding happiness: A theory of subjective well-being.* Melbourne, Australia: Longman Cheshire.

Helson, H. (1964). *Adaptation-level theory: An experimental and systematic approach to behavior.* New York: Harper & Row.

Henderson-King, D., & Veroff, J. (1994). Sexual satisfaction and marital well-being in the first years of marriage. *Journal of Social and Personal Relationships, 11,* 509–534.

Hetherington, M. M., & MacDiarmid, J. I. (1993). "Chocolate addiction": A preliminary study of its description and its relationship to problem eating. *Appetite, 21,* 233–246.

Higgins, E. T. (1987). Self-discrepancy: A theory relating self and affect. *Psychological Review, 94,* 319–340.

Higgins, E. T. (1997). Beyond pleasure and pain. *American Psychologist, 52,* 1280–1300.

Higgins, E. T., Klein, R., & Strauman, T. (1985). Self-concept discrepancy theory: A psychological model for distinguishing among different aspects of depression and anxiety. *Social Cognition, 3,* 51–76.

Hollon, S. D., & Kendall, P. C. (1980). Cognitive self-statements in depression: Development of an automatic thoughts questionnaire. *Cognitive Therapy and Research, 4,* 383–395.

Holmberg, D., & Holmes, J. G. (1994). Reconstruction of relationship memories: A mental models approach. In N. Schwarz & S. Sudman (Eds.), *Autobiographical memory and the validity of retrospective reports* (pp. 267–288). New York: Springer-Verlag.

Holmberg, D., Orbuch, T. L., & Veroff, J. (2004). *Thrice-told tales: Married couples tell their stories.* Mahwah, NJ: Lawrence Erlbaum Associates.

Hood, R. W., Jr., Spilka, B., Hunsberger, B., & Gorsuch, R. (2003). *The psychology of religion: An empirical approach* (3rd ed.). New York: Guilford.

Hormuth, S. E. (1982). Self-awareness and drive theory: Comparing internal standards and dominant responses. *European Journal of Social Psychology, 12,* 31–45.

House, J. S. (1981). *Work, stress and social support.* Reading, MA: Addison-Wesley.

Hughston, G. A., & Merriam, S. B. (1982). Reminiscence: A nonformal technique for improving cognitive functioning in the aged. *International Journal of Aging and Human Development, 15,* 139–149.

Ingram, R. E., & Wisnicki, K. S. (1988). Assessment of positive automatic cognition. *Journal of Consulting and Clinical Psychology, 56,* 898–902.

Inhelder, B., & Piaget, J. (1958). *The growth of logical thinking from childhood to adolescence: An essay on the construction of formal operational structures.* New York: Basic Books.

Isambert, F. A. (1969). Feasts and celebrations: Some critical reflections on the idea of celebration. *Humanitas, 5,* 29–41.

Isen, A. M. (1987). Positive affect, cognitive processes, and social behavior. In L. Berkowitz (Ed.), *Advances in experimental social psychology* (Vol. 20, pp. 203–253). San Diego, CA: Academic Press.

Isen, A. M. (2000). Some perspectives on positive affect and self-regulation. *Psychological Inquiry, 11,* 184–187.

Isen, A. M., Daubman, K. A., & Nowicki, G. P. (1987). Positive affect facilitates creative problem solving. *Journal of Personality and Social Psychology, 52,* 1122–1131.

James, W. (1981). *The principles of psychology.* Cambridge, MA: Harvard University Press. (Original work published in 1890)

James, W. (1985). *The varieties of religious experience: A study in human nature.* Cambridge, MA: Cambridge University Press. (Original work published in 1902)

Jamison, K. R. (2004). *Exuberance: The passion for life.* New York: Alfred A. Knopf.

Jevons, H. S. (1905). *Essays on economics.* London: Macmillan.

Ji, L.-J., Nisbett, R. E., & Su, Y. (2001). Culture, change, and prediction. *Psychological Science, 12,* 450–456.

Johnson, S. (1999). *The rambler.* Murietta, CA: Classic Books. (Original work published 1752)

Kabat-Zinn, J. (1990). *Full catastrophe living: Using the wisdom of your body and mind to face stress, pain, and illness.* New York: Doubleday Publishing.

Kahneman, D., Wakker, P. P., & Sarin, R. (1997). Back to Bentham? Explorations of experienced utility. *Quarterly Journal of Economics, 112,* 375–405.

Kavanagh, D. J., Andrade, J., & May, J. (2005). Imaginary relish and exquisite torture: The elaborated intrusion theory of desire. *Psychological Review, 112,* 446–467.

Keltner, D., & Haidt, J. (2003). Approaching awe, a moral, spiritual, and aesthetic emotion. *Cognition & Emotion, 17*, 297–314.

Kessler, R. S., Patterson, D. R., & Dane, J. (2003). Hypnosis and relaxation with pain patients: Evidence for effectiveness. *Seminars in Pain Medicine, 1*, 67–78.

Keyes, C. L. M., & Haidt, J. (Eds.). (2003). *Flourishing: Positive psychology and the life well lived.* Washington DC: American Psychological Association.

Kieras, J. E., Tobin, R. M., Graziano, W. G., & Rothbart, M. K. (2005). You can't always get what you want: Effortful control and children's responses to undesirable gifts. *Psychological Science, 16*, 391–396.

Killeen, P. R., Smith, J. P., & Hanson, S. J. (1981). Central place foraging in Rattus norvegicus. *Animal Behaviour, 29*, 64–70.

King, L. A. (2000). Why happiness is good for you: A commentary on Fredrickson. *Prevention & Treatment, 3*, Article 4, posted March 7, 2000. Retrieved July 1, 2005, from http://journals.apa.org/prevention/volume3/pre0030004c.html

King, L. A. (2001). The health benefits of writing about life goals. *Personality and Social Psychology Bulletin, 27*, 798–807.

King, L. A., Hicks, J. A., Krull, J. L., & Del Gaiso, A. K. (2006). Positive affect and the experience of meaning in life. *Journal of Personality and Social Psychology, 90*, 179–196.

Kitayama, S., Markus, H. R., & Kurokawa, M. (2000). Culture, emotion, and well-being: Good feelings in Japan and the United States. *Cognition & Emotion, 14*, 93–124.

Kleinke, C. L., Peterson, T. R., & Rutledge, T. R. (1998). Effects of self-generated facial expressions on mood. *Journal of Personality and Social Psychology, 74*, 272–279.

Klinger, E. (1982). On the self-management of mood, affect, and attention. In P. Karoly & F. H. Kanfer (Eds.), *Self-management and behavior change: From theory to practice* (pp. 129–164). New York: Pergamon.

Klinger, E. (1990). *Daydreaming: Using waking fantasy and imagery for self-knowledge and creativity.* Los Angeles: Jeremy P. Tarcher.

Koenig, H. G., Smiley, M., & Gonzales, J. A. P. (1988). *Religion, health, and aging: A review and theoretical integration.* Westport, CT: Praeger.

Kokkonen, M., & Pulkkinen, L. (1999). Emotion regulation strategies in relation to personality characteristics indicating low and high self-control of emotions. *Personality and Individual Differences, 27*, 913–932.

Kovacs, M. (1985). The Children's Depression Inventory. *Psychopharmacology Bulletin, 21*, 995–998.

Kraut, R. E., & Johnston, R. E. (1979). Social and emotional messages of smiling: An ethological approach. *Journal of Personality and Social Psychology, 37*, 1539–1553.

Krueger, R. F., Caspi, A., Moffitt, T. E., White, J., & Stouthamer-Loeber, M. (1996). Delay of gratification, psychopathology, and personality: Is low self-control specific to externalizing problems? *Journal of Personality, 64*, 107–129.

Kübler-Ross, E. (1969). *On death and dying.* New York: Macmillan.

Kubovy, M. (1999). On the pleasures of the mind. In D. Kahneman, E. Diener, & N. Schwarz (Eds.), *Well-being: The foundations of hedonic psychology* (pp. 134–154). New York: Russell Sage Foundation.

Kubzansky, L. D., Sparrow, D., Vokonas, P., & Kawachi, I. (2001). Is the glass half empty or half full? A prospective study of optimism and coronary heart disease in the Normative Aging Study. *Psychosomatic Medicine, 63*, 910–916.

Kuiper, N. A., & Martin, R. A. (1993). Humor and self-concept. *Humor: International Journal of Humor Research, 6*, 251–270.

Laird, J. D. (1974). Self-attribution of emotion: The effects of expressive behavior on the quality of emotional experience. *Journal of Personality and Social Psychology, 29*, 475–486.

Laird, J. D. (1984). The real role of facial response in the experience of emotion: A reply to Tourangeau and Ellsworth, and others. *Journal of Personality and Social Psychology, 47,* 909–917.

Lakein, A. (1974). *How to get control of your time and your life.* New York: The New American Library.

Lamb, C. (1823). *The essays of Elia.* London: John Taylor.

Lambie, J. A., & Marcel, A. J. (2002). Consciousness and the varieties of emotion experience: A theoretical framework. *Psychological Review, 109,* 219–259.

Langens, T. A., & Schmalt, H.-D. (2002). Emotional consequences of positive daydreaming: The moderating role of fear of failure. *Personality and Social Psychology Bulletin, 28,* 1725–1735.

Langer, E. J. (1989). *Mindfulness.* Reading, MA: Addison-Wesley.

Langston, C. A. (1994). Capitalizing on and coping with daily-life events: Expressive responses to positive events. *Journal of Personality and Social Psychology, 67,* 1112–1125.

Larsen, R. J., & Diener, E. (1987). Affect intensity as an individual difference characteristic: A review. *Journal of Research in Personality, 21,* 1–39.

Larsen, R. J., Diener, E., & Cropanzano, R. S. (1987). Cognitive operations associated with individual differences in affect intensity. *Journal of Personality and Social Psychology, 53,* 767–774.

Larson, R., & Csikszentmihalyi, M. (1983). The Experience Sampling Method. In H. T. Reis (Ed.), *Naturalistic approaches to studying social interaction: New directions for methodology of social and behavioral science* (Vol. 15, pp. 41–56). San Francisco, CA: Jossey-Bass.

Lazarus, R. S., & Folkman, S. (1984). *Stress, appraisal, and coping.* New York: Springer.

Lazarus, R. S., Kanner, A, D., & Folkman, S. (1980). Emotions: A cognitive-phenomenological analysis. In R. Plutchik & H. Kellerman (Eds.), *Emotion: Theory, research, and experience, Vol. 1: Theories of emotion* (pp. 189–217). New York: Academic Press.

Le Bel, J. L., & Dube, L. (2001, August). *The impact of sensory knowledge and attentional focus on pleasure and on behavioral responses to hedonic stimuli.* Paper presented at the 13th annual American Psychological Society convention, Toronto, Ontario, Canada.

Lefcourt, H. M., & Martin, R. A. (1986). *Humor and life stress: Antidote to adversity.* New York: Springer-Verlag.

Levin, J. S., & Schiller, P. L. (1987). Is there a religious factor in health? *Journal of Religion and Health, 26,* 9–36.

Levine, M. (2000). *The positive psychology of Buddhism and yoga: Paths to a mature happiness.* Mahwah, NJ: Lawrence Erlbaum Associates.

Levy, S. M., Herberman, R. B., Maluish, A. M., Schlien, B., & Lippman, M. (1985). Prognostic risk assessment in primary breast cancer by behavioral and immunological parameters. *Health Psychology, 4,* 99–113.

Lewin, K. (1951). *Field theory in social science: Selected theoretical papers.* New York: Harper.

Lewis, C. N. (1971). Reminiscing and self-concept in old age. *Journal of Gerontology, 26,* 240–243.

Lewis, M. I., & Butler, R. N. (1974). Life-review therapy: Putting memories to work in individual and group psychotherapy. *Geriatrics, 29,* 165–169, 172–173.

Lichter, S., Haye, K., & Kammann, R. (1980). Increasing happiness through cognitive retraining. *New Zealand Psychologist, 9,* 57–64.

Lieberman, J. N. (1977). *Playfulness: Its relationship to imagination and creativity.* New York: Academic Press.

Lindberg, T. (2004). *Enjoying the moment in the East and West: A cross-cultural analysis of savoring.* Unpublished doctoral dissertation. University of British Columbia, Vancouver, Canada.

Lindsay-Hartz, J. (1981). Elation, gladness, and joy. In J. de Rivera (Ed.), *Conceptual encounter: A method for the exploration of human experience* (pp. 163–224). Washington, DC: University Press of America.

Linville, P. W., & Fischer, G. W. (1991). Preferences for separating or combining events. *Journal of Personality and Social Psychology, 60,* 5–23.

Locke, J. (1995). *An essay concerning human understanding.* Amherst, NY: Prometheus Books. (Original work published in 1690)

Loewenstein, G. (1987). Anticipation and valuation of delayed consumption. *The Economic Journal, 97,* 666–684.

Loewenstein, G. (1994). The psychology of curiosity: A review and reinterpretation. *Psychological Bulletin, 116,* 75–98.

LoSchiavo, F. M., & Shatz, M. A. (2005). Enhancing online instruction with humor. *Teaching of Psychology, 32,* 245–248.

Lowe, G. (2002). *Data from the mass observation study of everyday pleasures.* Retrieved September 2002 from http://www.arise.org/lowepa.html

Lovallo, D., & Kahneman, D. (2000). Living with uncertainty: Attractiveness and resolution timing. *Journal of Behavioral Decision Making, 13,* 179–190.

Lykken, D. T. (1999). *Happiness: What studies of twins show us about nature, nurture, and the happiness set point.* New York: Golden Books.

Lykken, D. T. (2000). *Happiness: The nature and nurture of joy and contentment.* New York: St. Martin's Griffin.

Lykken, D., & Tellegen, A. (1996). Happiness is a stochastic phenomenon. *Psychological Science, 7,* 186–189.

Lyubomirsky, S., & Lepper, H. S. (1999). A measure of subjective happiness: Preliminary reliability and construct validation. *Social Indicators Research, 46,* 137–155.

Lyubomirsky, S., Sheldon, K. M., & Schkade, D. (2005). Pursuing happiness: The architecture of sustainable change. *Review of General Psychology, 9,* 111–131.

Macaulay, J. (2000). *Temporal savoring beliefs: Examination of the utility of a savoring scale to investigate the relationship between savoring and extraversion and the role of savoring in subjective well-being.* Unpublished honor's thesis, La Trobe University, Bundoora, Australia.

MacLean, P. D. (1990). *The triune brain in evolution: Role in paleocerebral functions.* New York: Springer.

Maccoby, E. E., & Jacklin, C. N. (1974). *The psychology of sex differences.* Stanford, CA: Stanford University Press.

Macfarlane, R. (2003). *Mountains of the mind.* New York: Pantheon Books.

Macht, M., Meininger, J., & Roth, J. (2005). The pleasures of eating: A qualitative analysis. *Journal of Happiness Studies, 6,* 137–160.

MacLeod, A. K., Pankhania, B., Lee, M., & Mitchell, D. (1997). Parasuicide, depression and the anticipation of positive and negative future experiences. *Psychological Medicine, 27,* 973–977.

Mandle, C. L., Jacobs, S. C., Arcari, P. M., & Domar, A. D. (1996). The efficacy of relaxation response interventions with adult patients: A review of the literature. *Journal of Cardiovascular Nursing, 10,* 4–26.

Markman, K. D., Gavanski, I., Sherman, S. J., & McMullen, M. N. (1993). The mental simulation of better and worse possible worlds. *Journal of Experimental Social Psychology, 29,* 87–109.

Marshall, A. (1891). *Principles of economics* (2nd ed.). London: Macmillan.

Martin, J. R. (1997). Mindfulness: A proposed common factor. *Journal of Psychotherapy Integration, 7,* 291–312.

Martin, L. L. (2001). Mood as input: A configural view of mood effects. In L. L. Martin & G. L. Clore (Eds.), *Theories of mood and cognition: A user's guidebook* (pp. 135–157). Mahwah, NJ: Lawrence Erlbaum Associates.

Martin, L. L., Ward, D. W., Achee, J. W., & Wyer, R. S. (1993). Mood as input: People have to interpret the motivational implications of their moods. *Journal of Personality and Social Psychology, 64,* 317–326.

Martin, R. A., & Dobbin, J. P. (1988). Sense of humor, hassles, and immunoglobulin A: Evidence for a stress-moderating effect of humor. *International Journal of Psychiatry in Medicine, 18,* 93–105.

Martin, R. A., & Lefcourt, H. M. (1983). Sense of humor as a moderator of the relation between stressors and moods. *Journal of Personality and Social Psychology, 45,* 1313–1324.

Martineau, H. (1833). *Cinnamon and pearls: A tale.* London: Charles Fox.

Maslow, A. H. (1954). *Motivation and personality.* New York: Harper & Row.

Matsumoto, D., Kudoh, T., Scherer, K., & Wallbott, H. (1988). Antecedents of and reactions to emotions in the United States and Japan. *Journal of Cross-Cultural Psychology, 19,* 267–286.

Mayer, J. D., & Salovey, P. (1993). The intelligence of emotional intelligence. *Intelligence, 17,* 433–442.

Mayes, F. (1996). *Under the Tuscan sun: At home in Italy.* San Francisco: Chronicle Books.

McAdams, D. P. (1985). *Power, intimacy, and the life story: Personological inquiries into identity.* Homewood, IL: The Dorsey Press.

McAdams, D. P. (1993). *The stories we live by: Personal myths and the making of the self.* New York: William Morrow.

McClelland, D. C. (1961). *The achieving society.* Princeton, NJ: Van Nostrand.

McCullough, M. E. (2002). Savoring life, past and present: Explaining what hope and gratitude share in common. *Psychological Inquiry, 13,* 302–304.

McCullough, M. E., Emmons, R. A., & Tsang, J. (2002). The grateful disposition: A conceptual and empirical topography. *Journal of Personality and Social Psychology, 82,* 112–127.

McCullough, M. E., Hoyt, W. T., Larson, D. B., Koenig, H. G., & Thoresen, C. (2000). Religious involvement and mortality: A meta-analytic review. *Health Psychology, 19,* 211–222.

McElrath, J. R., & Robb, A. P. (1981). *The complete works of Anne Bradstreet.* Boston: Twayne Publishers.

McMahon, A. W., Jr., & Rhudick, P. J. (1967). Reminiscing in the aged: An adaptational response. In S. Levin & R. J. Kahana (Eds.), *Psychodynamic studies on aging: Creativity, reminiscing, and dying* (pp. 64–78). New York: International Universities Press.

McWilliams, N., & Lependorf, S. (1990). Narcissistic pathology of everyday life: The denial of remorse and gratitude. *Contemporary Psychoanalysis, 26,* 430–451.

Meadows, C. M. (1975). The phenomenology of joy: An empirical investigation. *Psychological Reports, 37,* 39–54.

Medvec, V. H., Madey, S. F., & Gilovich, T. (1995). When less is more: Counterfactual thinking and satisfaction among Olympic medalists. *Journal of Personality and Social Psychology, 69,* 603–610.

Meehan, M. P., Durlak, J. A., & Bryant, F. B. (1993). The relationship of social support to perceived control and subjective mental health in adolescents. *Journal of Community Psychology, 21,* 49–55.

Meehl, P. E. (1975). Hedonic capacity: Some conjectures. *Bulletin of the Menninger Clinic, 39,* 295–307.

Meichenbaum, D. (1977). *Cognitive-behavior modification: An integrative approach.* New York: Plenum.

Mesquita, B., & Karasawa, M. (2002). Different emotional lives. *Cognition & Emotion, 16,* 127–141.

Metcalfe, J., & Mischel, W. (1999). A hot/cool-system analysis of delay of gratification: Dynamics of willpower. *Psychological Review, 106,* 3–19.

Middleton, R. A., & Byrd, E. K. (1996). Psychosocial factors and hospital readmission status of older persons with cardiovascular disease. *Journal of Applied Rehabilitation Counseling, 27,* 3–10.

Mill, J. S. (1873). *Autobiography.* London: Longmans, Green, Reader, and Dyer.

Miller, W. K., & Thoresen, C. E. (2003). Spirituality, religion, and health: An emerging research field. *American Psychologist, 58,* 24–35.

Mischel, W. (1974). Processes in delay of gratification. In L. Berkowitz (Ed.), *Advances in experimental social psychology* (Vol. 7, pp. 249–292). New York: Academic Press.

Mischel, W. (1981). Objective and subjective rules for delay of gratification. In G. d'Ydewalle & W. Lens (Eds.), *Cognition in human motivation and learning* (pp. 33–58). Hillsdale, NJ: Lawrence Erlbaum Associates.

Mischel, W., & Ebbesen, E. B. (1970). Attention in delay of gratification. *Journal of Personality and Social Psychology, 16,* 329–337.

Mischel, W., Ebbesen, E. B., & Raskoff-Zeiss, A. (1972). Cognitive and attentional mechanisms in delay of gratification. *Journal of Personality and Social Psychology, 21,* 204–218.

Mischel, W., Shoda, Y., & Rodriguez, M. L. (1989). Delay of gratification in children. *Science, 244,* 933–938.

Mitchell, T., & Thompson, L. (1994). A theory of temporal adjustments of the evaluation of events: Rosy prospection and rosy retrospection. In C. Stubbart, J. Porac, & J. Meindl (Eds.), *Advances in managerial cognition and organizational information-processing* (Vol. 5, pp. 85–114). Greenwich, CT: JAI Press.

Mitchell, T. R., Thompson, L., Peterson, E., & Cronk, R. (1997). Temporal adjustments in the evaluation of events: The "rosy view." *Journal of Experimental Social Psychology, 33,* 421–448.

Mobilia, P. (1993). Gambling as a rational addiction. *Journal of Gambling Studies, 9,* 121–151.

Moberg, D. O., & Brusek, P. M. (1978). Spiritual well-being: A neglected subject in quality of life research. *Social Indicators Research, 5,* 303–323.

Molière, J. B. P. (1992). *Les misanthrope.* Mineola, NY: Dover Publications. (Original work published 1666)

Moran, C. C., & Massam, M. M. (1999). Differential influences of coping humor and humor bias on mood. *Behavioral Medicine, 25,* 36–42.

Morgan, E. S. (2002). *Benjamin Franklin.* New Haven, CT: Yale University Press.

Murray, S. L., Holmes, J. G., & Griffin, D. W. (1996). The benefits of positive illusions: Idealization and the construction of satisfaction in close relationships. *Journal of Personality and Social Psychology, 70,* 79–98.

Myers, D. G. (1992). *The pursuit of happiness: Who is happy—and why.* New York: William Morrow.

Myers, D. G., & Diener, E. (1995). Who is happy? *Psychological Science, 6,* 10–19.

Nakamura, J., & Csikszentmihalyi, M. (2002). The concept of flow. In C. R. Snyder & S. J. Lopez (Eds.), *Handbook of positive psychology* (pp. 89–105). New York: Oxford University Press.

Nelson, T. D. (1992). *Metacognition: Core readings.* Toronto, Ontario, Canada: Allyn & Bacon.

Nichols, J. (1987). *A fragile beauty.* Layton, UT: Gibbs Smith.

Niederhoffer, K. G., & Pennebaker, J. W. (2002). Sharing one's story: On the benefits of writing or talking about emotional experience. In C. R. Snyder & S. J. Lopez (Eds.), *Handbook of positive psychology* (pp. 573–583). New York: Oxford University Press.

Noyce, W. (1958). *The springs of adventure.* New York: The World Publishing Company.

Oishi, S., Diener, E., Napa Scollon, C., & Biswas-Diener, R. (2004). Cross-situational consistency of affective experiences across cultures. *Journal of Personality and Social Psychology, 86,* 460–472.

Ostir, G. V., Markides, K. S., Black, S. A., & Goodwin, J. S. (2000). Emotional well-being predicts subsequent functional independence and survival. *Journal of the American Geriatrics Society, 48,* 473–478.

Orwoll, L., & Achenbaum, W. A. (1993). Gender and the development of wisdom. *Human Development, 36,* 274–296.

Paradiso, S., Johnson, D. L., Andreasen, N. C., O'Leary, D. S., Watkins, G. L., Ponto, L. L. B., & Hichwa, R. D. (1999). Cerebral blood flow changes associated with attribution of emotional valence to pleasant, unpleasant, and neutral visual stimuli in a PET study of normal subjects. *American Journal of Psychiatry, 156,* 1618–1629.

Pargament, K. I. (1997). *The psychology of religion and coping: Theory, research, practice.* New York: Guilford Press.

Pargament, K. I., & Mahoney, A. (2002). Spirituality: Discovering and conserving the sacred. In C. R. Snyder & S. J. Lopez (Eds.), *Handbook of positive psychology* (pp. 646–659). New York: Oxford University Press.

Parkes, C. M. (1996). *Bereavement: Studies of grief in adult life* (3rd ed.). New York: Routledge.

Pennebaker, J. W., Kiecolt-Glaser, J. K., & Glaser, R. (1988). Disclosure of traumas and immune function: Health implications for psychotherapy. *Journal of Consulting and Clinical Psychology, 56,* 239–245.

Pennebaker, J. W., & Seagal, J. D. (1999). Forming a story: The health benefits of narrative. *Journal of Clinical Psychology, 55,* 1243–1254.

Perry, S. D. (2001). Commercial humor enhancement of program enjoyment: Gender and program appeal as mitigating factors. *Mass Communication and Society, 4,* 103–116.

Peterson, E. H. (1997). *Leap over a wall: Earthy spirituality for everyday Christians.* New York: HarperCollins.

Pettit, J. W., Kline, J., Gencoz, T., Gencoz, F., & Joiner, T. E., Jr. (2001). Are happy people healthier? The specific role of positive affect in predicting self-reported health symptoms. *Journal of Research in Personality, 35,* 521–536.

Phillips, A. G., & Silvia, P. J. (2005). Self-awareness and the emotional consequences of self-discrepancies. *Personality and Social Psychology Bulletin, 31,* 703–713.

Piccard, B. (1999, September). Around at last! *National Geographic, 196,* 30–51.

Poloma, M. M., & Pendleton, B. F. (1990). Religious domains and general well-being. *Social Indicators Research, 22,* 255–276.

Pollock. R. (1828). *The course of time.* Philadelphia, PA: Claxton.

Pope, A. (1879). *Imitation of martial.* London: Macmillan. (Original work published 1730)

Provine, R. P., & Fischer, K. R. (1989). Laughing, smiling, and talking: Relation to sleeping and social context in humans. *Ethology, 83,* 295–305.

Putnam, S. P., Spritz, B. L., & Stifter, C. A. (2002). Mother–child coregulation during delay of gratification at 30 months. *Infancy, 3,* 209–225.

Ray, J. (1670). *A collection of English proverbs digested into a convenient method for the speedy finding of any one upon occasion.* Cambridge, England: W. Morden.

Reich, J. W., & Zautra, A. (1981). Life events and personal causation: Some relationships with satisfaction and distress. *Journal of Personality and Social Psychology, 41,* 1002–1012.

Reese, E., Haden, C. A., & Fivush, R. (1993). Mother–child conversations about the past: Relationships of style and memory over time. *Cognitive Development, 8,* 403–430.

Reker, G. T., Peacock, E. J., & Wong, P. T. (1987). Meaning and purpose in life and well-being: A life-span perspective. *Journal of Gerontology, 42,* 44–49.

Reker, G. T., & Wong, P. T. (1988). Aging as an individual process: Toward a theory of meaning. In J. E. Birren & V. L. Bengston (Eds.), *Emergent theories of aging* (pp. 214–246). New York: Springer.

Rilke, R. M. (2005). *Duino elegies* (G. Miranda, Trans.). Falls Church, VA: Azul Editions. (Original work published 1923)

Robbins, J. (Ed.). (1999). *The pleasure of finding things out: The best short works of Richard P. Feynman.* Cambridge, MA: Perseus.

Rodriguez, M. L., Mischel, W., & Shoda, Y. (1989). Cognitive person variables in the delay of gratification of older children at risk. *Journal of Personality and Social Psychology, 57,* 358–367.

Roese, N. J. (1994). The functional basis of counterfactual thinking. *Journal of Personality and Social Psychology, 66,* 805–815.

Roese, N. J. (1997). Counterfactual thinking. *Psychological Bulletin, 121,* 133–148.

Rothbaum, F., Weisz, J. R., & Snyder, S. S. (1982). Changing the world and changing the self: A two-process model of perceived control. *Journal of Personality and Social Psychology, 42,* 5–37.

Rotter, J. B. (1966). Generalized expectancies for internal versus external control of reinforcement. *Psychological Monographs, 80,* 1–28.

Rubin, Z. (1973). *Liking and loving: An invitation to social psychology.* New York: Holt, Rinehart & Winston.

Russell, J. A. (2003). Introduction: The return of pleasure. *Cognition & Emotion, 17,* 161–165.

Ryff, C. (1989). Happiness is everything, or is it? Explorations on the meaning of psychological well-being. *Journal of Personality and Social Psychology, 57,* 1069–1081.

Saarni, C. (1984). An observational study of children's attempts to monitor their expressive behavior. *Child Development, 55,* 1504–1513.

Saint-Exupéry, A. de (1942). *Airman's odyssey: A trilogy comprising Wind, Sand and Stars, Night Flight, Flight to Paris.* New York: Reynal & Hitchcock.

Salovey, P., & Mayer, J. D. (1989–1990). Emotional intelligence. *Imagination, Cognition and Personality, 9,* 185–211.

Salovey, P., Mayer, J. D., Goldman, S. L., Turvey, C., & Palfai, T. P. (1995). Emotional attention, clarity, and repair: Exploring emotional intelligence using the Trait Meta-Mood Scale. In J. W. Pennebaker (Ed.), *Emotion, disclosure, and health* (pp. 125–154). Washington, DC: American Psychological Association.

Salovey, P., Rothman, A. J., Detweiler, J. B., & Steward, W. T. (2000). Emotional states and physical health. *American Psychologist, 55,* 110–121.

Sarason, I. G., Levine, H. M., Basham, R. B., & Sarason, B. R. (1983). Assessing social support: The Social Support Questionnaire. *Journal of Personality and Social Psychology, 44,* 127–139.

Sartre, J. P. (1962). *Sketch for a theory of the emotions* (P. Mairet, Trans.). London: Methuen. (Original work published 1939)

Schaller, G. B. (1980). *Stones of silence: Journeys in the Himalaya.* New York: Viking Press.

Scheier, M. F., & Carver, C. S. (1985). Optimism, coping, and health: Assessment and implications of generalized outcome expectancies. *Health Psychology, 4,* 219–247.

Scheier, M. F., & Carver, C. S. (1992). Effects of optimism on psychological and physical well-being: Theoretical overview and empirical update. *Cognitive Therapy and Research, 16,* 201–228.

Schlosser, B. (1990). The assessment of subjective well-being and its relationship to the stress process. *Journal of Personality Assessment, 54,* 128–140.

Schoeneck, T. S. (1987). *Hope for bereaved: Understanding, coping and growing through grief.* (Rev. ed.). Syracuse, NY: Valley Press.

Schooler, J. W. (2001). Discovering memories of abuse in the light of meta-awareness. *Journal of Aggression, Maltreatment and Trauma, 4,* 105–136.

Schooler, J. W., Ariely, D., & Loewenstein, G. (2003). The pursuit and assessment of happiness may be self-defeating. In I. Brocas & J. D. Carrillo (Eds.), *The psychology of economic decisions. Volume 1: Rationality and well-being* (pp. 41–70) New York: Oxford University Press.

Schutte, N. S., Malouff, J. M., Hall, L. E., Haggerty, D. J., Cooper, J. T., Golden, C. J., & Dornheim, L. (1998). Development and validation of a measure of emotional intelligence. *Personality and Individual Differences, 25,* 167–177.

Schutte, N. S., Malouff, J. M., Simunek, M., McKenley, J., & Hollander, S. (2002). Characteristic emotional intelligence and emotional well-being. *Cognition & Emotion, 16,* 769–785.

Schwartz, B. (2000). Self-determination: The tyranny of freedom. *American Psychologist, 55,* 79–88.

Schwartz, B., Ward, A., Monterosso, J., Lyubomirsky, S., White, K., & Lehman, D. R. (2002). Maximizing versus satisficing: Happiness is a matter of choice. *Journal of Personality and Social Psychology, 83,* 1178–1197.

Schwartz, R. M. (1992). States of mind model and personal construct theory: Implications for psychopathology. *International Journal of Personal Construct Psychology, 5,* 123–143.

Schwartz, R. M., & Garamoni, G. L. (1989). Cognitive balance and psychopathology: Evaluation of an information processing model of positive and negative states of mind. *Clinical Psychology Review, 9,* 271–294.

Sedikides, C., Wildschut, T., & Baden, D. (2004). Nostalgia: Conceptual issues and existential functions. In J. Greenberg, S. L. Koole, & T. Pyszczynski (Eds.), *Handbook of experimental existential psychology* (pp. 200–214). New York: Guilford.

Seers, K., & Carroll, D. (1998). Relaxation techniques for acute pain management: A systematic review. *Journal of Advanced Nursing, 27,* 466–475.

Segerstrom, S. C. (2001). Optimism and attentional bias for negative and positive stimuli. *Personality and Social Psychology Bulletin, 27,* 1334–1343.

Seligman, M. E. P. (2002a). *Authentic happiness: Using the new positive psychology to realize your potential for lasting fulfillment.* New York: The Free Press.

Seligman, M. E. P. (2002b). Positive psychology, positive prevention, and positive therapy. In C. R. Snyder & S. J. Lopez (Eds.), *Handbook of positive psychology* (pp. 3–9). New York: Oxford University Press.

Seligman, M. E. P., & Peterson, C. (2003). Positive clinical psychology. In L. G. Aspinwall & U. M. Staudinger (Eds.), *A psychology of human strengths: Fundamental questions and future directions for a positive psychology* (pp. 305–317). Washington, DC: American Psychological Association.

Shakespeare, W. (1996). *The sonnets.* New York: Cambridge University Press.

Shakespeare, W. (2002). *Much ado about nothing.* New York: Oxford University Press.

Shapiro, D. H. (1980). *Meditation: Self-regulation strategy and altered state of consciousness.* Hawthorne, NY: Aldine de Gruyter.

Shapiro, S. L., Schwartz, G. E. R., & Santerre, C. (2002). Meditation and positive psychology. In C. R. Snyder & S. J. Lopez (Eds.), *Handbook of positive psychology* (pp. 632–645). New York: Oxford University Press.

Shoda, Y., Mischel, W., & Peake, P. K. (1990). Predicting adolescent cognitive and self-regulatory competencies from preschool delay of gratification: Identifying diagnostic conditions. *Developmental Psychology, 26,* 978–986.

Shulman, N. (1992). *Zen in the art of climbing mountains.* Boston: Charles E. Tuttle.

Silvia, P. J., & Duval, T. S. (2004). Self-awareness, self-motives, and self-motivation. In R. A. Wright, J. Greenberg, & S. S. Brehm (Eds.), *Motivational analyses of social behavior: Building on Jack Brehm's contributions to psychology* (pp. 57–75). Mahwah, NJ: Lawrence Erlbaum Associates.

Simpson, J. A., & Weiner, E. S. C. (Eds.). (1989). *Oxford English dictionary* (2nd ed.). Oxford: Oxford University Press.

Singer, J. L. (1981). *Daydreaming and fantasy.* Oxford, UK: Oxford University Press.

Smith, A. (2000). *The theory of moral sentiments.* Amherst, NY: Prometheus Books. (Original work published in 1759)

Smith, J. D., & Washburn, D. A. (2005). Uncertainty monitoring and metacognition by animals. *Current Directions in Psychological Science, 14,* 19–24.

Smith, R. H. (2000). Assimilative and contrastive emotional reactions to upward and downward social comparisons. In J. Suls & L. Wheeler (Eds.), *Handbook of social comparison: Theory and research* (pp. 173–200). New York: Plenum.

Smyth, J. M., Stone, A. A., Hurewitz, A., & Kaell, A. (1999). Effects of writing about stressful experiences on symptom reduction in patients with asthma or rheumatoid arthritis: A randomized trial. *Journal of the American Medical Association, 281,* 1304–1309.

Snyder, C. R. (1994). *The psychology of hope: You can get there from here*. New York: The Free Press.

Snyder, C. R. (2002). Hope theory: Rainbows in the mind. *Psychological Inquiry, 13*, 249–275.

Solomon, R. L. (1980). The opponent-process theory of acquired motivation: The costs of pleasure and the benefits of pain. *American Psychologist, 35*, 691–712.

Spielberger, C. D. (1973). *State-Trait Anxiety Inventory for Children (STAIC)*. Redwood City, CA: Mind Garden.

Spinrad, T. L., Stifter, C. A., Donelan-McCall, N., & Turner, L. (2004). Mothers' regulation strategies in response to toddlers' affect: Links to later emotion self-regulation. *Social Development, 13*, 40–55.

Stevenson, R. L. (1881). *Virginibus puerisque and other papers*. London: Kegan Paul.

Stone, A. A., Greenberg, M. A., Kennedy-Moore, E., & Newman, M. G. (1991). Self-report, situation-specific coping questionnaires: What are they measuring? *Journal of Personality and Social Psychology, 61*, 648–658.

Strack, F., Martin, L. L., & Stepper, S. (1988). Inhibiting and facilitating conditions of the human smile: A nonobtrusive test of the facial feedback hypothesis. *Journal of Personality and Social Psychology, 54*, 768–777.

Strack, F., Schwarz, N., & Gschneidinger, E. (1985). Happiness and reminiscing: The role of time perspective, affect, and mode of thinking. *Journal of Personality and Social Psychology, 49*, 1460–1469.

Strube, M. J., Berry, J. M., Goza, B. K., & Fennimore, D. (1985). Type A behavior, age, and psychological well-being. *Journal of Personality and Social Psychology, 49*, 203–218.

Stuck, H. (2004). *The ascent of Denali: A narrative of the first complete ascent of the highest peak in North America*. Santa Barbara, CA: The Narrative Press. (Original work published in 1914)

Styles, E. A. (1997). *The psychology of attention*. Mahwah, NJ: Lawrence Erlbaum Associates.

Swinkels, A., & Giuliano, T. A. (1995). The measurement and conceptualization of mood awareness: Monitoring and labeling one's mood states. *Personality and Social Psychology Bulletin, 21*, 934–949.

Syrjala, K. L., Donaldson, G. W., Davis, M. W., Kippes, M. E., & Carr, J. E. (1995). Relaxation and imagery and cognitive-behavioral training reduce pain during cancer treatment: A controlled clinical trial. *Pain, 63*, 189–198.

Syrus, P. (1856). *The moral sayings of Publilius Syrus*. (D. Lyman, Trans.). Cleveland, OH: [n.p.]. (Original work written 42 B.C.)

Tannen, D. (1991). *You just don't understand: Women and men in conversation*. New York: Ballantine Books.

Tellegen, A. (1992). *Note on structure and meaning of the MPQ Absorption scale*. Unpublished manuscript, University of Minnesota, Minneapolis, MN.

Thera, N. (1972). *The power of mindfulness*. San Francisco: Unity Press.

Thompson, C., Barresi, J., & Moore, C. (1997). The development of future-oriented prudence and altruism in preschoolers. *Cognitive Development, 12*, 199–212.

Thoresen, C. E. (1998). Spirituality, health, and science: The coming revival? In S. Roth-Roemer, S. R. Kurpius, & C. Carmin (Eds.), *The emerging role of counseling psychology in health care* (pp. 409–431). New York: Norton.

Thornton, S., & Brotchie, J. (1987). Reminiscence: A critical review of the empirical literature. *British Journal of Clinical Psychology, 26*, 93–111.

Thrash, T. M., & Elliot, A. J. (2004). Inspiration: Core characteristics, component processes, antecedents, and function. *Journal of Personality and Social Psychology, 87*, 957–973.

Tietjens, E. (1919). The most sacred mountain. In J. B. Rittenhouse (Ed.), *The second book of modern verse: A selection from the work of contemporary American poets* (pp. 95–96). New York: Houghton-Mifflin.

Tiger, L. (1992). *The pursuit of pleasure.* Boston: Little, Brown, & Company.

Tolle, E. (1999). *The power of now: A guide to spiritual enlightenment.* Novato, CA: New World Library.

Tomkins, S. S. (1962). *Affect, imagery, consciousness, Vol. 1: The positive affects.* New York: Springer.

Torrance, E. P. (1969). *Creativity.* Sioux Falls, ND: Adapt Press.

Tracy, J. L., & Robins, R. W. (2004). Show your pride: Evidence for a discrete emotion expression. *Psychological Science, 15,* 194–197.

Trope, Y., & Liberman, N. (2003). Temporal construal. *Psychological Review, 110,* 403–421.

Turner, V. (Ed.). (1982). *Celebration: Studies in festivity and ritual.* Washington, DC: Smithsonian Institution Press.

Uchida, Y., Norasakkunkit, V., & Kitayama, S. (2004). Cultural constructions of happiness: Theory and empirical evidence. *Journal of Happiness Studies, 5,* 223–239.

Vaux, A. (1988). *Social support: Theory, research, and intervention.* Westport, CT: Praeger.

Veenhoven, R. (1988). The utility of happiness. *Social Indicators Research, 20,* 333–354.

Veroff, J. (1999). Commitment in the early years of marriage. In J. M. Adams & W. H. Jones (Eds.), *Handbook of interpersonal commitment and relationship stability* (pp. 149–162). New York: Springer.

Veroff, J., Douvan, E., & Hatchett, S. J. (1995). *Marital instability: A social and behavioral study of the early years.* Westport, CT: Praeger.

Veroff, J., Douvan, E., & Kulka, R. (1981). *The inner American.* New York: Basic Books.

Veroff, J., & Veroff, J. (1980). *Social incentives: A life-span developmental approach.* San Diego, CA: Academic Press.

Vilaythong, A. P., Arnau, R. C., Rosen, D. H., & Mascaro, N. (2003). Humor and hope: Can humor increase hope? *Humor: International Journal of Humor Research, 16,* 79–89.

Warthan, M. M., Uchida, T., & Wagner, R. F., Jr. (2005). UV light tanning as a type of substance-related disorder. *Archives of Dermatology, 141,* 963–966.

Waterman, A. S. (1984). *The psychology of individualism.* Westport, CT: Praeger.

Waterman, J. (2002). (Ed.) *The quotable climber: Literary, humorous, inspirational, and fearful moments of climbing.* Guilford, CT: The Lyons Press.

Watson, D. (2000). *Mood and temperament.* New York: Guilford.

Watson, D. (2002). Positive affectivity: The disposition to experience pleasurable emotional states. In C. R. Snyder & S. J. Lopez (Eds.), *Handbook of positive psychology* (pp. 106–119). New York: Oxford University Press.

Wegener, D. T., & Petty, R. E. (1994). Mood management across affective states: The hedonic contingency hypothesis. *Journal of Personality and Social Psychology, 66,* 1034–1048.

Weiner, B. (1992). *Human motivation: Metaphors, theories and research.* Thousand Oaks, CA: Sage.

Weiner, B., Frieze, I., Kukla, A., Reed, L., Rest, S., & Rosenbaum, R. M. (1971). Perceiving the causes of success and failure. In E. E. Jones, D. E. Kanouse, H. H. Kelley, R. E. Nisbett, S. Valins, & B. Weiner (Eds.), *Attribution: Perceiving the causes of behavior* (pp. 95–120). Morristown, NJ: General Learning Press.

Weinfurt, K. P., Bryant, F. B., & Yarnold, P. R. (1994). The factor structure of the Affect Intensity Measure: In search of a measurement model. *Journal of Research in Personality, 28,* 314–331.

White, K., & Lehman, D. R. (2005). Looking on the bright side: Downward counterfactual thinking in response to negative life events. *Personality and Social Psychology Bulletin, 31,* 1413–1424.

White, R. W. (1959). Motivation reconsidered: The concept of competence. *Psychological Review, 66,* 297–333.

Wickwire, J., & Bullitt, D. (1998). *Addicted to danger: A memoir about affirming life in the face of death.* New York: Pocket Books.

Wild, T. C., Kuiken, D., & Schopflocher, D. (1995). The role of absorption in experiential involvement. *Journal of Personality and Social Psychology, 69*, 569–579.

Wilson, T. D., Centerbar, D. B., Kermer, D. A., & Gilbert, D. T. (2005). The pleasures of uncertainty: Prolonging positive moods in ways people do not anticipate. *Journal of Personality and Social Psychology, 88*, 5–21.

Wilson, T. D., Lindsey, S., & Schooler, T. Y. (2000). A model of dual attitudes. *Psychological Review, 107*, 101–126.

Wilson, T. D., Lisle, D. J., Kraft, D., & Wetzel, C. G. (1989). Preferences as expectation-driven inferences: Effects of affective expectations on affective experience. *Journal of Personality and Social Psychology, 56*, 519–530.

Winokur, J. (Ed.) (1987). *The portable curmudgeon.* New York: New American Library.

Wong, P. T., & Fry, P. S. (Eds.) (1998). *The human quest for meaning: A handbook of psychological research and clinical applications.* Mahwah, NJ: Lawrence Erlbaum Associates.

Wood, J. V., Heimpel, S. A., & Michela, J. L. (2003). Savoring versus dampening: Self-esteem differences in regulating positive affect. *Journal of Personality and Social Psychology, 85*, 566–580.

Wright, F. L. (1958). *The living city.* New York: Horizon Press.

Young, K. S. (1998). Internet addiction: The emergence of a new clinical disorder. *CyberPsychology and Behavior, 1*, 237- 244.

Yovetich, N. A., Dale, J. A., & Hudak, M. A. (1990). Benefits of humor in reduction of threat-induced anxiety. *Psychological Reports, 66*, 51–58.

Zika, S., & Chamberlain, K. (1992). On the relation between meaning in life and psychological well-being. *British Journal of Psychology, 83*, 133–145.

Zillmann, D. (1988). Mood management: Using entertainment to full advantage. In L. Donohew, H. E. Sypher, & E. T. Higgins (Eds.), *Communication, social cognition, and affect* (pp. 147–171). Hillsdale, NJ: Lawrence Erlbaum Associates.

Zimbardo, P. G., & Boyd, J. N. (1999). Putting time in perspective: A valid, reliable individual-differences metric. *Journal of Personality and Social Psychology, 77*, 1271–1288.

Zimmerman, J. E. (1964). *Dictionary of classical mythology.* New York: Harper & Row.

Zuckerman, M. (1979). *Sensation seeking: Beyond the optimal level of arousal.* Hillsdale, NJ: Lawrence Erlbaum Associates.

Appendix A

Self-Report Items Assessing Perceived Control Over Positive and Negative Events and Perceived Control Over Positive and Negative Feelings in Response to Events

Avoiding

1. In general, how much control do you feel that you personally have over whether or not bad things happen to you?

    1 = none at all; 2 = a little bit; 3 = some; 4 = a lot; 5 = a great deal.

2. Over their lives most people have something bad happen to them or to someone they love. By "something bad," we mean things like getting sick, losing a job, or being in trouble with the police; or like when someone dies, leaves, or disappoints you. Compared to other people you know, have things like this happened to you a lot, some, not much, or hardly ever?

    1 = a lot; 2 = some; 3 = not much; 4 = hardly ever.

*3. In general, how likely or unlikely do you think it is that bad things will happen to you?

    1   2   3   4   5   6   7
    very unlikely   very likely

Coping

1. When bad things have happened in your life, how well do you feel that you have typically been able to cope?

    1 = not at all; 2 = a little bit; 3 = some; 4 = a lot; 5 = a great deal.

*2. Compared to most other people you know, how much have these bad things typically affected you?

    1 = not at all; 2 = a little bit; 3 = some; 4 = a lot; 5 = a great deal.

*3. When something bad happens to you, compared to most other people you know, how long does it usually affect the way you feel?

1   2   3   4   5   6   7

not for very long   for a very long time

Obtaining

1. In general, how much control do you feel that you personally have over whether or not good things happen to you?

   1 = none at all; 2 = a little bit; 3 = some; 4 = a lot; 5 = a great deal.

2. With respect to good things that have occurred in your life, to what extent do you think that you have typically been responsible for their occurrence?

   1   2   3   4   5   6   7

   I have typically   I have typically
   not been responsible   been responsible

*3. Over their lives most people have something good happen to them or to someone they love. By "something good," we mean things like receiving an honor or award, getting a good grade in school, getting a promotion or raise, or going on vacation; or like when someone does something nice for you or a good friend comes to visit. Or maybe just something important you wanted to happen did happen. Compared to other people you know, have things like this happened to you a lot, some, not much, or hardly ever?

   1 = a lot; 2 = some; 3 = not much; 4 = hardly ever.

4. In general, how likely or unlikely do you think it is that good things will happen to you?

   1   2   3   4   5   6   7

   very unlikely   very likely

Savoring (*Perceived Ability to Savor Positive Outcomes* scale (PASPO; Bryant, 1989)

1. When good things have happened in your life, how much do you feel you have typically been able to appreciate or enjoy them?

   1 = not at all; 2 = a little bit; 3 = some; 4 = a lot; 5 = a great deal.

2. Compared to most other people you know, how much pleasure have you typically gotten from good things that have happened to you?

   1 = none at all; 2 = a little bit; 3 = some; 4 = a lot; 5 = a great deal.

3. When something good happens to you, compared to most other people you know, how long does it usually affect the way you feel?

   1   2   3   4   5   6   7

   not for very long   for a very long time

*4. When good things have happened to you, have there ever been times when you felt like everything was really going your way; that is, when you felt on top of the world, or felt a great deal of joy in life, or found it hard to contain your positive feelings? How often would you say you felt like that?

   1 = many times; 2 = rarely; 3 = once in a while; 4 = never.

5. How often would you say that you feel like jumping or shouting for joy?

   1 = never; 2 = rarely; 3 = sometimes; 4 = often.

*Reverse-scored item.

Reprinted from Bryant, F. B. (1989) A four-factor model of perceived control: Avoiding, coping, obtaining, and savoring. *Journal of Personality, 57,* 773–797; with permission from Blackwell Publishing, Oxford, UK.

Appendix B

The Savoring Beliefs Inventory (SBI)

SBI

Gender: _____
Age: _____

Instructions: For each statement listed below, please circle the one number that best indicates how true the particular statement is for you. There are no right or wrong answers. Please be as honest as you can.

	strongly disagree					strongly agree
1. Before a good thing happens, I look forward to it in ways that give me pleasure in the present.	1	2	3	4	5	6	7
2. It's hard for me to hang onto a good feeling for very long.	1	2	3	4	5	6	7
3. I enjoy looking back on happy times from my past.	1	2	3	4	5	6	7
4. I don't like to look forward to good times too much before they happen.	1	2	3	4	5	6	7
5. I know how to make the most of a good time.	1	2	3	4	5	6	7
6. I don't like to look back at good times too much after they've taken place.	1	2	3	4	5	6	7
7. I feel a joy of anticipation when I think about upcoming good things.	1	2	3	4	5	6	7
8. When it comes to enjoying myself, I'm my own "worst enemy."	1	2	3	4	5	6	7
9. I can make myself feel good by remembering pleasant events from my past.	1	2	3	4	5	6	7
10. For me, anticipating what upcoming good events will be like is basically a waste of time.	1	2	3	4	5	6	7

		strongly disagree					strongly agree	

11. When something good happens, I can make my enjoyment of it last longer by thinking or doing certain things.

1 2 3 4 5 6 7

12. When I reminisce about pleasant memories, I often start to feel sad or disappointed.

1 2 3 4 5 6 7

13. I can enjoy pleasant events in my mind before they actually occur.

1 2 3 4 5 6 7

14. I can't seem to capture the joy of happy moments.

1 2 3 4 5 6 7

15. I like to store memories of fun times that I go through so that I can recall them later.

1 2 3 4 5 6 7

16. It's hard for me to get very excited about fun times before they actually take place.

1 2 3 4 5 6 7

17. I feel fully able to appreciate good things that happen to me.

1 2 3 4 5 6 7

18. I find that thinking about good times from the past is basically a waste of time.

1 2 3 4 5 6 7

19. I can make myself feel good by imagining what a happy time that is about to happen will be like.

1 2 3 4 5 6 7

20. I don't enjoy things as much as I should.

1 2 3 4 5 6 7

21. It's easy for me to rekindle the joy from pleasant memories.

1 2 3 4 5 6 7

22. When I think about a pleasant event before it happens, I often start to feel uneasy or uncomfortable.

1 2 3 4 5 6 7

23. It's easy for me to enjoy myself when I want to.

1 2 3 4 5 6 7

24. For me, once a fun time is over and gone, it's best not to think about it.

1 2 3 4 5 6 7

See Bryant, 2003.

Appendix C

Instructions for Scoring the
Savoring Beliefs Inventory

Four scale-scores can be derived from the SBI:

(1) *Anticipating* subscale score;
(2) *Savoring the Moment* subscale score;
(3) *Reminiscing* subscale score; and
(4) *SBI Total* score.

There are two different scoring methods for the SBI. The first scoring method is the one used in the original article reporting the development and validation of the SBI (Bryant, 2003, Table 3, p. 185). With this original scoring method, positively anchored items are summed, negatively anchored items are summed, and then the sum of the negatively anchored items is subtracted from the sum of the positively anchored items. This scoring method is used both for each subscale and for the SBI Total score. With this scoring method, scores on each SBI subscale can range from -24 to +24; and SBI Total score can range from -72 to +72. Using this scoring method enables researchers to compare SBI scores for their samples with "normative" SBI scores reported in the original validation article (Bryant, 2003).

The second scoring method converts scale-scores back into the 1–7 "metric" of the response scale for the SBI, by summing the positively anchored items, reverse-scoring the negatively anchored items, adding together these two sums, and dividing the resulting total by the number of constituent items. This scoring method provides average scores for the Anticipating, Savoring the Moment, and Reminiscing subscales, as well as an average SBI Total score. With this scoring method, scores on the three SBI subscales and SBI Total score can range from 1 to 7. This scoring method makes it easy for researchers to interpret SBI scores in the "absolute" terms of the original 1–7 response scale. With this scoring method: 1 is the lowest possible "absolute" score (0th percentile); 2 lies at the 16.67th percentile on the absolute scale; 3 lies at the 33.33rd percentile on the absolute scale; 4 is the midpoint on the absolute scale (50th percentile); 5 lies at the 66.67th percentile on the absolute scale; 6 lies at the 83.33rd percentile on the absolute scale; and 7 is the highest possible "absolute" score (100th percentile).

The two scoring methods provide equivalent sets of scores that are perfectly correlated with each other. In other words, both within each subscale and for SBI Total score, an individual's score using the first scoring method correlates perfectly with that same individual's score using the second scoring method. However, the two scoring methods provide different "metrics" for evaluating SBI scores — the first scoring method yields summed scores, whereas the second scoring method yields averaged scores. Researchers may choose one or the other scoring method, depending on their purpose or preference.

Scoring the SBI Using the Original "Summed Score" Method

I. *Anticipating subscale score*
  A. Sum responses to the following four items: 1, 7, 13, 19.
  B. Sum responses to the following four items: 4, 10, 16, 22.
  C. Subtract the total obtained in Step B from the total obtained in Step A, to get a summed score for the SBI *Anticipating* subscale.

II. *Savoring the Moment subscale score*
  A. Sum responses to the following four items: 5, 11, 17, 23.
  B. Sum responses to the following four items: 2, 8, 14, 20.
  C. Subtract the total obtained in Step B from the total obtained in Step A, to get a summed score for the SBI *Savoring the Moment* subscale.

III. *Reminiscing subscale score*
  A. Sum responses to the following four items: 3, 9, 15, 21.
  B. Sum responses to the following four items: 6, 12, 18, 24.
  C. Subtract the total obtained in Step B from the total obtained in Step A, to get a summed score for the SBI *Reminiscing* subscale.

IV. *Total SBI score*
  A. Sum responses to the following 12 (odd-numbered) items: 1, 3, 5, 7, 9, 11, 13, 15, 17, 19, 21, 23.
  B. Sum responses to the following 12 (even-numbered) items: 2, 4, 6, 8, 10, 12, 14, 16, 18, 20, 22, 24.
  C. Subtract the total obtained in Step B from the total obtained in Step A, to get a summed SBI *Total* score.

Scoring the SBI Using the "Average Score" Method

I. *Anticipating subscale score*
  A. Reverse-score the following items: 4, 10, 16, 22.
  B. Sum responses to these four reverse-scored items.

    C. Sum responses to the following four items: 1, 7, 13, 19.

    D. Add together the sum obtained in Step B and the sum obtained in Step C.

    E. Divide the resulting total by 8, to get a mean score for the SBI *Anticipating* subscale.

II. *Savoring the Moment subscale score*

    A. Reverse-score the following items: 2, 8, 14, 20.

    B. Sum responses to these four reverse-scored items.

    C. Sum responses to the following four items: 5, 11, 17, 23.

    D. Add together the sum obtained in Step B and the sum obtained in Step C.

    E. Divide the resulting total by 8, to get a mean score for the SBI *Savoring the Moment* subscale.

III. *Reminiscing subscale score*

    A. Reverse-score the following items: 6, 12, 18, 24.

    B. Sum responses to these four reverse-scored items.

    C. Sum responses to the following four items: 3, 9, 15, 21.

    D. Add together the sum obtained in Step B and the sum obtained in Step C.

    E. Divide the resulting total by 8, to get a mean score for the SBI *Reminiscing* subscale.

IV. *Total SBI score*

    A. Reverse-score the following 12 (even-numbered) items: 2, 4, 6, 8, 10, 12, 14, 16, 18, 20, 22, 24.

    B. Sum responses to these 12 reverse-scored items.

    C. Sum responses to the following 12 (odd-numbered) items: 1, 3, 5, 7, 9, 11, 13, 15, 17, 19, 21, 23.

    D. Add together the sum obtained in Step B and the sum obtained in Step C.

    E. Divide the resulting total by 24, to get a mean SBI *Total* score.

The following is an SPSS syntax file for computing the *summed versions* of the SBI subscales of Anticipating, Savoring the Moment, and Reminiscing, as well as SBI Total score:

```
COMPUTE anticsum = (sbi1+sbi7+sbi13+sbi19)-(sbi4+sbi10+sbi16+sbi22).
VARIABLE LABELS anticsum 'Summed score for SBI Anticipating subscale'.
COMPUTE momntsum = (sbi5+sbi11+sbi17+sbi23)-(sbi2+sbi8+sbi14+sbi20).
VARIABLE LABELS momntsum 'Summed score for SBI Savoring the Moment
    subscale'.
COMPUTE reminsum = (sbi3+sbi9+sbi15+sbi21)-(sbi6+sbi12+sbi18+sbi24).
```

VARIABLE LABELS reminsum 'Summed score for SBI Reminiscing subscale'.
COMPUTE sbitot24 = (sbi1+sbi3+sbi5+sbi7+sbi9+sbi11+sbi13+sbi15+sbi7+
    sbi19+sbi21+sbi23)-(sbi2+sbi4+sbi6+sbi8+sbi10+sbi12+sbi14+sbi16+sbi18+
    sbi20+sbi22+sbi24).
VARIABLE LABELS sbitotal 'Summed SBI Total score'.
EXECUTE.

The following is an SPSS syntax file for computing the *averaged versions* of the SBI subscales of Anticipating, Savoring the Moment, and Reminiscing, as well as SBI Total score:

RECODE
    sbi2 sbi4 sbi6 sbi8 sbi10 sbi12 sbi14 sbi16 sbi18 sbi20 sbi22 sbi24
    (1=7) (2=6) (3=5) (4=4) (5=3) (6=2) (7=1) INTO sbi2r sbi4r sbi6r
    sbi8r sbi10r sbi12r sbi14r sbi16r sbi18r sbi20r sbi22r sbi24r.
COMPUTE anticavg = (sbi4r+sbi10r+sbi16r+sbi22r+sbi1+sbi7+sbi13+sbi19)/8.
VARIABLE LABELS anticavg 'Mean score for SBI Anticipation subscale'.
COMPUTE momntavg = (sbi2r+sbi8r+sbi14r+sbi20r+sbi5+sbi11+sbi17+sbi23)
    /8.
VARIABLE LABELS momntavg 'Mean score for SBI Savoring the Moment
    subscale'.
COMPUTE reminavg = (sbi6r+sbi12r+sbi18r+sbi24r+sbi3+sbi9+sbi15+sbi21)
    /8.
VARIABLE LABELS reminavg 'Mean score for SBI Reminiscing subscale'.
COMPUTE sbitotav = (sbi2r+sbi4r+sbi6r+sbi8r+sbi10r+sbi12r+sbi14r+sbi16r+
    sbi18r+sbi20r+sbi22r+sbi24r+sbi1+sbi3+sbi5+sbi7+sbi9+sbi11+sbi13+sbi15+
    sbi17+sbi19+sbi21+sbi23)/24.
VARIABLE LABELS sbitotav 'Mean SBI Total score'.
EXECUTE.

See Bryant (2003).

Appendix D

The Ways of Savoring Checklist (WOSC)

WOSC

Date: _____
Age: _____
Gender: _____

We would like you to think back to a positive experience that you recently had. Please describe the circumstances: _____
_____
_____
_____

Please estimate the date that this particular positive event occurred:
_____

A. How desirable was this particular event? (circle one number)

    1   2   3   4   5   6   7   8   9   10
    The worst thing   The best thing
    that could happen   that could happen

B. To what extent were you personally responsible for the occurrence of this event?

    1   2   3   4   5   6   7   8   9   10
    I was not   I was very
    at all responsible   much responsible

C. How expected or unexpected was this particular event?

    1   2   3   4   5   6   7   8   9   10
    I did not expect   I expected
    it to happen   it to happen

D. How long did this particular event last, when it occurred?

     1   2   3   4   5   6   7   8   9   10
     It lasted a   It lasted a
     short time   long time

E. How rare would you say this particular event is in your life?

     1   2   3   4   5   6   7   8   9   10
     It does not   It happens
     happen very often   very often

F. To what extent did you look forward to this event before it occurred?

     1   2   3   4   5   6   7   8   9   10
     Not much   A great deal

G. How much did your enjoyment of this event depend on what YOU were doing?

     1   2   3   4   5   6   7   8   9   10
     Not at all   Almost entirely

H. How much did your enjoyment of this event depend on what OTHERS were doing?

     1   2   3   4   5   6   7   8   9   10
     Not at all   Almost entirely

The following pages contain a list of things that people might think or do while they are going through positive events. Please read each of the following statements and indicate how much each of them applies to what you thought and did the last time you went on vacation.

When this event happened . . .

	Definitely Doesn't Apply		Applies Somewhat		Definitely Applies	
1. I thought about sharing the memory of this later with other people.	1	2	3	4	5	6	7
2. I tried to take in every sensory property of the event (sights, sounds, smells, etc.).	1	2	3	4	5	6	7
3. I reminded myself how long I had waited for this to happen.	1	2	3	4	5	6	7

	Definitely Doesn't Apply		Applies Somewhat			Definitely Applies	
4. I reminded myself how transient this moment was — thought about it ending.	1	2	3	4	5	6	7
5. I jumped up and down, ran around, or showed other physical expressions of energy.	1	2	3	4	5	6	7
6. I thought back to events that led up to it — to a time when I didn't have it and wanted it.	1	2	3	4	5	6	7
7. I tried to focus on certain sensory properties in particular (perhaps blocking out others).	1	2	3	4	5	6	7
8. I thought only about the present — got absorbed in the moment.	1	2	3	4	5	6	7
9. I reminded myself how lucky I was to have this good thing happen to me.	1	2	3	4	5	6	7
10. I told myself why I didn't deserve this good thing.	1	2	3	4	5	6	7
11. I looked for other people to share it with.	1	2	3	4	5	6	7
12. I thought about how I'd reminisce to myself about this event later.	1	2	3	4	5	6	7
13. I reminded myself what a relief it was.	1	2	3	4	5	6	7
14. I thought how I wished this moment could last — reminded myself how I must enjoy it now because it would soon be over.	1	2	3	4	5	6	7
15. I laughed or giggled.	1	2	3	4	5	6	7
16. I thought about ways in which it could have been worse.	1	2	3	4	5	6	7
17. I opened my eyes wide and took a deep breath — tried to become more alert.	1	2	3	4	5	6	7
18. I closed my eyes, relaxed, took in the moment.	1	2	3	4	5	6	7
19. I thought about what a lucky person I am that so many good things have happened to me.	1	2	3	4	5	6	7
20. I thought about ways in which it could have been better.	1	2	3	4	5	6	7

	Definitely Doesn't Apply		Applies Somewhat			Definitely Applies	
21. I expressed to others present how much I valued the moment (and their being there to share it with me).	1	2	3	4	5	6	7
22. I consciously reflected on the situation — took in details, tried to remember them, made comparisons.	1	2	3	4	5	6	7
23. I told myself how proud I was.	1	2	3	4	5	6	7
24. I reminded myself that it would be over before I knew it.	1	2	3	4	5	6	7
25. I tried to speed up and move more quickly.	1	2	3	4	5	6	7
26. I focused on the future — on a time when this good event would be over.	1	2	3	4	5	6	7
27. I tried to slow down and move more slowly (in an effort to stop or slow down time).	1	2	3	4	5	6	7
28. I made myself relax so that I could become more absorbed in the event or activity.	1	2	3	4	5	6	7
29. I said a prayer of thanks for my good fortune.	1	2	3	4	5	6	7
30. I withdrew and inhibited my feelings (stiffened up).	1	2	3	4	5	6	7
31. I hung around with others who know how to have a good time.	1	2	3	4	5	6	7
32. I labeled specific details of the situation explicitly — tried to find out what it was that I was enjoying and note each aspect explicitly.	1	2	3	4	5	6	7
33. I told myself how impressed others must be.	1	2	3	4	5	6	7
34. I reminded myself that nothing lasts forever so I must enjoy this now.	1	2	3	4	5	6	7
35. I sighed or made other verbal sounds of appreciation to help myself savor the moment (e.g., saying mmm, aahh, humming or whistling).	1	2	3	4	5	6	7
36. I reminded myself that others who were involved in the event were also thinking and feeling the same way.	1	2	3	4	5	6	7

	Definitely Doesn't Apply		Applies Somewhat			Definitely Applies	
37. I concentrated and blocked out distractions; I intensified one sense by blocking another.	1	2	3	4	5	6	7
38. I just went through the experience one moment at a time and tried not to look too far ahead.	1	2	3	4	5	6	7
39. I told myself how it wasn't as good as I'd hoped for.	1	2	3	4	5	6	7
40. I physically expressed my feelings to others (hugging, touching).	1	2	3	4	5	6	7
41. I took mental photographs.	1	2	3	4	5	6	7
42. I thought about what a triumph it was.	1	2	3	4	5	6	7
43. I thought about how fast the time was passing.	1	2	3	4	5	6	7
44. I screamed or made other verbal expressions of excitement.	1	2	3	4	5	6	7
45. I compared myself to others (asked myself "Am I enjoying this as much as they are?").	1	2	3	4	5	6	7
46. I reminded myself of other places I should be or of other things I should be doing instead.	1	2	3	4	5	6	7
47. I talked to another person about how good I felt.	1	2	3	4	5	6	7
48. I tried to memorize my surroundings.	1	2	3	4	5	6	7
49. I told myself why I deserved this good thing.	1	2	3	4	5	6	7
50. I touched myself—rubbed my stomach, clapped my hands, etc.	1	2	3	4	5	6	7
51. I made associations with other past pleasant events and reminded myself of them.	1	2	3	4	5	6	7
52. I thought about other things that were hanging over me, problems and worries that I still had to face.	1	2	3	4	5	6	7
53. I took photographs with a camera to capture the experience.	1	2	3	4	5	6	7
54. I thought about what a good time I was having.	1	2	3	4	5	6	7

	Definitely Doesn't Apply		Applies Somewhat			Definitely Applies	
55. I thought about how things might never be this good again.	1	2	3	4	5	6	7
56. I thought about things that made me feel guilty.	1	2	3	4	5	6	7
57. I thought or did something entirely different from any of the above. (Please describe).	1	2	3	4	5	6	7
58. I got high or intoxicated to help me enjoy it.	1	2	3	4	5	6	7
59. I imagined a whole sequence of good events that could arise as a consequence of this event.	1	2	3	4	5	6	7
60. I tried not to think too much — just relaxed and enjoyed.	1	2	3	4	5	6	7
61. I thought or did something entirely different from any of the above. (Please describe).	1	2	3	4	5	6	7

_____

_____

_____

_____

Now think again about this particular positive event.

When this event occurred, how much
did you enjoy it?

    1   2   3   4   5   6   7
Very little   A great deal

After this event occurred, for how long
did you continue to enjoy it?

    1   2   3   4   5   6   7
Not for   For a very
Very long   long time

Appendix E

Instructions for Scoring the
Ways of Savoring Checklist (WOSC)

The WOSC provides quantitative information about 10 different dimensions of savoring in the form of 10 subscale scores (i.e., Sharing With Others, Memory Building, Self-Congratulation, Comparing, Sensory-Perceptual Sharpening, Absorption, Behavioral Expression, Temporal Awareness, Counting Blessings, and Kill-Joy Thinking), as follows.

I. *Sharing with Others:*
    A. Sum responses to WOSC items 1, 11, 21, 31, 40, and 47.
    B. Divide this sum by 6 to obtain a mean subscale score for *Sharing With Others.*

II. *Memory-Building:*
    A. Sum responses to WOSC items 2, 12, 22, 32, 41, 48, and 53.
    B. Divide this sum by 7 to obtain a mean subscale score for *Memory Building.*

III. *Self-Congratulation:*
    A. Sum responses to WOSC items 3, 13, 23, 33, 42, 49, and 54.
    B. Divide this sum by 7 to obtain a mean subscale score for *Self-Congratulation.*

IV. *Comparing:*
    A. Sum responses to WOSC items 6, 16, 26, 36, 45, 51, and 55.
    B. Divide this sum by 7 to obtain a mean subscale score for *Comparing.*

V. *Sensory-Perceptual Sharpening:*
    A. Sum responses to WOSC items 7, 17, 27 and 37.
    B. Divide this sum by 4 to obtain a mean subscale score for *Sensory-Perceptual Sharpening.*

VI. *Absorption:*
    A. Sum responses to WOSC items 8, 18, 28, and 38.
    B. Divide this sum by 4 to obtain a mean subscale score for *Absorption.*

VII. *Behavioral Expression:*
    A. Sum responses to WOSC items 5, 15, 25, 35, 44, and 50.
    B. Divide this sum by 6 to obtain a mean subscale score for *Behavioral Expression.*

VIII. *Temporal Awareness:*
    A. Sum responses to WOSC items 4, 14, 24, 34, and 43.
    B. Divide this sum by 5 to obtain a mean subscale score for *Temporal Awareness.*

IX. *Counting Blessings:*
    A. Sum responses to WOSC items 9, 19, and 29.
    B. Divide this sum by 3 to obtain a mean subscale score for *Counting Blessings.*

X. *Kill-Joy Thinking:*
    A. Sum responses to WOSC items 10, 20, 30, 39, 46, 52, and 56.
    B. Divide this sum by 7 to obtain a mean subscale score for *Kill-Joy Thinking.*

The following is an SPSS syntax file for computing mean scores for the 10 savoring subscales of the Ways of Savoring Checklist (WOSC):

```
COMPUTE sharing = (woscl+woscll+wosc21+wosc31+wosc40+wosc47)/6.
VARIABLE LABELS sharing 'Sharing: WOSC (1,11,21,31,40,47)/6'.
COMPUTE membuild = (wosc2+woscl2+wosc22+wosc32+wosc41+wosc48
    +wosc53)/7.
VARIABLE LABELS membuild 'Memory-Building: WOSC (2,12,22,32,41,48,
    53)/7'.
COMPUTE scongrat = (wosc3+woscl3+wosc23+wosc33+wosc42+wosc49
    +wosc54)/7.
VARIABLE LABELS scongrat 'Self-Congratulation: WOSC (3,13,23,33,42,49,
    54)/7'.
COMPUTE compare = (wosc6+woscl6+wosc26+wosc36+wosc45+wosc51
    +wosc55)/7.
VARIABLE LABELS compare 'Comparing: WOSC (6,16,26,36,45,51,55)/7'.
COMPUTE sensharp = (wosc7+woscl7+wosc27+wosc37)/4.
VARIABLE LABELS sensharp 'Sensory-Perceptual Sharpening: WOSC
    (7,17,27,37)/4'.
COMPUTE absorptn = (wosc8+woscl8+wosc28+wosc38)/4.
VARIABLE LABELS absorptn 'Absorption: WOSC (8,18,28,38)/4'.
COMPUTE bexpress = (wosc5+woscl5+wosc25+wosc35+wosc44+wosc50)/6.
VARIABLE LABELS bexpress 'Behavioral Expression: WOSC
    (5,15,25,35,44,50)/6'.
```

COMPUTE temporal = (wosc4+wosc14+wosc24+wosc34+wosc43)/5 .
VARIABLE LABELS temporal 'Temporal Awareness: WOSC (4,14,24,34,43)/5'.
COMPUTE cntbless = (wosc9+wosc19+wosc29)/3.
VARIABLE LABELS cntbless 'Counting Blessings: WOSC (9,19,29)/3'.
COMPUTE killjoy = (wosc10+wosc20+wosc30+wosc39+wosc46+wosc52
    +wosc56)/7.
VARIABLE LABELS killjoy 'Kill-Joy Thinking: WOSC (10,20,30,39,46,52,56)/7'.
EXECUTE.

Appendix F

The Children's Savoring Beliefs Inventory (CSBI)

CSBI

Instructions: For each statement listed below, please circle the one number that best indicates how true the statement is for you. There are no right or wrong answers. Please be as honest as you can.

	strongly disagree						strongly agree
1. I know how to have a good time.	1	2	3	4	5	6	7
2. I don't like to look forward to good times too much before they happen.	1	2	3	4	5	6	7
3. It's hard for me to hold onto a good feeling for very long.	1	2	3	4	5	6	7
4. It makes me happy to think about good things that are about to happen.	1	2	3	4	5	6	7
5. I don't look back on good things after they are over.	1	2	3	4	5	6	7
6. It is a waste of time to think about good things that may happen.	1	2	3	4	5	6	7
7. I enjoy looking back on happy times that have already happened.	1	2	3	4	5	6	7
8. I often stop myself from having a good time.	1	2	3	4	5	6	7
9. I feel excited when I think about good things that are going to happen.	1	2	3	4	5	6	7
10. When I remember good memories, I feel bad or let down.	1	2	3	4	5	6	7
11. When fun times are over, I can make good feelings from those fun times last longer by thinking or doing certain things.	1	2	3	4	5	6	7

	strongly disagree				strongly agree		
12. It's hard for me to get excited about fun times before they happen.	1	2	3	4	5	6	7
13. I feel happy when I think about good things from my past.	1	2	3	4	5	6	7
14. I can enjoy good things before they happen.	1	2	3	4	5	6	7
15. It is a waste of time to think about good things that happened in the past.	1	2	3	4	5	6	7
16. I am able to enjoy good things that happen to me.	1	2	3	4	5	6	7
17. It bothers me when I think about good things before they happen.	1	2	3	4	5	6	7
18. I like to remember fun times so that I can think about them later.	1	2	3	4	5	6	7
19. I am not able to feel joy at happy times.	1	2	3	4	5	6	7
20. I can feel good by thinking about a good thing that is going to happen.	1	2	3	4	5	6	7
21. When a fun time is over, I don't think about it anymore.	1	2	3	4	5	6	7
22. I don't enjoy good things as much as other people do.	1	2	3	4	5	6	7
23. It is easy to bring back the good feeling from happy memories.	1	2	3	4	5	6	7
24. When I want to, I am able to enjoy something.	1	2	3	4	5	6	7

From Cafasso, 1994.

Appendix G

Instructions for Scoring the Children's Savoring Beliefs Inventory

Four scale-scores can be derived from the CSBI:

(1) *Anticipating* subscale score;
(2) *Savoring the Moment* subscale score;
(3) *Reminiscing* subscale score; and
(4) *CSBI Total* score.

There are two different scoring methods for the CSBI. The first scoring method follows the procedures used in the article reporting the development and validation of the adult version of the SBI (Bryant, 2003, Table 3, p. 185). With this original scoring method, positively anchored items are summed, negatively anchored items are summed, and then the sum of the negatively anchored items is subtracted from the sum of the positively anchored items. This scoring method is used both for each CBSI subscale and for CSBI Total score. With this scoring method, scores on each CSBI subscale can range from −24 to +24; and CSBI Total score can range from −72 to +72.

The second scoring method converts scale-scores back into the 1–7 "metric" of the response scale for the CSBI, by summing the positively anchored items, reverse-scoring the negatively anchored items, adding together these two sums, and dividing the resulting total by the number of constituent items. This scoring method provides average scores for the Anticipating, Savoring the Moment, and Reminiscing subscales, as well as an average CSBI Total score. With this scoring method, scores on the three CSBI subscales and CSBI Total score can range from 1 to 7. This scoring method makes it easy for researchers to interpret CSBI scores in the "absolute" terms of the original 1–7 response scale. With this scoring method: 1 is the lowest possible "absolute" score (0th percentile); 2 lies at the 16.67th percentile on the absolute scale; 3 lies at the 33.33rd percentile on the absolute scale; 4 is the midpoint on the absolute scale (50th percentile); 5 lies at the 66.67th percentile on the absolute scale; 6 lies at the 83.33rd percentile on the absolute scale; and 7 is the highest possible "absolute" score (100th percentile).

The two scoring methods provide equivalent sets of scores that are perfectly correlated with each other. In other words, both within each subscale and for CSBI Total score, an individual's score using the first scoring method correlates perfectly with that same individual's score using the second scoring method. However, the two scoring methods provide different "metrics" for evaluating CSBI scores—the first scoring method yields summed scores, whereas the second scoring method yields averaged scores. Researchers may choose one or the other scoring method, depending on their purpose or preference.

Scoring the CSBI Using the Original "Summed Score" Method

I. *Anticipating subscale score*
   A. Sum responses to the following four items: 4, 9, 14, 20.
   B. Sum responses to the following four items: 2, 6, 12, 17.
   C. Subtract the total obtained in Step B from the total obtained in Step A, to get a summed score for the CSBI *Anticipating* subscale.

II. *Savoring the Moment subscale score*
   A. Sum responses to the following four items: 1, 11, 16, 24.
   B. Sum responses to the following four items: 3, 8, 19, 22.
   C. Subtract the total obtained in Step B from the total obtained in Step A, to get a summed score for the CSBI *Savoring the Moment* subscale.

III. *Reminiscing subscale score*
   A. Sum responses to the following four items: 7, 13, 18, 23.
   B. Sum responses to the following four items: 5, 10, 15, 21.
   C. Subtract the total obtained in Step B from the total obtained in Step A, to get a summed score for the CSBI *Reminiscing* subscale.

IV. *Total CSBI score*
   A. Sum responses to the following 12 items:
      1, 4, 7, 9, 11, 13, 14, 16, 18, 20, 23, 24.
   B. Sum responses to the following 12 items:
      2, 3, 5, 6, 8, 10, 12, 15, 17, 19, 21, 22.
   C. Subtract the total obtained in Step B from the total obtained in Step A, to get a summed CSBI *Total* score.

Scoring the CSBI Using the "Average Score" Method

I. *Anticipating subscale score*
   A. Reverse-score the following items: 2, 6, 12, 17.
   B. Sum responses to these four reverse-scored items.
   C. Sum responses to the following four items: 4, 9, 14, 20.
   D. Add together the sum obtained in Step B and the sum obtained in Step C.

E. Divide the resulting total by 8, to get a mean score for the CSBI *Anticipating* subscale.

II. *Savoring the Moment subscale score*
    A. Reverse-score the following items: 3, 8, 19, 22.
    B. Sum responses to these four reverse-scored items.
    C. Sum responses to the following four items: 1, 11, 16, 24.
    D. Add together the sum obtained in Step B and the sum obtained in Step C.
    E. Divide the resulting total by 8, to get a mean score for the CSBI *Savoring the Moment* subscale.

III. *Reminiscing subscale score*
    A. Reverse-score the following items: 5, 10, 15, 21.
    B. Sum responses to these four reverse-scored items.
    C. Sum responses to the following four items: 7, 13, 18, 23.
    D. Add together the sum obtained in Step B and the sum obtained in Step C.
    E. Divide the resulting total by 8, to get a mean score for the CSBI *Reminiscing* subscale.

IV. *Total CSBI score*
    A. Reverse-score the following 12 items:
       2, 3, 5, 6, 8, 10, 12, 15, 17, 19, 21, 22.
    B. Sum responses to these 12 reverse-scored items.
    C. Sum responses to the following items:
       1, 4, 7, 9, 11, 13, 14, 16, 18, 20, 23, 24.
    D. Add together the sum obtained in Step B and the sum obtained in Step C.
    E. Divide the resulting total by 24, to get a mean CSBI *Total* score.

The following is an SPSS syntax file for computing the *summed versions* of the CSBI subscales of Anticipating, Savoring the Moment, and Reminiscing, as well as CSBI Total score:

```
COMPUTE anticsum = (csbi4+csbi9+csbi14+csbi20)-(csbi2+csbi6+csbi12
   +csbi17).
VARIABLE LABELS anticsum 'Summed score for CSBI Anticipating subscale'.
EXECUTE.
COMPUTE momntsum = (csbi1+csbi11+csbi16+csbi24)-(csbi3+csbi8+csbi19
   +csbi22).
VARIABLE LABELS momntsum 'Summed score for CSBI Savoring the
   Moment subscale'.
EXECUTE.
```

```
COMPUTE reminsum = (csbi7+csbi13+csbi18+csbi23)-(csbi5+csbi10+csbi15
    +csbi21).
VARIABLE LABELS reminsum 'Summed score for CSBI Reminiscing subscale'.
EXECUTE.
COMPUTE csbitot = (csbi1+csbi4+csbi7+csbi9+csbi11+csbi13+csbi14+csbi16
    +csbi18+csbi20+csbi23+csbi24)-(csbi2+csbi3+csbi5+csbi6+csbi8+csbi10
    +csbi12+csbi15+csbi17+csbi19+csbi21+csbi22).
VARIABLE LABELS csbitot 'Summed CSBI Total score'.
EXECUTE.
```

The following is an SPSS syntax file for computing the *averaged versions* of the CSBI subscales of Anticipating, Savoring the Moment, and Reminiscing, as well as CSBI Total score:

```
RECODE
    csbi2 csbi3 csbi5 csbi6 csbi8 csbi10 csbi12 csbi15 csbi17 csbi19 csbi21 csbi22
    (1=7) (2=6) (3=5) (4=4) (5=3) (6=2) (7=1) INTO csbi2r csbi3r csbi5r
    csbi6r csbi8r csbi10r csbi12r csbi15r csbi17r csbi19r csbi21r csbi22r.
EXECUTE.
COMPUTE anticavg = (csbi2r+csbi6r+csbi12r+csbi17r+csbi4+csbi9+csbi14
    +csbi20)/8.
VARIABLE LABELS anticavg 'Mean score for CSBI Anticipation subscale'.
EXECUTE.
COMPUTE momntavg = (csbi3r+csbi8r+csbi19r+csbi22r+csbi1+csbi11+csbi16
    +csbi24)/8.
VARIABLE LABELS momntavg 'Mean score for CSBI Savoring the Moment
    subscale'.
EXECUTE.
COMPUTE reminavg = (csbi5r+csbi10r+csbi15r+csbi21r+csbi7+csbi13+csbi18
    +csbi23)/8.
VARIABLE LABELS reminavg 'Mean score for CSBI Reminiscing subscale'.
EXECUTE.
COMPUTE csbitavg = (csbi2r+csbi3r+csbi5r+csbi6r+csbi8r+csbi10r+csbi12r
    +csbi15r+csbi17r+csbi19r+csbi21r+csbi22r+csbi1+csbi4+csbi7+csbi9+csbi11
    +csbi13+csbi14+csbi16+csbi18+csbi20+csbi23+csbi24)/24.
VARIABLE LABELS csbitavg 'Mean CSBI Total score'.
EXECUTE.
```

Author Index

Subject Index